Krotona, Theosophy & Krishnamurti
1927–1931
Archival Documents of the Theosophical Society's
Esoteric Center, Krotona, in Ojai, California.

Volume V of the Krotona Series

Joseph E. Ross

Krotona, Theosophy, & Krishnamurti, 1927–1931: Archival Documents of the Theosophical Society's Esoteric Center, Krotona, in Ojai, California.
Volume V of the Krotona Series.

First Edition, 2011

Library of Congress Catalogue in publication data
Ross, Joseph E., 1943-
Krotona, Theosophy, & Krishnamurti, 1927–1931: Archival Documents of the Theosophical Society's Esoteric Center, Krotona, in Ojai, California.
Volume V of the Krotona Series.

ISBN: 978-0-925943-15-6

1. Ojai Region (Calif.)-History. 2. Theosophical Society-History

Cover images, from top, left to right: The "Tent City" of the Star Camp, May 1928; C.W. Leadbeater with several young women of The Manor group, 1928; early Krotona's formal gardens; J. Krishnamurti as Head of The Order of the Star in the East. (Painting by Alfred Hitchens, 1913. The original painting hangs in the E.S. Shrine Room of the Adyar Theosophical Society, Chennai, India); First International Star Congress, Ojai Valley, May 1928.

www.krotonaarchives.com

In memory of Albert Powell Warrington
and his wife Betty
whose devotion to an ideal, and whose courage in attempting to
carry out that ideal, has made Krotona possible.

Table of Contents

Author's Preface

Material for this volume has been drawn from the documents the author has collected during his many years traveling around the world to Theosophical centers. Extensive reading, especially perusal of early theosophical and secular journals and books, has rounded out the history contained in the quaint and curious letters now in the author's archives, which are to be housed in the future at the Krishnamurti Foundation of America, Ojai, California. Letters here printed contain priceless bits of information and sidelights on the writers' personalities, which will enable the reader, however distant in time or space, to become acquainted with the leaders of the theosophical movement as they actually lived the events portrayed in their writings.

The letters included in this volume have been transcribed directly from the originals and without omission, except for the occasional correction of obvious errors of spelling and punctuation. When a magazine or book is mentioned in a letter, it is printed here in italics, whereas the original letters in such cases often simply have initial letters capitalized. In some letters commas have been added for clarity.

Whenever I have quoted something written by another, I have attempted to use the quoted words in the same context as the original writer used them—aware that even slight alterations, such as changing a single word, or omitting a part of a sentence, may change the meaning. Alas, many writers (even among trained scholars) break this rule, and in so doing, do violence to the original meaning of the original writer. An ellipsis (three dots or points) within a quotation indicates that something has been omitted, but the context should be unchanged.

The author has been asked, Why another book on the history of Krotona (for it has all been said in the other publications)? This book is written in chronological order in the format of a diary, using rare archival documents describing entirely authentic and factual events taking place at Krotona, giving insight behind the scenes that have never been made public. The letters contained herein hold information about, and shed light on, the personalities around the founding of the Krotona Institute, as well the evolving relation between Krishnamurti and Theosophy during this time. Many of the letters are controversial; some are contradictory, and some, confusing.

And, the past is past: except that its shadow still falls on the present, perhaps thereby overshadowing and creating a pre-determined future.

The author acknowledges and take full responsibility for making public the letters and documents presented to him by Betty Warrington and others that are in this publication.

———————————

The following resolutions regarding *Early Works of J. Krishnamurti* are included here because throughout the publications of the Krotona history, (Volumes 1–4), many of J. Krishnamurti's lectures and private talks were included without making a needed disclaimer that they are not verbatim reports of J. Krishnamurti, even though they seek to represent his thinking. They were modified or edited by recorders as notes from the period described, so they can not necessarily be taken as the authentic words of J. Krishnamurti.[*]

———

[*] One example of similiar innacuracy is in the publishing of the statement made by Dr. Annie Besant regarding the Teaching of Krishnamurti. C. Jinarajadasa writes that he came across an address by Dr. Besant at Adyar on May 11, 1928, to celebrate the birthday of Krishnamurti. The typescript of her address was corrected by Dr. Besant herself. That which was published, however, was from an uncorrected copy of emendations. C. Jinarajadasa does not make the corrections until they are made public in a publication in *The Theosophist*, Vol. LIV, n12, September 1933, pp.638-642.

Early Works of J. Krishnamurti Access Policy

Pursuant to the resolutions by the trustees in 2006 and 2008 at International Trustees Meetings the following public access to the *Early Works Collections* in the archives of the KFA, KFT, and KFI will be determined by the following policy.

POLICY:

Upon application to study, read, research, or review Krishnamurti Archives collections of Early Works [1915-1933] scholars and readers will be informed of the following rationale:

Krishnamurti, during his lifetime, opposed the publication of the 'Early Works.' There is the anecdotal testimony of trustees and close associates to whom he mentioned his reasons for not wanting to republish the works prior to 1933 with some exceptions specifically approved by him, like the 1929 speech on the Dissolution of the Order of the Star. These reasons were:

A.) That what he said and wrote and was published before 1933 may not be accurate representations of his teachings.

B.) That several of his writings and speeches were heavily edited and modified by others.

C.) That some of the works published in his name were to some extent written by others and he was not sure of their authenticity.

To avoid all questions of censorship, repression, or cover-up the archive collections of early [1915-June 1933] Krishnamurti works [unpublished, published, unedited, edited, printed, and handwritten] housed in the archives of the three Krishnamurti Foundations [KFA, KFT, and KFI] will be available to the general public upon standard application-for-access to an archive collection following the agreed individual Foundation archive procedures and with a signed copy of this POLICY is kept on file.

Copyrights to the collection are vested with the Krishnamurti Foundation of America for pre-1933 materials where established. 'Public Domain' Bern Convention rules apply to all other materials in the collection.

Unanimously voted on by the Krishnamurti Foundation of America on November 20, 2010.

Acknowledgements

The author extends his deepest gratitude to all the many writers of the letters, left as a record of Krotona's history. My special thanks to the staff of the Krishnamurti Foundation of America Archives for being exceedingly helpful in giving me access to their archives, and permission to reproduce documents for this volume, and also to Edwin House Publishing. Especially to those who have granted the author personal interviews, offered their documents, photographs and other information to complete this and future volumes. Words will never convey the debt of the author's gratitude.

Special mention must be made of Robert Boyd's painstaking and careful work in checking the original documents with the printed proofs. The author also thanks him for his superb editing skills making valuable suggestions toward the completion of the final version, and his Foreword as well.

Special mention must be made of W.G.M. Beumer who provided us with a publication about J.J. Van der Leeuw and family.

Joseph E. Ross, author is solely responsible for any imperfections remaining. Throughout the documentation, please be advised that the letters and memos form a narrative which is broken by "transitions bars" which are really inserted miscellanea!

Foreword
By
Robert Boyd

It has been suggested that the incipient growth of the Theosophical Society from the date of its founding in New York in 1875, owed in part to an attempt to synthesize the Eternal Wisdom of the Eastern World for the benefit of those in the Western World whose spiritual insights would be enhanced by an addition to their already cherished traditions.

Perhaps this quest led the heirs of H.P. Blavatsky to try to satisfy a spiritual longing in the Western World by way of esoteric lessons for an inner core of Theosophical Initiates in teachings enunciated by the Liberal Catholic Church. The latter, it should be noted also, sought to promote a belief in the coming of a new Messiah in the person of the young Jiddu Krishnamurti.

As we shall read in the pages of this work, the agenda of the renewed Theosophical Society had a broad spectrum of social goals, not only in India, but also in Australia and the United States of America, to serve its purposes. Indeed, the formation of an Esoteric Center in America provided resources for the Society's programs in general.

The story of the founding of the Esoteric Section of the Theosophy at Ojai, California, is one of infinite possibilities that would satisfy the changing requirements of the leadership abroad to harmonize gradually for the greater good of the Society. Early members' prosaic expressions, and daily contributions helped Krotona to ingratiate itself with, and give much to, the social milieu of the Ojai Valley in the late 1920's. That is, essentially, what this sequence of events records. Personalities come alive, as they give their all to the building and enfoldment of their dreams.

An Open Letter to Fellow Theosophists

The author feels that it may be important to examine what is meant by the word *religion* in the statement, "the Theosophical Society is to be a cornerstone of a new religion." Is *religion* a matter of churches, temples, rituals and beliefs? Or is it the moment-to-moment discovery of Life's movement? A movement which may have any name, or no name at all.

As the author understands it, the great purpose of the Theosophical Society, as originated by H.P. Blavatsky, is to exemplify and foster Brotherhood. She brought from the storehouse of the past the great teachings of the Wisdom-Religion, Theosophy, that man is divine in essence. Life is that which binds not only all men, but all beings, all things in the entire Universe into one great whole, an essential divine wholeness, differing in form as expressed in plants, animals, human beings, planets and stars.

So, is a *religious* life one that is lived fragmented by organizations and beliefs, or a life, a movement, that is integral, not fragmented and so whole, holy, sacred? What does Theosophy foster?

The first Theosophical magazine in America was William Quan Judge's *The Path*, begun in 1886. In 1894, W.J. Walters of San Francisco began a magazine for children called *Mercury*. *Mercury* was adopted and remodeled as the Section Journal with its second volume in August 1895 after the Judge Secession. By October 1899, it was replaced by *The Theosophic Messenger*. In January 1913, the title of the Section's Journal was expanded to *The American Theosophist* and *Theosophic Messenger* continuing for five issues, so that by June 1913, the journal was split into two periodicals, *The American Theosophist*, which continued the volume numbering of the old title, and *The Messenger*, which began a new series of volume numbers. Seventeen months later, *The American Theosophist*, was discontinued and combined with *The Messenger* beginning in October 1914. *The Messenger* was renamed *The Theosophical Messenger* in December 1927, and kept that title until January 1933, when it returned to the title of *The American Theosophist*. From 1933 onward, *The American Theosophist* kept the title, although the volume numbering continued that of *The Messenger* and *The Theosophical Messenger*, not that of the earlier *American Theosophist*.

By November 1961, *The American Theosophist* began to publish two special thematic issues a year. In the middle of 1988, the two special issues were converted into a new journal, *The Quest.*[*]

What is the *quest* behind Theosophy, and how is it best fulfilled by Krotona?

———————— ❧❧ ————————

Krotona Institute as a Study Center

Krishnamurti held that study centers should be beacons of light in the years to come. He raised many issues in that light, such as: *"How do they become truly religious places? How does a physical place become sacred space? What is the ambience that will hold the sacred?"*

Krishnamurti said in 1983, regarding Brockwood, that today and in the future a Study Center must be more than a school. (And why can this statement not apply to the Krotona Institute?)

> It must be a centre for those who are deeply interested in the Teachings, a place where they can stay and study. In the very old days an ashrama — which means retreat — was a place where people came to gather their energies, to dwell and to explore deeper religious aspects of life. Modern places of this kind generally have some sort of leader, guru, abbot or patriarch who guides, interprets and dominates. Brockwood must have no such leader or guru, for the Teachings themselves are the expression of that truth which serious people must find for themselves. Personal cult has no place in this. [†]

* Algeo, John, "What's in a Name: The Quest", *The Quest*, Vol.85/number 1, January 1997, p.2. History by John Algeo, National President of the Theosophical Society in America in 1977, and then editor of *The Quest*, the official journal of the Theosophical Society in America.
†Krishnamurti, J., "Brockwood Today and in the Future", *On Study Centres*, 1983, p.49.

Krishnamurti felt that the very word *ashrama* had traditional connotations, for it was too much a part of the Hindu consciousness, although Dr. George Arundale used the name for his organization at Adyar, and published pamphlets under that heading. Let's read what Krishnamurti dictated to Sunanda Patwardhan at Vasanta Vihar on January 26/27, 1984 regarding his insights on study centers:

> They [these centers] must last a thousand years unpolluted, like a river that has the capacity to cleanse itself; which means no authority whatsoever for the inhabitants. And the teaching in themselves have the authority of the truth. It is a place for the flowering of goodness, where there is a communication and cooperation not based on work, an ideal, or personal authority. Cooperation implies not around some object or principle, belief, and so on, but a sharing of insights. As one comes to the place, each one is his work, working in the garden or doing something [else], may discover something as he is working. He communicates and has a dialogue with the other inhabitants, to be questioned and doubted in order to see the weight of the truth of his discovery. So there is a constant communication and not a solitary achievement, a solitary enlightenment or understanding. It is the responsibility of each one to bring about this sense—that if each one of us discovers something basic anew, I is not personal but it is for a all people who are there to share.
>
> It is not a community. The very word 'community' or 'commune' is an aggressive or separative movement [away] from the whole of humanity. But it does not mean that the whole of humanity comes into this place. It is essentially a religious center according to what K has said about religion. It is a place where not only is one physically active but there is a sustained and continuous inward watching. So there is a movement of learning where each one becomes the teacher and the disciple. It is not a place for one's own illumination or one's own goal of fulfillment, artistically, religiously, or in any other way, but rather a place for sustaining and nourishing one another to flower in goodness.

This is not a place for romanticists or sentimentalists. This requires a good brain, which does not mean an intellectual [brain] but a brain that is objective, is fundamentally honest to itself, and has integrity in word and deed.

This place must be of great beauty, with trees, birds, and quiet, for beauty is truth, and truth is goodness and love. The external beauty, external tranquility, and silence may affect the inner tranquility, but the environment must in no way influence the inner beauty. Beauty can only be when the self is not; the environment, which must have great wonder, must in on way be an absorbing factor like a child's toy. Here, there are no toys but inner depths, substance, and integrity that is not put together by thought. *

Should Krotona be a community or a Study Center? I question whether Krotona should be a community, and whether there should be permanent inhabitants. When people live permanently in such a place, it generally becomes a community with its hierarchical, dependent nature of relationship and routines and ritualized way of meditation and living. A Study Center is a place where people come for a short stay, for a few weeks, and go back with a deep awakening to meet life anew.

And, I would like to remind fellow theosophists, that no organization, including Krotona, can be religious; only people in an organization can be religious. Throughout history, religious organizations have been sectarian, divisive, and hierarchical. If Krotona is to be a place of deep honesty, the awakening of intelligence in the midst of confusion and conflict that is taking place in the world today, it depends on the people of Krotona, their awareness, attention and affection.

Patwardhan relates that when there were strained working relations between some colleagues at Krotona, Krishnamurti wrote to him:

* Patwardhan, Sunanda, *A Vision of the Sacred; My Personal Journey with Krishnamurti*, Edwin House Publishing, 1999, pp.110-111.

You should all work together, help each other to grow, to flower. If there are any misunderstandings among you, as here are sure to be, they should be dissolved immediately by talking things over, and not postponed to the next day or even the next hour. If postponed, the misunderstandings will grow and become barriers between you. I would most strongly urge you, if I may, not to keep each other's work in separate, watertight compartments. We are all working together, either externally or inwardly. [*]

———————————————

Also by Joseph E. Ross

Krotona of Old Hollywood Volume I 1866-1913
Krotona of Old Hollywood Volume II 1914-1920
New Krotona from Hollywood to Ojai Volume III 1921-1922
Krotona in the Ojai Valley Volume IV 1923-1926
Spirit of Womanhood: A Journey with Rukmini Devi
Krishnamurti: The Taormina Seclusion 1912

Contact: joseph@krotonaarchives.com
www.krotonaarchives.com

---

[*] Ibid., p.82.

Eugene Munson in white suit; Dr. Besant and Henry Hotchener on Krotona Hill.

Chapter 1
1927

Dr. Arundale, General Secretary in Australia, suggested that the Theosophical Society members throughout the world should unite in giving an "80 years gift" in 1927 celebrating the joint 80th birthdays of Dr. Besant and Bishop Leadbeater; Dr. Arundale suggests they are just now beginning the greatest part of their life work as their leaders—full of fire, wisdom, and active service.

Before she went on to Hollywood New Year's Eve to give an address at the midnight service in St. Albans Liberal Catholic Church prior to the blessing of the city as the New Year came in, Dr. Besant gave a short message to her Esoteric Section (E.S.) students at Krotona. She mentioned that "Adyar stands today something more than the headquarters of the Theosophical Society. It is a symbol of a great achievement, the restoration of the Ancient Wisdom to a world grown musty with materialism." *

---

* After the services, Sarah Wetherill Logan of Eddington, Pennsylvania, accompanied Dr. Besant on her return to Ojai, and moved into one of the new houses on Krotona Hill. From correspondence it seems Dr. Besant expected Robert Logan, Sarah's husband and President of the American Anti-Vivisection Society, to join them at Krotona.

The following is in Dr. Besant's own handwriting regarding the World-Teacher.

To my dear students in the E.S. (Esoteric School)

A new year is beginning for us, and I wish to send you all a greeting of good-will, and to ask you to join with me in joyful greeting to the opening year. For the waiting time is over and the World-Teacher has revealed Himself in a way more beautiful and more inspiring than we had dreamed of. Efforts have been made in the creeds of the Christian Church to put into human words the Eternal Relation of the Father and the Son in the unity of the Divine Nature, and in one of these it is written that although the Son be God and Man, "yet He is not two but one Christ," and that that union was effected "by taking the Manhood into God." In the Christ is the union of God and Humanity, "the Manhood" being blended with Divinity. So on a much lower plane, in our mortal world, does the World-Teacher, the Christ, raise the consciousness of His chosen disciple into this own, blending it with His, so far as is possible within the limits of a human body, and we behold Him "full of grace and truth."

Shall we not then rejoice for the coming year, in that the world is once more blessed with the presence of the Lord, coming to help the new sub-race and to lay the foundation of the new civilisation through those who are willing to work under His direction.

Annie Besant*

Documents among Warrington's papers show that Dr. Besant gave a series of weekly E.S. Talks during her stay at Arya-Vihara, at the East end of the Ojai Valley with her beloved Krishnaji. It had been many years since Oaji had the privilege of the Presence of the O.H., Dr. Besant.

---

* Besant, Annie, "To My Dear Students in the E.S.", *The American E.S.T. Bulletin*, n50, February 1927, p.i.

One bright sunny Sunday morning, January 3, 1927, at Arya-Vihara, Dr. Besant called her coworkers together to share her vision and thoughts on buying a piece of land in Ojai. A.P. Warrington, Captain Max Wardall, an American theosophist, Robert and Sara Logan, two prominent Philadelphia theosophist, Henry and Marie Hotchener, C.F. Holland, Attorney at Law, John and Nanea Roine and George Hall, an active realtor and Krotona manager who was pushing for a tract of land adjacent to Krotona. They did not know at the time that this tract of live evergreen oaks of the type found in Southern California would one day become a special spot known as "the Oak Grove" where Krishnamurti would speak regularly over many decades. By 1975, a primary day school, the Oak Grove School, was started adjacent to it.

About ten o'clock, they left Arya-Vihara* in two cars to see the land on the west side of the Krotona property first, since George Hall and some of the members thought that this piece of land, covered with large evergreen oak trees, would be just the right place for what Dr. Besant had in mind. They came to a high open place on the property, "Outlook Point," on the peak of the hill overlooking the surrounding countryside, later to be the location for the Starland Camp fires.

It is reported that they all gathered around Dr. Besant and expressed their ideas about the site. Some were very much in favor of it; others seemed to be waiting to hear what she or Krishnamurti had to say, but neither seemed impressed or keenly interested at the time in this location. Although, some 160 acres were bought by Krotona later to become the Oak Grove from which Krishnamurti give his dialogues until his death in 1986. The land was dedicated to the work of the World-Teacher.

Meanwhile, Krishnamurti persuaded Annie and the whole group to look at the Upper Ojai Valley region where there was

---

* The "Brothers Association" had been originally formed around April 1923 in order to hold title to the property known as Arya-Vihara.

another larger tract of land for sale. As they reached the lower part of the Upper Valley property they stopped at a spot where there was a spring from which water was running continuously. From there the party, including Dr. Besant and Krishnamurti walked up a steep hill to view the property that was for sale, and they liked it very much; they got in touch with the owners and the negotiations began for about 465 acres plus the oil rights. This will be one of the most important transactions to take place in the Ojai Valley for many years. It comprised 314 acres of the Tucker farm, 80 acres, known as the Gentry place and 71 acres of the Nick Walnut Mesa, until recently owned by A. Sarzotti. A land use plan of this original 465 acres was drawn up by Sterling Hoag, A.I.A., of West Los Angeles.

At 80 years young of age, Dr. Besant was just beginning the greatest part of her life work. She had once again made herself personally responsible for the foundation, and been chosen by the Hierarchy as the herald of the movement of paramount importance to the world. She desired to found a center for the new civilization in the Ojai Valley of California. She dreamt of an utopian colony running on educational lines which would be a great factor in the progress of the world. The foundation would be non-sectarian, but a belief in the ideals of the founders would be a requirement for residence.*

Dr. Besant came to Ojai for a visit during October 1926. During her stay in Ojai, plans were being discussed for the building of a camp for the Order of the Star of the East on the site that Fritz Kunz had bought in 1925 in the Upper Ojai Valley for the purposes of a camp and possibly a school to be run by the Order of the Star. (An organization created for Krishnamurti by Dr. Besant in 1912, which later he disbanded in 1929.) It was discovered, however, that that site was unsuitable for a camp as it had no water, and it was

---

* A personal note: more and more as the years roll on I have learnt to appreciate Dr. Besant's many facets and in how many different ways she towered above average humanity. We cannot but admire her amazing versatility, her extraordinarily complete grasp of a vast number of subjects, and her power of dealing instantaneously yet effectively with any and every emergency.

decided to establish the Star Camp on the acreage near Krotona Hill at the west end of the Ojai Valley.*

Meanwhile, Dr. Besant bought the 150 acres from the Order for her project which came to be known as the Happy Valley community scheme. Dr. Besant then formed the Happy Valley Foundation for the express purpose of holding title to the land she bought from the Order of the Star in the East and also an additional large acreage known as the Tucker Farm which she expressly acquired for the future Happy Valley community. Dr. Besant believed that the new race was here and multiplying rapidly in California. The Foundation would include a school, later a college as a World University, which would endeavor to train young people to be good citizens in the New Civilization.

The idea of the World University began back in 1925. Dr. George Arundale said, "The World University that we are going to start is *not* the Theosophical World University. The Theosophical World University does not exist at least on the physical plane. Krishnaji said it existed only on the mental plane, and so it does. It is not what you and I think the University ought to be, it is not our conception of the University that matters. We have not yet received the word of the Master (The Mahachohan) that it is to be instituted in His Name, and yet we must work in affiliation with it. Our task is the preparatory work that will render possible the Master's command."… "If I have understood rightly the speeches that were made at Ommen by those who are going to found the University, the Theosophical World University will represent 'the Mysteries in Education.'" George Arundale goes on to say, "Our University will be the University of the Elder Brethren, in which the Masters will take direct and personal interest. Indeed, They will guide it, insofar as we are wise enough to leave it in Their hands."

---

* Today, there are four theosophical camps in the United States: Pumpkin Hollow Farm, founded in 1937, Far horizons Theosophical Sierra Camp founded in 1954, Ozark Theosophical Camp founded in 1970, and Indralaya in the Orcas Island founded in 1927. All these camps are on acres of woods and meadows and were founded by members of the Theosophical Society to form the nucleus of communities striving to live in harmony with nature and with each other. Consistent with this approach, vegetarianism, and harmlessness to all life are practiced at the camps.

In 1926 Krishnamurti disclaimed that he was the "New Messiah." He explained, and several times later, that he had found himself of a new personality, not his own, speaking to those of his faith and to the world. He said, "It is like a dream. If you have a dream you can recall it, but some parts are vague. I remember, but not definite or concisely. But since the first manifestation of the Great Teacher I feel the ecstasy of purpose which comes from something I want to share with everybody — a joy of living, a feeling of happiness that I want to give to others."

Dedication of the Outtdoor Amphitheater by Rukmini Devi Arundale.

Who can tell where a story begins, or when the seed of an idea, which perhaps has long lain fallow, first sends out its tendrils? Such was the dream and vision of A.P. Warrington's, to use drama to synthesize the emotional forces in the world of art to portray the revelation of man's inner life. He thought that if he could accomplish this, such drama would stand unsurpassed in history. The theater was in some respects the most important of Greek institutions and the chief source of culture for the populace. Pageants and ceremonies of many kinds took place in outdoor Greek amphitheater, and it became the venue of great religious dramas.

The performance of "The Light of Asia," in 1918 in Hollywood, left a mark that carried over to Ojai, where Dr. Besant in 1926 sparked again the enthusiasm to build another outdoor amphitheater at Krotona. A.P. Warrington started on it immediately. It was completed in a natural ravine shaded by large California Oaks on the East side of the Krotona estate. Dr. Arundale and Rukmini were staying at Krotona for part of their American tour when A. P. Warrington asked Rukmini to dedicate the amphitheater with an ancient Sanskrit ritual with Dr. Besant present, and over the years it was used for musicals, lectures, and weddings.

There is no document that Krishnamurti gave any talk that day, but, may have been present with Dr. Besant when she gave the following speech on January 7, 1927 at 1 p.m.

The Great Colony in Southern California
Dr. Annie Besant

There is just one point that I would like to mention, because it is important for all of you, that is the question of the Great colony in Southern California, a thing that you must not regard as a matter of indifference to you. Indeed, the Sixth Sub-Race are being born, and there is no reason why we should not develop the qualities that are wanted to make us fit to be chosen. Only 600 years off — very short years.

If you would learn to think in hundred of thousands of years, you would remember. They plan out years literally 100,000 years before hand, and if you could realize how you could be adaptable, never mind if they are not harmonious, that does not matter a bit. The more disagreeable they are, the better for you. Very useful, because when a nice tempered person meets one who is very cross and snappy, instead of getting a little bit ruffled, he will think I am very glad to see you, because here is a chance for me to develop. You might welcome the most unpleasant person and then you would improve him.

As we have go to prepare to live in that colony, if you are going to be there, remember then that you will be living among very Great People, THE MANU, the HEAD of it, will be there. The Master who is to be the MANU of the Sixth Root Race, and who is now the CHOHAN MORYA, and Master K.H. who will be the BODHISATTVA of that Colony, will be there. You have all got an opportunity. You have come into the E.S. because your Monad ages ago have ordered you in. Don't think you have come in because your lower self wanted to come in, but because of the Inner-man, so make the most of your opportunities. Cultivate the Colony Spirit first, which is not easy for the Fifth Race people.

Be Harmonious and Friendly just as Hard as you can.

On January 11, 1927 at Arya-Vihara, Annie Besant gave a talk that became an article for the Theosophical Society in America titled, "The New Civilization," and published as an article in a four page pamphlet titled "The Happy Valley Foundation." It was also published in the January issue of *The Server* (magazine of the Order of the Star), reprinted in *The Messenger*, Vol. XIV, n10, March 1927, pp. 218-220, and reprinted in *The Magnet* Vol. VIII, n1, April 1927, pp. 7-13, *The Herald of the Star*, Vol. XVI, March 1927, pp. 94-98. Much of the information in the article is repetitive and contains information already elaborated.

Krishnamurti also gave a special members' meetings at Krotona titled "What are You Seeking?" as January 11, 1927 was the anniversary of the founding of the Order of the Star in the East. We do not know if this talk was given in the open-air amphitheater at Krotona, or in the Music Room, for no record has been found where it was given.

Warrington on that Sunday reminds the colony of Krotonians, what the fundamental purpose of Krotona is:

It is to make a centre. You can do that by living together, working together. Things don't just happen. They occur because you make them occur, have to have a purpose. I want to suggest just one step whereby we can make a little deeper effort to bring about the Centre. What is a centre? First, a centre is a spiritual and mental concept. It is an idea, a thought, something created on the mental plane and vivified by spiritual motive. Unless the thing we are doing here on the physical plane has a splendid counterpart on the mental plane, and its counterpart on intervening planes, what we are doing will be to some extent soulless, without a proper vantage in the worlds where things are permanent. I believe that many things arise and flourish for a time and disappear simply because they have been built without proper thought, proper feeling, and you have a shell without the soul. Then, its building on lower planes ought to be almost an automatic action. If you are going to the city, you make a list of things to be done; you wonder if the car is in proper condition; you clean it a little; when you get to the city, you plan to go to certain places. First all all you make a schedule of the whole business. It is marvelous to realize how you have thought things out. If you do not think things out, the whole business seems lacking. How to do that, making of Krotona, which we are now trying to build, a centre for the Masters, is the thing that confronts us. We want, in order to make this a centre, to form ourselves into a group of human beings who will form for Him a collective vehicle. That group has got to have for its very essence the feeling and spirit of brotherhood.

Another aspect which I have not mentioned, an aspect peculiar to Krotona, and that is the teaching side here. The Charter which we have for the promotion of this centre requires that we shall make a college here. The meaning for us is that we shall, as we are able to organize it, have to start a teaching institute or centre. We shall need to get the proper instructors here and need to have the proper people to take the instructions. We can see how that would be worked out. Effort is along the line of the restoration of the Mysteries. Promotion of school, institute, or college here will be the activity along that line in the revival of the Mysteries.

Members present: Miss E. Honold, Mrs. Mattie D. Munson, Mr. Wm. M. Mayes, Mr. J.P. Ascott, Mrs. Mary Coldy, Mrs. Sarah C. Mayes, Mr. Eugene W. Munson, Mr. George H. Hall, Miss Marie Poutz.*

Since Dr. Besant announced the foundation of the "New Civilization," in the Upper Valley of Ojai, California, C. Jinarajadasa picks it up, and explores the place of intuition in the new civilization in his lecture delivered at the Fifty-Second Anniversary of the Adyar Theosophical Society, December 1927. The lecture is published in a small pamphlet by Spring of 1928.

Miss Marie Poutz reported that she had read with much interest the various letters and articles which appeared in *The Messenger* about Krishnamurti saying that he had attained liberation, an inexpressible state. Thus, questions concerning his statements regarding whether he was a Theosophist. He said, "he was." He is Life, and nothing is exterior to him. This made confusion doubly sure.

She hoped that the members should heed the following warning. On a slip of paper dated February 7, 1927 among her other documents she wrote:

> On this date Krishnaji told Dr. Besant, that he feared that Theosophists, because of intellectual pride, would not receive the new message. That message will be *simple*, and on hearing it, they may think they have that in Theosophy — and more, and will not think it worth while.

———————————❧———————————

While Dr. Besant was in Omaha in the fall of 1927, a song entitled "Alma Mater," the words of which were written by Beatrice Rakestraw and the music by Warren Watters was sung and presented to Dr. Besant.†

---

* Warrington, A.P., meeting of the Krotonians called by Warington, at his residence. Taken from his rough draft of handwritten notes.
† All the music sheets, written throughout the history of Krotona, can be found in the Ross Collection, www.KrotonaArchives.com.

Krotona set the scene of a delightful wedding in idyllic surroundings. It was normally a quiet and unexciting life on Krotona Hill, until Miss Susan L. Warfield, of Hollywood, wed the Right Reverend Irving S. Cooper, Regionary Bishop of the Liberal Catholic Church in the United States. The ceremony, held in the charming open-air amphitheater, was conducted by the Right Reverend John Tettemer, Auxiliary Bishop of the Liberal Catholic Church. Miss Warfield had many friends in the Ojai valley, and was one of the most prominent and popular members of the St. Albans Church in Hollywood, where her singing had given great pleasure for several years past.

Bishop Cooper, who had presided over the destinies of the Liberal Catholic Church in this country almost since it's founding, was widely known throughout the United States and other countries. As author, lecturer and world traveler he was one of the prominent leaders in the Theosophical Movement for many years. Mrs. Anne E. Surr attended the bride, and the Rev. John Ingelman also of Hollywood, supported Bishop Cooper. Two little flower girls, Patricia Gooder, daughter of Mrs. Leslie M. Gooder of Winnetka, Ill. and Mary Louise Gerard of Ojai, conducted the bride to the lovely open-air altar, converted into a veritable bower of flowers and ferns, which was prepared beneath the overhanging oaks.

Immediately after the ceremony, Warrington was host at a wedding breakfast in honor of the distinguished couple. Other guests were: Dr. Besant, Krishnamurti, Dr. and Mrs. John Ingelman, Mrs. Anne L. Surr, Mrs. May S. Rogers and Bishop Tettemer.

Bishop and Mrs. Cooper now take their residence in one of the new houses on Krotona Hill.

Annie Besant consecrated the Order of International Co-Freemasonry in the Ojai Valley as Lodge #551. Also known as Le Droit Humain or Human Rights, it was founded in 1893 in Paris, France specifically to support the initiation of women as Freemasons. Today, the order has spread over the world and is comprised of women and men who work together in service to humanity, and who promote freedom of thought and inner growth. The order expresses the widest tolerance for all religions, races and nationalities, providing a place where people can share equality and the bonds of unity.

A.P. Warrington sent out the following letter to members who were interested in joining the E.S. They could not belong to any other body, association, or organization for the purpose of mystic study or occult training (Masonry excepted), as this would interfere with progress in the Eastern Esoteric teachings. Warrington told aspirants that nn important thing for them to consider at this juncture was what their attitude should be towards their teacher, Dr. Besant, the Outer Head of the School. Mr. Warrington also instructed them that to make the most progress one needd to form a warm, personal link with the teacher and his fellow-students, and by so doing, help to bring about an inner unity which makes up any organized body, and much more so an occult one, a concentrated power.

> Your application for membership in the E.S. is received, and before considering your admission to the initial stages, it is best that I should remind you of the ends which the School is intended to subserve.
>
> During the early days of the T.S., an unbrotherly attitude had developed among the members, and it was decided, as H.P.B. has told us, "to gather the 'elect' of the T.S. and call them to action." The School was then a Section of the T.S., as it is now, and she wrote of its formation thus: "It is only by a select group of brave souls, a handful of determined men and women hungry for genuine spiritual development, and the acquirement of soul-wisdom, that the Theosophical Society at large can be brought back to its original lines. Disappointment is sure to come to those who join this Section for the purpose of learning 'magic' art or acquiring 'occult training' for themselves, quite regardless for the good of other people less determined." Again, "developed powers— except those which crown the efforts of a black magician— are only the culmination of, and reward for, labors bestowed unselfishly upon humanity, upon all men, whether good or

bad. Forgetfulness of the personal self and sincere altruism are the first and indispensable requisite in the training."

I would remind you also that the great passion of H.P.B.'s life was her devotion to the Masters, the Elder Brothers of humanity whose sublime renunciation advances the spiritual upliftment of the race; and since the E.S. is Their School, and its duties tend to bring members nearer to Them according to the degree of their earnestness, it is well that only those should seek entrance who believe in the overshadowing Presence of the Great Brotherhood over the School, and eagerly desire a "closer walk" with Them in Their Service.

The motive of the applicant, therefore, should be unselfish; he should be determined to work for humanity, with no desire on his own part to benefit or gain something for himself alone; he must realize that the E.S. is a body set aside for service; that he is to offer a whole-hearted devotion to it and give a sincere loyalty to the Outer Head; that he seeks training only in order to help and teach others. This he must see as the ideal to be striven for, and moreover he should be willing to undertake a rigid discipline of study and meditation and strict obedience to the rules of the School, and he should be reasonably sure beforehand that he has the time and health to enable him to do the required work, as when once in, he is expected to live up to the established regulation.

If in the light of these facts you still feel that you can conscientiously ask for membership in the School, then please fill in and return the blank sheet which accompanies this letter, and after its receipt by me, your application will be duly considered according to the rules laid down by the Outer Head. Let me caution you, however, not to attempt to go further, unless your motives be pure and in accordance with the objects set forth. To come for personal gain, would simply result in painful disappointment. Do not, therefore, decide the matter hastily, but take ample time for searching thought, as the step is not one to be lightly made.

Faithfully yours,
A.P. Warrington
Corresponding Secretary

Letters around this date also track the work by Annie Besant to secure land in Ojai for great purposes:

Feb 2 1927
Private and Confidential
Arya-Vihara
Ojai, California

> To all pledged Members of the E.S.T.
> Dear Co-Worker:
> At the wish of the Inner Head I have secured a tract of land, 465 acres, in the Upper Ojai Valley, and have to obtain a large sum of money as quickly as possible, to meet the cash demand. After that, the price is to be paid by a yearly rental secure on mortgage: as to that there is no difficulty. The part of the Valley bought will form the valley of the nucleus of the sixth Sub-Race, out of which will be chosen the sixth Root-Race, with its colony in Lower California. I earnestly ask your help in raising the amount needed, $40,000, and to send me as soon as possible your gift, large or small according to your power, for this splendid task. Some have given, and this does not apply to them.
> Personally I feel this to be a unique opportunity of service, one of the reasons of my coming to America, and I am giving to it all I have, outside obligations already incurred. I am sure I shall not ask your help in vain.
> Your faithful servant in His Work,
> Annie Besant, O.H.

Thompson Bros. in Hollymont paid for all the property purchased so far in full up to the last note amounting to $50,000. This note matured around February 2, 1927. Attention was given to George Hall, that the Thompson Bros. were interested in having this note paid in full at maturity, or at least in part. They were asking George at this time for an official letter of extension for one year. They had a deal to complete the sale of the Ternery and hilltop. George Hall had to present this to Warrington and receive his full approval, and to secure the signature.

Miss Poutz in the following letter was now put on probation and accepted by her Master, after many years as a devoted student of the Theosophical Society and the Esoteric Section.

February 14 1927
Orient Line
England & Australia
S.S. Otranto

My dear Miss Poutz,
Thank you very much for your kind letter of January 4. Allow me to congratulate you very heartily upon your Acceptance by our Master. I am sure that you will find that this closer link with Him gives you far more power in the work which you have been carrying on so faithfully for so many years.

I do not think that it is in the least likely that I shall visit the United States again in this incarnation. Our great President, though only six months younger than I, is still going most magnificently a great deal of public lecturing work; but I do not think that that is the best line of usefulness for me. I can do better by remaining quietly at home, helping our young people to become workers for Theosophy, and writing occasionally such books as are within my power.
With all heartiest good wishes and affectionate regards,
I am every yours most cordially,
C.W. Leadbeater

A letter by Dr. Besant that speaks to the intention of Happy Valley as a college, and World University:

February 18 1927
Arya-Vihara
Ojai, California

Dear Miss Sommer: (Miss Julia K. Sommer)
I think it is quite probable that the school in the Happy Valley will become a College and a branch of the World University. I do not know what are the rules of your Theosophical World University Association, but I doubt if it would be legitimate to use money

contributed for the University for the building of a school. The money from the Open Gate School which was voted to myself will, of course, be used for the proposed school in the Happy Valley. With kind regards,
Annie Besant

From a letter from Annie Besant in March of this year, we get a sense of the internal conversation:

27-3-15
Adyar

> My dear Charles, (C.W. Leadbeater)
> Enclosed is confidential, but it is necessary that you should see it. Mr. Walton is living in the Ojai Valley at Krotona, and he may mislead many. The absurdity of his pretensions is obvious, but he should not, in my E.S. centre, talk of our Krishna as he does and take on himself the training of an old body for the Lord. He told Kulkarni many other foolish things; luckily Kulkarni did not believe him. You might send the other back. I fear, that Warrington is under Walton's influence.
> Very affectionately yours
> Annie Besant

The above letter regarding Mr. Robert Walton, is referring to the letter found in Volume IV, *Krotona in the Ojai Valley* written by Krishnamurti, January 14, 1924 to his beloved "Mother", Dr. Besant.

Through Mrs. Kiningale Cook, (Mabel Collins) spent the major part of her life in work as a humanitarian supporting the Anti-Vivisection cause, and associated with Miss Cobb, the founder of the British Union for the Abolition of Vivisection until she closed her eyes on this world March 31, 1927. She is known by most Theosophists as the transmitter of *Light on the Path, The Idyll of the White Lotus, When the Sun Moves Northward, The Story of Sensa,* and many more titles.

On April 6, 1927, papers of incorporation of the Order of the Star in the East were filed in the Country Clerk's office, Ventura, California as part of the Theosophical Society. The organization was to have seven trustees who were to serve seven years, one trustee to be elected a year. The first board of trustees consisted of: Fritz Kunz, Ernest Stone, Alma Kunz Gulick, Maysie S. Rogers, F.R.H. Gerard, H.J. Budd, and R.W. Davis.

Dr. Besant was making an appeal for funds back in February from the E.S. members, and those who responded to her request, received the following message as she was leaving Ojai. Reference is to the February 2, 1927 letter.

April 14 1927
Ojai, California

Dear Co-Workers:

I am exceedingly grateful to you for your generous response to my appeal to you to help me in buying the large tract of land in the Ojai Valley, needed for the Great work.

I am enclosing to you a list of donors to the Happy Valley foundation Fund; if any of you find your name omitted or any other error in the text, will you kindly notify me, directing your letter addressed: Dr. Annie Besant, care of Mr. George Hall, Krotona, Ojai California.

We have made the cash payment on the land as required, the sum of $40,000. We have also paid sums due on three plots of land — 80, 70 and 15 acres respectively — and have paid for and are completing a partly built little house, erected on the land.

The main avenues and roads have been fixed, and trees are to be purchased and planted along these — the beginning of making habitable the land with its public buildings. At a meeting last week of the organizing committee, Mr. Louis Zalk of 300 East Michigan Street, Duluth, Minn. was appointed to carry on the collection of funds; well known persons have been selected in most of the States of the Republic to circulate information and collect the large sum necessary for establishing the Happy Valley Foundation; and I am sure that those who have started the work so successfully by their own generous gifts will form groups to help the State Representatives in the heavy task of collecting the big sum necessary to prepare the land they have secured to be a fitting cradle for the infant sub-race. Much has to be done before any inhabitants can settle in the Happy Valley, and we must build the foundations strongly and wisely before we can welcome any settlers.

A work, which has to endure for centuries, cannot be hurried in its early stages; we work under Master-Builders, who plan wisely, before they execute with strength and adorn with beauty.

So, brothers mine, let each of us do his part in the work to which we are called, and let each take his share in the common duty of preparing worthily the Home for the new men and women who shall dwell therein. It is a splendid task, and we are all sharers in the work and in the success which will crown our labors. While I am away in other lands, I shall eagerly watch and help in the building of the new Home, and when I return next year, I hope to see great progress and many changes; for the Blessing of the Holy Ones will make us strong as they watch the preparations to give fitting reception to the great souls whom They will send to the Ojai Valley, to shape and fashion the civilization of the New Age.

Annie Besant.*

Louis Zalk of Duluth, Wisconsin, was active in Star Camp preparations from the beginning with George Hall, and ran an iron and steel business in Wisconsin.

Dr. Besant appointed George Hall her representative in all matters in Ojai, and appointed Fritz Kunz an International Lecturer for the T. S., and Krishnaji had asked him to work in a similar capacity for the Order of the Star in the East.

April brought Warrington sad news when he received word the death of his mother, Mrs. Emily Ann Warrington, a National Member of the Theosophical Society. The month of April Warrington replied to inquiries regarding the continuance of the "Krotona Drama."

In view of the widely circulated and properly authorized Associated Press story announcing the loose mystic union which now exists between the World-Teacher and His chosen vehicle, the natural reply to these inquiries is the "Krotona Drama" has done its work; its mission is finished; for, the event it was intended to herald is now taking place. Thanking those who have done so much to make it the beautiful

---

* Besant, Annie, "To the E.S. members who Responded to my Request," *The Server*, Vol. IX, April 1927, nXI, separate insert.

success it was, I suggest that we now look to other
useful activities.

After a stay of several months in the Ojai Valley, Dr. Besant,
Krishnamurti and a large party of their friends were to leave around
April 29th. D. Rajagopal, Dr. van der Leeuw, Max Wardall, Mrs.
Sarah Logan, Miss Rosalind Williams, Miss Eurth Goold, Miss
Marion Courtright and Mr. Fen Germer left Ojai with brief
stopovers in Los Angeles, Chicago and New York from where they
sailed for Europe on the S.S. Republic, arriving in London May 9.

Lady Emily Lutyens and Miss Lutyens left Ojai a few days
later to join Sir Edwin Lutyens in the East and accompany him to
England.

Who was Dr. J.J. van der Leeuw (Koos)? He was born August
26, 1893. His family held controlling interest in the van Nelle
Company,* a tea, coffee, and tobacco merchant in Rotterdam, which
was managed by his brother, the industrial magnate C.H. van der
Leeuw (Kees). As the President of the International Congress of
Modern Architecture, C.H. van der Leeuw was one of the most
influential patrons of modern architecture in the world in the 1920's
and 1930's.

As it turned out Dr. J. J. van der Leeuw did not build anything
to Griffin's design, although he persuaded several other members
of the Theosophical Society to do so. Koos became member of
the Theosophical Society in 1914, and became a personal friend
of Krishnamurti. It was in 1924 that Koos went to Australia for
occult training with C.W. Leadbeater, becoming a priest in the
Liberal Catholic Church, and treasurer of The Manor (the villa of
the Theosophical community in Sidney) where he also founded the
King Arthur's School for boys, which existed for only one year. By
1925 he published *The Fire of Creation*, for which he was awarded the
Subba Row Medal. The book, however, considered his masterwork,
is *The Conquest of Illusion* which is dedicated to Krishnamurt and to

---

* The Nelle factory is one of the most important historic industrial buildings in the Netherlands.

in memoriam to Krishnamurti's brother Nityananda.

The famous lecture in which Koos supports Krishnamurti in 1929 after Krishnamurti dissolved the Order of the Star in Ommen with the words "Truth is a Pathless land," is entitled *Revelation or Realisation: the Conflict in Theosophy*. The result of this conflict caused George Arundale, International President, to remove Krishnamurti from the grounds of Adyar. Krishnamurti never returned to Adyar until December 1985, a few months before his death on February 17, 1986.

On a return-flight from a series of lectures in South Africa on August 23, 1934, Dr. van der Leeuw's airplane ran into a sandstorm above Tanganyika and hit a mountain. He did not survive. For those interested for further research, please see a book entitled, *Beyond Architecture* by Marion Mahony and Walter Burley Griffin.

The following letter from C.W. Leadbeater is to Miss Eugene Honold, a resident of Krotona occupying the same house with Miss Marie Poutz.

April 27, 1927
The Manor, Mosman
Sydney, Australia

Dear Miss Honold,

I was glad to receive your letter of March 17th, and to hear that you have had such beautiful experiences. I think, however, that with regard to them you had better deal with the Esoteric leaders in your own country; even though we are old friends, I must not interfere with them, for it is not well to mix currents of magnetism, though I assuredly send you general and very earnest good wishes, and surround you with strength which you may absorb as you will and as you can, but according to the methods which they have prescribed for you. It is indeed a wonderful blessing to live at one of the great Centres of our movement, and I am sure that under such conditions you will make the most rapid progress which karma renders possible.

With all affectionate remembrances and hearty good wishes,
I am ever,
Yours most cordially,
Presiding Bishop: C.W. Leadbeater

The Manor , Mosman
Sydney, Australia
April 27 1927

Dear Miss Poutz,
Very many thanks for your kind letter of March 22. I rejoice greatly to hear that you have been able to take a further step, and that you are now a member of the Inner Temple as well as of the Great White Brotherhood. Our President has said in her letters that the Masters have been wonderfully gracious, and have drawn a large number into touch with Them; but I have not up to the present seen a list of names, nor have I heard any details. But they will come all in good time. The work is being wonderfully stimulated all over the world; here at least it is simply overwhelming, and I do not know how we shall get through it now our General Secretary has left us as an ambassador to your Convention.
With all heartiest good wishes,
I am ever,
Yours in true affection,
C.W. Leadbeater

———————————⚑⚑———————————

Meanwhile, in the America, L. W. Rogers makes a public statement in the April issue of *The Messenger*, regarding the community life at Wheaton. He says:

"Only workers with exceptions, will be students staying temporarily for the training school and library. The reason it didn't work at Krotona, was: The trouble at Krotona was idleness — too many people with nothing to do but call upon each other and gossip about trivial things. Wheaton will be one of the busiest spots on earth, and not see the fate of Krotona."
"Another one of our Headquarters workers was resigned

21

to accept a position in Ojai. Mr. Vernon Hill, in charge of the shipping room of the Theosophical Press — who was with us several years. He was asked to take charge of the gardening on the Star grounds adjoining Krotona. I am beginning to wonder if Ojai is playing a practical joke on the Theosophical Society Headquarters by taking most of our experienced workers! Well, if it is a joke it is a double-edged one for, as good as these resigning workers were, we are getting better ones in their places! So it is a jolly good joke and everybody is happy.

Seriously, while we are sorry to lose Mr. Hill we are all happy in the thought that he is to have the open air and sunshine of the outdoor work. His war experience in France left his health much impaired and the work he is taking up in the Ojai is the best fortune that could come to him. At Krotona he will meet Lieut. William Mayes — or at least most of him! Some of him was left on the battlefield when a bursting shell interfered with his plan of leading a charge!"[*]

Vernon Hill

It is at this time period that Dr. Besant is one of the first celebrities to make use of the airplane for travel as she goes to Berlin by way of Amsterdam.

Now a letter from Annie Besant that speaks to the dynamics with Dr. van Hook, previously discussed in this chapter.

---

[*] Rogers, L.W. "Community Life", *The Messenger*, Vol.XIV, n11, April 1927, p.243.

May 28 1927
West Side House, Wimbledon Common,
London, S.W. 19

Dear Parthe, [A.P. Warrington]
Your letter of the 26th April.
No member of Dr. van Hook's E.S. group can be admitted to
E.S. gatherings unless he leaves Dr. van Hook. The only, so far,
who has resigned Dr. van Hook's group, who is also a Pupil, is
Mr. Brinsmaid; he remains a Pupil. I have received letters saying
that they hold to Dr. van Hook from Miss Cutler, Miss Trueblood
and Mrs. Kockersperger. I will notify you when I receive other
resignations, or statements that they remain with him. The others,
who were Pupils, must be suspended until I hear from them.
My visit to Chicago makes no difference, except as stated above.
Every yours,
Annie Besant

Warrington, now at Castle Erede, reports that he observed
Dr. Besant striving to understand the meaning of Krishnamurti's
talks. She gave Warrington the impression that she was watching
Krishnamurti's every utterance for some new word for the New Age;
and he remembered how she made use of one thing he said, namely,
"Behaviour is righteousness." It was at this Camp that Dr. Besant
delivered her address in which she indicated that there would be no
liberation for her until everybody else had first reached that lofty
state. We shall see her return to America for the last time in 1929,
and then, but a fragment, as it were, of her old self. Her forces were
feeble then, and there was not that grand completeness in her.

On June 23, 1927, Krotona Institute states that they have granted
permission for The Pacific Telephone and Telegraph Company to
place and maintain 17 poles, and 6 anchors with the necessary wires
and fixtures, upon the Krotona estate so that Star Camp can start
their 200 acre tract improvement by January 1, 1928.[*]

---

* According to the blueprint map in the author's collection.

Castle Erede Ommen
June 28 1927

My dear George,

I have been pondering the thought that it would be desirable to have none but pupils at Krotona; and I have come to the conclusion that, while the plan is highly desirable and we must try to add here to it as closely as possible, we must never-the-less prove the rule to be good by making intelligent exceptions. Do it as worthy cases come up, otherwise the very thing will happen which we want to avoid, namely, practically an official, public announcement (through gossip, of course) that there is such a group as Pupils on the hill and that the place is sacrosanct for them alone. And that wont do! Rather let us never mention the rule, but make wise exceptions to it while living up to it as nearly as possible.

I don't know of any exception to it just now unless it should be young Hill, but of course there has been no place for him. If there had been I should have taken him in, and any differences could have been explained to him as Masonic.

All goes wonderfully well here. We are all so very happy. I wish all Krotonians could have come. But next year will be your favoured year, and hundreds will then be enjoying your opportunities at the Camp.

I am sending this through Miss Poutz, so that she may see my decision.

Heartily

A.P. Warrington

Fritz Kunz and Dora van Gelder wed in Chicago on May 16, Dora keeping her own name. They had a baby boy named John in April 1929.

On August 2, Krishnamurti delivered a noteworthy address "Who Brings the Truth?" at Eerde, the International Headquarters of the Order of the Star, This talk is noteworthy as marking the beginning of Krishnamurti's break from the influences which have up to this point surrounded him.

Maude Couch contacts Louis Zalk that Warrington has been quite ill with arthritis for over a week, but seems to be improving, while Hazel Crowe gave a weekly report to Zalk regarding Warrington moving furniture to Santa Barbara for three months.

Edd Mathews loaned the truck to transport the luggage, etc.

Hervey and Alma Gulick are moving into the old ranch house on Krotona, while Goldy and Mrs. Rosner are taking their apartment. George reminded them that he was going to charge them a good stiff price and donate the money to Star Camp.

Louis Zalk reminded George Hall that he should suggest to Warrington that he would be glad to sell to Krotona all the land they needed on very easy terms. In fact, Zalk proposed that if Krotona assumed interest and taxes plus a small annual payment to reduce the contract, they could act now, before the land was sold to others.

There are many letters in the archives, regarding the starting of Star Camp, only a few are used here. The many unsorted boxes regarding the Star Camp history are still at Krotona. Louis Zalk announced his Camp organization sheet as follows:

L.W. Shattuck, assistant to Frank Gerard. Louis B. Cassell and E.W. Munson in reserve for further consideration as possibilities for the positions of Camp Superintendent and Asst. Superintendent. Mr. Munson could also act as chief mechanic under Ray F. Goudey, with in reserve Mr. Holstead and Mr. Paul A. Fisher. Mrs. Anita Jones Huckaby for looking after the meals. Anita knew the chemistry of foods with ten years experience, and the kitchen equipment and management under Mr. Huckaby. Others mentioned were Dr. John A. Ingelman, Henry and Marie Hotchener, Wm. F. Mayes, Mrs. Ellen S. Hooper, Dr. E.B. Beckwith, Mr. Toluboff, Mrs. Galgier, Dr. Geo. F. Lake and so many others.

August 31 1927

Dear Louis,

LANDSCAPING

If this matter has to be referred to Krishnaji, it should be done at once, so that we can start the planting of trees during the rainy season.

Please refer to your map in connection with the following recommendations.

I have consulted Mr. Toluboff as instructed, but because of the vagueness of his recommendations and his apparent lack of interest, with regard to which, of course, I may be mistaken, I have consulted two landscape architects.

I quote from Mr. Toluboff's letter as follows: "The trees that would fit the landscape of Starland Camp in the future, generally speaking, should be trees typical of California: No.1, Oak Trees; No.2, Sycamores; No.3, Eucalyptus; No.4, Cypress. For the borders on the roads, Oak trees and Eucalyptus should be used in preference to others; for groups in the camp we could use any bushy low type of local growth with couple of real good Cypress pointing to the sky in each group. At the buildings we should have as much as possible of southern, even tropical, palms and cactuses. The cactus every where against the white walls."

Regarding the recommendations of Mr. Peragnell, I will quote from my letter of July 28th, as follows:

"Mr. Pragnell, who is the landscape gardener for the Libby Estate, and does an extensive business from Santa Barbara to Los Angeles, has recommended to me the following combination of trees to be planted along the roads:

"First, Eucalyptus Citriodora alternating with Eucalyptus Sideroxyton Rosea. The first of these has a white bark which does not peel, and is commonly called the lemon scented Eucalypts. The other one has a pink flower. This is his first choice.

"He also suggests another combination. The first of these is the Eucalyptus Viminalis, which has a pnkish white flower, which is to be alternated with the Cucalyptus Ficifolia (scarlet flowered), or with the Ceonothu Thyrsiflorus (deep blue flowered)."

Mr. T. Barrons is doing very wonderful work in the beautifying of Arya-Vihara. He spends the whole of Wednesday there each week. He has been very successful in securing many hundreds of dollars worth of trees and shrubs as gifts. He has very kindly offered his services to the Star Camp, free of charge, and will be able to furnish to the Camp a large number of threes for the cost of transportation from Santa Barbara. He has already secured the promise of 300 Palms, five years old. His recommendations (please refer to map) are as follows:

Bordering road No.1, 30ft. Apart, palms; bordering road No.4, pepper trees; bordering roads Nos. 5and 6, Acacias, Melanocylon; bordering road No.3, Eucalyptus, Ficifolia (scarlet green blossom), Eucalyptus Polyanthema (white blossoms), alternating these two varieties; bordering road No.2, Pinus Canariensis (blue pine); for the grove of trees near the boundary line (green figures No.8), Monterrey Cypress.

I am enclosing herewith a map which I furnished to Mr. Barrons, and his memorandum thereon.

Perhaps with these three recommendations before him, and the map for reference, Krishnaji himself could decide this problem of landscaping, and send us his instructions.

You will notice that Mr. Barrons says nothing about the buildings, but only deals with the main features which should be started as far as possible this year. If the palms which he suggests or the main entrances are not wanted for that purpose, perhaps they could be used around the buildings as suggested by Mr. Toluboff.

Since we would probably get a different suggestion from every artist consulted, it seems to me that the decision lies with Krishnaji, who will, of course, be in a much better position to judge of the work of Mr. Barrons when he has returned, and sees that has been accomplished at Arya-Vihara. I do not believe that sufficient funds will be available to do all of this work the first year, but we ought to take advantage of our opportunity of securing these 300 palms at so little cost. I am not supposed to know anything about this subject, but I have done the best I could to furnish preliminary information from those who are supposed to know.

Cordially yours,

George Hall

By October 18th, the welder started welding the Star Camp pipe lines, the road grading was nearly finished, and a Ventura contractor was discussing the bath house problems and the room construction costs.

It was at this time George Hall announced that he had for the past few months been endeavoring to purchase from the Ranch Company the old ranch house. This transaction was mixed up in a very complicated way with George Hall's own real estate activities. He was able to secure the property of about eight acres with the old ranch house at a remarkably low figure. This would allow the Star to move the National Headquarters office from Hollywood, and allow the moving of the Star Camp office to the same location. Warrington was rather anxious to keep Krotona isolated and undisturbed by all of this; it was quite impossible with all this business being transacted in the E.S. Office building at the Krotona Institute. Possession of the building could not be had until January 1st, 1928.

The records show a statement of Star Camp land indebtedness, including payments of principal and interest totaling $10,000. Adding to the costs in the monthly statement is the following figures: $1000 barrel water storage tank, complete, $640; preliminary grading costs outstanding and unpaid, about $200. The bridge was finished costing $350. George wanted to ensure that the bridge be straight with the road, and because the man entrusted with the work did not get it initially right, it cost another $50 to correct.

The large expenditure ahead of them was the cost of the bath houses and kitchen units plus the grading of the ground for the tents.

It was in March 1922 that Dr. Besant addressed a circular to all members, in which she outlined the events which had led to the problems in America and Australia. She said, "The super-physical line of communication," had never been broken. She had always explained that she could "Obtain, whenever necessary, the approval or disapproval" of her Master on any point on which she was in doubt.

Before leaving the United States For the Ommen Camp in August, Dr. Besant and her beloved Krishnaji, were traveling throughout the country on an E.S. tour giving talks to E.S. members that the World-Teacher had arrived. Most of the talks were published in *The American E.S.T. Bulletin*.

G.S. Arundale while at Huizen wrote down a conversation with Dr. Besant concerning her predictions of the World-Teacher's coming. It also appears in the book *Krishnamurti: The Taormina Seclusion, 1912.*

---

*Edwin House Publishing, 2003, pp. 158-161.

In August 1927 I stayed at Eerde Castle for a month before the Ommen Camp. It was the first year during which difficulties became serious, or took a serious turn between Krishnamurti's teaching and the predictions made for 15 years previously by the leaders of the T.S. and particularly Dr. Besant and C.W.L. According to these predictions, a recurrence was to take place of what had been before, the Lord Christ was to "occupy" Krishnamurti's body and give out the new message through his lips.

Indeed, some corroboration of these predictions had already taken place at Benares in 1911, at Adyar in 1925, at Ommen in 1926. For a short time while Krishnaji was speaking he seemed to lose consciousness, a mighty voice seemed to speak through his lips and a tremendously powerful influence was felt by all those who listened, yet in 1927 all was changed. We knew that in January 1927 important occult events had taken place in Ojai when changes had been brought about in Krishnaji's physical and inner being, we knew that he had reached union with the lord and we could see, and he told us that no occupation of his body was taking place, nor would take place any more, that whenever he spoke it was he, Krishnaji, and no other who experienced the thought and thought out the words. The turmoil and confusion during that month were great. There were those who, knowing of the change, resented the faulty description given by our leaders and expressed their resentment bitterly; there were those who not perceiving the difference, or uninformed as to changes, spoke high in their loyalty to the leaders. Endless discussions took place between them and Krishnaji finally asked me to go to Dr. Besant and tell her definitely all the truth, such as it was, and therefore of the error made until then.

It was only some months later that during Dr. Besant's stay in London I carried out that mission, and had wither at Wimbledon the conversation, which I now wish to record:

I began by revising the whole position, the predictions made, the occupation of the body theory, the clear denial now brought both by the evidences of our senses and by Krishnaji's definite statement. He had said that there was no occupation of him, that there would be no such occupation in the future and he was the one who knew. Was it not imperative then that we should "drop the occupation of the body theory" and conform our description to the truth.

I then said, while Dr. Besant was silent, waiting for my exposition to proceed, that Theosophical teachings might support the facts as they were if one considered the process followed in the foundation of sub-races. It is when a root-race is to be founded that the Lord Manu and the Lord Boddhisattva come personally to earth in order to evolve the type of body necessary for their race, that body remaining established for the whole duration of the race; but when a new sub-race comes to be formed the Lords choose out of their race one disciple who in advance had developed to perfection the consciousness of the future sub-race. Up to that level the disciple is perfect, from that level upward to the Atmic where the Lords can be said to reside, the disciple is as yet imperfect; so that in order that perfection itself should appeal to men the Lord Boddhisattva lends his own perfection for those levels where the disciple is imperfect, and we have at the same time "occupation of the disciple" and "union with the disciple," at the level where his perfection ceased, i.e. 2nd level for the 2nd sub-race, 3rd for the 3rd, 4th for the 4th, 5th for the 5th. In the case of Jesus, therefore, the Lord lent his Buddhic principle between the disciple's perfect manas and the atmic level, and indeed all Christian symbology is indicative of the identity of the Christ with Buddhi.

But in the present case the same law demanded that the chosen disciple (Krishnaji) having achieved perfection as to his Buddhic Consciousness, there was no longer any gap between his perfect Buddhi and the Lord's Atma. Of the two factors of the previous comings, therefore namely union and occupation, only one was now existent, i.e. union and there was no longer any occupation.

There I stopped. Dr. Besant then asked the question, "How do you know these things?" and I answered, "I do not know how but they seem to me certain." At that moment her eyes emptied of light and she was motionless. I knew she had gone out of her body and she remained for a while absent. When she returned she said simply "As I have never had the experience of being present near the Teacher when a new sub-race was founded and therefore could not know from my own memory how he was to return, my Master showed me the previous comings and I described the future one in terms of the former."

No more was said on the subject, but I thought that the nature of her error was very clear to me, and that although it had led to tragic consequences, it was a trifling one, and of such spiritual beauty as to be easily disregarded if rightly understood. It seemed to me that while looking at the contemplation of the duality; Lord-disciple, she, a disciple, had ignored the disciple lost in the glory of the Lord (as a star is not seen in the radiance of the sun), that the presence of the Lord had been to her the one factor worthy of note, and the other factor, that of union, had not been taken into account at all. Had she given any value to the union factor and described the new coming in terms of union, there would have been no mistake for indeed there was union, the union of Krishnaji with this Beloved, of which he sung in his "Love Lyrics." There my mission ceased and I remained silent leaving Dr. Besant to act or speak as she thought fit. To my knowledge she mentioned her mistake in describing the future coming at an E.S. meeting in Amsterdam. Whether she mentioned it elsewhere and to others I do not know. I have not even reported that conversation to Krishnaji, leaving her to do so if she wished, but I could not help feeling all this while that it would have been well if, while some of Krishnaji's followers were led to abuse of our leaders because of their misunderstanding the truth might have been known, the mistake brought back to its reality, to its beautiful reality. Then would it be possible to bridge over the gap between Krishnaji's message and the T.S. For there need have been no discrepancy at all between his message and Theosophy. Not only can we understand him in the light of Theosophy if the mistake is suppressed, but there can be no richer corroboration of Theosophical teachings than Krishnaji's description of

31

his own experience regarding the consciousness of the 6th sub-race. Has not the Society been rent by a needless, by an artificial division?

It may be that the further part of my conversation with Dr. Besant that day could help in understanding the former part. I said to her "Mother, since we have this conversation about difficulties, might I speak of another one?" She acquiesced and I said, "I heard you say not long ago that Christianity was a religion of the lower mind, is it not one of the higher?" She replied with tremendous force: "Lower." I rejoined "Is not the 5th race at the level of the 5th principle, the higher mind, and is not this 5th sub-race peculiarly intended to perfect that 5th principle and accordingly do we not see that Christ's teaching is on the higher mind plane, that of the ego as a spiritual unit and of the ego's social links with other egos. The Christian God is a social God, a Father, Christ a social Saviour, the first born among many brethren; Mankind is spiritual democracy, all egos having an equal right in the eyes of the Father." Then again I saw her withdraw from her body; her eyes lost their light; she remained so for a while; then on returning she said these very words: "You are right. I was told a religion of the mind and I made it of the lower mind."

It seems to me that these two mistakes of our Beloved Chief are very much alike. In both cases reverence for the Masters led her to overlook some of the factors involved. She was then at a period of her life when avowedly she knew her brain to be tired and she trusted less to her own reflections and thinking, and therefore remained unflinchingly near to what she had seen and heard. However that may be, I consider it my duty to consign my remembrances of that conversation by writing, to be used by the leaders of our Society as they may think wise.*

George Arundale's great success as a lecturer and writer was not due merely to his deep occult lore, and to the fact that he spoke from personal knowledge, but also because of the abundant sense of humor that lit up his discourses, his happy and incisive style of

* Arundale, G.S. Statement with Dr. Besant in the Author's archives.

"putting it across," and that indefinable magnetism which gave a special charm to some lecturers. He wrote from his own experience to justify that the Lord is here. Traveling from Amsterdam to Paris, en route for Cherbourg and New York, he wrote a small pamphlet "The Lord Is Here."

Warrington arrived back at Krotona bringing with him George and Rukmini Arundale whom he accompanied from the American Theosophical Convention held in Chicago at the Stevens Hotel. He spent the months of June and July in Holland where he was the guest of Krishnaji, and where he attended the International Camp Congress of the Order of the Star.

When Dr. Arundale arrived for the first time on American soil, he realized that he was touched with something different from anything he had so far experienced. He had wondered whether he lived in America before. In a curious sense he felt familiar with the whole spirit of the country.

Warrington reminded Dr. Arundale that they needed him to help America, the nation that was at the present moment receiving special attention from the Masters of Wisdom, and that the Society needed vigorous, high-caliber leaders, those who would come to their work with energy and vision. They believed that in American the garden would grow many Sixth-Race flowers, asking Dr. Arundale to stay and be the master-gardener.

He reported that their party for the tour was a most happy little circle, and that Warrington, about sixty years of age, was as young as the youngest, and made all the arrangements for the party. What they would have done without him he did not know. He made Dr. Arundale the official Theosophical courier of the United States.

Building begins at Krotona; water tower.

The following was recorded at the home of Betty and A.P. Warrington when the Lord Vaivaswatta Manu* and the World-Mother gave an audience to George and Rukmini Devi on September 20, 1927. The meeting was confirmed by Maude Couch, Miss Poutz and Betty Warrington. Maude N. Couch had a copy of this in the E.S. office, and with her permission and at the request of Miss Poutz, the messages was read to E.S. members at Krotona in 1965 with the name of the recipients not given. It is published here to show how far off the mark they had gone, before Krishnamurti dissolves everything in 1929, by making everything into world-theatre and theatrics, rather than reverence inspired by revelation.

> They welcomed us and talked of the future of the work. We were told, the Lord represents the Father, She the Mother. As He is the Father of the Aryan Race, She is the Mother. As He sows the seed of a new civilization, She tends to its growth, for She is the Mother of all things. They showed Themselves in Their Divine Offices and in Their work together for the New Race. Together They represent the Logos, each individually representing one Aspect, one Manifestation of the Logos. The Lord Vaivasvatta spoke and explained these things and said how He hoped that we two could help in His work as we too represent the two aspects,

---

* (Sk.) Name of the Seventh Manu, the forefather of the post-diluvian race, or our own fifth humankind.

while, through our love for each other, the unity between the two Great Departments of work could be made manifest. He went on to say that He had desired George in America for His Work and that He is using him. George prostrated as the Lord said these words and there flashed a brilliant Light, the Light of the Logos himself unifying George with the Lord Vaivasvatta. For a moment George was non-existent, and it was as if an initiation, Divine Blessing, a Consecration had taken place which made George officially the Son of the Lord Vaivasvatta Manu. He told George that in future He would direct George's work in America and use him. The Lord then spoke to this effect:

"My Son, I have consecrated you that you may help me in My Work. I have seen with pleasure the harmony of Love and Power you are able to produce in the hearts of My American children, and I have the authority of Our Lord to use you as My Own. I shall stand behind you in ever-increasing measure and help you to give My Message to the Citizens of America. They must be helped to stand on a sure foundation to perform their Dharma to their own nation, to their younger brothers and to the World at large. They have the foundation of true Citizenship, true Freedom, and true happiness. The time has come to give them final stage of citizenship—a sense of their Power and a true Aryan Dignity of Culture and the poise of understanding. In the name of Our Lord the Sun, I accept and bless you, My Messenger and Son."

Then He spoke to me (Rukmini) and said that I would also be needed to help Him through helping the Women of the World and of America to a truer realization of Womanhood, and Our Lady said:

That as George has had the preparation all these years by his nearness to Dr. Besant and C.W.L., he could well go out into the World to work. But I had to prepare myself yet for the work She had for me. She was glad I am staying on at Ojai for during every day of quiet that I could have She would help me to come nearer to herself. She mentioned the fact that the Lord Vaivasvatta had already pointed out to me the Centre for the World-Mother and She showed me that in the new civilization, the true Woman and Mother would have a great place. She would hold a position of graceful womanhood respected and loved, and She would be a priestess in the home and a splendid part in all the activities of her country.

The Lord Vaivasvatta Manu:

I have brought you to My new home, in which I am glad to know you have been happy. I thank you for the help you have given My people, and now I send you forth again to continue the good work you have already done.

I shall guide and direct you so that through you America may the more swiftly travel along the road on which I have set her. It is My Message that you give so well, as our brother Krishnaji speaks the World of the blessed Maitreya.

You have nobly fulfilled the hope with which I sent you, and I shall need you for further service in My new country and in My Ojai home, O traveler through the worlds.

I will watch over your two loved comrades until they rejoin you, and as you travel from place to place My power rest on My Messenger and Son."

The Master Jesus talked to Warrington, Rukmini and myself and explained the mechanism of the using of a vehicle by The Lord, to what extent the Lord could identify His consciousness partially with that of the vehicle, and the extent to which the individuality of the vehicle must necessarily to some extent have play and make a certain unavoidable complication, the right which must not be lost and which calls for wisdom and common sense on the part of all.

He told us to guard against the people of today being confused or misled by the setting of the Coming 2,000 years ago. For each Coming there is the appropriate setting — the Word is spoken in the form most suitable to the times. The well-to-do shall be justified, if they spread their well-being abroad, for we must learn that there is as much possibility of spiritual growth through material prosperity as through following the usual code of morality, in learning, for example, not to tell a lie. Our Lord may be surrounded by well-being, may live a material ease and comfort, and will be no less the Christ. He will spread the Gospel of material well-being and take advantage of the very spread of material prosperity in America — a prosperity in the plan for America — to guide it to its true purpose. Material well-being must become universal, and the well-to-do may well "enter the Kingdom of Heaven" provided they use a purely acquired wealth in the service of their fellow-men.

We should remember that Our Lord is all things to all men and that He will exhort each people according to that people's need and destiny. It may be that He will deem it wise to assume the role of the Sannyasi, and some He may exhort to the renunciation of worldly goods and of the worldly life, yet others the Great Sannyasi may exhort to the pursuit of material welfare, for His work needs the Vaishya as well as the Brahmana, the Sudra as well as the Kshattriya. India is the world Brahmana, but America shall be the world Vaishya, each country holding up and practicing its own mode of Divine Activity, both of which are equally vital to the welfare of the world.

The Master directed me to give everywhere my lecture on "America: Her Power and Purpose," for "you are knocking at the door of the heart of the American people with your finely delivered message. You are helping them to receive Our Lord as He will come to them, understanding the genius of their civilization and molding it to its great purpose. There should be little argument about the Coming. Appeal to hearts rather than to minds. State the Great Fact, let it speak for itself, and declare what Our Lord calls no man from prosperity or from comfort or even from luxury, but exhorts that these be won at no cost of pain to others and that they be used to help others to gain the same well being. Impress the people with the eagerness of the great fathers of the American nation, those who have lived for her and died for her in days gone by, brood over their people today, and eagerly hope they may seize the wonderful opportunity now before them, before America —

the child of their hearts and the creation of their sacrifice. As the Master Jesus said this, I felt that I entered into the group-soul of these great servants of American and received their benediction upon my work for them and for Those who sent them forth.

The Master was good enough to thank Mr. Warrington for the great help he was rendering the work and us by sharing the tour with us. "He is a great example of a true American gentleman. His fine atmosphere uplifts the tone of all with whom he comes into contact, and makes more possible both the appropriate delivery of your message and its cordial reception."

The Lord Maitreya was good enough to grant us an audience. I set down my impression in my own words of His Blessing:

Tell My American children that I come to them in their daily lives, in their homes, in their daily occupations, for I want to enter into their joys and hopes, into their grief's and sorrow. I want to enter into the hearts of My American children that they may move swiftly to their great destiny and mission. For what have they been born of sacrifice, nurtured in freedom and brought to prosperity, but that they may stand on My Left Hand as My Indian children, of their birthright, stand on My Right Hand, that together We may journey (wander) through the world and bring to Me My other no less cherished children.

The Lord explained that from the beginning America had been dedicated and consecrated to this great purpose — that she might be His trusty servant on his return to the outer world. Every great step she has taken has been in preparation for this, and the Hand of Destiny has been in each great episode of her birth and youth.[*]

---

* Author's archives.

Meanwhile, books are still needing to be kept.

October 5 1927

> Dear AP:
>
> For some time I have been urging AB to repay the Krotona loan while she has the money. Today she authorized to write Hall to pay back $15,000. Please do it at once, and get your securities released. She is very busy and I am sure you will be happy to be rid of the burden of the interest.
>
> I will write you more fully on the boat, sailing for home on 8 Oct. Will be at Parobia for 2 weeks.
>
> Parthe please have Hall send receipt from Krotona on bank for $15,000 payment with nice words of thanks. I told her Krotona needed the money to keep its expenses up. Much love to you and Kotonians.
>
> Max.

Dr. Mary E. Rocke, who was by profession a gynecologist of some standing in London conceived and carried through the erection of a magnificent Star Amphitheater for the Star Organization at Balmoral Beach, Australia, and offered it to Krishnamurti, but he declined to accept it. (The Amphitheater had no connection at all with the Theosophical Society, apart for the fact that all those associated with it were eminent members of the TS, that the foundation stone was laid and "consecrated" by Leadbeater, with Theosophist and Co-Masons enthusiastically participating, that it contained a Shrine Room for the ES of the TS, and that TS members were urged to contribute to the building of the Amphitheater in TS publications, etc.) Mary, a member of the Order of the Star in the East (founded in 1911 in Benares, now Varanasi, India), was made Organizing Secretary in 1911. She was a member of the Co-Masonic order, and wrote rituals for the World-Mother movement, and Co-Masonic using music composed by Mozart, an active Freemason. She had spent a year at Eerde, Holland, and was travelling with Dr. Besant, Krishnamurti, Dorothy and C. Jinarajadasa on their way to India. when she fell down the saloon companion stairway on the P & O lines "China". The party had seen her the day before, and had noticed nothing wrong with her except that she seemed a little vague in her talk, but not sufficient to cause alarm. She died instantly while at sea, on the way to India presumably from her injuries from the fall.

Beatrice Wood writes her experience for *The Messenger*, October 1927, that the first time she attended a theosophical lodge room meeting, no one welcomed her at the door, no one bothered where she sat, no one smiled, no one seemed conscious of the thrilling excitement of coming into contact with members of the Society for the first time. She sank into a seat by an empty row of chairs, while others avoided the places beside her; they had friends they preferred to sit by. After the lecture was over she did not leave immediately, but stood in the middle of the room, hoping that one or two people might talk to her. However, the members were too busy discussing occult progress, and their self-interest in comparing notes. There was nothing left for the woman to do but to walk home, more lonely than when she had come. Beatrice states that this is a true story. She felt that the Masters would not allow one hungry soul to pass unwelcomed, if They did, they were failing in their sacred duty.[*]

October 24 1927
C/O Miss Cora M. Allen
17 Beverly Road
Buffalo, N.Y.

> Dear Mr. Warrington:
> Enclosed is a map of the pergola south of our house, and the typewritten copy of Mr. pragnell's recommendation for the planting. Will you please note your approval or any changes you wish made, and return the map to me. But you need not return the typewritten specifications.
> Mr. Pragnell is also working on a map of the library grounds, and a map of the grounds around your house, but this is not yet finished. I expect to be able to send you the library plan the last of this week. Mr. Munson has started the excavation work around the pergola, beginning this morning. I think we shall be able to show considerable results with this work in the next three or four months.

---

[*] Wood, Beatrice, "Our Attitude to New Members", *The Messenger*, Oct., 1927, Vol.XV, n5, p.109..

It seems to me that Mr. Pragnell is taking hold of this matter most efficiently.

Mr. Ascott turned over the key of his house about the 15th, and is occupying a room in Mr. Fey's house at the foot of the hill. Vernon has moved his personal effects into No.9, but will continue to sleep at Siete Robles until I can find some one else to occupy the house. I am expecting Mr. Danskowski to do this about the first of November.

Everything seems to be moving very satisfactorily at Krotona. I hope you are having an enjoyable trip.

Most cordially yours,

G.H. Hall

Love and best wishes from us both G.G. [George & Grace]

"Taj Mahal"; the Pleiades center dome is the Shrine Room.

Warrington hadn't had any time alone for weeks and weeks, and his correspondence piled up with no acknowledging of it.

Headquarters Staff
Theosophcial Society
Wheaton, Illinois

Dear Friend:

We send you herewith a copy of an open letter addressed to Dr. and Mrs. George S. Arundale. For weeks we have been harbouring the idea that Dr. Arundale should remain in this country, and at last this idea has been kindled into a living flame. Around the country in ever widening circles we hear the clarion call sounded and resounded, Dr. Arundale shall stay and help us in this dawn of a new day. Remember, leaders will never thrust themselves upon us, but will come only in answer to our appeal for them. Let us, therefore, all unite in one ringing invitation.

To keep our Comrades in America, and to prove to them that the call for their services is urgent, we propose this letter, which you will please sign and mail to the address given below immediately. Persons on the pacific coast should telegraph, time is pressing and we do not want Dr. Arundale and his dear wife, Rukmini, to sail from America on the 19th of this month. We want them both, we need them both. They have grown very near and dear to us.

Because we cannot possibly reach all our members at this late date, won't you please sign, securing as many additional signatures as possible?

We need not point out the needs of the Section, you already know, they are many. New life is needed, and greatness is all that that word signifies. Dr. Arundale is that GREATNESS, let us show him that we want his services.

Faithfully yours,

Signed by the Headquarters Staff:

Ernest Stone, Elise Atwood, Ben Harris, Mary E. Moutz, Angele Davis, Bessie B. Maxson, Marion C. Peterson, Doris Lincoln, Lillian Boxell, Allan Boxell

Mr. Ben Harris, one of the signatures in the above letter, who was one of the most popular people who ever came to Headquarters, completed the two years of service by handing in his resignation and returned to his native California living in a mountain cabin near the Ojai Valley. We will find him later on becoming very involved with Krotona, and the Taormina Community.

Around October 22nd and 23rd, Dr. and Rukmini Arundale along with Warrington honored Headquarters at Wheaton after dinner one evening as they all gathered in the library with only the light from the fireplace illuminating the room. Dr. Arundale talked of various impressions of Wheaton, and all those present, at their good fortune in living at Headquarters and taking an active part in the very important work being done there. He told them that the "atmosphere" of the place was impressive and he could personally testify to its peace and serenity.

The following letter was received from George and Rukmini Arundale on the eve of their departure for Europe, from whence they would sail shortly to India.

S.S. Olympic, New York

Dear Friend:

We are indeed grateful to you for your appreciation of our stay among you and for your warm and brotherly invitation to us to remain for some time longer in America.

We can assure you that this visit has been to us of absorbing interest and of very great inspiration, and the more we have contacted the American people the more we have realized the wonderful destiny in store for your great country if she will seize her opportunity. In particular stand out, as you will, of course, agree, our visit to glorious Ojai, to Wheaton, your noble Headquarters, and to Washington, where are so many great memorials of the past, above them all towering the shrine to your greatest citizen, Abraham Lincoln.

We long to return to contact yet more intimately the soul of the American people, but for the time being we must be home once more in India for the Annual International Convention, thence proceeding to visit our beloved brethren in Australia, so wonderful in their sacrifices in the cause of Theosophy. After the Australian Convention in April, at which one of us hands over his office to a more worthy successor, plans for the future have to be made in consultation with our elder brethren, Dr. Besant and Bishop Leadbeater, for we must go where we can be most useful in the common work.

We both most earnestly hope, however, that good karma and the needs of the work may before very long bring us back to you. We want to come back, though we think the need for us is not quite as great as, in your generosity, you suggest. You have many fine workers, a devoted band at Headquarters, and a president in Mr. Rogers whose devotion and quite outstanding ability place him in the front rank of theosophical workers throughout the world. Nevertheless, it would give us the greatest happiness to join them in helping to theosophize America, for we have found here a real home and have cherished memories of visits to many centres throughout the land. You gracious wish that we should remain will, we most earnestly hope, bring us soon back again. In the meantime

43

we thank you from our hearts for all you have done for us and for all you have been to us.
Au Revoir.
Affectionately and fraternally,
Rukmini Arundale
George S. Arundale

October 26 1927

Dear Mr. Warrington,
Mr. Hall has asked me to enclose another note to you to let you know that the Star organization through Dr. Ingleman has purchased eight more acres of land from the Ojai Ranch & Development Co., which includes the old ranch house. This latter will be used for a Star Headquarters building for the time being, and Mr. Ingleman says he expects to move the offices up here by January. Mr. Hall plans to move the Star Camp office there at the same time. The move cannot be made sooner because of the fact that possession of the building cannot be had until January 1st.
With every good wish for your happiness and comfort on this strenuous trip,
Most sincerely yours,
Maude N. Couch

The Ranch House mentioned in the letter above, located in Meiners Oaks on South Lomita Avenue, was on land originally called "Cheery Acres" owned by the Meiners Family dating back to the 1870's. The Meiners family raised fruit trees, wheat, oranges, lemons, apples etc., and on the rest of the ranch raised hogs. After Mr. Meiner died in 1898, the land was kept by his heirs until 1924 when it was subdivided, and George Hall bought for Krotona the Ranch House building along with several acres. Warrington found this information very interesting as the purchase completed the tract and would be more than very useful during the Star Camp. He felt this surely would make the Star workers very happy to be in the Valley.

The Ranch House played a role in the subsequent history of Ojai. Allan Hooker was a well known Theosophical lecturer in

Columbus, Ohio. After hearing Krishnamurti, he left his old home where he worked as a baker in a pie factory, and bought the Ranch House from Krotona around 1949. Initially it was run as a boarding house with room for 16 guests. His wife Helen helped with the serving and housekeeping. Needing money, they expanded the small dining room into a vegetarian restaurant in the living room using card tables and folding chairs. Then it could seat a very cozy 30. Though Allan wrote arguably the cookbook that initially defined California vegetarian cuisine, *Vegetarian Gourmet Cookery*, eventually, they had to change the Ranch House menu to include meat in order for the restaurant to work as a business. Today, the Ranch House has expanded into one of the most desired outdoor wedding locations in the area with a lush garden setting bursting with color, serving up to 100 guests easily.

The Halloween party on October 31, was a great success at Krotona. The feature of the evening was a book contest, each person represented the title of a book and then each had to guess what the other represented. Mr. Kirk, of the Publishing Co., was the most amusing. He came as "Lavender and Old Lace," and wore a dainty party gown of the proper shade with a picture hat to match. George Hall was the only book that nobody could get. He represented "From the Unconscious to the Conscious" wearing an original drawing of a knock-out in a prize fight. Miss Poutz fittingly represented "The Ancient Wisdom" and equally fitting was Gene Munson's portrayal of "Peck's Bad Boy", while Mrs. Hall in enormous rubbers and workman's gloves caused a great deal of fun as "So Big," from the Edna Ferber novel of 1927, and the others were more or less cleverly portrayed. They played games, popped corn, toasted marshmallows in the fireplace and danced in the Hall.

Nov 1 1927

Dear Mr. Warrington,
    Answering your questions in letter of the 28th received today, I had an order from Dr. Besant sent me by Max, to pay Krotona $15,000, which I accordingly did on Oct. 27th. I do not know why

she paid this amount or why she did not pay the balance of the loan. Guessing at it, I should say she perhaps did not need this much any longer and wanted to stop the interest. You know the note is not due for two years.

I immediately applied $10,000 on our note at the Hollywood bank, and paid $4000 in notes at the Ojai Bank. I then applied fro a %15,000 load at the Ojai Bank, which I think will go thru. If it does, I will pay up the $15,000 loan balance in Hollywood and our Thompson note will be released. It comes due Feb. 2, 1928. With the garden development at Krotona and the new road, I will probably have to borrow again before Feb. but it was good business to pay up our short time notes here when I get the chance.

Mrs. Hall and I are now quite well, although I was "out on my feet" as the fighters say, for about a week about the middle of the month. Grace has gone to Hollywood for a few days rest. Louis will arrive in Hollywood about the 6th, and I shall have to go down soon after for a few days. i should have gone before to see my Father, but the well at Arya-Vihara stopped pumping water and I have had to give it immediate and constant attention. I thought it had gone dry at first, but we found on examination the pipe had rusted thru and the water was leaking back. I have had it repaired and it should be pumping again by the last of this week.

Clark starts grading the new road at Krotona tomorrow. Laborers are working at the pergola near your house. I am still waiting for color instructions, to do the calsomining at your house. I shall also have to do Miss Poutz's office and bedroom and Billy's bedroom at the same time. We have just had a three day rain and the roofs don't leak.

I made a strenuous effort to locate the land you asked me to option, but so far I can't find it. I shall try again this week, taking my maps with me, and hope to find it. Then I will have to determine the owner and see what we can do about price and an option. I shall try to have this done before you return.

I am making an effort to go slow as you suggested, and already I see the great value of your advice. I shall keep at it until I have become so deliberate you will hardly believe your eyes. And I am not joking.

I have arranged for Mathews to take over the Camp books Dec. 1st, and relieve Mrs. Couch for Miss Poutz on that date. Dankowsky arrived yesterday but declined to live at the Siete Robles farm house. I can't blame him, and found him a place in the village. He will help Reihl at Arya-Vihara and at the Press for the present. Miss Freeman has returned to Ojai, and if she does not want to go to the farm house, she will take a cottage at Blairs Court. No other news of interest.

Much love to you always from G.G. (George and Grace)

Nov 9 1927

My Dear George,

Ethel Barburn wants a job. Maysie is urging me to take her as cook. She is a good one, and able in many lines. Healthy too!

But if I do, what about Mrs. G.? It's complicated. You see, I shall have much company from time to time, and Mrs. G. can't do the job. Nor is it right to call on willing Mrs. Mayes. I really must have some one who can efficiently carry the load. Yet I can't move tell I hear from you about Galdy.

Won't you please have a talk with Mrs. Mayes and then till her what to wire me.

Many thanks, dear George.

Heartily

A.P.W.

Sarobia

November 21 1927

My dear George,

Thank you for your telegram. Maysie was urging me for an answer, and I had, of course to hear adequately from Krotona first. In the end I decided to wire her that Ethel had better get some job somewhere, and so let me wait to decide my problem after I get back home and can better look into all sides of the matter.

I have now decided that I am to go down to Porto Rico for a week or ten days (and the trip takes four days each way), and I may go from there to Cuba and thence home. It all depends upon how badly they (Cubans) may need me. I shall certainly be very glad when it all is over and I can once more return to my beloved Krotona. I have come through the strenuous hopping about none the worse for it. We all found that if we insisted upon being allowed to take a long nap just after luncheon every day, rain or shine, we could get along without any scars and bruises. The result was, that at the end of the trip we were not all wearied out. The secret of successful traveling is in living regularly the important features of the home routine without interference. That satisfies the poor old body and he is willing to do a reasonable amount of slaving for you.

I feel quite lost without the Arundales. We did grow so very close together. It will be very nice if we can have them back with us again.

I hope all goes well with you, my dear George, and with your dear wife. My very best wishes, always.

Affectionately,

A.P.W.

New Orleans
Nov. 15, 1927

Dear G.S.A. and Rukmini:

I am sorry I cannot go in person to wish bon voyage. May all good fortune attend you until your return. And may that be soon! We shall await with impatience the indication of Dr. Besant's desire in the matter. We shall all be delighted if it is in the Plan for you to live in America. There is wonderful scope for theosophical work here, and we will be delighted to give you any of it from the position of chief executive to that of perpetual lecturer!

Please let me hear from you soon and often.

L.W. Rogers

Don't they wish they may get you! Yet who knows? You may practice for the Staff by visiting different countries as General Secretary instead of planets!

Under the supervision of Eugene Munson, superintendent of Krotona, a new road was constructed from the entrance to the administration buildings. Will Clark of Ojai was responsible for the grading and Lawrence Le Valley furnished the shale. The road is a great improvement on the old one, being wider and on a better grade. The entrance from the State Highway has been considerably widened and the obstruction of railroad poles cut down to permit vision in each direction along the road. It is at this time that construction begins on Star Camp.

Guests of A.P. Warrington at Krotona were Mr. and Mrs. Kendell Jenkins of San Francisco.

In November 1927, The first number of the *International Star Bulletin* was a unique magazine issued as the direct instrument of Krishnaji for uniting and coordinating his workers throughout the world.

Catharine Gardner Mayes is one of a great American family, the Gardners of Boston. Born on June 25, 1885, she was the great-niece of Isabella Stewart Gardner whose Victorian mansion is now one of the leading Renaissance art museums in the East.

Catharine, however, came to the health spa at Wheeler Springs, California in 1927 and immediately fell in love with it. After five years, around 1932, she fell in love with and married Billy Mayes, another theosophist, and together was idyllic as they helped build Krotona to the establishment it is today. She also wrote many small pamphlets such as *Need We Grow Old* published in 1931.

On the evening of December 28 at the 52nd Annual Convention of the Theosophical Society known as "Star Day" meet under the Banyan Tree in a semi-circle for a Platonic Symposium on "Happiness and Liberation." C. Jinarajadasa attempted to create a new kind of Theosophical propaganda by means of Platonic Symposium. Those taking part in the Dialogue, were, Yadunandan Prasad; C. Jinarajadasa, J. Krishnamurti, N.S. Rama Rao, A. Schwarz, D.K. Telang, B. Sanjiva Rao, Mrs. Malati Patwardhan, Jamnadas Dwarkadas, B. Subba Rao, K.S. Chandrasekhara Aiyar, the Chief Judge of Mysore. The full report was published in the *Star Review* for August 1928.

The first Theosophical Lodge to be formed in the Ojai Valley came into existence with the title "Ojai Valley Oaks Lodge of the Theosophical Society" with Mr. Frank Gerard, Mr. Jack Hislop, Miss Ruth Hart and Mrs. Alberta Kirk as provisional officers. Their first public lecture was to be held in the Woman's Club on November 24, 1927. The author was told that the certificate was held by the President of the Lodge. The Krotona Lodge was formed on January 9, 1930.

Closing the first chapter, I would like to suggest that the Theosophical Society was broken during these years, not because Krishnamurti left, but because members were not ready to listen and face the fact that their self-interest was the only problem which existed; self-interest which produces fear, love of power, conflict, attachment, and **the desire for continuity.**

Tents dot the Krotona Meadow for the Star Camp Congress, 1928.

Chapter 2
1928

The Ojai Valley has been the scene of many interesting and notable events, but it is doubtful if anything has taken place as unique and distinctive as the First Star Camp Congress on the meadow near Meiners Oaks, west of the Ojai village. Not often, in this comfort-loving age, do we see such a phenomenon as the gathering of a thousand people, to live in tents for a week or so. Their sole object to get away from the pressure of domestic and business life, to be quiet and to listen to the words of a modest young man who offers to share with his audience the ending of sorrow and suffering, and to be happy. Quietly and without brass bands or parades of any kind, this great party of campers settled into its magical city of brown tents, known as "Tent City".*

Soon after the First Star Camp Congress, in 1928, Krishnamurti would officially dissolve the Order of the Star, and the land and facilities would be temporarily abandoned. In 1946 the idea for a school based on Besant's original vision became a reality and the first Happy Valley School, before it moved to other land in the Upper Ojai, was established in the vacant buildings of the Star Camp. The

---

* Krotona had two entrances, one the south entrance was the back entrance and is opposite the entrance to the Villanova Preparatory School. There is no sign there, but a fence with a gate. The main entrance is about 100 yards further north, opposite Hermosa Road, or Krotona Road.

camp cafeteria became the school auditorium, and a carpentry shop and ceramic studio were installed directly behind it. This building still stands today and is now a private residence on Besant Road in Meiners Oaks. Mignon Casselberry's written report of May 1972 says that though the actual starting of the Happy Valley School was located on Besant Road in Meiners Oaks on 33 acres, that in 1946 it was re-located in the Upper Ojai Valley. She reports that the school was never inhabited at Besant Road due to lack of suitable personnel available, lack of knowledge of how to proceed, lack of leadership, and lack of money.

The Star Camp gathered in "Tent City". The building in the foreground would be the first location of the Happy Valley School.

As the history continues, we shall read how Krishnamurti, Aldous Huxley, Dr. Guido Ferrando and others helped in the actual developing of the Happy Valley School. The motto of the school was "Aun aprendo—I am still learning."

———————————⚓———————————

Annie Besant writes to Warrington regarding financing centers and her desire to give her "80 years gift" to fund Happy Valley School.

Jan. 13, 1928

My dear Parthe, [A.P. Warrington]
I should like, if you agree, to let the interest on the loan advanced to The Manor (Sydney) to continue for 10 or fifteen years, and the capital sum advanced to be made a gift instead of a loan. As you know, the Masters, when I was in Australia, in 1922, I think, discussed among themselves a Center for the Southern

Hemisphere, considering in this respect, Rio de Janeiro and Sydney. Sydney was chosen. It is supplied with spiritual forces directly from Shamballa, and these radiate from it in all directions. There is some barrier (which the equator represent) making it difficult to overleap the live shadow physically by the equator. I do not know its nature.

Under the circumstances we were told to strengthen Sydney as much as we could. That is why I wanted Krotona to keep it, when it was endangered. If we can do this, canceling the loan but making the yearly payment of interest for one of the periods named, Dr. Van der Leeuw will pay off the remaining £3500 owed for the property, and make it free from debt, except for the interest. If this would seriously cripple Krotona, then I must try to earn the necessary money, and pay off the loan. I think I could do it in four or five years. As I could pay it off out of the money given me the other day as an "80 years gift". But I wanted to give that to the Happy Valley.

You might cable me yes or no. I shall understand that the latter means that Krotona would be seriously crippled.

With affectionate wishes for the New Year.

Annie Besant

A letter captures preparations for the Star Camp:

Jan 16 1928
Ojai

Dear Sir,

In reference to the planting at Star Camp after going over the ground, I believe the very best course to follow would be to plant the trees in position without regard to clearing the full width of planting at this time, but properly clear about one square yard for each tree, and basin as we plant, then later in the season cut the weeds and grass, or better still plow these planting spaces to prevent grass fire danger.

If you will kindly arrange to send me about 300 1x1x4 long redwood stakes, I will mark out the planting position with them and each plant can be staked and tied as planted.

These stakes should be dipped in creosote before used.

I will later submit total cost of plants, have sent out for quotations from several firms. I was surprised at the conditions of the ground and entered to go right ahead at once.

Respectfully

F.C. Pragnell

53

F.C. Pragnell, landscape architect for the Libby Estate in Ojai did an extensive business from Santa Barbara to Los Angeles, as well as the Star Camp, Krishnaji's home at the East end of the valley called Arya-Vihara off of McAndrew Road.

Warrington appeals for funds to develop the Krotona Library, and its need to serve different roles in historical events:

Library Appeal
Ojai, Krotona Institute of Theosophy
February 11 1928

Dear Fellow-worker,

When the Krotona Centre was removed from Hollywood to Ojai, only such improvements were erected on the new land as were rigidly necessary to make a start. Since then much has happened. The declarations of Dr. Besant and Bishop Arundale, concerning the immediate future of the Valley, have fired our membership with keenest interest, and many developments are taking place around us.

It now becomes necessary for Krotona to keep pace with the progress of events and to provide the facilities which it is its duty to do; chief among these is a proper hall for meetings. We have never had a hall here and, therefore, when Dr. Besant, Krishnaji and Bishop Arundale came they all spoke out of doors, and when the weather was inclement the small library had to be used, often much to the discomfort of the audience.

Krotona adjoins the Starland; the date for the Camp is approaching rapidly, and many hundreds of members will soon be here, a large number of whom will be members of the E.S. For them we have no hall for meetings; nor for T.S. members; nor Co-Masons; but if we begin very soon, we can build one suitable for all purposes, adjoining the library, by the time of the Camp. The cost will approximate $12,000, including improvements incidental to its construction, and necessary adaptations of the library building.

I am giving these facts to E.S. members only, inviting them to cooperate with us in the speedy collection of funds wherewith to make this necessary improvement.; The Krotona Estate has not asked for upkeep, and does not expect to do so. It takes care of that (albeit on a scale of bare necessity) partly from the rents of cottages to the workers and partly from its small capital otherwise active for income purposes.

But if Krotona is to expand and meet the increasing demands upon its usefulness, it must seek the financial cooperation of those who may wish to have a hand in its upbuilding. Hence this appeal.

Those who can cooperate with us in making these improvements are asked kindly to send their subscriptions to Mrs. Maude N. Couch, Cashier, "Krotona," Ojai, on any basis they may be able to do. But those who cannot may send us their thoughts of goodwill for this too will be useful cooperation.

There may be a few who will consider sending $1,000, some $500, others $100, and still others less, according as they may have the means. But there is always that larger group whose funds are low, and these should remember that even $1.00 subscribed monthly for six months, say by 1,000 people, would amount to one-half the sum required.

If, fortunately, members should feel moved to act quickly, we could, as stated, have the hall ready for our first future important need for it.

Ever fraternally,

A.P. Warrington, *Vice-President*

Corresponding wtih Annie Besant on the Southern Hemisphere Center.

February 15 1928

My dear Amma,

I have sent you by cable the word "Writing." In response to your inquiry of the 12th ultimo, in spite of the fact that our reply to you is substantially, "yes." The reason is this:

Krotona wishes to and will see that a 4,000 pound contribution is made to the Southern Hemisphere Centre, if you should approve the proposal herein made; and it will feel greatly honored to have the privilege of doing so. But, as naturally you would not have had all the local facts hitherto laid before you, you could not be mindful of the fact that Krotona could not "renounce any claim on the principal" of 4,000 pounds which it has loaned to that Center without placing itself in a position to be criticized by those who gave the money, for they gave it understanding that it would be used in the up building and support of Krotona itself.

Therefore, I would venture to propose that you allow me to lay before our American E.S. membership the nature of the plan for the Southern Hemisphere Centre—you to indicate how much I may say—inviting them to contribute the needed sum over a period of 10 years. As we have over 2200 members in this Division (540 of whom are living in Latin America) this would mean less than $1.00 per year per member during the 10 years.

I am sure it would fire our members with enthusiasm to be privileged to contribute to so hallowed a plan, and the money would surely be produced in joy and gladness. I think we could reduce the principal at the rate of $2,000.00 per year, and that would mean a gradual reduction of Sydney's interest, thus making the plan a better one financially for them. Spiritually, it would seem better for it would give our members the rare privilege of cooperating in a big work at an outlay easily within their means.

May we have your approval of the plan, lading as it does to the same end that you have in view? And would you kindly sketch out how much of what you have told me of the purpose for the Centre may be disclosed to the E.S. in my appeal to them?

I hope this suggestion may be pleasing to you, for we live to do the will of the Great Ones as voiced by you, Their agent.
Devotedly,
A.P. W.

Bishop Iriving S. Cooper and A.P. Warrington arrived Havana, Cuba, taking the island republic by storm with a series of lectures on behalf of the Liberal Catholic Church. Warrington gave several excellent lectures for the members of the Esoteric Section and for the public as well.

It is noteworthy that the Republic of Cuba granted free railroad passes to all Editors, to do propaganda work for the Society.

April 15, Krishnamurti arrives by train to Los Angeles in the company of Baron van Pallandt, Dutch nobleman of Ommen, Holland, Mr. Tristram and Mr. Prasad, professor of physics at the University of Madras. Among those greeting them were Mr. and Mrs. D. Rajagopal, chief organizer of the Order of the Star, Dr. and

Mrs. John A. Ingelman, National Organizer for the United States, Mrs. Marie Russak Hotchener, editor of *The Star* magazine.[*] Mr. Louis Zalk, Ojai Camp Manager, James Montgomery Flagg, the distinguished illustrator, whose best known work was a World War One recruiting poster, depicting a stern Uncle Sam pointing his finger and demanding, "I Want You." [†] Bishop John Tettermer of the Liberal Catholic Church and many others who were especially devoted to Krishnamurti's ideals were also at hand to welcome him. C. Jinarajadasa, former tutor of Krishnamurti in his teens, and in 1928 International Vice-president of the Theosophical Society, arrived a few days later.

Roy C. Wilson, architect from Santa Paula reports that for the sum of $400 he would prepare complete plans for the lecture hall, at least once a week consultation during the construction, and working details for the additions and alterations to the library building. For the sum of $500 he would prepare complete plans with full size drawings, and to supervise the construction relating to the harmonizing of the old work to the new, including color scheme and furniture layout for the entire building.

This addition also consisted of a vestibule 32 x 74 feet in size, to be erected on the north side of the Library, extending lengthwise from east to the west where it will form an angle in the rear with the main building, in which angle a cloistered arcade will be added.

With the erection of a kind of monastery wall at the corresponding situation at the south of the old building a patio will be formed ending in a student's garden, already planted on the three remaining sides with cypress.

In the rear of the south portion of the Library building there is now an open terrace with an out-of-door fireplace. This will be

---

[*] The first number of the new magazine was released February 1928.
[†] Krishnamurti sat for his friend James Montgomery Flagg to have a profile ink sketch done in 1928. Flagg died May 27, 1960 in his New York apartment at the age of 82.

enclosed and used as a service kitchen for such occasions as receptions or other social gatherings. The broad terrace in front of the Library will be partly covered by the addition of an arcade, and the present entrance vestibule will be enlarged.

All has been skillfully carried out by Roy C. Wilson, the talented young architect from Santa Paula. Mr. L.G. Schuller was in charge of the construction work and promised, if all went well that it would be finished by the time of the Star Camp.

C. Jinarajadasa gave a public lecture stating that Krishnamurti cannot be labeled. "I don't want to label him and I don't want to label his message; I want to look at it and admire it." The message titled: "Krishnamurti's Message" given in March 1928 was published in February 1930 in the series "Adyar Pamphlets," n134.

———————————————

April 24, 1928

> My dear Partha, [A.P. Warrington]
> I think your idea of suggesting to members the idea that Sydney is the chosen Centre for the Southern Hemisphere is very good. The paying towards its release from debt a dollar a year, would probably arouse much enthusiasm. It is curious that the equator forms a barrier, over which a force must leap. But Sydney can be charged from Shamballa, and then distribute the force over the Southern Hemisphere. You can tell E.S. degree members this, but do not write it.
> With love to Krotona
> Herakles [Annie Besant]

Annie Besant reports on a Convention to C. Jinarajadasa.

> Dear Raja, [C. Jinarajadasa]
> I was glad to read THE MESSAGE from THE KING written down by the President April 23, 1928 and thank you for letting me see it. One wonders if it ought to have any less publicity than the others which have been received from Him and if so why.
> May I call your attention to my late annual report and closing

Convention address in this connection? Since it adverts practically to each point of THE MESSAGE which naturally I had not seen this is <u>for me</u> evidence that the Vice-President must have "tapped the same wire," an also that the President's transcription was accurate, only differing in the word "ideals" where I used "forms" which the Lord was shattering. In reality "ideals" does not tie in with "forms" appearing twice later in THE MESSAGE as would the latter word.

The Message:	My Convention Report:
My Messenger, the Lord of Love, is with you, shattering outworn ideals. Let the Life shatter every form that binds. New forms will be created to express the new Life.	For it is my conviction that the teacher is here to revitalize all true and useful forms of life that can withstand it and to shatter those that cannot; and that those which can prove their value will go forward and fulfill their mission helping always, to bring forth the blessing of life in a variety of ways.
Stand round Him.	I hope that Theosophists through-out the wide world will open their heats their Lodges and Sections as hospitably as they can to the great guest that we are now entertaining in our household here at Adyar, whenever he comes to them.
Protect Him.	The time may come, who knows? When he may need protection. Who is going to protect him? What greater Theosophical op-portunity could we have than to observe and study, under our Sec-ond Object, the life and works of this teacher as we have been in the habit of doing as to other teachers in the days gone by.

Could I be other than deeply impressed by these parallels? But I cannot feel it reasonable that the President should say, as stated (Convention Closing Remarks) "that when He came He would not

say the thing that we expected Him to say," and then after He had come should tell you she was "disappointed" in what was said; and I can only explain this upon the ground of her failing health. In the full vigour of her days she would have been valiant in carrying out the intent of THE MESSAGE without reserve. Nor would she (you will pardon me) have permitted the KING'S MESSAGE to be footnoted, especially if that tended to rob it somewhat of its force. Your interpretation and mine of Krishnaji's references to Gurus, etc., differ radically. To me he is only saying what H.P.B., A.B., and C.W.L. all have said, that ultimately no Master may help, but that one must attain for oneself.
Every yours,
A.P.W.

The founding of Oaks Lodge of the Theosophical Society was formed at Meiners Oaks on Poli Ave, Ojai, at the home of the President, Marianne C. Thomas, within sight of the Star Camp grounds and Krotona Hill. There were sixteen members to begin the Lodge. On May 28, a program was given under the direction of the Arts and Crafts Committee with Monica Ros, Louise Hancock, Rebecca Eichbaum, Alice Bonnell Green, Patricia Huntington and Patricia Brown. Krotona has a lodge also called the Ojai Valley Lodge.

Construction of the buildings at the Star Camp went ahead at full speed. In accordance with the plans of Louis Zalk, Manager of the Camp, and with the approval of Krishnamurti, the first buildings to be finished were the bath houses and kitchens, the contract for which was granted to L.G. Schuller & Co., of Ventura, California. There were twelve bath houses with a capacity to serve over a thousand persons, the first few of which was ready for the coming Star Camp. Every building was equipped with the latest and most modern appliances for the convenience of the guests. Mr. D. Rajagopal arrived in February, followed later by the Countess de la Warr, Lady Emily Luytens, and several other members from Europe.

The first International Star Camp Congress was held at Ojai, May 21 to 28. They expected a much greater gathering in 1929. Louis

Zalk, Manager ,planned to still further improve the great tract and buildings, the property of the Order. The roads were much improved and landscaping undertaken among other things.

Krishnamurti gave a public address on May 15 at the Hollywood Bowl with an audience of 16,000, which seats 20,000 people. This was a new avenue by which to reach the public.

The special passenger train from Chicago to Ventura, California, of eight cars, brought a large party of Theosophists. The cars were switched at Ventura to the branch line to Ojai. The train had the first vegetarian dining car that ever crossed the American continent, according to one of the travelers. Hundreds of autos from every state in the union, plus Mexico and Canada, arrived for the camp. There seems to have been created a problem between the Star organization disagreeing with the Theosophical Society. Krishnamurti made it quite clear: "It is rather fascinating to think that there should be diversity about Truth. As we are all looking at form and its various expressions, or rather trying to understand Truth from the form side, naturally then there is apparent diversity in Truth."

Krishnamurti continually tried to make simple and clear every point. "In helping others to attain Liberation and happiness, we must look to all forms of life—religion, politics, science, and art. Every human being, whether he be of a far-off country or of our own, desires to attain this Liberation and happiness, and any one of the forms may be his means of attainment. Those who would help really and lastingly must find out along what lines they can best give their creative energies."

———————————— ❧ ————————————

May 3 1928

> My dear A.P., [Warrington]
> The President is anxious to considerably improve the *Theosophist*, and I am endeavouring to carry out her wishes in all possible ways. Will you be so good as to send me monthly a chatty dealing with affairs at our great Ojai. These may well be quite personal, but should be of general interest. If snapshots are available, so much the better.

I should also be very much obliged if you could put some one on to send me monthly a review of Theosophy in the various American fields—international, national, religious, educational, industrial, social, economic, etc., showing how Theosophy is active in these various fields and is modifying the life of the American people. Also, any specially notable cuttings suitable for the *Theosophist* would be very much appreciated.

We hope to make the *Theosophist* bright and really attractive. Affectionately,
George (Arundale)

———————— ❧ ————————

This is an important document, included here at length, because it gives a first-hand account of the Star Camp.

Impressions of The Ojai Camp
By Ernest Wood

It is with considerable diffidence that I write about Krishnaji at the Ojai camp. Only my own impressions and thoughts are possible, or indeed permissible, for Krishnaji desires that only officially passed and authorized reports of his talks should be published. Therefore, it is necessary fro me to say that I quote from memory, and give only my own impressions and experience.

I will speak first of the setting of the Ojai Star Camp or Congress of 1928. There is, in the newest part of the new world of Southern California, where all eyes are now turned to see what this new civilization can make of itself, a secluded valley entirely surrounded by peaceful mountains. Some years ago Mr. A.P. Warrington, moved by an impulse for which he could not account, decided to settle there the new home of the American administration of the Esoteric School of Theosophy, where the workers might enjoy calm life and the pure beauty of nature, and perhaps at some future time members of the School might come to carry out their study and meditation under the best conditions.

This centre, Krotona, consists of several small dwellings

arranged in a circle not far from the top of dome-like hill, which is crowned with a picturesque tower surmounting one corner of a courtyard built and ornamented in the Spanish style. About this there is the illusion of an old-time *hacienda*—but inspection reveals that behind the slits of the tower are no sentinels with ready rifles, and in the stables no impatient *caballos*, but above there is a water-tower and below are "parked" Billy Mayes' old Ford—the Krotona postal van —and the more respectable "oil-wagons" of Mr. Warrington and some of his residents and helpers. Outside the circle of little houses, slightly down the hill, lie the office of the Esoteric School and the new and wonderfully beautiful Krotona hall and library building, with its garden of streams somewhat on the old Mogul plan. So rare is the "composition" of Krotona that the buildings seem almost to have grown there, to be part of Nature's plan rather than man's. Probably it is part of God's plan, which can harmonize both of these.

Behind Krotona hill the promoters of the Star Camp have purchased some hundreds of acres of land. I say behind, because the main road, which runs through the middle of the valley, is on the other side, and one must make a considerable detour by side roads to approach the Star camp lands, if one does not enter direct through the Krotona grounds. Behind the Krotona dome there is an eminence, a little table-land, flat, but sloping up to a point. At its edges flanked by bushes, on three sides cliffs go down, and on the fourth a saddle-back connects it with Krotona hill. From one side of this table-land—the place of the camp-fires—paths lead down by zigzag ways among the trees, into the oak grove—the place of the morning talks. Continue, and you come to the wide-spread pasture lands on which there arose almost in a night a forest of five hundred tents, not in serried, ranks, as in a military camp, but—at the suggestion of Krishnaji—in "Studied disorder," so to say. These tents were most luxurious, providing not only room for beds and chairs—real iron beds with spring mattresses—but also a little verandah in front by the flap of the tent supported on two poles. The tents were clustered in large groups round the bath-houses—according to the law in California, which is very strict in its supervision of camps—which represented the last word in sanitation.

Crossing now a tiny stream—still moving away from Krotona and towards the road which leads to the Starland and the pretty little village of Meiner's Oaks on the other side of that road—we come to the kitchen and serving counters of the cafeteria, and to the two large dining-tents just outside that building. In these particulars also the management (Mr. Zalk and Mr. Hall) brought civilization to its full modern attainments—the layman could only marvel at the many ingenious mechanical devices, mostly electrically driven, employed for the preparation of the food and the cleaning and storing of the dishes. Could even a thousand people empty those huge cauldrons of soup?

The food was plentiful, varied and excellent, so much so indeed that there was a general demand for a simplification of the meals. It was not suggested that the delegates were dining not wisely but too well, but it was felt that two meals a day of the sort here provided were not requisite even for the labours which many delegates performed as police, servers and officials of various kinds. And how these worked— without distinction of sex, race, creed, caste or colour, or even money! It was said that there were serving in the kitchen, dish-washing and what not, one bishop, four priests, four lawyers, one banker, one army captain, one chemist and I do not know many ladies, or what their distinguished careers in ordinary life. Krishnaji himself, visiting this centre of industry, said that he would be very happy if permitted to take a share in that work as his function in the camp.

The psychology of this camp was itself a remarkable thing. Here were something approaching a thousand Star members, taken away from their normal life of settled routine and worldly contact, sleeping in tents, seeing the stars and the morning, and for the most part sitting or reclining on the ground while listening to talks or answers to questions, or to poems ready by Krishnaji, containing his feeling and thought as well as his words. Imagine these human beings released from the adaptations of their daily lives, wending their way in twos and threes up the little path leading to the camp-fire ground on the hill-top, as the evening shadows wrapped the trees about them in mystery, a darkness rendered visible by the coloured lanterns which lined the route. Surely here was a masterpiece, though unintentionally so, of practical psychology, for these Star members felt like pilgrims mounting to a shrine where all the world was left behind and the Teacher would be found. And as we sat in the darkness, lit only by the flames of the faire, we felt each one of us somehow separated from the rest and alone with the Master Singer.

For what seems a long time now Krishnaji has been telling us to clear away all attachments and prejudices, that we may respond to the life within. Here every assistance was given to that process—mind and body were prepared for the new light. Most of us had never seen a fire like that before. It was piled with consummate skill, so that after Krishnaji applied the torch it soon blazed up, and flying flames torn by the wind into a hundred fantastic forms flew separately into the air, lingered a moment, and vanished after another into the night.

For these camp-fire talks each evening Krishnaji was dressed in Indian clothes. He stood before the fire and chanted Sanskrit mantras, first telling us that we must regard these merely as his son—like the songs and the music of the hired performers who opened each evening's session—and not as intended to have magical or mystical significance. He was anxious that we should not make a ritual of the camp-fire, which might then degenerate into a superstition.

For the most part at these evening camp-fires, while we sat on the sloping top of the hill, away from the world, Krishnaji recited some of his poems, though two or three times he spoke to us also for a little while. I cannot remember his words or the sequence of his thoughts on those occasions, but I can recall their effect. There was nothing that we have not heard before, or have not read in his published works. But we were all intent upon catching the life in those words, which were all too soon gone, like the flying flames of the fire. He stopped always with a sense of loss to us.

By some effect which I do not understand Krishnaji makes us live with him. He does not speak to us from the outside, at least he does not speak to me from the outside. His "I" is not easily to be separated from our "I." With him we are in the presence of ourselves (I do not like to say our higher selves) to a rare degree. His poems always produce this effect. I, for one, cannot read them without feeling them also to be my own.

The Teachers seem always to have taught thus, with life itself rather than with words. We find the same thing in the *Gita* where Shri Krishna tells his pupil to "come to me," and yet to find himself. Patañjali has the same teaching—control the mind (sutra ii) and you will reside in your own true state (sutra iii), which is the goal of yoga or union with the divine. In reading or hearing Krishnaji's poems I have always felt that the "I" in them is myself, and the poems are somehow my own. I think I have found that he is not a teacher telling us something from the outside; in this "teaching" the teacher effaces himself (has it not been said that the Ego of a Master is only an illusion?) and the pupil alone is there, tasting the truth and the life.

At those camp-fires Krishnaji did not teach or instruct us in any ordinary sense of those words. I doubt if it can be said with accuracy that he gave us a message. If he had an extensive description of some occult branch of science to give to us as our need we might hear something new from him each day. But he insists upon the One Truth, the Life; we must agree as to that before he can propound any particulars. Why discuss the way until we have caught a glimpse of the goal, sufficiently clearly to make us desire that above everything else? He seems to say that the lesson of life can be learned under any circumstances, and from a little flower as well as from a universe of suns.

To my mind, trained on somewhat scientific lines, he seems to give confirmation of a long believed truth, that the reality of objects lies in their properties, not in their substance, their matter or form. Thus the reality of water is not to be found in oxygen and hydrogen, nor the reality of oxygen or hydrogen in electrons. Thus also the reality of man is not to be found in the body or mind of man. The life is manifest in the forms, and if we will we may take the life and let the matter go.

So I cannot tell what Krishnaji said at those meetings, but I think that he wants us to forget his words and take their life, so perhaps I have given a not impossible account of those camp-fire talks.

Speaking to the public in the great amphitheater at Hollywood a few days before camp, * Krishnaji formulated his object more definitely than usual, perhaps because he was speaking to "outsiders" (may I be forgiven this word?). It was supremely logical. First, he said to the people give up your prejudices. Recognize that it is comfort which you usually seek, and realize that that comfort is stagnation. For half-an-hour he emphasized this in a variety of ways, with many beautiful and expressive similes. He asked the people to put aside all their preconceptions, so that they might be open to consider what he would then say. Afterwards he told them about the life, and came as near as he has ever been to an announcement of what we should do. One of his auditors at once pronounced it "a noble three-fold path." What would conduce to the realization of life, to liberation? For the body beauty should be the rule—not external decorations, but essential beauty. For the feelings, detached emotions—not the absence of emotions. Presumably our emotions should be as strong as is consistent with circumstances, but they must not attach us to particular forms, which come and go. Thirdly, for the mind the rule is: fix your goal, visualize your goal.

Krishnaji did not say it, but I see in these the fructification of Discrimination. Desirlessness and Good Conduct. Good Conduct is nothing but that skill in action, of mind and body, which always produces beauty; feelings without personal desire are detached emotions; and to see our true life so that we may fix our goal is Discrimination. In fact, in Sanskrit books that first of the four Qualifications is usually called not merely *viveka*, or discrimination, but *iha-mutra-vastu-*

---

* On this occasion he had an audience of twelve thousand people.

67

viveka, or discrimination between "here" and "there," the material and the spiritual selves. Truth is the understanding of life. It is the same for all. Therefore there is only one goal. But each must fix his goal as if it were his alone.

All through the camp talks Krishnaji brought us back and back to these things. He does not bring peace to the body, but a sword. There is nothing left of the old self when Krishnaji has done with it. He strikes at every error with instant and deadly precision. One old Theosophist said that he felt as if a steam-roller had gone over him and flattened him out. Even those who are least excitable pronounce themselves "impressed," often "deeply impressed." I had an opportunity in New York, as Chairman of Krishnaji's big meeting there, to watch the faces of his auditors, and could in many cases see the effect in their expression. Veils were torn away, chrysalides were cracked, men and women (especially men, I thought) were freed from particular bondages to which they had not realize before that they were subject. They would go away making a deeper search, hearing a new song of life.

Krishnaji cuts the old self away from its moorings and sets it adrift on an ocean, the waves of which most people wait until they are dead, when in the astral plane they learn to drop the valueless objects of desire, and in the heaven-world they realize a fuller and richer quality of the really valuable relations between man and man and between man and the world. He would put death under us by anticipating its action. He has been careful to specify that attachment through feeling and thought is as binding as clinging to the body, if not more so. So he says: "Away with your explanations and your consolations!"

The body, we know, is a passing thing. The world shudders at this, and hides the fact of death as much as possible, but when forced to face it, cries out: "But nevertheless my loves shall not perish." We must face the fact that they will, so that loves may become love, not attached to form. Even the Teacher must go; there shall be no clinging emotion even there. Krishnamurti says: "I have no disciples. I will recognize no followers." To me he said laughingly, as is often his way, after I had not seen him for two years: "Wood, I hope you are not acquiring any followers." I said I had tried not to, but I could not quite help being one myself. I spoke of those who had helped us, and of gratitude. "Gratitude!" He came at me like a shot from a bolt, "Why gratitude?" I understood. It is of this world, though probably among its best products. Like devotion, it is a bond if it binds thought or action, or stands in the way of our being ourselves. We must learn the lesson of the flower and the Sun. And sympathy may fall into the same class, for superstitions seem to be endless. We must not be unhappy because another is unhappy—a simple and obvious proposition, the contrary to which in practice would breed evil from evil and sorrow from sorrow.

But consolations and hopes come in for the greatest measure of scorn. Explanations must go. You have explained a difficulty and brought comfort to the mind. You have solved the problem. There is comfort once more, and some peace, or at least hope. Hope! For what? Possibly for the thing from which experience has been trying to release you. How often people hope for the worse, for the past to come again. They will not let go. They say, "When my karma is gone I shall have the opportunity, the affection, the power which is now denied me." So it brings consolation and hope, and for the present some contentment in a waiting state. Such knowledge is bondage and stagnation. It is refusing the lesson of experience. But reincarnation taken as opportunity, tacitly agreed upon, finds its place in Krishnaji's world of thought.

He will leave us no place of rest whatever, on any plane. He says "I was bound; I am free. I was unhappy; I am happy. Let go your bonds. Come away. Be free. Be with me." I questioned whether it was necessary to bring more unhappiness into peoples lives. He answered: "The world will bring that to them." No one must be urged. I remain with the feeling that he would not desire to disturb the ignorant, attached to action, but to those who knock he will respond with shattering words. Such were my impressions from his talks besides the camp-fire and on some few mornings standing on the mound-like platform under the trees in the oak-grove, while we all sat and reclined around. His exact words will appear in print, reported in due course.

In the question meetings under the same trees, again and again queries were put relating to teaching given by others—was such and such a statement true or false, should we follow this or that line of activity? In every case he answered the thought, not the form. In all cases, he drew the questioner's attention back to the life. Apparently he has no business with those who do not want to seek that life, at least not at this stage of the unfoldment of his programme.

Never would he pronounce upon another's teaching, but always assert his own. As to a course of action, if you think best, do it. If not, do not. Do not stifle your own best life. Ceremonies are not necessary (how often have we heard this from Dr. Besant and Bishop Leadbeater?)—but perhaps, if we put the question specifically, all things are unnecessary. Ceremonies are crutches—but we must decide whether we need them or not. He will not decide for us. He refuses to do so. But one thing was emphatic—there is no God outside ourselves.

At the end of one of these question meetings he said with great dignity and sorrow: "I wish you would be more friendly." Most of those present took it to mean towards himself, but on reflection I think it referred to the many and sometimes hard questions relating to the activities of others. They came perilously near to intolerance and the desire to set authority against authority. Krishnaji is not to be used as a cudgel, even to fight against a wrong or an error. Each man must decide for himself what is right, using only the light within. Each man is competent. It reminded me of Emerson's sayings that imitation is suicide, and that each man has the key to his own problems if he would but use it. Nothing could be more dramatic than these periods of questioning, and among these stood out one breathless minute when, apparently hurt by the hardness of the questions, Krishnaji drew himself up and asked "Who do you think I am?" The climax to that dramatic scene came when Krishnaji answered the question as to whether he knew himself to be the World-Teacher with the simple statement: "Yes, even more than that."

I will sum up. Krishnaji has brought us back to the first chapter of the Gospel of St. John. He says n effect: "Look within yourself. There is the light that is true life, and is free and happy. It exists in everything, everywhere. Release yourself from bondage, darkness, obscuration, and you will find that you are free. Nirvana, freedom, happiness are all the same thing. To be yourself is liberation and it is to be God and to be the World-Teacher yourself." The Gospel tells us about the Word who was with God and was God, without whom nothing was made, in whom was the life that is the light that lighteth every man that cometh into the world, that gives the power to become sons of God to those of us who recognize and respond. E.W. [Ernest Wood] *

The original Ranch House with Star Camp tents in foreground.

On Saturday afternoon, May 28 at three o'clock, the Krotona Institute held their Krotona Garden Program out of doors, on the terraced lawn in front of the Library with the gorgeous mesembryanthemum, a prostrate succulent plant native to Africa as a background. Those who took part were Monica Ros on the violin,

---

* Wood, Ernest, "Impressions of the Ojai Camp", *The Australasian E.S.T. Bulletin*, n42, July 1928, pp. 293-300.

Louise Hancock dancing, Rebecca Eichbaum vocal, Alice Bonnell Green on the violin, Patricia Huntington and Elizabeth Price Coffey. The program was under the direction of the Arts and Crafts Committee of the Ojai Valley Oaks Lodge, .

On June 3, Warrington welcomed all the members to a general E.S. meeting in the new hall. He was asked if he was going to dedicate the building today. His reply was, "I somehow do not come along that line." He felt that if they just allowed their appreciation and gratitude to perform the dedication. He told them, "I believe that when we meet here in the name of the Masters, when we turn our thoughts and our hearts to Them, and invoke Their blessing in the silence, there is a point of meeting between Them and ourselves. Then something is born in the place that is of precious value to us, and that, I hope, is the thing that is happening here today."

Correspondence between the local Ojai paper of the time "The Ojai", and the *Theosophist* magazine.

June 20 1928
Ojai Publishing Company
Publishers of "The Ojai"

Dear Mr. Warrington,

Mr. Kilbourne informs me that it will be my duty to collect and write a budget of news each month which he has promised you for the *Theosophist* magazine. Certain things occur to me in this connection and I'll list them below for your consideration:

In order to secure accurate news notes it will be necessary for me to have access to yourself or to someone at Krotona who has knowledge of persons and events here—also of plans. Once a month, say, if I could have thirty or forty-five minutes of intensive planning and fact-gathering from your memory, your correspondence or from you plans. Or you might designate someone who know well what is on foot and I could confer with this person.

Second point—I want to know if you think the Theosophist would welcome news of Star activities in the valley—such as the plans for the building of the amphitheater at Ojai Camp and such matters?

Third point—Bishop Arundale mentions snapshots as being acceptable. Is there a camera fiend at Krotona whose co-operation I could enlist? For instance it seems to me that one of the most interesting things would be to immediately "snap" the new library with yourself and a few other most prominent American officials— (whoever is available and suitable)—in its porch and send that on. Can you think up someone who would rush about with me one afternoon a month, say, snapping persons and things so that we might send a picture or two each time?

Fourth point—Is there a special date for sending news to reach them for publication any given month? Or do we simply send them a budget of news as soon as we can—perhaps next week—and then a month later follow it with another?

Here are some items I have in mind for the first budget— perhaps they will suggest others to you that should be sent—or perhaps for some reason you will think best to eliminate some of them.:

The presence of the Woods in Ojai and his work on a new book:

Picture of new library with some persons and article on it:

C.J.'s visit here: the fact that he and Prasad and Krishnaji were invited and did speak at Thacher:

Improvements planned for Star grounds next year: perhaps a picture of Messrs. Zalk and Hall and a building there.

Mrs. Rajagopal's visiting here this summer:

Plans for Krotona Institute to enable students to come:

Bishop Cooper's plans for a tour and perhaps a little about his recent one.

If you think best I could come to Krotona some evening early and make plans or whoever is to give me data could meet me in the village or at our house. Probably it is not easy for your people to come down town often though. Thursday evening is the one that is practically impossible for me. At other times I am fairly free.

Fraternally,

Blanche Kilbourne

The *Ojai Valley News* began in 1887 and by 1891 it had become known as *The Ojai*. After having presided over the destinies of *The Ojai* for the past three years, Mr. Frank Gerard severed his connection with the paper. Mr. Gerard came to the Ojai Valley in the summer of 1924 and served on the faculty of the Thatcher School during 1924-1925. In the summer of 1925, together with Fritz Kunz and Ernest Stone he purchased *The Ojai* from Train Brothers and took over the editorship of the paper. In the spring of 1927 Dr. Besant, at whose request Mr. Gerard remained on as editor, purchased the business of the publishing company. Mrs. Gerard gave birth to a daughter in January 1928. The business management of the press was placed in the hands of Mr. George Hall and in January of 1928 Mr. Frank Kilbourne was brought from Seattle to take over the general management of the publishing end of the concern, taking over the editorship in which he had the assistance of Mrs. Kilbourne, who had years of journalistic experience.

Meanwhile, Harold A. Kirk, became the Advertising Manager and Assistant Editor.

The Ojai began publication of a two-edition newspaper. There was the usual edition for citizens of the valley and the county, and then a second edition with some of the more purely local news deleted and additional news and features of a purely theosophical nature replacing it; this second edition was published for the many friends of Dr. Besant all over the world who wanted to read *The Ojai* since was published in the valley containing the headquarters of the Esoteric Section of their society as well as the headquarters for the annual Star Camp.

———————————— ❦ ————————————

The following letter regarding the World-Mother movement, can be found in the book: *Spirit of Womanhood: A Journey with Rukmini Devi,* by Joseph Ross, 2009 (www.krotonaarchives.com).

The Manor, Mosman
Presiding Bishop
May 8 1928

> My dear George,
>   Many thanks for your letters of April 13th and 16th. It is evident that you will be increasingly busy for a long time to come,

and the daily edition of *New India* seems to be beginning nobly. I should hardly think it likely that the Message from the World-Mother could possibly influence the election of the President; why should it? I was very much interested in the suggestions which you made as to the way in which the work of the World-Mother was complementary to that of the World-Teacher. I am sure that you are quite right as the intended cooperation, although I do not quite understand in detail some of the remarks which you make. I know how fully our Lord the Bodisattva, as we know Him, approves our attempts to work for the World-Mother; but I am afraid that there may be a certain amount of difficulty in the outer work, arising from the fact that in his physical brain our Krishnaji knows nothing of all this. It would seem that some sort of epitome of what our President said must have been telegraphed to America; and of course reporters at once descended upon Krishnaji and demanded further elucidation. Equally of course, Krishnaji, knowing nothing whatever about it, was obliged to say so, and to remark that he could offer no comment upon what the President had said. You and I, understanding fully how tremendous, how incredibly great is the limitation produced by the descent into a physical body, would not be in the least surprised or perturbed by his ignorance; but I am afraid that it may be a knotty problem for some of the more foolish of our members. It may offer quite a good opportunity to the darker powers to try to create a division in the Society, to set up Krishnaji as against the President, and possibly the Star against the Theosophical Society as a whole. I should say that a great deal will depend upon the attitude which we ourselves take with regard to the matter. I should be very glad to hear at once of any pronouncement that our President may make; for myself, I shall take it perfectly calmly and philosophically, and say that while perhaps it may appear a little remarkable that in the physical body Krishnaji knows nothing about these developments, the whole situation is unparalleled; we have no criterion by which to judge how much of the higher plan should be known through the physical body, and consequently it would be foolish to allow ourselves to be upset or greatly surprised by anything whatever that may happen, Here are certain facts, and there is not the slightest doubt as to their accuracy; it is not our business to dispute about them, but simply to note them and to go on with the work which is definitely given to us to do. That seems to me the wisest line to take, but I should be glad to now whether our President approves of it, or whether she has any other suggestion to make.

75

With love to you and Rukmini.
I am ever,
Yours most affectionately
C.W. Leadbeater

————————⋙⋘————————

Warrington called for an informal talk with the Krotonians at his residence on Monday night, June 11, 1928 where Miss Poutz read a clipping from *The Los Angeles Examiner* alleging a break between Dr. Besant and Krishnamurti, and Mr. Warrington made the following remarks:

There is no break. Here is the idealism we have been working with and his is the new.

The new message seems to be an expansion of Theoosphy. Theosophy, so far as it represents the truth about the cosmos and man, naturally would not be changed by any lofty coming; but what is to be changed is our attitude towards life, our approach to life. Take the point that was made in the clipping about authority; when questions were asked of Krishnaji in which the expression was used "we are told thus and so," he politely almost jeered at the idea of people believing because they were told; and it seems to me if that is taken at its significant value, it means that all teachings given on authority is valueless in his eyes to promote the evolution of the person who believes only on authority.

How a great deal of theosophical teaching has been given out on the authority, or tradition, and I have no doubt that there are thousands of theosophists whose grasp of Theosophy can only be that of custodians of the knowledge, just as a book is, and it is even not unlikely that when born in some other life they may reject that same teaching, if meanwhile they have become bound to a contrary authority, all because their reverence for authority makes them accept that which is given rather than that which is evolved from within.

Take the E.S. as an approach to Krishnaji's message. It would be, perhaps, in his eyes wanting in freedom, because it proceeds along pathways that might be thought to limit one—that of authority, pledges, stern discipline, reports on conduct and daily observations, work required for the T.S., the L.C.C., or Co-Masonry. It is possible that none of these things lies within the scope of Krishnaji's thought. He may see in the E.S. plan a sacrifice of one's liberty, of one's action, of one's initiative. I do not know. But this is a wonderful instrument that Dr. Besant has built up with so much labor, patience, understanding and breadth of ability—this E.S. Fundamentally, as a structure, it has been successfully used as an approach to the ideals which Krishnaji presents, even though it may seem to be bound by authority.

Question: Did not the Master Morya found the E.S.?

Answer: My judgment is that the Master Morya looks on within limits and lets His pupils express their own uniqueness in their own way, reaching out a restraining hand when there is danger; and that He always makes the best of what they do, being pleased that they do the work in their own way.

Then there are these Orders that so many people have gone into from a stern sense of duty and not voluntarily. I am not so sure but that the pressure would need to be withdrawn there, if these people were to work with true spontaneousness, rather than upon authority. Spontaneity has fire in it, and you seldom get it from one who is urged.

The ancient Oriental method of yoga is in some measure in operation in our E.S. the spirit of it is different from that of the modern Occidental world. It was logical that it should have been adopted at the time the E.S. was formed, for it has within it the glamour as well as the wisdom of the Orient, and it has been wonderfully inspiring to us all. But a new generation is coming on, and that may be less and less thrilled by Oriental modes, and more inclined to for the way of life in newer channels.

Another thing. Mr. Louis Zalk is sending out a letter calling the attention of the members of the fact that Krishnaji has expressed a very vital interest in the drama, especially *The Light of Asia* which was produced during the Camp, and he wishes to make permanent the little theatre at the Camp.

Take that and lay it along side the prophecy that we are coming to a time when the Seventh Ray will find beautiful expression among the masses of the people; and the thought that Krishnaji has been expressing, that religion, rites and ceremonies are not necessary, but that self-expression is important.

One thing I believe to be true, and that is, that Krishnaji's fundamental views have come to stay. I don't believe he will have anything to take back. I believe he will build on the things he has already said. If his teaching does not bring about any change in our lives, in our consciousness, then we are dead to it. The message is a message of happiness. [*]

June 15 1928

My dear Amma,

I thank you for your kind consent to allow me to try to raise $2,000.00 per year in the E.S. over a period of ten years in order to enable Sydney to retire the mortgage indebtedness on The Manor.

I am planning to take the matter up early next year, and have so written to Bishop Leadbeater, after a full conference with Dr. van der Leeuw and C.H. Dr. van der Leeuw has taken his departure from the Valley, and caries with him my letter.

I often wonder about you these days. My devoted thoughts go to you frequently. I cannot fail to observe the trend of opinions and events as they transpire at Star Camps, and relate them with all I know of the past and its Great Leaders.

Krishnaji was very wonderful at the late Camp. There were questions which drew out some fire and deep sincerity. I think most members were disturbed. It was clear that he had struck out in a new direction, leaving the old things behind. This I am sure made many feel as if they had been left dangling in the air. It seemed that the Theosophy that they had made the mainspring of their lives was being put to one side with churches and the rest—this that is the most real and tangible fact in life for them. There were some who felt the hope that there might after all be a simpler and more joyous way, and so the "discontentment" of which Krishnaji speaks, was born in many a heart.

*Warrington, A.P., Informal talk to Krotonians only, June 11, 1928, at his residence, taken from his handwritten rough draft of notes.

As to Krishnaji's attitude toward the E.S., I have no knowledge. I can only repeat a conversation reported to Miss Poutz by Philip Rheil, Krishnaji's faithful man at Arya-Vihara. No doubt you will prefer to keep it as confidential.

Krishnaji: You belong to the E.S., I think?

Rheil: Yes.

Krishnaji: You intend to remain in it?

Rheil: Yes.

Krishnaji: Why?

Rheil: Because I like it. It has helped me, and I may be able to help others better.

Krishnaji: Well—half shrugging his shoulders.

The above suggests the possibility that the E.S., with its many disciplines, and gradations of degrees and years; its several obligations; its duties towards T.S., Star, church, and Masonry may not appeal to Krishnaji as a useful approach to the simple ideals which he is spreading. And Krishnaji is one of the Initiates. What will this mean? Will the O.H. attempt to adapt her more or less Orientally constructed plan of spiritual training to the conditions and life of the modern Western world to which Krishnaji is beginning to appeal?

Well, these are questions that have invited me to examine them and estimate their worth. Naturally I have no opinion to express. I am only having a comfortable little chat with you as I sit in my office at home looking out at the sunshine and the flowers and recalling the dancing memories of the late Camp.

We were all so sorry you were not here. Some of us missed you greatly. But some of our little group will see you in Europe and bring back tidings of you.

With much love, I am,

As always,

A.P.W.

———————————— ❧ ————————————

By July, Miss Julia K. Sommer left for Chicago in company with Marie Poutz to attend the national convention of the Theosophical Society, and from there Miss Poutz made an extended tour of the U.S. while Julia went to New York where she joined Mrs. Charlemagne Tower of Santa Barbara and embark on the "Berlin" of the North

German Lloyd line for a lengthy tour of Europe.

C. Jinarajadasa, International Vice-President of the Theosophical Society has been visiting at Krotona for some weeks giving a symposium on the subject "The Value of the Arts to a Community" with about 200 guests; they were bidden to a concert of rare excellence. Mr. and Mrs. E. J. Reunitz of Santa Paula, Mrs. Vida Reed Stone, who accompanied Mrs. Orline Moore of Briningham Alabama, in her solos. Mr. & Mrs. William Worth Beiley, Mrs. Elizabeth Price Goffey, Miss Rebecca Schuyler Eichbaum are all members of the faculty of the Southwst Studios of Musical Art in Fort Smith, Arkansas, and soloists of unusual reputation. During the Sam period, Reginald Pole shared his idea regarding the theatre as an art. "The Theater is the playground of the human soul. Upon its stage all dreams of beauty that are expressible in terms of the physical brain of man may be brought into visible realization. It is the focusing point where can be merged the experiences of varied units of consciousness. For the Theater is the congenial host of all the arts." *

Louis Zalk, a prominent business man of Dultuh, Minn., general director of the Camp, extended a warm greeting to over 800 guests, for the first congress. One of the best entertainments at the camp during the free periods was the production of *The Light of Asia* by Reginald Pole and Beatrice Wood. A company of young people gave "A Dreamer of Dreams" one afternoon and folk songs and dances of various nations were much enjoyed. Krishnamurti drew thousands to the Ojai Valley. A building boom was soon on in the valley, advertised as "the Beauty Spot of the Ojai." Excursions were arranged each day permitting visitors from every part of the United States to view the beauties of the Valley.

Because the Starland was in Meiner's Oaks it held a special interest for most of the followers, who were buying lots within a short walk of the Starland.

* *The Star*, "The Theatre as an Art", Vol.1, n6, June 1928, p.56.

A symposium on "What a Camp Means" was participated in by C. Jinarajadasa, Warrington, Dr. Ingelman, Marie Russak and Henry Hotchener. The opening meeting of the Star Camp Congress, the Campfire, was held under the starry canopy of night, in an ideal setting, on Outlook Point, on the peak of the hill overlooking the surrounding countryside. Here the stillness and majesty of the approaching twilight of the evening was broken by the quiet murmur of voices as the great crowd gathered almost noiselessly to await the opening numbers of the musical program arranged by Mrs. Glen Ellison of Hollywood, the musical director of the week. The delicate beauty of the Levings trio (violin, cello and piano), the organizers of the delightful annual summer concerts in the Eagle Rock Bowl, assured their listeners of many musical treats during the camp week. The soloist of the evening was Rosalie Barker Frye, English concert contralto of London and New York, accompanied by Elise Watkin-Mills, famous throughout Canada and England as concert artist accompanist and already well known in the same capacity in California. Inspired by the surrounds and the occasion, Mrs. Frye's glorious voice was an inspiration to her hearers.

After the music, Krishnamurti stepped forward and touched the torch to the campfire, chanting a prayer to the fire, an ancient Sanskrit hymn, as the flames leapt skyward. Warrington spoke poetically of the dream of a dreamer, saying that the first Star Congress of Ojai was the realization of a long-cherished vision held by one man, Krishnamurti.

By May 31, Warrington hosted an informal reception in honor of Krishnamurti who would be leaving the following day with his party, Mr. & Mrs. Rajagopal, Professor J. Prasad, Dr. J. van der Leeuw and others enroute to London. (Some publications report enroute to Holland.)

Published in 1928, a small pamphlet *Jesus and Krishnamurti: Their Lives and Teachings*, by Harriet Tuttle Bartlett, National Lecturer for Theosophy, attempted to throw light upon the present day Advent of a great teacher.

Dr. Besant announces America gets Vice-Presidency:

An official notice from Dr. Besant, which will give much satisfaction to American members, reads as follows:

"I have the pleasure of informing you that I have appointed Mr. A. P. Warrington of Krotona, Ojai, U.S.A., Vice-President of the Theosophical Society. He represents our largest National Society. He has accepted the appointment. The announcement has been delayed by my illness.
Yours fraternally,
Annie Besant."

To E. S. Members
of the American Division, E.S.T.

Dear Friends,

In appointing me to the Vice-Presidency of our Theosophical Society, the President-Outer Head has relieved me of the Corresponding Secretaryship of American Division of the E.S.T., and has appointed Miss Marie Poutz my successor.

And so I take leave of you, my friends and co-workers, as the official representative of the O.H. in this Division. In doing so I wish to express to you my appreciation of the hearty and dependable way you have worked with me all these one and twenty years, and to say I lay down my reins of office with feelings of no little regret. You have made me proud of you in many instances, many emergencies, and my happy work with you cannot be forgotten.

My successor needs no introduction to you. She already has endeared herself to you by her wise helpfulness through long years of devoted and capable service. You are fortunate that she can still be with you. I ask for her at least as faithful and sincere cooperation as you have given to me; then all will be well.

After all we do not part. Only for me the scene changes in the drama and a new character has been assigned. Doubtless we shall still have our contacts in some form.
With real affection,
A.P. Warrington

To E.S. Members of the American Division, E.S.T.

Dear Friends,

In accepting the post so graciously offered me by our beloved O.H., I do so realizing fully what the loss of Mr. Warrington's never-failing understanding and wise guidance will mean to the E.S.

But in union there is strength, and if, as I trust, you give me as hearty a co-operation as you have always given him in the past, we may hope to aid one another to make of Master's School an ever more efficient instrument of service to the world.

There will be no change in the work of the School as outlined for the new E.S. year. May we labor faithfully side by side in the service of Those Who rule and guide the world, and may Their blessing rest upon everyone of you.

Every your faithful friend,

Marie Poutz

———————————⟡———————————

A document showing AP Warrington grappling with the 'new message' Krishnamurti is communicating.

Musings
By the Corresponding Secretary

I went up to the top of the Mount of Oaks today, the place of the late Camp-fire. [also called Pilot Point] The charred remains of the fire were still visible, reminding me of the striking picture made when the audience of a thousand gathered upon this site night after night and listened to Krishnaji, and watched the flames of the great fire surge upward into the heavens. Today, I looked over the valley and up to the tops of the mountains, and with the memory of the Camp-fire still fresh in mind, I drifted into many musings.

Down the valley and out into the world, which is an extension thereof, I could conceive the play of forms, forms of life of every character—life rushing into form after form—forms both entangling and helpful, intended always to be helpful, but ever ending in some degree of thralldom.

Star Camp-fire on the top of Mount of Oaks, also called Pilot Point.

Up here on this Mount of Oaks, where Krishnaji had stood and taught the pilgrims of the Star, all outer forms were missing. I could see nothing but my own poor self, insignificant and unimportant. That self seemed to open out into a larger Self, also myself; and that, in turn, into a Self still larger, and beyond that just life—all life. (Was this a picture of my threefold self—my earthly, heavenly, and eternal self, and were the three together my own expression of the One Self?) Nothing else seemed to exist but myself, manifesting in these aspects—the pilgrim, the way and the portal—and then, the goal beyond.

If the true way of life be within and upwards, from lesser self to greater, within one's own being, as I felt it to be, on this mount of many memories, then the complicated systems that obtain down in the valley would seem unessential. What are they for? If life is so simple, so personal in plan; if its goal is found within one's own self, then wherefore all the search outside?

Or, can it be that the outer search is essential after all? May it not be that it is at first essential go give solid proof that the way lies in another direction? Is it possible that strength, goodness and beauty are gained only thereby? It has taken

84

me a long time on the journey of life to see how beautiful, how wonderful is this immediate path which lies within myself. Could it have been those complications of form that served as a preparation for the awakening, bringing to me some realization of the great simplicity which lies within?

What now should I do to take advantage of the opportunity that comes to me with this fleeting glimpse? "Unify your three-fold nature—the body, the soul and the spirit. Make them one. Work constantly from the centre of their unity; strike down all the barriers that have been erected between them. In tis the eternal will be realized."

I sounded over and over the Sacred Word, symbol of that unity, and it seemed that I could feel a oneness never before realized.

I can reflect now more clearly upon Krishnaji's meaning when he says that religious and other forms are *not necessary* to the eternal life, which he calls the Beloved; for, is not the need solely this, that we shall bind together our three-fold nature—the earthly, the heavenly, and the eternal—and live in the unity of these three in all simplicity and perfection of effort? Perhaps the outer forms exist for those who do not see this. The sacred atmosphere and mystery thrown round them may be helpful to those who as yet are blind to the inner way. Perhaps they may thus be helped to realize it in time. But sad it is that such forms should be used to separate man from man and to create all manner of distinctions and barriers within the great human family.

Perhaps the explanation of things as they are lies in this: human growth exists in various stages of immaturity. Throughout these stages man is rushing out hither and you in search for truth and happiness. His senses are crude, able to apprehend vibrations of form only. Therefore he seeks truth in form. As he succeeds in glimpsing a stage ahead he erects a form to lead his brethren to that stage. What is its value, this form he has built up? Its ultimate personal value lies n the degree that it awakens aspirants to a knowledge of the simple way to the eternal self. Throughout the earlier stages, perhaps, this reminder is very vague, and may be it is inevitable that the immature man shall take form for substance and build up all his hopes thereupon. Perhaps it is only as he grows through experience that he begins to see beyond his religious form, and discovers the truth that the way lies within himself.

Perhaps there is another explanation of forms, one having an occult significance. The world in its great preponderance of material activity must gradually become filled with unworthy thoughts and emotions—the creative energies of man ever expressing themselves in such crude ways as hatred, jealousy, envy, anger, resentment and other vices that separate man from man. Doubtless these accumulate in great centres of undesirable influence. Obviously then something has to be done to counteract such hosts of world-wide, crude, destructive, embodied energies, else they would more than ever precipitate war, famine, destruction. And what can help to counteract this?

It is well attested that the magic of the Mass and of Masonry become dynamos of force, creating great currents of beauty and upliftment which pour themselves out into the world with beneficent results. May it not be, then, that these beneficent forces are necessary as a measurable foil for those cruder forces created in these days of humanity's immaturity? Without the finer forces would not the grosser creations overwhelm the race in an eonian catastrophe? I do not know, but these are reflections which come to me as I sit here on the Mount of Oaks and ponder the contradictions which I knew arose n the minds of many on hearing Krishnaji's message.

To me it all seems so simple. Krishnaji has not condemned religions or ceremonial forms, whatever they may be. He has simply stated a cosmic truth—that they are not necessary to the ascent up through ones higher self into the life eternal.

He has not said, and one would seem to doubt that he ever would say, that rites and ceremonies have no use in the world as purifying channels, channels purifying the world in some measure of the dross of emotion and thought produced by humanity in its ugliest moods. These channels may be of the very greatest use in holding the balance and in assuring the hope for humanity at large. They may be an invaluable means of service to the world in keeping it swept measurably clean of the invisible filth produced by undeveloped humanity.

But is [it] does not mean that, because these outer forms may be useful as purifying agencies tot the world at large, they also are necessary to one's own personal liberation. They could hardly be necessary since one's liberation is known to be attained by turning within and unifying the three-fold man, until he becomes the united self and passes through the portal to the eternal life which is his Beloved.

If these musings shall have led to the realization of even a fragment of truth, then I can truly see why in Krishnaji's message I see no contradiction, no condemnation, nothing to puzzle even those who are immersed in form. Let them use their forms, if they like, to help make the word clean; it is such a fine and useful thing to do. But if they want liberation, let them remember that the record shows that the Lord comes again and again to restate the simple, royal way, which is within. Even though it may be that in the past He may have established, or inspired others to establish, many forms for the helping of the world in certain ways; who knows? Yet when His task comes to state the way of liberation, has he not always pointed out the way within? Perhaps it is not His chosen work to be the builder of forms, but rather to be the giver of life. Perhaps there are others who take his message of the life and cast it into forms believed to be useful in leading one toward that life. So, his message ever remains the message from the snow-capped peak, set forth from time to time into the valley of life, lest we forget; lest we forget!

A.P.W.*

———————————❧———————————

On June 10, Warrington gave his E.S. talk at the Krotona open-air amphitheater. It contains gems of insights that he had at the time the E.S. members of the Theosophical Society were going through

* Warrington, A.P., "Musings", *The American E.S.T. Bulletin,* September, 1928, n53, pp.1-4.

such conflict regarding Krishnamurti and his message.

The members seemed to prefer that we meet here today, under the trees, rather than in the new auditorium. That I feel is a good choice for E.S. members to make. I believe the closer we keep to nature, the nearer we come to the true line of human progress. It seems to have been the peculiar egotistic tendency of the human type to try to separate himself, insulate himself, from the other kingdoms and to antagonize them and himself. I feel, therefore, that the rue line of evolution for us lies near to nature; we should recover the lost friendship with the nature forces, an recovering that friendship, we shall gain an impetus that will help us in evolution. We Theosophists might do well to cultivate all the various nature friendships.

Well, I have heard a great many doubts and opinions and remarks generally with regard to Krishnaji and his message. I think some of the brethren have been a bit upset, but I don't quite see why they should be. It may have been because they jumped to conclusions, and have not see a big enough picture.

Yesterday I was up again at the Camp-fire place and indulged in these musings.

It would be interesting to hear from some of the members present, if they have any thoughts to express, for many are puzzled, and do not understand. It is a habit of many to think in terms of extremes. They would see on the one hand a wonderful teaching explaining life to their complete satisfaction. That for them would be Theosophy. They would see on the other hand Krishnaji, whom, they believed to be the World-Teacher, speaking in a way that implied to them that he did not recognize Theosophy as having the importance in their lives which they believed it to have. They therefore jump to the conclusion that their great philosophy that had been so carefully built up now had no value.

Let us also take an extreme view and suppose that it was the World-Teacher who established all the useful religions and other uplifting, organized forms in the world, and do limit your imagination in picturing them. Let us believe

He is putting His life into these forms, that He has created elemental powers to vivify them regularly upon proper invocation. Each has its peculiar function, no two being just alike. Now He comes and vitalizes the Star, which is an added form to those existing in the world. It is to do a particular thing, apparently through that form He desires to build up no philosophy, to establish no technical form of cosmology, or to employ no rite; but, avoiding details He puts the eternal truth before the minds of the people in a capsule of simplicity. Naturally, if He is creating an additional form through which to express is life, a form that is different from the rest, He will not repeat what He has done before, but will take a new course. This new form has its own uniqueness and value of all the others that have been formed. There is something curious in a certain type of the religious mind that when it accepts one form, makes it deny everything else in the world apparently at variance with it; a bigoted narrow-mindedness. In this lies the cause of much of the religious troubles that have ever existed in the world. The priestly mind is a very one-pointed mind; focuses on minute details. The priest is more apt to have a microscope at his eye than a telescope.

In one of the letters from the Masters, if I remember correctly, He speaks of religions as having done a large part of the harm in the world. Is that only because they have been mismanaged, that they have not been in wise hands? The power of the magic that exists within them, we have been told, can go on quite independently of the character of the priest. But that has to do with the inner usefulness, and some believe that that has worked continually for the blessing of the world. But think of this. Most people now realize that thoughts are things and emotions are things, and since the world population is creating, besides the good, huge centres of evil force, the aggregate of such centres becomes a kind of world devil, a great Frankenstein monster, dominating its creators until they pray to it—make sacrifices to it—the thing they have created. This accumulation of thought force throughout the world probably at times gets very hectic, inflamed, and has to break out in war. I have no doubt that this creature is really the centre of the real impulse that drives men to war—the elemental created by the thinking and feeling of the people of the world.

In my "musings" it was this force that I had in mind as being weakened by the magic of the Mass and Masonry, the Magic that exists in any of the religions of the world that have that power.

I now invite opinions from those present.

Marie Poutz: I may, perhaps, add my own idea as to the value of these forms, rites and organizations employed at an earlier stage than when liberation can be looked forward to. Man begins by being selfish within himself; then his selfishness extends to the wife and children and those who are dear to him. Is it not good to have organizations to take him beyond that family selfishness, influencing him to unite with others from whom he desires no immediate benefit? It seems to me that those forms teach him to work with a group rather than a family. So, to my mind, those organizations are useful as they help people to widen their selfishness. Everything that broadens is useful.

A.P.Warrington: It is just as if some wise One had said: The world is full of forms, religious and otherwise. They are all right as far as they go. They help you to develop your civic virtues; they improve your social status; they are educationally broadening, refining; but when the Lord comes, He comes with a new Message and hope that lies beyond there. He comes with a promise of liberation. If you want that, you must find it outside these forms and within yourself. That makes it clear. The form exists for a definite thing, not specifically for liberation. But if one wants liberation, one must have come up along these ways, and then turn within and find it within yourself. I see no confusion in that.

Marie Poutz: There is no shadow of any confusion, but I should like to know, when we decidedly want liberation and accept the hints given by Krishnaji, and work to grain liberation for ourselves, is it necessary when we get that vision to give up the work we are doing in the organizations of men which lead them a little bit nearer to their own goal?

90

It is necessary to give up the work we are going along those lines when we seek liberation for ourselves?

A.P. Warrington: I should think that would be a temperamental matter. Take the priesthood. It lays down definite lines as to what is spiritual and unspiritual, what is worthy and unworthy, and make the beautiful realm of duty a place of slavery; and it is possible that if we were psychoanalyzed, we should find, in a higher sene, that unless we wanted to do that authorized duty from within, we were enslaving ourselves to something that would tie us and prevent liberation.

I noticed in Krishnaji's message that impulse. If duty springs from within and we should be unhappy without fulfilling it, then we should be very foolish to drop it; but if we have been brought up along ecclesiastical lines and everything we have done along such lines has been from a strict sense of religious duty—the proper thing to do—then, I think, if we were to drop those things and do what we wanted to do from within, throwing our whole nature into something of our own unique design, we should make more progress than if we did the dutiful things on somebody else's authority.

I think we shall need to readjust our viewpoint by what he said of authority and tradition.

Then there is the higher selfishness. A young man having the financial independence to go to college has before him the problems as to whether he shall go and qualify himself for a higher, a trained service, or remaining illiterate and working side by side with the best trained masses. He has to make that choice. No doubt if he were all aflame with the desire to help, he could be very useful remaining where he stood and working there. On the other hand, it is a question if he could not wield a far wider and more helpful influence by going through a period of through training and building up his own nature. By doing this he would not merely be developing himself, for selfish ends; he would be aiding a fragment of the consciousness of the Logos Himself, would he not? He would be carrying out the task coming to him from a primal impulse coming from the One in Whom we live and have our being. We have a duty to a group of elementals—to train them to be useful instruments. And when they are useful, to whom are they useful? To the Logos, to the One Life.

These are just thoughts that run through one's mind, aroused by this almost new doctrine of Krishnaji's. It might be profitable if we should allow ourselves to think ourselves into new fields of thought; if we should readjust our position in view of what we have heard, and see if we do not start out in a fresh direction—not dropping what we have acquired, but using it to widen our field of observation and experience.

K.L. Same thing we have been taught all along. Nothing new, but it comes with a new emphasis.

A.K.G. I think the Message has given courage to those people who have belonged to organizations as a matter of duty. It has set them free from a certain unconscious hypocrisy.

H.G. There is one point that has seemed curious. To go way back, we are told that the First Outpouring from the Third Logos builds matter from which forms are made; that the Second Logos is the builder of form, the ensouler of form, and is the life of all form until the Third Outpouring from the First Logos comes and liberates, to a certain extent, life from its close attachment with form. Then life goes on in the human kingdom a very long time, all through the Path of Outgoing, and it proceeds some distance along the Path of Return before that stage is reached. That Initiation is reached when the Causal Body is broken and life is really liberated from form.

Now, the World-Teacher is considered as the representative of the Second Logos in this world, and it comes with rather a shock to hear that particular One say that form is entirely unnecessary. It seems like a denial of what we have been taught is His own particular function.

A.P.W. But is He not dual? There is a dual quality to the Second Logos, is there not? If that suggests an explanation, then the thought follows that there should be an even balance between life and form; that each should be serving the other. But when life becomes entangled in form, and the balance is lost, then He comes to restore the balance. So that might be a process that takes place within the field of the Second Logos Himself, if one may speculate—the restoration of the balance in that Cosmic field. However, these are only philosophical speculations, yet very interesting to some.

D.R. Since we have been leaning more to the side of form so long, might it not be that Krishnaji wants to restore the balance and give a lean to the life: bad to be unbalanced.

A.P.W. Krishnaji is using form every day in everything he does. The Star is just as much a form as the Church, but it is a simple form, direct form, and one that probably leaves out occult machinery, so to say. It is a kind of Protestant movement. I think, however, that the Star, as a form, looks to Krishnaji as authority. It is only in the individual that one can wipe away authority. If a form, an association did that, it would lose guidance.

D.R. Is it not true that our whole life is based on authority? The world is round, etc.

A.P.W. To be told that the earth is round, that the planet Mars is inhabited, should never mean more to us than a suggestion, because the course that one person has found to be the true, may not at all be the way I have found; but if he tells me what his way is, it is a suggestion to me as to how I shall find my way, and I am sure I should find it along a little different road. When we regard all the so-called authorities as merely sign-post, suggestions, and take out of them what we can and find our own way, then we shall be following the way of our own uniqueness. But when we follow instructions, step by step, point by point, the authority dominates.

E.W.M. Two facts stand out in my mind: 1st: The fact of our existence in the world here proves the absolute necessity of forms to earth life. We cannot be here without their use, we cannot get along without them as humans. 2nd: Our functioning as spiritual beings working toward liberation should ever be to learn the non-essentiality of any particular form; learn to work in the form and be free of it. We cannot be here and be without the forms, but we can be here and be without any dominance of form over ourselves.

A.P.W. After all, these things grow out of social instinct,

the desire to get together in some combined effort. If we image man as being alone, without social contacts he would be liberated from the possibility of liberation if forms were essential. They are more or less artificial and man-made.

Bishop Leadbeater has shown the difference between the Lord in His fullness and that fragment of Himself that is finding expression now through Krishnaji. I have felt that if Krishnaji remains with us, say 20, 30 or 40 years, as we hope he may do, we shall find an enlargement of His expression and shall observe an extension of the scope of his message. It is not reasonable to expect that for decades there will be no variation. Therefore one comes to the conclusion that the material instrument of the Lord will itself evolve in His hands as He uses it.

So, I do not think those critical minds should feel discouraged because Krishnaji has not appeared as the greatest musician, the greatest artist, the greatest everything in the world. Perhaps they might wait. This is just the beginning. Who is it that has the genius to say how much the Lord wishes to express of Himself at this time?

A.P. Warrington [*]

Fundraising through the ES:

June 15 1928

Friends:

To fifty members well-known to me, I am sending this letter. I am sending it on behalf of our beloved E.S. Centre, "Krotona," the heart of all the outer T.S. Movements. It needs you just a little at this time.

The officers were recently pressed to expand construction to keep pace with the sudden growth and progress developing in Ojai Valley. This I now completed—done adequately for you and your work here, and in such taste and beauty as will enable you to feel proud of it. And it is already being used by full audiences. As the

* Warrington, A.P., "E.S. Meeting Amphitheatre, Krotona", Sunday June 10, 1928, pp. 5-11.

returns have not been adequate to cover the cost of improvements made, and as I am the custodian of the fund, I take the liberty of asking fifty of my well-known friends if they would not like to have a further hand in this work by contributing to help finish the payments?

Much of Krotona's value lies in the strength of its tranquility. This should not be disturbed by financial anxiety.

The letter which Mr. Warrington recently mailed to E.S. members is giving to those who have not already contributed the opportunity of sharing in the Krotona building expenditures by a payment of $1.00 per month for a period of months. And while this is the most that some members can do, I believe that there are others who would deem it a privilege to give more if the opportunity were given to them; and so I am writing to you, because I believe that you will either find it possible to aid substantially yourself, or will be able to put the facts clearly to others who can.

Often our members forget that, even as the E.S. is the Heart of the T.S., so has it been the means for fostering those other movements which have been established in connection with the tremendously important future which now confronts us. Undoubtedly it was foreseen that the membership of the Inner School would consist of a band of people who, because they had been proved in past lives, could be depended upon to meet the varied demands of the work at this particular time.

This role of "mother" to the allied activities has linked Krotona with all the plans which are being developed in the Ojai Valley. And in order to keep pace with the requirements of this work, and to provide for the gatherings which have become a part of it, an auditorium and other additions to the Library Building became a necessity.

Krotona, as a centre of peace and tranquility, beauty and culture, is of inestimable value to the work in general, and ought never be harassed by financial anxiety; in tranquility lies much of its strength. So, the least we can do at the present time is to cooperate with its officers in such manner as to relieve them from the pressure of financial responsibility.

You, I know, will readily see, that to us of the present day there has come a great privilege, and with it a responsibility.

Would you not like to assist further by becoming one of a group of 50 each of whom makes himself responsible for the payment of $100 to $200? As Mr. Warrington has appointed me custodian of the fund, I am taking the liberty of approaching fifty members will

known to me with this letter, and I hope you will be pleased that I have done so.
Sincerely yours,
George H. Hall

House building and finances at Krotona:

The Ojai Camp
June 27 1928

Dear Mr. Warrington:

Following yesterday's conversation as to the general problem of T.S. and E.S. members building house on Krotona grounds, I take the liberty of offering a few points for your consideration. I do this because naturally I would wish Krotona safe-guarded from certain troublesome circumstances.

A few things occurred to me that would make it very undesirable to loan money from individuals with which to put up houses for them. The term "loan" itself has a particular psychological influence which would be present in the transaction during its whole life. In the event of the person getting hard up or suffering a disaster the idea of a loan to Krotona might imply a certain kind of a claim towards getting the loan repaid, and however clearly a contract may be worded it is difficult to talk to unfortunate people who have the term "loan" in their minds. They might demand repayment, even though unjustly or against the terms of the contract. On the other hand should they build the houses themselves on leased ground that factor of a loan would not be in their consciousness. All they could ask would be that Krotona help them sell their houses, which Krotona would do, subject to proper consideration for its own interests.

Another factor involved is the experience of building houses itself. Assuming that a certain type of architecture is agreed upon, together with an amount to be spent and a standard of building, it is usually the case that the owner of the house, during the process of building, wants added features put in, and these sundries first of all amount to a considerably higher sum than the estimate, and there would be this negotiating and conferring between the prospective tenant and Krotona during the process of building, and the sum finally spent would generally compel various modifications of the contract entered into.

There is also possible difference of opinion as to the standard of material put in. If the tenant does not build his own house there is the possibility of a dispute as to workmanship and material. If the roof leaks his claim is apt to be on Krotona.

Another factor to follow this plan, where a great many tenants would be involved would demand a great deal of careful bookkeeping, accounts would have to be kept with each person, entailing a great many items which would throw a considerable burden on Krotona as far as clerical work is concerned.

Still another factor is that loaning the money from individuals and building houses for them entails a rather complicated contract with many items to be gone into, and wherever a contract is complicated there is generally afterwards room for dispute and the possibility of legal controversy.

Contrasted with all the above the simple land contract of leasing the land to the tenant and letting him build his own house, subject to the conditions you lay down, does away with practically all of the above objections, keeps things simple and easy to handle, and accomplishes the same result eventually as far as revenue is concerned. Revaluations should be, in my opinion, eliminated in favor of a straight 20 year valuation, which should average well the possibilities of the land from every standpoint and yet be fair to the tenant.

I understand that you might have some difficulty as to the water question because of a technical draw-back, etc., in your own water rights, however it seems to me that that might be arranged. After all, where there is no actual difference in final results but only a nominal and technical phraseology involved, then an agreement should be easy. After all the same water is used whoever is the technical owner of the house, and my experience with ordinary people is that they do not impose restrictions arbitrarily in those cases where their own pocketbook is not affected one way or the other.

I hope you will pardon the liberty I take in offering this. No doubt all of these reasons have occurred to you also.

With good wishes, and thanking you for your courtesy, I am,
Cordially yours,
Louis Zalk

Meanwhile, George Arundale, who was beginning to find it difficult to understand Krishnamurti as the World-Teacher, wrote a booklet of 39 pages, which did admit the connection between Krishnamurti and the World-Teacher:

A word by way of Explanation

From time to time even the most beautiful of instruments need tuning—what to say of others. In January last I found my own poor instrument needed turning. It was out of tune, unmelodious, unharmonious. I could have gone on playing it in its disharmonious condition, but I should have constantly been making a noise; and there is already enough noise in the world. So I decided to tune the strings of my instrument anew, to tune them a little more in unison with Myself. To this end I went into Retreat, into a meditation, into what I like to call a brooding, and I remained in it for many months. I did this partly because I hate to be out of tune, and partly because there is a special melody I want to play these coming years, and an ill-tuned instrument would ruin it. Not that I claim my instrument now to be in perfect tune. My ear is not yet perfectly developed. But it plays better than it did, at least I hope it does. I draw my bow across a string or two in this little series of booklets. How do the notes sound to your ears? Do they ring true to you? Or, if your own instrument has been recently tuned, is there, in your judgment, still need of a little adjustment? Or perhaps you have another octave, another chord, another note, in the Universal Scale of Life? I may not agree with you, but what does that matter?

I draw my bow across a string—
> *No. 1. Krishnaji: Light-Bringer.*

I draw my bow again—
> *No. 2. The Joy of Catastrophe.*
> *No. 3. Go Your Own Way.*
> *No. 4. Fanaticism—Wholesale and Retail.*
> *No. 5. Shadows and Mountains.*

I shall draw my bow again if the above receive sufficient welcome.

George S. Arundale

Krishnaji: Light-Bringer

During the last six months and more I have been in the fortunate position of being able to dwell out of the world, though still living in it, and to go through the furniture of my mind, feelings, and of other states of my consciousness, both for purposes of re-arrangement, of a bonfire where possible— note, please, I do not say "where necessary," of replacing the old with new, of having the least amount of furniture in the various rooms of my house, so that there may be room, space, freedom for movement.

I have endeavoured to be for the time being in contemplation, in meditation, before the Altar of the Real, so that in this Vigil I might realise Myself in greater measure than before. I do not for a moment pretend that total realisation has come. It would be absurd so to pretend, but I do feel that I have come somewhat nearer to the Real. I feel a readjustment to Reality. I feel that Life has been re-valued. I feel renewed. Old values have given way to new values, or have become clearer, less formal, less restricted, less of the substance of Time and more of the nature of Eternity.

I have taken stock of myself as ruthlessly as I could. I have tried not to consider my feelings or prejudices or superstitions or convictions. I have tried to remember my weaknesses. I have tried to look myself frankly in the face, or, if you will, frankly in the mind, frankly in the feelings, frankly in my views and opinions frankly in my truths. I have a fairly clear idea of the criticisms which from time to time have been levelled against me. I read them carefully whenever they are written, and sooner or later the oral criticism comes to my ears. It is astonishing how quickly such criticism travels. I am thankful for the critics. I have been weighing it.

The whole process of the readjustment has been a most delightful experience. It is like travelling to a part of the world one has never visited before. The unfamiliar scenery, the strange conditions, the peculiar circumstances, prove extremely fascinating. I suppose I have been looking at all these things before. They may have been present in my consciousness. But though I may have been looking I certainly have not see. And now to perceive is a tremendous uplift, is a most refreshing expansion of my consciousness, gives me a feeling of being able to breathe more freely where hitherto I have been half suffocated, though I may possibly have not been a ware of the fact. If I am not accustomed to take deep breaths I may think I am breathing splendidly, with my full lung capacity, when, in fact, I may hardly be breathing at all. In this prolonged brooding through which I have been going I have tried to see how deeply I could breathe, whether I could expand my spiritual lungs far more than I have ever expanded them before. And the result has been that in certain directions I find I have hitherto been only half breathing, if as much as half. What a difference it makes to take deep breaths! How tremendously exhilarating and vitalising!

I have tried to be ruthless. I have sought to challenge, with all the impersonality at my command, every belief and opinion I have held, my normal judgments and understandings, my habitual ways of looking at life, in fact the Arundale outlook generally. I said to myself: Let the old Arundale, however constructed, die. Let him descend into the waters of death for baptism into truer Life. I have hoped, most sincerely and ardently hoped, that the old Arundale has indeed died, yielding place to anew Arundale, an improvement on the latest of the series of Arundales which have been running their course through the ages. What is the use of living if one cannot die? What is the use of dying if one cannot live? And are not all times times for dying into a new life?

I have looked for the origins of myself. I have looked to see where there has been genuine Arundale and where only imitations of other people. I will not say that these imitations have been worthless, spurious. I will not say that the genuine Arundale has been true. But I will say that though imitation may be the sincerest form of flattery of others, it is by no means the sincerest form of flattery of oneself. One must in the long run be oneself, even though it is but in the nature of things that others should help us to become ourselves. I have been feeling very strongly that I do not want other people to hand me vessels into which the Life is to be poured. I am glad that they should suggest to me the best shape for the Life, the best shape for this Life, the best shape for that. But I want to make my own vessels myself, even though I may make them in the likeness of vessels brought before my eyes. Interestingly enough, I have found myself in possession of quite a considerable number of vessels originating with other people which I have, perhaps out of laziness, perhaps out of difference, taken into my own use, putting them upon the shelves of my mind and emotions, and no doubt exclaiming: See what beautiful vessels I have! The longing has now come upon me to have vessels of my own fashioning, and as far as possible to have few or none which are not of my own fashioning. I wanted, in other words, to see how I could get on without taking for granted that which hitherto I may have taken for granted, which hitherto I may have deemed essential to my wellbeing. Could I get on by myself, to the extent to which anyone can get on by himself in a world in which all is indissolubly united?

It would take a number of dull volumes—dull, that is, to others, though not dull to myself, for I should have known the delight of writing down in them the records of a phase of my evolution—to describe the many deaths of attitudes and beliefs and opinions, and the nature of the births into a newer life. There has been a holocaust in some directions. Some parts of the old Arundale have not reincarnated at all. Other parts have been reborn in forms altogether different. I will, therefore, select just one evolutionary phase as an example. I will take the case of my reaction to Krishnaji, to the very wonderful force he is, or of which he is the channel—which you will.

I had grown up, as it were, to believe, practically without any question, certain statements which had been made with regard to the World-Teacher and to Krishnaji's relation to Him. As time passed, and I began more and more to think for myself, I naturally began to judge with such small judgment as I possessed. Hitherto I had not judged, and because I did not judge I did not really know. Until I began to judge I seemed to now more than I really did know. When I began to judge for myself I have no doubt I began to divest myself of what was really truth. In the eyes of many I shall have seemed to know less. I ceased to "know" that which apparently I had hitherto "known." But I think I have lately been beginning at last to take my stand upon that which I could truly say I know, though it may well be that some day I shall know that which I had previously played with, not understanding the nature of it, that which I must not at present say I know. But for the time being I had to restrict the circumference of my understanding within its true limitations.

Frankly, I found some of the statements made with regard to Krishnaji difficult to accept, not because I knew them to be untrue, but because I knew nothing about them, or only a little. They were beyond my own experience, such as this was. Doubtless my experience was at fault. it was obviously less both in quality and in quantity than that of my elders. Still, it was all I had, and I felt I must rely upon it. On the other hand, I had been accustomed, with very great profit to myself, to accept as working hypotheses many teachings given by my elders. I thus found myself in a most tiresome tangle. Tradition was leading me in one direction. Experience and the desire to stand on y own feet were leading me in another direction. Orthodoxy was obviously along one pathway. Heterodoxy was along another, and what kind of excommunication might not come if I travelled thereon: not excommunication by my elders, I hoped, but possibly self-excommunication.

Suppose I were to speak out boldly and say: "After all, I do not understand what is said with regard to the relationship between Krishnaji and the World-Teacher. I do not understand the identity of consciousness. I am not able yet to say he *is* the World-Teacher. I see things otherwise." Suppose I were to say this frankly, should I not be calling down upon my head the anathemas of many and the sad disapproval of a few whose approval means much to me? Might it not be said that here is the traitor? Might I not, in fact, apart from what people might be saying, be thwarting in a small yet definite way work which I knew and know to be the work of a Great Being? Might I not thus show myself unworthy of the favours I have received, guilty of the basest sort of ingratitude?

Mind you, I am not saying that the form in which I have set forth my bold speaking expresses what I actually believed in the light of such wisdom as I possessed. I have purposely exaggerated. What I did believe I set forth at the time, to the strong disapprobation of many, in a little pamphlet entitled "The Lord is Here." But even this pamphlet I felt to convey less than that which I wanted to convey. It was true for me at the time. It still remains for me substantially true. But there was something lacking. It was not what it ought to be. It fell short. And ever since I wrote it I have been feeling its shortcomings. What was the matter with it? Not that it was untrue according to my own particular standard and understanding. What was, then, the matter?

I think I have since discovered what was the matter. I was not looking Krishnaji straight in the face. I was not looking at him face to face. I was looking at him either through other people's spectacle, or through spectacles of my own made in pat of glass coloured for me by other people, and in part of glass which I had myself coloured in order to see him in the colouring in which I thought I wanted to see him, or ought to see him. It was all unreal. It was all a matter of labels. And now I have been feeling that I must see him not as in a glass darkly, but face to face. I had, as a result of having my thinking done for me largely by others, expected Krishnaji to flow into certain moulds carefully prepared beforehand. He must be the slave of these moulds, fit them with all obedience and even servility. All I expect him to say, he must say. All I expected him to do, he must do. All I expected him to be, he must be. What a fool I was! I admit this without the slightest reservation. I had expected the World-Teacher, for then as now I had no doubt of a definite relationship, to subordinate Himself to my conceptions of the role He ought to play in the world. Why, if I were so certain as to what He should do, I might as well have realised that someone else could do the work. He comes just because there is no one else to do the work. He alone can do, and, even more, there is no one else who can *know* what is to be done.

I expected Krishnaji to fit himself to my measurements just as I should expect to fit perfectly into a suit made for me by a competent tailor. With much care and trouble I had made a suit, and Krishnaji did not fit into it, and did not wear it. A little disconcerting? No, hardly that. Rather, extremely amusing. *I had forgotten I had not his measure!* What a fool again! A tailor may take my measure. Perhaps anybody can take my measure. But to take the measure of Krishnaji and of Him Whom he represents . . . ! Well, as events showed only too clearly, I was not a competent tailor, and I only had myself to blame.

But what a muddle it all was for the time being. Here were splendid gifts, piercing probings, magnificent tearings away of outworn veils hiding the Truth we ought to know, towering simplicities. And there was I almost ignoring the gifts spending my energy in clumsily fumbling about the source whence they were derived. I occupied myself in studying the interpretations of others with regard to their source. I tried to study their source for myself. And I found others engaged in the same activities. I found many appraising these gifts in terms of their supposed source. I found that many valued the gifts not for their intrinsic value but for their supposed hall-mark. I found many not really caring for the fits at all, still less using them; but jealous of any irreverence towards them, not for the sake of the fits themselves but for the sake of the hall-mark they were supposed to bear.

I found some setting forth the following:

1. Krishnaji is the World-Teacher.

2. When he speaks the World-Teacher speaks.

3. Those who do not accept these statements are rejecting the World-Teacher.

This attitude, which I confess I regard as in the highest degree fanatical, inquisitorial and cruel, troubled me. I may know him to be the World-Teacher, but how or why should others know this highly abstruse fact, assuming it to be a fact? It is a part of a post-graduate course of studies, and most of us are little more than matriculates. It troubled me that certain people were erecting Krishnaji into a dogma of sorts, so that it became blasphemous to treat him as an ordinary human being. It became, that is, blasphemous to be ignorant, not to know what other people might happen to think they knew; and, after all, how many of those who say he is the World-Teacher know what they mean when they say it, or know for themselves and have not borrowed the statement from others? It is not a crime to be ignorant. It is not a crime to be young. It is not a crime to have a coloured skin, or hair of such and such a hue. And I felt strongly that labels, however true, must on no account be permitted to stand in the way of Krishnaji being all things to all. He may be the World-Teacher. But let him be supremely Krishnaji, someone whom we can see and know with the ordinary eyes of the body, of the mind, of the feelings. Let him be supremely understandable, naturally understandable. Let us be with him face to face, without having to subscribe to articles of belief, or to be subjected to tests of conformity with man-made standards.

What a waste of time! How silly! How wrong! With what tremendous delight I suddenly came to the conclusion that hall-marks did *not* matter, that labels did *not* matter, that authority did *not* matter, that descriptions did *not* matter, that there was no question either of orthodoxy or of unorthodoxy, of loyalty or of disloyalty. Some who read this booklet may say that they knew this all the time and rejoiced accordingly. Maybe. All I can say is that I suddenly awoke to the fact. It was borne in upon me as in a flash that I might well leave alone al questions of source. I could take these up at my leisure. But I should do well simply and naturally to look Krishnaji, and that is his Gifts, his truth, his Message, straight in the face and do the best I could with them both for myself and for others.

It was a wonderful relief and a great inspiration. And I am going to be quite frank about it. I have tried to put aside all that has confused me, side-tracked me, bothered me, troubled me. I have brushed aside all that has come to me from without, and I have tried to rely exclusively upon that

105

which is within me. I have said to myself: Never mind what others have said, whoever they may be. Never mind what you yourself have thought. Just be straight with Krishnaji; but straight from yourself, not from anyone else whatever. Go straight to him from yourself and not *via* anybody else. You owe this to him and you owe this to yourself. I do most sincerely hope I shall not be misunderstood, except by those whose business seems to be wilful misunderstanding, when I say that I put on one side all that has been said by the two people I most revere and who have helped me most—Dr. Besant and Bishop Leadbeater. I have not the slightest doubt that all they say is profoundly true. My experience has always been of their most extraordinary accuracy, wherever I have had the means of judging. But I made up my mind that I must go to Krishnaji myself, in my own straight line, in no line of anyone else's drawing. I do not for a moment question the wisdom of the declaration of these two revered elders, nor the need for such declarations; God forbid I should question their truth. But I have found I wanted to get to Krishnaji in another way, leaving this particular way aside for the moment. This is, I know, what they would wish me to do, for any statements they themselves may make with regard to the occult side of the phenomenon of Krishnaji have, for them too, infinitely less significance than the Truth which comes. They give us the occult side because it is true. Let those who have the eyes to see, see. But there is that which matters even more, infinitely more.

I have put aside the ecstasies of the fanatical devotee, as I put aside the fulminations of the fanatical opponent. I have put aside those who, for the moment, are blinded by the dazzling Light into those dangerous extravagances which so often tend to turn away people who are ready to see. I have put aside the hatred of those who virulently deny the Light because they happen to be blind. I put aside all questions as to the relation between Krishnaji and the World-Teacher, simply because I have not sufficient material wherewith to build my Truth. I am quite ready to hear him say: "I am . . . " this or that. Doubtless he knows. Who should know this if not he? But I want to be free even of this. I want to soar into the infinite expanse of formless Truth, bathe in it, be renewed in it, so that in the world of forms I may myself build forms as near as I can in its likeness, in its Life, in its Spirit. The wonders as they are are enough of me at all events for the time being. They are more than enough for me. It will take me all my time to understand what I can understand. I must grope first after all this, and only play, as it were, with that which is somewhat beyond my ken. Surely I must cast my eyes about for the Light beyond. Yet the Light Present must enter welcoming eyes and fill my being with its effulgence. Let me not, for the sake of that which is farther off, loosen my hold of that which is immediate to my grasp. It was this consideration which made me brush aside that which I have enumerated above, and no less, I must add, myself as I was. I knew I must get at Myself from myself, for only by getting at Myself could I come face to face with Krishnaji, or, for the matter of that, with any Reality whatsoever. For I should like it to be distinctly understood that while I am in this particular experience brooding in terms of Krishnaji, my conclusions apply no less to anyone or to anything else. To reach the naked Truth one must divest oneself of clothing. One must travel to Oneself on rails of one's own laying, if rails one needs at all. And one has not travelled to Oneself, or one has not reached Oneself, if crutches remain, if labels remain, even if dogmas and doctrines remain: in other words if one remains particularised and has not become universalised.

Furthermore, I am not thinking of Krishnaji in any other way than in the way in which I should think about any other outstanding personality with a Message to deliver— from himself or from Another matters not at all. There is no question in my mind of fitting myself to him or to this teaching. There is no feeling in me that acceptance is the best policy—open-eyed acceptance if possible, blind if not. The whole value of Krishnaji to me lies in his power to make me more Myself. X may set my feet on the Path of discipleship. Y may draw me near to a Great Teacher. Z may help me to develop occult powers. And so on. Krishnaji helps me to know Myself—capital M. He helps me to find Myself. He aids me to distinguish between my many selves and My Self. How he does it I do not quite know. Probably because he is so very much Himself—capital H. But his power does not, to my mind, lie in statements or in the disclosure of Truth, or in definitions. As it seems to me, it lies in his attitude of pointing the way, so that we may perceive that *the* way is our way. He suggests how the knife may be made tremendously sharp, and he stirs in us the intuition or the instinct to ferret out the places where incision is needed. Then he says: CUT. But we must find out the places, and we must use a sharp knife.

If I were to set forth the nature of Krishnaji's teachings I should have to write all about myself, for however general these teachings may be from one point of view, from another their application is supremely individual. And each one of us, recognising the generalisation and therefore it applicability to our individual selves. I dare not set forth the generalisation. It is exactly what I cannot do. Nor would I venture to particularise if for others. But since the cap fits my head as every other head too, I am learning to put it on. Each one of us must understand for himself. It does not matter who Krishnaji specifically is. I do not know whether he cares who he is specifically. He knows who he is, and he knows that supremely he is, as we all are, *LIFE*. This knowledge must come to us too. How it comes to each one of us, when it comes, these are individual matters. Above all, there must be guarded borrowing of the Life of others, guarded introducing of it into ourselves knowing it to be borrowed, and therefore without that vital fact of its being part of us. There must be no prefacing of statements with the words: Krishnaji says. We must on no account sue him to bludgeon others into mental or emotional insensibility. Nor must we bludgeon ourselves. We must use our own judgments, or rather, perhaps, our own intuitions, our own best understanding. There is no greater reverence or gratitude than honest and sincere judgment, decision, made in the light of our highest powers. "I take this. I leave that. This appeals to me, That does not." No pretence, whether to ourselves or to others. What has become part of ourselves will live. That which is not part of ourselves, however much we may try to deceive ourselves or others, even honestly, into the belief that it *is* ourselves, will die because it has no contact with the flow of our life's blood. May I say without offence that I sometimes wonder how much longer the same people will have to go on attending Camp Fires, and either on the physical plane or in some other way—mentally and emotionally, perhaps—following Krishnaji about, before they learn to grasp the Real for themselves? I suppose the surest sign of successful discovery lies in the rising of an overwhelming urge to help to awaken in others that Life which he has awakened in us. We shall then be satisfied with being Ourselves and shall know our nearness to him, if we desire this, be physical distances what they may. Perhaps the first sign of the dawning life—I wonder—is impatience with others who do not see that which we ourselves have taken no little time to see. We shall want to use force, forgetting that Nature uses Time with far greater effect. We shall, perhaps, go raging about with narrow conviction and with all the intolerance of the newly converted. After a time, if we really have found the Life, we shall become sure and wise. We shall cease to render people unconscious in trying to awaken them. We, too, shall use the weapon of Time with the hand of Understanding. If we have not found the Life, we shall shortly become as violent in opposition as we have been fanatical in support. A fanatic can so easily be superlative in any way, since any particular way for him or her is, I was almost going to say, a matter of chance, or a matter of temperament and stage of evolution. And in general a fanatic roams over a number of superlatives, many of them at opposite ends, before he settles down to wise and ordered enthusiasm. When a person goes into superlatives about Krishnaji, or about anybody or anything else, I can only hope for the best. Superlatives are no doubt good servants, but they are terrible masters.

Now what am I gong to do with the results of all this brooding, be they right or wrong? What can I myself say that will be useful to others? First, I shall not go into ecstasies of adjectival admiration. I shall avoid labels and definitions. If I am asked what I believe about him, I shall reply that such beliefs do not matter in the least, and that in any case my own beliefs are certainly of no importance at all; that his message does matter, and that my belief with regard to him, be it what it may, might well cloud the issue, which is that here is a Man with a Message which he delivers with supreme conviction and which he himself lives, a message which has profoundly influenced large numbers of plain commonsense straightforward people. I shall not mind describing my personal beliefs, but I shall most heavily discount them.

Next, I shall urge people to listen to him when the opportunity occurs, to listen without prejudices or preconceptions. I shall *not* say: "You must listen in this way and in that. It is this. It is that. You will not understand unless you know this and that. Remember he is this and that." I shall also endeavour to give people an idea as to that which they may expect to receive him. They will be disturbed, perhaps perturbed. They will be shaken. They will feel that here is someone who is not afraid to tell the truth. They will see that here is someone who has the courage of his convictions. They will see that here simplicity, unaffectedness, burning straightforwardness, relentless fire, deep insight, the calm assurance of self-realization. They will realise themselves to be in the presence of someone different. They will find themselves beginning to say: Yes, it is true.

What is true? It is just at this point that I shall stop. This they must and will find out for themselves in his presence and under his influence. If I could tell them what they will know to be true the world would not need Krishnaji. I should suffice, and, therefore, anyone else. And even if I could tell them they would not say: "Yes," for I am not that which Krishnaji is, whatever that be. Let us take refuge in sublime vagueness.

I shall proceed to point out that there is no question of accept in his teachings or being damned. He brings the Truth, a truth if you will. He may say: I know. Well and good. He offers freely. Let us receive gratefully in the spirit in which he gives. We may say the fit is not for us. We may for any reason even reject the gift. Yet can we remain grateful to him who offers. And if we are wise we shall never forget that our understanding is still microscopic, that we know so little, that there is an infinitude of wisdom waiting for us, and that the little we already have has not really made us happy, calm, peaceful, at ease. Perchance, that which Krishnaji tells us....? Perchance the way into the Kingdom of Happiness which he discloses to us is after all *the* way? Is he happy? Is he utterly at peace? Does he know no sorrow? What are his answers to these questions? If he is happy, if he is utterly at peace, if he *has* ceased to know sorrow, there surely must be so unusual value in his pathway. He is like ourselves. He is a human being. He has known, perhaps, that which we know now of sorrow, trouble, unhappiness. He has transcended these. Perhaps we can see for ourselves that he has transcended these. Are we afraid to change? Are we slaves to that which holds us impotent in its strangling grip? Are we so "set" that we have become adamant? Have we no vision? Then indeed are we in danger of perishing. Without revolution in ourselves, no evolution of ourselves. If we are not afraid of change, if we are not the slaves of inertia, then will Krishnaji's power be to us of priceless value, for it will inspire us to change from our centres for ourselves, and not under the influence of external forces which may affect the circumference but which can never reach the heart.

If his power challenges our preconceptions, so much the better. All these, the very best of them, are probably but resting places on the Road to Truth. Useful resting places, but nothing more than resting places. Have they not often left us in the lurch? Have our beliefs and convictions, our opinions and conclusions, saved us, protected us, from sorrow, from anxiety, from grief, from trouble? Have we sufficient of the spirit of adventure in us, of the spirit of determination to reach the goal, of the spirit of will to understand the meaning of life, of immense and unquenchable longing to be eternally happy, to experiment with ourselves, to take a suggestion, from one who says he has discovered, as to how to play this

Game of Life so as to win all the time and ever?

If our house tumbles in ruins about us, can we not build another? The home now fallen to pieces has by no means been storm proof, it has not even been rain proof, we have had to huddle in it as best we could with little if any protection. Is it not worth while for someone to pull our house to pieces, so that we may be forced to build another? We can always build the same old leaky structure if we are fools; and there is just the possibility of our profiting from past experience. Or we can demolish our house ourselves, seeing what a fine dwelling place Krishnaji has, how airy, how free, yet how wonderfully safe. If someone tearfully bewails the fact that his house is now in ruins about him, the answer is—perhaps a little brutal: So much the better. Now build a really better one. And if he asks on what plan? Listen to Krishnaji, a master-builder as you can see with your own eyes. And then build a house for yourself according to your own wise plans.

I should also point out that we must be annoyed neither with Krishnaji nor with ourselves if at first much of what he says is beyond us. He does not come into our midst just to repeat that which we already know. He does not come to tell us that we are going on splendidly, and that all we have to do is to remain just as we are. I do not know quite where he would be were he to speak thus to us all. He comes to exhort us to be different, to change, to give up the outworn, to break away. We may not be ready. We may not quite see. There may be a variety of reasons why as we hear him at any particular time we are not in tune, we are not in accord. We need neither blame him nor ourselves. It may just be that part of his message does not apply to us, though I should think this unlikely. In any case, we need not be troubled. We need not be worried about ourselves when we stand aside of the time. We need not be afraid we are losing an opportunity, though some of our friends will doubtless shake their heads at our obtuseness, prophesying to us that such an opportunity as this comes but rarely in the history of the world, and that we shall remain, at the best, stationary in our evolution if we do not seize it now. If we are eager to know, if we are sincere and honest, we are missing no opportunities, even though we are not for the time being able to say "Yes" to Krishnaji as others may be saying "Yes." In order that we may be able to say "Yes" tomorrow it may well be inevitable that some of us should be saying "No" today. I doubt if Krishnaji is anxious for us to say "Yes" to anything he says. He desires us, I should think, to consider deeply and not to reject simply because we are too set to move; not to reject out of obstinacy and perversion, on general principles, but only if we feel we must. If we feel we must, well and good. We then say: "This is not for me." We shall, of course, not be such fools so to say: "This is not for anybody." And if we are really wise we shall say: "This is not me at present. Later on, who knows? I shall keep it in mind." We need never reproach ourselves with courteous, honest, heartfelt disagreement, whatever people may say. And surely it is clear that we have nothing with which to reproach Krishnaji. He discloses to us his store of precious jewels. He points out to us the beauties of each. Even if we do not desire to wear some of them, or any of them, nonetheless have we every reason to be grateful to him for so freely offering. Yet there will probably be ignorant people who will be angry with him for bringing gifts they do not happen to want. Perhaps they are blind. In any case, there may surely be others who will be thankful for that which we may reject. As Krishnaji comes to our doors we may say to him: "Thank you, friend, I need nothing today." But surely we shall have enough nobility of heart to add: "Godspeed to you on your mission." And fortunately for us, there is every hope that though he may today have done no business with us he will call again before long, when we may be thankful to say: "Enter, friend. I have business with you."

Before the Life that is Krishnaji can truly enter our hearts we must open our homes to it, throw open the doors, unbar the gates, unclose the windows. Indeed, doors, gates, windows should ever be left open, or we shall be suffocated by air which has become impure, by air we are gradually using up. What doors, which gates, which windows? Each one of us should know his own house well enough to have no difficulty in finding them, through in many cases they have become more like part of the solid wall, for want of use, than openings, and we may have no little difficulty in opening them. We may even hesitate to open them for fear of the draught, for fear of the fresh air, to which we are not accustomed. Creeds are often closed and heavily barred doors or windows. So are beliefs, opinions, convictions, self-satisfactions of all kinds. Because of these we often remain stultified in our houses when we might take walks abroad, when we might even while at home breathe the pure air circulating around us. There is nothing we should be unable to open. There is nothing in us which is perfectly free, perfectly true, unchangeable. We cannot stop where we are, either physically, emotionally, mentally or otherwise. We must grow. Why not rapidly? The only obstacles in the way are ourselves. The only road is ourselves. The obstacle is myself. The barrier is myself. The road is myself. The end is My Self.

If we are big enough to perceive greatness and to recognise the supreme value of greatness, of whatever nature, in a world suffering from widespread mediocrity and fearsomeness, we shall — whatever we may be able to understand or not understand—be thankful that a Light is shining in the darkness, even though it may not dispel our darkness. What matters it if our darkness remains, so that somewhere darkness is dispelled? If some are able to say that Krishnaji has brought them Light, and there are thousands to say this, tens of thousands, what matters it if we still remain in darkness? By the testimony of others, he is a Light-Bringer, and we may well be thankful that Light shines in the darkness, dispelling it here and dispelling it there, even though it may not dispel our darkness. Other Light will come to us, or this very Light. Light comes to all. Light shines upon all. We have but to let it in. Each one of us is Light. We have but to shine. Today these shine. Tomorrow those. Today you. Tomorrow I.

So, for the world's sake, and because witnesses are everywhere acclaiming the Light-Bringer, we who are happy in the joy of others, we who perhaps are among those who acclaim, we who are thankful that darkness here and there recedes before the advancing Light, rejoice in Krishnaji, welcome him, hear him gladly, and are with him thankfully in our hearts as he carries his Light into the dark places.

There are other Light-Bringers. The world is never left without Light-Bringers. Let us cherish all who bring Light, be it brought to us or to others. I write of Krishnaji because I have been thinking about him. I might write of others similarly. I know many great Light-Bringers, and there must be many, very many, whom I do not know. I say: Let us cherish Light-Bringers and make them welcome, come they to us or to others, whether they bring Light which enters our hearts or Light which for the time passes us by. The world needs Light, more Light. Some day all Light will enter all hearts.[*]

A.P. Warrington writes an article for *The Star* under the title "A Growning Work" for the July 1928 issue. He did a review of Krishnamurti's latest work, *The Immortal Friend*. He reports that the poem opens with a disclosure of how the author met his Beloved. He believes the immortal poem parallels that of *The Light of Asia* in spirit. He closes by relating an incident:

> If my memory serves me, the opening verses of this poem were read by Mr. Krishnamurti soon after they were written, and under rather striking circumstances. It was at Krotona, in Ojai Valley, and the date was January 11, 1927. A few days before (December, 1926) he had spoken in the Music Room of the Krotona Library, as it happened, standing under the beautiful picture representing Eternal Peace. He had on this occasion shone forth the radiancy of a Presence—a Presence which we believed to be that of the World-Teacher—had shown it so clearly that at the conclusion all left the room in great silence.
>
> Naturally, therefore, as Mr. Krishnamurti stood on the

---

[*] *Krishnaji: Light-Bringer*, published by Theosophical Publishing House, Adyar Madras, 1928.

terrace on January 11th facing the valley and its impressive wall of mountains, the audience gathered at his feet were keenly expectant. He read. And, as said, I think the lines were those in the beginning of *The Immortal Friend.*

But on this occasion when all were so expectant, there were those among us who believed that the Presence we felt was not as before, but was that of another—even the Buddha Himself. And then the striking incident occurred.

While Mr. Krishnamurti was reading the closing lines, there fell a few drops of rain. Suddenly, as if out of the mountainside, a rainbow appeared. And then all was over.

When the audience had gone, and while I felt still under the spell of the occasion, a friend came to me and said that he had somewhere read, or heard the tradition, that once when the Lord Buddha had spoken, and the audience had gone, a woman came and begged of Him comfort because of the loss of a relative. Before the Lord replied, He drew her attention to a little sprinkle of rain that had begun to fall, and then to the rainbow that followed. The Lord then spoke to the woman, using this occurrence to show the transitoriness of earthly existence, and the beauty and delight that follow for those who understand.

And ever after that, it is said whenever the Buddha appears in person to inspire the words of a true teacher, there falls a sprinkle of rain, and appears a beautiful rainbow. [*]

A letter shows, meanwhile, in August of that year, Krotona improving its grounds, and administrative work by George Hall.

Ojai, California
August 13 1928

Dear Mr. F. C. Pragnell,

At my request, you seem to have looked pretty thoroughly into the question as to whether it would be possible to establish at Krotona some productive activities, including in the beginning a nursery, and the reports which you have made as the result of

---

[*] Warrington, A.P., "A Growning Work", *The Star*, July 1928, Vol. I., n7, pp.11-13.

several weeks' consideration and investigation are so favorable that I should like to have you make an initial experiment along the line of a nursery business, and let us see what the promise may be of an ultimate, fine business of this nature. You have been kind enough to tell me that Krotona's highest good is very dear to you and that you would like to undertake the demonstration of the practical establishment of a nursery on Krotona grounds, giving as much time as you could to it, without compensation for the first year.

You have assured me that Mrs. Marie L. Hancock (who has also given me the same assurance) would be glad to do her best in assisting you to make the venture a success.

I also am assured by Mrs. Sarah C. Mayes that she will be willing to handle the office end of the business for the same period, without salary, and this would relieve you of a side of the work which you have told me you could not undertake.

I am also assured by you that in the beginning, and for very many months, you will only need $500. to start up activities at the old lath house; and also to make a beginning in some way for planting under a more extended plan down in the bottom lying West of the "Street in Spain." This $500. I understand can all be contributed by those who will have a hand in this work on a basis with which we are already familiar, and which will be mentioned herein a later paragraph.

The conditions, therefore, seeming so favorable, I have decided to make the experiment of creating a Department of Production here at Krotona, the same being a Department of the Krotona Institute of Theosophy; but it is my thought that this plan will in nowise affect the present organization of Krotona, nor demand any duties whatsoever of the present officers of Krotona, nor involve Krotona n any financial liability; the idea being that the Department will work under the aegis of Krotona, and for the benefit of Krotona, but operating as a separate activity.

I would be willing to head the Department as the sole member of the Krotona Board who would be active in the work of the Production Department.

I have asked Mrs. Maude N. Couch to join forces with us in this undertaking as Assistant Department Head to meet with us in our councils, and to represent the Department Head when away.

Since the Production Department will be required to do its own financing, and incur no financial liability involving Krotona, it has been understood between the five workers who will undertake the beginnings of this activity, namely, myself, Mrs. Couch, yourself,

Mrs. Hancock and Mrs. Mayes, that each will contribute $100. to make up the fund mentioned in a previous paragraph, and this money will be forthcoming within the next three weeks, as required.

As to water: It is understood that the Department will take water out of Krotona's present system, which comes from the Ojai Mutual Water Co., and that the Department will be obligated never to use the water between the hours of nine A.M. and five P.M. with the exception of the noon hour, from twelve to one. I will try to get Krotona to put in a separate water meter at the proper place, so that we may know just what water we consume in this business, and can pay Krotona for it.

I suggest that the nursery end of the Nursery Department be called The Valley Nursery and that you go ahead with the scheme as soon as you may wish, using for the present the old lath house and the grounds adjacent thereto for your work. When the time comes a little later you may begin down in the bottom, lying West of the "Street in Spain," at such localities within said grounds as you may find to be the best suited for your purposes.

As to any profits which the Department may make, these may all be turned back into further developments and growth of the enterprise until the time when the business will justify proper salaries to those who are actually doing the work. When that time comes, after deducting from the gross income all the proper expenses and overhead, including also salaries, which would be rightful under the circumstances, ten per cent of the net profits shall annually be turned over to the official treasurer of Krotona, and the remaining ninety per cent shall be used for further development of the Department.

This letter constitutes a memorandum of understanding between the five parties who are willing to begin the work of the Department non the one hand, and the Krotona officers on the other. From time to time, by mutual understandings similarly entered into, this present understanding, which I am hereby addressing to you, may be amended, abridged or expanded according to the mutual wish of all concerned, with a view to further benefiting Krotona through the enhancement of the power and usefulness of the Production Department.

Fraternally,
George H. Hall

Memorandum of Understanding signed by department heads, and the Krotona Institute of Theosophy Trustees.

The Krotona Institute of Theosophy recognizes the formation of a Nursery Department to do business as a separate department from Krotona's general activities, under the name of The Valley nursery, with A.P. Warrington, Mrs. Maude N. Couch, Mr. F.C. Pragnell, Mrs. Louise Hancock, and Mrs. Sarah Mayes as the present officers.

Krotona leases to the Valley Nursery the present lath house and glass house on the estate and the land appurtenant thereto within the enclosure, save and except the dwelling therein.

Krotona also leases the strip of lowland extending the full length of the property lying immediately adjacent to the railroad track and West of the so-called street in Spain, including the well. Likewise, a strip adjacent to the aforementioned strip and extending up an ascent to the North thereof for a distance of 400 feet in width, and lying West of the dumping barranca.

The terms of the above lease are as follows: The Valley Nursery must finance all of its activities and return to Krotona as an annual rental ten percent of al the net profits it makes, after deducting all expenses, including reasonable salaries. The remainder of 90 per cent of the aforementioned improvements, developments and extensions. The said lease shall extend for a period of ten (10) years.

It is understood that for the first year no salaries are to be paid to the officers of The Valley Nursery and that no charge shall be made by Krotona for water supply to the Valley Nursery through its present meter during the said period of one year.

If any misunderstanding should arise at the end of the lease as to the proper terms for a new lease, the question or questions that cannot be agreed upon are to be submitted to arbitration, each of the two parties to chose an arbitrator, and the two arbitrators to choose a third, the majority of whom shall make the decision which shall be binding upon both of the aforesaid parties.

Going to Adyar was Mrs. May S. Rogers, the wife of the National President L.W. Rogers, to be secretary to Dr. Besant for an indefinite period.

August 26

My dear Warrington,

I arrived in London, only to find that the President and Dorothy were leaving for Bombay the next day. However I had my talk with the President. I was of course too late for Ommen. Krishnaji asked me to come here with him, especially as John was not fit to travel, he has kidney trouble. Rajagopal comes today, and I leave in two days for the Blecks in France, and after to London.

Biascoechia has cabled advising that I go <u>direct</u> from London to Brazil, so I sail from Southampton on Oct 5. So my tour will be Brazil, Urugnay, Argentina, Chile, Bolivia, Peru, Costa Rica, Mexico, Cuba and Porta Rico. After that, movements are uncertain, but I shall be in Chicago for the World Congress.

I gave the Krotona address for mail. Till Sept. 20, at Ojai, I think the mail can be sent to London after that, for a while, till I notify you again, to Buenos Aires, care the General Secretary. I hope the rheumatic trouble is passing off rapidly.

Every yours
C. Jinarajadasa

A pamphlet was published by Miss Julia K. Sommer, formerly a teacher in the Chicago elementary schools and later principal of the School of the Open Gate in Hollywood which gave a frank discussion of the need for more radical reforms in the elementary school policy and practice.

A document from September 1928, showing the concern with the relation between Theosophy and education.*

September 1928
Theosophical World University Association
Chicago, Ill.

To the President and Secretary of
Dear Associates in Theosophy,
Fundamentally to be a theosophist means to hold a certain attitude toward life, which may be designated a Theosophical attitude, expressing itself in Theosophical behavior. One need not necessarily talk in Theosophical terms nor be a member of the T.S. to be a Theosophist.

One of the most powerful means for bringing to pass the theosophizing of the world in this sense of the word is thru the proper education of children. The enclosed pamphlet [Educational Ideals] presents ideals of education that are Theosophical in the truest sense of that word and presents them in a form acceptable to the average layman, within or outside of the T.S.

The ideals put forth form the standpoint of educational psychology are well worth serious consideration, for in the opinion of the author if these ideals were put into practice more generally a Theosophical civilization would be more speedily realized on earth.

You will note that a dollar will buy ten of these pamphlets which sell for 15¢ a piece retail. Would you not like to consider putting these pamphlets among your other literature that is on sale? Your lodge would make a profit of 33 1/3% on the sale of them.

We have also the same pamphlet without the Theosophical World University Assn. label for those workers who might prefer to distribute them unlabelled. These may be had at the same price. Or you may have some with the label and some without.

Trusting we may have an order from you, we remain
Yours, for *Education as Service*
Theosophical World University Assn.
Miss Seidell, Secretary

Dr. Besant suggests an international visitor for Happy Valley.

---

*Cf., Krishnamurti's later concern with education and the founding of schools.

Sept. 11, 1928
Adyar

Dear fellow worker,

This is to introduce to you Mrs. Sarojini Naidu, of the most eloquent of women, a poetess, an Ex-President of the Indian National Congress, and a charming personality. She is not one of our members, but is an idealist and a servant of India. She shows a very fine type of Indian womanhood, and is a good answer to Miss Mayo's slanders. Please take her to the Happy Valley, and introduce her to Mary Gray, who will, I am sure, be glad to meet an exceptional woman.

As ever,

Annie Besant

I think John Ingleman and Hilda would like to meet her.

———————————————

September was the opening of the new enterprise for Ojai Valley a nursery on Krotona Hill near the tower, under the direction of F.C. Pragnell, expert landscape architect. The nursery was already equipped to meet the demands of the Christmas trade and it is specializing among other things in the living Christmas tree, potted plants, Christmas baskets, holly wreaths and poinsettias. A booth was established down in the village at Hart's Theatre Building during the week before Christmas. Krotona's plans included productive activities for the future and the starting of the nursery as one of the first moves.

Late September, Mr. & Mrs. Hervey Gulick and Miss Mina Kunz removed from their residence on the Hill to the old farmhouse.

Krishnamurti may have thundered, let us say, against ceremonies, but George Arundale remarks that if he participated in ceremonies, he could bring to them a greater life. George writes to C.W. Leadbeater exhibiting his confidence in the work and the future of the Liberal Catholic Church.

In the following letter Jean Delville is mentioned. Delville was born in the Belgian town of Louvain in 1867. He lived most of his life in Brussels where his training at the age of twelve began at the Academy of Fine Arts. Sometime during the mid to late 1890's, Delville joined the Theosophical Society, and in 1910 he became the secretary of the Theosophist Movement in Belgium. In the same year he added a tower to his house following the ideas of J. Krishnamurti, painting the meditation room at the top entirely in sky blue. Only photographs and drawings still exist, the house, no longer stands. He died in 1953. Delville's works are also remembered at the Theosophical Society headquarters in Madras, where the Hall of Religions was decorated during the 1960's in a style which, according to Philippe Jullian, imitates that of Delville (the Symbolists, 1973).

The following is an excerpt of an letter by George Arundale to C.W. Leadbeater.

Adyar,
October 4 1928

My dear Bishop,

I was very happy to receive your letter. I cannot for the life of me make out why people are so much troubled, and why Jean Delville, for example, should bother to write a pamphlet of the kind he has written. Surely the whole teaching of Krishnaji is that we should take our stand upon ourselves, and be our own authorities. He challenges authority and form and ceremony just because we are slaves to them. And now Jean Deliville tells us that we must be slaves to a particular interpretation which happened to suit him, and this whole pamphlet reeks of authority. Personally, I am wholeheartedly with Krishnaji. I agree with what he says, and I feel more than ever attached to my bishopric and to my membership of the Liberal Catholic Church, for what these can do. I have been told that Tettemer has been on the verge of resigning his bishopric. Well and good. Let everyone resign who wants to. Let all go who want to go. Our church has a magnificent piece of work to do, of which I feel more and more proud as the time passes, and I am thankful that we are being unloaded of our dead weight. It is a real service Krishnaji renders to the Liberal Catholic Church—and I am not in the least sarcastic. Let all go who cease to be wholehearted. They may not in reality be suited of this particular form of service, and it is as well that they should have found this out.

But why be annoyed with others who have not—shall I say "yet" found it out. More and more I come to the conclusion that the safest kind of life to lead is one's own life, and not a caricature of someone else's, which is what many of these fanatics are doing. I do not blame them. I have been a fanatic in my time. Perhaps I am one still. But I see clearly the importance of not being as tyrannical fanatic, of not being an inquisitorial fanatic, a fanatic who has a bed of Procrustes on which all and sundry must lie down, and which they must fit.

I have just written a pamphlet *Krishnaji: Light-Bringer* in the course of which I say that I do not know he is the World-Teacher. I admit the Connection between him and the World-Teacher. I see that. But I do not see more than this. And I say that it does not in the least matter what one see in this respect. Let us take him as he is. Let us use what he gives. What helps, we can take. What does not help, or what we cannot understand, we simply leave. And that is all there is to it. Above all no excitement, and no inquisition, and no being troubled. There is reason why people are troubled is because they do not know. If they knew they would not be troubled. So what they are troubled about is their own ignorance, not really at all about what X or Y says. X might say what he liked and no one would be troubled if he had knowledge about the matter or at all events what he considered knowledge. Only a few days ago the Lord spoke to me desiring me to thank a few workers for their service of His church at Adyar. I had had no communication from Him for a very long time, almost years. I was overwhelmed, and the message He gave was only a fragment of the wonderful influence by which I was pervaded. He spoke to me as standing there thinking of Him and in His glorious consciousness. I knew. I knew the power and purpose of the L.C.C. I knew the valuable nature of the work we are doing. I knew it and I know it. I knew it before, of course. But I know it more fully than ever. What can anyone say—Krishnaji or the President or anyone else —which can compare with such an experience, untranslatable in words. But I am happier than ever in my membership of the L.C.C. and more determined than ever to be all I can to her.

We probably leave India in January, possibly to go to Java and to Australia, then to the U.S.A.—you must be there for the World-Congress of the T.S.—and then afterwards we all will travel <u>home</u> to Huizen where we shall want to be for some months, perhaps a year, if we may, making it our headquarters. The President entirely approves. I think there is work for us to do in Europe.

124

The rest of the letter is missing.

———————————◆◆———————————

Oct 6 1928
R.M.S.P. Almanzora

My dear Warrington,
As possibly mail for me may come to Krotona, I enclose the addresses to which to forward. I started from Southampton yesterday and get to Rio on the 20th. I expect to be there a month, and then go on to Monte Video.

Just before leaving London, I saw the last issue of the American *E.S. Bulletin*. It was news to me that you had given up the Corresponding Sectary, and that Miss Poutz was taking your place. I noted your saying that you had been <u>appointed</u> Vice-President. The General Secretaries for England and Wales made the same announcement. It was in the letter the President sent to the Gen. Secs., but I think owing to her illness she did not recollect that she can only <u>nominate</u>, and not appoint, the Vice-President. The nomination has then to be voted upon by the General Council. The President <u>can</u> appoint the Treasurer and Recording Secretary.

Last news of the President from Adyar says that she is fit again, and has much travelling ahead of her in India, lecturing.

Krishnaji, Jadun and Rajagopal who were in London, left on the 4th for Eerde, the former two to sail for India in two weeks.
Ever yours,
C. Jinarajadasa

———————————◆◆———————————

Annie Besant writing an exuberant letter about the World-Teacher, in 1928, prior to Krishnamurti dissolving the Order of the Star.

October 31, 1928
Adyar
E.S.T. Private

To The Corresponding Secretaries of the E.S.
My dear Colleagues,
We are living in a wonderful and glorious time, a time when

125

the World-Teacher lives among us in the body of His Disciple Krishnaji. We have very sensibly and rightly promised to serve Him by spreading His Ideals. That promise must, of course, be kept. My own position is a responsible one, since I am the Outer Head of the E.S., the Inner Head being my Guru. I have been pondering how best I could perform that double duty, and I act with the approval of the Guru I adore.

Once in a long term of years the blessed Lord Maitreya, the World-Teacher, pays a visit to our World, to proclaim the Ideals on which the civilization of the new sub-race shall be built. He has come, as He promised in 1909, and He is proclaiming those Ideals. He proclaims the "direct Path"— which, if I understand Him aright, is open to all by virtue of His presence among us. Each must find it for himself, since it is in his own heart. Each can find it for himself, since God is that Self, the Free, the Fetterless. He is then a Mukta, he is Liberated. To that, as the goal, Krishnaji calls us. Let us hear and obey the call.

Under these circumstances, so rare, so precious, we need naught else. The new wine must not be poured into the old bottles. So I, as the outer Head of the E.S., in obedience to the Inner Head, and in the service of the beloved Teacher, suspend the institution which has prepared us for the freedom to which we are called and into which we enter.

We are dedicated to the spreading of the World-Teacher's Ideals, and we take up that service. All members should study His writings; try to attune themselves to the Song of the Lord. Let us rejoice in the Life He pours out in such splendid streams; let us full ourselves with it. Let us let go of all that impedes its entrance, its permeating of every fiber of our being. Let us trust ourselves fearlessly to its guidance, for it is the Life of the Lord.

Please print—if necessary translate—this message, and let every member of the E.S. pledged and unpledged, have a copy. What may be hidden in the future I know not. But our present duty is clear. For every member of the School who wishes it, I remain his link with the Inner Head. Thus we "keep the link unbroken," as was ordered by H.P.B.

Members can keep or return their papers to the corresponding secretary, as they prefer.

Annie Besant
O.H.

Nov 3 1928

My dear Raja,

Your letter from Steamship Almanzora, dated October 6, has just come, and your mail will be promptly dispatched as received, according to the addresses your enclosed.

You are quite right. My expression should not have been "appointed" in respect of the Vice-Presidency. The note which you saw in the American *E.S.T. Bulletin* was written in July, a few minutes after the cable came asking if I would accept the Vice-Presidency. I did then as I frequently do, dictated the thing to get it off my mind, not using special care about my expressions but intending later to carefully check the matter up before publication. I became quite unwell, however, and this latter precaution was not taken: hence the expression. I see there are others who have dropped into the same expression, showing that we all might study the rules of our Society a little more carefully, the former Vice-President excepted.

I have at last been prevailed upon to leave home and take a course of treatment under a very modern specialist whom John Ingelman recommended, along with others who knew something of his success; and here I am in Santa Barbara with Mr. Mayes and Miss Barbour in a nice little cottage for at least three months; at all events until I can get all right again.

The X-ray photograph showed that the descending colon was nothing but a little thin passage about the size of a rubber tube and without the usual muscular development; the transverse colon was festooned downward below the naval; and the ascending colon was likewise in trouble but better off than the other two parts of this offending passageway.

After six weeks of treatment another X-ray photograph shows the ascending colon in fine condition, the transverse had shortened and lifted even, indeed an inch, above the navel, and the descending colon with a development of muscles and enlargement of the passage that was truly remarkable. I did not know such things were possible; nor did I know before I came that I had this particular difficulty. Therefore, I am hoping now that we know what the trouble was, how very bad it really was, and how easy it is to correct it, I shall be able to pull myself out of this difficulty and have a more useful body in the future. However, it will take time and I am giving time to it. All that is necessary.

We have just started a nursery at Krotona. It is in the hands of a little group of most enthusiastic members. Please be assured it is not a baby nursery, although it is a baby industry. We are hoping that by the cultivation of trees, shrubs, flowers and plants generally to establish a beautiful occupation for members that will bring in a profitable income to Krotona and help it on its way to doing good in various directions.

I hope your tour down South will be a great pleasure to you. Those dear people in the Spanish American countries are so very, very hospitable and generous in their kindness that I am sure everything will be done for you that generous hearts can suggest.
Every yours,
A.P.W.

While Warrington is staying at 12 Ocean Ave, in Santa Barbara for treatment and rest, he is asking George Hall not to impose any charge of rent upon the Star members for meeting at Krotona once a month until he could talk it over with him what is on his mind regarding this group. He is trying to be back at Krotona for Thanksgiving if all goes well. Meanwhile, Warrington asked George to have Mr. Schuller to repair a bad leak over the hall at the library from a heavy down pour of rain which needed fixing immediately.

Krishnamurti arrived at Adyar on November 5, while Dr. Besant arrived on the 10th. She said, that when she knew that the World-Teacher would soon take possession of His vehicle, she asked permission of her own Guru to resign the presidency of the Society, so that she might go with him everywhere. The request was refused, and she was told to go on with her own work. Her life lies in utter obedience to her Guru, and no more was said.

Gladys Hall writes an article for *The Occult Digest*, in November, titled: "The Second Christ", subtitled, "Who says "I have no name. I do not believe in names and labels I have attained to life." The title for the second page is "Alcyone Judges Hollywood". "He Calls The Movie Screen A Muddled Pool of Truth." It was again published in the September issue by the courtesy of *Motion Picture Magazine*, "The Second Christ Weighs Hollywood".

A series of letters in November - December 1928 giving a picture of the ongoing work and internal daily workings of Krotona and the TS.

Nov 22 1928

Dear Mr. Warrington:

I have been after Mr. Schuller steadily since the rain, but have been unable so far to get the leaks at Krotona fixed. Yesterday afternoon I found Mr. Schuller at his shop and I happened to know that the roofing men were in the Valley, and Mr. Schuller got into his car immediately to see if he could not get them on the job but so far they have not appeared. The roofing company that did our work is the best in the county, and as they are responsible for fixing the leaks without charge I shall keep after them until I get it done.

I also spoke to Mr. Schuller about going to Santa Barbara to talk over with you the costs of the new cottages you contemplate building at Krotona, and he said that he would try and get away to do so.

Referring to the plan you mention in your letter: I have never heard of exactly this arrangement and I am afraid that it would not work out satisfactorily to either party. We had a contract at Star Camp on one of the bathhouses whereby the cost was guaranteed to be a certain amount, but the work was done with a 10% of the cost as supervision charge. The arrangement was that if the cost ran over the guaranteed amount the supervision charge for the excess cost would be 5% only, instead of 10%, and that if one-quarter more. Even this did not work out satisfactorily and was not enforced, the contractor accepting 10% of the estimated cost of the building regardless of the actual cost. I think when we come to build these little cottages we shall find it most advantageous to get competitive bids and let the contracts for a fixed price, as the cost of simple buildings of this kine, if completely planned before hand, can be very accurately estimated. The contractor then carries the gamble and if he has any hard luck it comes out of his profits.

I suppose you have heard about the big fire by this time. Gene, Vernon, Ed, Reihl and I were out practically all night Tuesday, but nothing at Arya-Vihara or Happy Valley was harmed and now the fire has apparently been conquered.

Hoping you are making satisfactory progress with your treatments, and that we shall see you at our community dinner on

thanksgiving Day, I remain ever,
Most cordially,
G.H. Hall

Dec 5 1928

Dear Mr. Warrington:
    I do not personally remember ever having met Feliz Maruenda Suares or Charles Weber. Of course I know Comez, who was at Krotona when I first went there in 1919. I cannot remember exactly how long he stayed, but I do remember that he moved away to the beach, or some place where he had a cabin, and did not come back to Krotona while I was there.
    I asked both Mrs. Goldy and Mrs. Rosner if they remembered either of the other two people ever having been at Krotona. Neither of them remembered Mr. Weber, and I am quite sure he was not there at any time after I came. Suares, however, was there for a very short time, and as near as I can find out it was in the early part of 1919. Both Mrs. Goldy and Mrs. Rosner remember him and that he lived in the bachelor's cottage. Mrs. Rosner says he was quite an impossible person and the most conceited man she ever knew. He must have left before I took charge because I remember quite clearly the bachelor's cottage and the different men that occupied it. Also from Mrs. Rosner's description of this man I am quite sure that I never saw him. When he left Krotona he went to some Spanish country to teach in a college and wrote back to the Krotona office asking that we kindly furnish him with a copy of all the books in the Krotona library for his college library.
    This is all the information that I can furnish and I hope it may be of some use to you.
Ever most cordially yours,
G.H. Hall

"Krotona" E.S.T. American Division
Ojai, Calif.
December 10, 1928

Friends,
    The words of the Outer Head will, I trust, awaken in you the same glad response which sings in my own heart. The E.S. has worked faithfully; but now, the Lord is with us, and when He

speaks of the Direct Path, there must be undivided attention.

As the Outer Head says, what maybe hidden in the future we know not. Meanwhile many will rejoice that she is still the link with the Inner Head for those who wish it, and that the link made by H.P.B. remains unbroken.

The warm links of friendship formed between us during those years of our common work also remain unbroken, and I shall always be glad to hear from any of you who wish to write to me. My address remains unchanged, for while the future of the E.S. is unknown, Mr. Warrington and I intend to hold this center for any work that may be required in the future and to devote our energies to trying to make of Krotona an ideal community center; we are also making plans for the re-opening of the Krotona Institute sometime in the future. That explanation was due to those who have contributed in the past, financially and otherwise, to the up building of Krotona and who may still be interested in its welfare and progress.

This closes all E.S. groups and ends the work of the Secretaries of Discipline; but members individually are free to follow any practice they want or none at all. However, to those who in their new freedom might be tempted to put aside all practices including meditation which is the food of the spiritual nature, I will quote these words of Krishnaji's:

"You must meditate regularly. What kind of meditations of no importance . . . the result is the important thing, not the system." (The Spark and the Flame. *The Star* for September, Vol.1, n9, page 7, 1928.)

I will ask all group officers to kindly return to this office the Group Pictures, without frames. Members who prefer to return their own individual papers will please keep their boxes and send the papers in parcels.

Brothers, let us eagerly and joyously go forward into the glorious future ahead of us.

All is well!

Every your old friend,
Marie Poutz,
Corresponding Secretary

Dec 11 1928

Dear Mr. Warrington:
Hervey [Gulick] drew his usual perfect map covering accurately

and minutely every feature of the building site. The slope of the land varies slightly according to the distance back from the highway, but roughly the ground slopes toward the railroad track with a drop of 10 ft. in 250 ft. This is approximately the length required for five units of two apartments each and four garage spaces.

I have only had an opportunity for one interview with Mr. Schuller, and he said that it would not be practical for him to make an estimate of cost without more definite specifications as to the method of construction. My own judgment is that it would be inadvisable to plan for tile roofs, as such roofs properly go with the same kind of construction we already have, and it is my understanding that you wish to build these apartments at a much less cost per square ft. than our other buildings. The ordinary composition roof, covered with red, green or gray colored gravel, will cost about $7.00 per square and the Johns, Manville asbestos gravel, will cost about $10.00 per square, if I remember correctly. Tile shingles cost about $10.00 to $28.00 per square and do not seem to me appropriate to an otherwise cheaper class of construction. Of course there is an argument the other way since the outward appearance of any stucco finished building can have the appearance of the highest type of construction as well as to appear less costly. The saving in cost being in interior finish. However, it is well to remember that a tile roof requires extra heavy framing to support the weight, which adds materially to the cost of the building in addition to the difference in cost of the roof itself.

If you will kindly send me the detailed specifications you have in mind for these buildings I will endeavor to obtain definite estimates of cost and submit to you for your changes and approval. Or if you prefer I will suggest the specifications and summit to you for your approval.

I hope that when you come down for Christmas you can plan to have sufficient time for us to discuss and decide the details of these plans in order that we may have a definite and final proposition before the board meeting on the 12th.

I am happy to hear through Miss Poutz that you are definitely and steadily gaining in health and that after another month we shall have you with us again.

Ever most cordially yours,

G.H Hall

Dec 12 1928

My dear George,

I had thought the other day that we should ask Miss Poutz to store the E.S. stock as closely as convenient and let us use the rest of the E.S. building on the main floor for bachelor quarters. Now Miss Poutz writes to me and says that she thinks that two rooms could be released for this purpose.

Would you not kindly look into the situation and let me have your suggestions?

I am expecting to be home on the 24th and may even remain a week. Am getting along very nicely. The doctor wishes me to stay until the 19th of January.

You will remember that you told me that our new houses could easily be put on one level, and I so informed the architect, but your letter which has just come shows that there is a drop of 10 feet in 250 ft. I will, therefore, hold up the drawings until I can see the map. Kindly mail the same to me as soon as you can.

As to Schuller: I don't think we need to approach him again until after the last item of details is included in a bill of specifications. I will talk all this over with you when I get home. Meanwhile, please send me Hervey's plat.

With best wishes to you and Mrs. Hall, I am,
Cordially,
A.P. Warrington

December 13, 1928

My dear Amma,

Miss Poutz has shown me your E.S. circular declaring the Suspension of the School for a time. May I say you have met the situation in your usual magnificent way?

Miss Poutz and I are in sympathy with the step. Neither of us was surprised, though I think some our membership will be, and will now feel like sheep without a shepherd. To our members the E.S. means everything that is best and highest in life, and I am not sure that all of them can be left to find their own way alone. Therefore, one can but look forward with hope to possible future plans for the E.S.

If the School were to be re-organized on the basis of Krishnaji's teachings, it could still serve as the heart of the T.S., could it not? My thought was, when I wrote to you last summer on the subject,

133

that you would no doubt wish sometime to adapt the teachings and methods of your School to the new Evangel, while still retaining undisturbed its integrity as an organized group of pupils. In spite of the weaknesses and failures of its personnel wherever they may have been, I do feel that your E.S. as a cohering body has been a power for good, a real weapon in your hands against the powers of reaction, both in this world and the other. And as to the T.S., one wonders what it could do with it.

Now that Miss Poutz is to be set free for a time, I shall ask her to help us with the work of the Krotona community. She would be admirable in the Library, and also as the head of the Institute when finances place us in position to open it again. Perhaps now more than ever the Krotona idea should be pressed forward, in the Manu's service complementing and paralleling Krishnaji's work.

Perhaps too, if we press forward now and develop, the ideal industrial and cultural community for those fittest types drawn to us through their interest in *Theosophy* and *The Star*, we shall probably do a useful service, however slight, to both the Manu and Boddhisattva of the future. We have already taken two industrial steps here, one the book business, which is even now doing well, and the other, our garden nursery, of which I have already written you. Since the summer the value of our new nursery stock has increased to over $2,500. And the members who have been drawn here to help with this new business are exhibiting enthusiasm in their work, pouring new life into our centre, and adding to its needed fluidity. These two activities are only the beginning of what I can see could become a thriving hive of Theosophical work of substantial value to the movement.

But if these my Krotona ideas should not lie within your plan, I shall of course be duly informed by you, otherwise I expect to go forward with them. Practically from the beginning we have worked toward the idea of creating, as stated, a cultural and industrial, spiritual centre having a hoped for relationship to the Manu's plan for the future.

I find the impressive Indian political drama in which you are playing so powerful a part of absorbing and thrilling interest. If this interest and my fullest good will could be of help to you, my dear Amma, that would be my mite contributed to the situation.
Always devotedly,
A.P. Warrington

Dec 14 1928

Dear Mr. Warrington:

Mrs. Hall suggested the idea of utilizing the E.S. building for living quarters almost immediately that we knew the E.S. was to be suspended. I did not write you about it, or speak to Miss Poutz, but intended to take it up with you the next time you came down. On receipt of your letter of the 12th I went to see Miss Poutz and she showed me the arrangements that she was willing to make which would release the two rooms on the south side of the building, between Mrs. Couch's office and Miss Poutz office, where Miss Kimball and Miss Honold have been working. These will be very pleasant rooms especially in the winter time. One of them has a closet and the other has a large set of shelves which can be easily changed into a wardrobe. Miss Poutz also suggested that if the E.S. should re-open that at first it probably would not be necessary to use these rooms anyway, as an extra desk for E.S. work can easily be placed in my office. I shall try to get time very soon to remove the bulk of the Krotona property from the storage room in order that the entire space may be available for Miss Poutz to store the E.S. things from the two rooms mentioned. She says she thinks she can bet these two rooms will be emptied by the first of the year.

I remember telling you that I thought there was not much difference in elevation on the building site you described, and that if that were the case it would not be difficult to grade the building site to one level, and I was surprised when Hervey gave me the map to find that the fall was 10 ft for a building 250 ft long. I am mailing the map as you request with this letter.

If I remember correctly you were intending to get the complete working drawings from the architect, and I did not at that time have any other suggestions to make. Since then I have come across a plan taken from an apartment house, the interior arrangements of which I consider much more convenient in many little details than the one suggested by your architect. The shape of the room is somewhat different to accommodate these built-in features but the actual floor space is practically the same. From rather general preliminary estimates I am quite sure that these apartment could be built for less than $2,000. each, even with tile roofs. I would like very much for you to see the plan of this apartment but it would be difficult to explain the built-in features by letter. I have asked Mr. Schuller to get me a blueprint of the floor plan and I already have pictures of the built-in features. Perhaps when you come down and see these plans and pictures you may wish to incorporate some of the ideas in your plan, and therefore I would suggest that you do not order the final drawings until after our next conference.

Will your remaining in Santa Barbara until the 19th of January interfere with the date set for our board meeting on January 12th? If so could the board meeting not be postponed to January 19th without risking the chance of missing Mr. Wardall? As the notices for this board meeting should go out soon please let me know.

I am most happy to hear that you may be able to remain with us several days at least when you come down for Christmas.

With cordial good wishes, I remain ever,

Most sincerely yours,

G.H. Hall

December 15 1928

Dear Mr. Warrington,

Enclosed please find original of draft No 794B on the Canadian Bank of Commerce, San Francisco, Calif., dated 14 December 1928, to the amount of 200 dollars in payment of interest on The Manor Loan.

Another draft to the amount of 300 dollars will follow in about ten days. This makes a total of 500 dollars which will bring the payments of interest to date of January 1st. 1929.

Owing to a misunderstanding between Dr. J. J. van der Leeuw and the previous Manager of The Manor Trust the payments have not always been on time. Since Dr. van der leeuw's visit to Sydney this difficulty has been cleared away and I trust that in future every payment will arrive in Ojai on or before the date it is due.

With all best wishes, I am,

Cordially yours,

H. van der Veen, Manager

Krotona Institute of Theosophy
Ojai Calif
To the E.S. Members of the American Division

Dear Friends,

Now that the E.S. has been suspended by the O.H. "for a time," the E.S. members will no doubt wish to know if Krotona is effected, and this circular is to inform them.

Krotona was originally intended to be a communal centre providing industrial, cultural and spiritual opportunities for those earnest students who might wish to withdraw from the strain of city life and do their work in a Theosophical atmosphere under ideal conditions. But before it was possible to concentrate on this plan further than to conduct the Krotona Institute regularly up to 1919, the great privilege came to us of furnishing a headquarters for both the T.S. (8 years) and the E.S. (17 years). The work required by these two headquarters and the lack of adequate funds to carry out our plans served to delay the one pointed development of the original idea until the present time.

Since neither of the headquarters offices needs to claim our attention for the time being, Krotona can now concentrate its activities in the direction of the original plan. Already a book shop has been opened. A garden nursery has been established (called the Krotona Hill Nursery) with M.N. Couch, Business Manager, S.C. Mayes, Secretary, Treasurer, F.C. Pragnell, Landscape Architect, and M.L. Hancock, Nursery Supervisor. Arts and crafts are being considered and other activities will be engaged in as time goes on. Also residence sites will be discussed with those who may wish to build and bring their families here to live.

Before everything we need now to increase our housing facilities. At present we have only a cluster of small houses with a capacity just equal to the activities going on at Krotona at this time, and so we cannot even reopen the Krotona Institute until we can build proper accommodations for the students.

But Krotona is in debt. It owes the Bank $10,000. which was borrowed for Dr. Besant, and is still short on the enlarged Library Building. One can but wish that Dr. Besant's friends in America would get together and relieve her of this $10,000. obligation. As everybody knows, when she incurs a debt it is never for herself, but for the work—our Theosophical work. Can't her American friends volunteer to pay this off, thus enabling us to return the cancelled note to her soon?

If they did no more than this, they would in truth do a fine thing; for that Great Leader is now carrying the tremendous burden of helping to set India free, and while doing that, it does seem that her friends might set her free from at least this obligation, thus incidentally giving Krotona relief at Bank. I put it up to you.

A further statement of Krotona's affairs will have been found in two circulars issued by me a few months ago. Conditions have not greatly altered since then.

It may interest those who do not know, to learn that the Krotona estate and the Star estate adjoin one another, making one continuous property, and this nearness makes for mutual helpfulness. The teaching side of the work of Krotona will naturally include the ideals as given by the Lord who has come, while all other aspects will be dedicated to the Manu, for Krotona seeks service along this parallel line. It is most fitting that the activities devoted to the two lines represented by the Manu and the Boddhissattva should be established happily side by side in useful cooperation, and those of us who are helping in the work feel that we are most privileged.

Offering to you, as in the past, our glad services in every way, and hoping there may be those who will make it possible for us to cancel our Head's paper, as suggested above, I am,
Fraternally yours,
A.P.W.

On Christmas Eve, 1928, a deed was secured to two lots in Meiners Oaks for a Liberal Catholic Church site. At this time, Meiners Oaks was a small suburb of Ojai with about 200 families, a comparative wilderness offering peace and quiet and a field in which there were no other churches.

Joining the Liberal Catholic Church in 1923, Bishop Edward M. Matthews was born in Terrell, Texas in 1898. Serving in the U.S. Army from 1916-1917, he joined the U.S. Marine Corps in 1918. Moving to Ojai, California in 1927, he co-founded the Church of Our Lady and all Angels, now the cathedral church for the province of the U.S.A.

The Liberal Catholic Church was founded in 1916 by Bishop James I. Wedgwood and Bishop Leadbeater—both Englishmen— the first a bishop in the Old Catholic Church (which had split off from Rome after the First Vatican Council proclaimed the dogma of Papal infallability in 1870) and the second a leader of the Theosophical Society. Their aim was to present a Theosophical interpretation of Christianity, although the Liberal Catholic Church leaves its members free in matters of belief, it claims to have a purpose, to show humanity's place in the great plan. By Wednesday, October 30, 1929 the lines were laid out for the foundation.

Early services of the Ojai church met at the residence of Lavilla Humason on Foothill Road, and several clergy were residents in the Ojai Valley. Bishop Irving Cooper appointed the Rev. Frank E. Kilbourne, newly arrived from Seattle, as priest in charge. Frank Kilbourne also operated *The Ojai* newspaper, printing plant, stationery store and gift shop until September 1947 when he retired.

Frank Gerard, Community Development Company offers complete real estate service with maps, blue-prints, and information on contractors such as John Roine, along with Margaret H. Deaderick, resident representative for the Star Camp sub-division. Everyone was taking advantage of being in Real Estate business and publishing. Frank Gerard Real Estate offering members a complete list of land and homes in Ojai, plus drawings and building construction by John Roine.

Several large oak trees on the property made an attractive frame for the edifice, and church members and their friends literally built the redwood church in less than two months. Rev. John Roine became the first priest ordained in the redwood church. Architect and builder John Roine, well-known for his unusual and high-quality work, including the Madeline Baird Mansion in Meiners Oaks, designed and supervised the construction sparing no expense to bring the finest materials from Europe to create this stunning work of art. The dramatic entrance is round with pink marble stars, pillars, and beautiful stained glass windows. The ceiling is covered with gold leaf, while the formal dinning room is covered in silver leaf, all applied by hand

The men organized working parties on weekends and women served picnic meals on piles of lumber. Among the workers who helped put up the building, either by hammer or saw, or by cooking the meals, were Harold Kirk, for many years associated with *The Ojai* in an executive capacity; Frank E. Kilbourne Jr.; Vernon C. Hill; Edward Matthews; A.F. Knudsen; Eugene Munson; Blanche Kilbourne; Alberta Kirk; May Grant; and Nanea Roine.

The church, which had a pleasing, Gothic doorway with three similarly arched windows on the front and could accommodate 100 people, held its first two services on Tuesday, December 24, 1929. Father Kilbourne celebrated the 8 a.m. Holy Eucharist, with Blanche Kilbourne at the organ. At the evening service, Monica Ros played a violin solo.

By 1948, buildings had gone up on both sides of the Liberal Catholic Church in Meiners Oaks, so the congregation voted unanimously to move to another location.

Sarah Peacock Rogers made a gift to the parish of nearly half an acre of land east of Gridley Road, a meadow with many aged oak trees and an inspiring view of Topa Topa.

On December 8, 1948, J.R. Brakey, a Ventura housemover who had moved more than 200 church buildings, moved the church to the Rogers' property.*

---

* In 1969, the larger church was built on the property, a short distance to the north, by George Thomas, an experienced contractor in building churches. The little redwood church was then remodeled and today serves as the social hall and meeting room.

Looking back then, we would see the Meeting Hall in Ojai is in progress. Bishop Pitkin looks on from the side, something he has done ever since the beginning of the several projects in progress here in Ojai. Young Master Chase on the other side of the age scale also can be counted among the observers. Edgar Wylie and Donald Chase are putting a new wall partitioning in along the south wall.

Additional work in the Meeting Hall will be two rest rooms, air conditioning and another door in the north wall. An arbor is contemplated on the north side of the Meeting Hall to provide shade for members who leave the church of Our Lady and All Angels just across the way.

All the work contributed is voluntary and when completed, it will be the Silent Evidence of Regular Voluntary Efforts. Note that spells S.E.R.V.E.!

Deacon Henry W. Dawn, very active in the Ventura County Democratic Central Committee, arranged an interview with then California Gov. Edmund G. Brown, pleading for a mutual arrangement of tax exemption for religious and non-profit corporations in the state of California and the state of Maryland, where ever the Liberal Catholic Church in the United States is incorporated.

Warrington called the Krotonians to the Music Room on December 28 as it was a very significant date, and always will be for them.

I remember so well how on this day, with Dr. Besant and very many others, Krishnaji stood about where Mrs. Douglas is sitting under that picture of the "Infinite Peace", and for the first time the Lord Maitreya used his body. It was so new to him (Krishnaji) that he would not use the first person pronoun. He told Dr. Besant that he resisted because he was afraid we would not understand. She came up to me afterwards with tears running down her cheeks saying, "This is the beginning of all that I have prophesied. It has all come true."

I shall always remember this room, and I think a little brass bowl should be put there.

I do not know what we could do tonight with greater profit to ourselves than to discuss some of the aspects of Krishnaji's longings for us. I say longings because I believe he has a real longing that we should understand what he is saying to us: but what I may say tonight, hope you all will take sort of in the family. I make no claims for myself. Some claims have been made for me and they stand for what they are worth, but as to the goal which Krishnaji is holding before us, the goal of liberation, I know of none who has attained it in the sense he has done, and I do not care who may claim to have gained that liberation of which he speaks.

Some years ago when I was visiting Dr. Besant in Washington I recall that she was surrounded by a group of

This arrangement saved the church a large sum of money when the church received 50 adjoining acres from the Sarah Peacock Rogers' bequest for the development of an educational center for the clergy.

The Mary Gray Chapel in 1961 was to be held once a month by Father Roine from Los Angeles. It was served by the late Bishop Hampton. Services were reestablished in the Chapel primarily for the benefit of pupils at Mrs. Houghton's School for retarded children. Mrs. Houghton being a member of At. Alban's for many years. Since Father Roine commenced his regular visits, interest has spread to adults living in the neighborhood, so that of late attendance at the Eucharist has averaged about 16, with 9 at the Healing Services.

pupils, and one woman, a very earnest woman who evidently wanted to synthesize the virtues into one, asked Dr. Besant to tell her which of all the virtues she might specialize on; and Dr. Besant answered, "perfect accuracy." I realized at the moment she had made truth her great goal in life, but she put it very simply and said "perfect accuracy."

Now the liberation that Krishnaji is holding before us as the ideal goal is something that begins just as simply as the acquisition of the habit of truth. The first freedom that we must attain for ourselves is the freedom of the little things that hold us back from being noblewomen and noblemen. We are bound up in this temple of fancies, likewise weaknesses and limitations. Think what a wonderful thing it would be if we could gain freedom from the qualities in us, say the qualities of jealousy, anger, resentment, petty revenges, freedom from other people's opinions. I simply tell you I was richly rewarded, and I found out, it came to me then, what it is that Krishnaji wants us to do. Krishnaji wants us to be free, to be master at the moment of a situation in which at the moment we are placed. *

---

* Warrington, A.P., informal talk to Krotonians only, at his residence, December 28, 1928, taken from his handwritten rough draft of notes.

Krotona Library before the hall is built

Chapter 3
1929

It was known by E.S. members that to attack a religious form (such as the Liberal Catholic Church) which helps large numbers of people could lead one to be removed from the E.S. This meant that the members who challenged Dr. Besant's direct statement as to the World-Teacher in relation to the L.C.C. could be put out of the E.S. From the author's point of view, nothing could have been better for an E.S. member: he would then find himself in a position where he would have to use his powers of discrimination, his own understanding, as a guide rather than on any self-proclaimed leader. (It is worth remembering that only through freedom can one learn the truth). We will see in this year how the L.C.C. reacts to the new messsage of Krishnamurti.

In February, A. P. Warrington, who had been staying in Santa Barbara at the Paso Robles Hot Springs* for several months, returned to his home at Krotona after a week or two in splendid health.

---

* #12 Ocean View Ave.,Santa Barbara, California.

Jan 4 1929
Mr. A.P. Warrington
12 Ocean View Ave.,
Santa Barbara, California

Dear Mr. Warrington:

I am sorry you did not have time to see me after my return from the city and so I will have to write to you. Thompson Bros. deal for the Ternary property is progressing satisfactorily, and they do not seem to think there is any possibility of the deal not being closed in the near future, although the money may not be paid by the 2nd of February.

Dr. Besant's note is not due until the 14th of February, 1930.

I found upon investigation in the city that I can buy the best bath tub for only $4.00 more than I would have to pay for a second and so I have today ordered this tub from Los Angeles. As soon as it comes Mr. Munson will install it at the office building.

The water hearing at Ventura yesterday was continued to Jan 15th, which is the last possible date that the matter can be postponed. At that time the county board will have to take final action upon the petition presented for the formation of this district. From the numerous protests presented to the board yesterday by many of the prominent property holders in the Ojai I would not be surprised to see the petition denied. The Ojai Land & Development Co., Mr. Mead Gosnell and Judge Daley were among the prominent ones to refuse to include their property in the district. Judge Daley made a rather long winded speech in which he brought out considerable information about the water situation in the Valley and the past history of attempts to get water. Also a number of questions were asked of the engineers, and as a result of the meeting I gathered the following facts:

Water cannot be obtained from the Matilija and Ventura rivers by means of a storage tank for a number of reasons, chief of which are: (1) The legal difficulties are very great. (2) There is no proper foundation for such a dam and it could not be constructed without great danger of breaking and flooding the Valley.

Water cannot be obtained from the Sespe for the reason that it is a tributary of the Santa Clara river and the inhabitants of the Santa Clara Valley from the ocean to Saugus would all have objections to the diverting of this water to the Ojai. The legal difficulties in this case are practically insurmountable. There is also

144

this practical difficulty that if the survey now being made by the state should establish a surplusage of water for the Sespe and it could be obtained for the Ojai, it still would cost more to bring the water over or through the mountains than the quantity of water available could possibly be worth.

I talked with Mr. Mead Gosnell about this matter, and he is emphatically against it on the grounds that any such attempt to obtain water for the Ojai would require a bond issue of so large an amount that the land involved could not sustain the burden, and if such a project could be put across it would absolutely kill the Valley. Those were the exact words he used.

Another point that came out very clearly was that the promoters of the formation of this district did not have any practical proposition to make as to any method of obtaining a water supply, but apparently based their action entirely upon the argument that it was necessary to form the district in order to have an organization through which to work. The discussion of this argument brought out clearly the fact that even such an activity would place a burden of taxation upon the lands involved without any guarantee of ultimate benefit to be obtained therefrom.

I shall of course attend the meeting on the 15th, and unless the developments at that meeting materially change the situation I will not feel justified in including any lands belonging to myself or to our Theosophical organizations unless I have definite and specific instructions to that effect from the board of directors of such corporation. Please let me know at your early convenience what you think I should do with regard to Krotona.
Ever most cordially yours,
G.H. Hall

Around January 11, 1929, Miss Mina Kunz removed from Hollywood and made her permanent home with Mr. and Mrs. Hervey Gulick in the old Krotona farmhouse on the east side of the hill.

January 12, 1929 trustees were: E.W. Munson, Max Wardall, Fred Smith, Walter J. Field, Thomas Talbot, Miss Marie Poutz, George H. Hall, Grace S. Hall, Fred Hart, A. P. Warrington, Miss Rita Miklau, Bishop Irving Cooper, C.F. Holland.

---

65 Warrington Crescent, W.9.
London, England
January 1929

Dear Fellow Pupil,

You will doubtless have heard that Bishop Wedgwood, with Dr. Besant's warm approval, has agreed to start a Centre here in England.

The Huizen Centre, Holland, will still be carried on, though on a somewhat smaller scale, under the general direction and guidance of Bishop Wedgwood, but his main work, for several years at any rate, will lie over here. He intends to continue with the oversight of the Church in continental countries, and other work, but feels that the change of residence will in no way affect this.

The plan is that all activities shall be included in the work of this Centre, T.S., Church, Masonry, World University, and various subsidiary activities, and it is hoped that it will grow into a very powerful instrument for the furthering of the work of the Masters in the Outer World.

A good deal of money will be required to start this work, and we are therefore appealing to our Fellow Pupils in the hope of enlisting their interest, and their help, in either of the following ways.

a. by donation

b. by subscribing an annual sum, however small, for three years.

Our aim is to make this Centre entirely self-supporting. A certain number of workers will live at the Centre and help to build up the various activities, and in addition to special Pupils' gatherings from time to time we hope also to throw everything open to T.S. and Masonic and Church workers at certain seasons of the year. Properties are being inspected, though nothing entirely suitable has up to the present been found.

Those of you who have had the privilege of visiting Huizen, or of attending Pupils' gatherings over which Bishop Wedgwood has presided will be able to estimate the possibilities of more extensive work over here, and be in a position to appreciate what it will mean to England, and indeed to the whole world, to have Huizen duplicated on a larger scale in England.

In order to help us to formulate plans more definitely we would very much appreciate an early reply this letter.

Yours sincerely and fraternally,
Margaret Jackson
Edw. L. Gardner

P.S. Until the Trust is formed and a permanent Treasurer appointed, we shall be glad if you will kindly send your reply to this letter to Colonel Powell, Pan's Garden, Little Austin's Rd, Earnham, Surrey.

Bishop Wedgwood was busy by 1929 creating another center at Tekels Park in England, founded and owned by the Adyar Theosophical Society. It was dedicated to the ideals of Universal Brotherhood and to the uplifting of humanity, "the great orphan," to quote the Brother KH in one of his letters.

Thirty-five miles southwest of London, Tekels Park lies on the border of the town of Camberley (about 15 minutes walk from there). The estate started out with about 50 acres of woodlands and now has over eighty acres including a hill-side, a brook, and extensive meadowland surrounded by a belt of trees, old and young.

Following the purchase in 1930, Dormy House was soon built with restaurant, lounge and rooms for temporary residents and visitors. The large Lecture Hall, and the St. Francis Liberal Catholic Church was a gift from the late Miss Josephine Chambres who herself built and occupied the first house to be erected.

Today, it has been sold to a developer.

A series of letters in January and February of 1929 give a cross section of activity:

Krotona, Ojai, CA
Jan 17 1929

Dear Mr. Warrington
I had Roine come up Monday night to arrange for his concert and to talk over the plans of the new buildings. He asked to have the concert on Tuesday night and promised to telephone me from Los Angeles yesterday confirming the date. So far I have not heard from him, I hope he will telephone today, as the advertising should go out not later than tomorrow.
I called up Mrs. Gray to find out if the lodge would give way for

Tuesday night and discovered that they have changed their meeting date to Friday, so there is no conflict. After talking about the lodge date Mrs. Gray brought up the subject of the apartments and said that she had a talk with Mrs. Gardner and that they had decided to drop the whole matter so far as Krotona is concerned. She asked me to inform you of this fact, and she explained to me further that they were not seeking to rent property or to secure a place to run a tea room, but that they had understood that you had promised to lease them a piece of property where they could carry out their own ideas. Under these circumstances I presume it would be best for me not to press the matter further with Mrs. Gardner.

Mr. Roine and I went over the plans for the new building in a preliminary way, and he said that on his return from the city he would be glad to put in a bid for the construction. I explained to him that before the bids would be asked for I would be glad to have his advice and suggestions as to any changes in the specifications in order that we might not have to revise the bids after they had been made, and that after these changes and suggestions had been placed before you for your approval that the bids would then be asked for. Immediately, and from only a preliminary examination of the plans, he brought up a number of points, the most important of which is the roof. He emphatically disapproves of the style roof suggested as he says he has never seen one that does not leak badly, and that if a tile roof is to be used at all it should be a Mission tile rather than the hand made Spanish. I would not mention this objection now but rather wait until I submit a final report except for the fact that my first readying of the specifications shows that the architect is requiring the most expensive construction throughout for this type of building.

When this project was first proposed to me by you your strongest argument in its favor was that we needed a cheaper type of building than we now have in order that the rental return might bear a much higher proportion to the investment, and I have understood from the beginning that it was your purpose to build the building at a comparatively low cost per square foot. While I have had time to study the plans and specification s only slightly I am quite sure that the building proposed is fully as expensive, and probably much more expensive, than the ones we already have. If this is the case there are still two other points you might consider. If such an expensive building is to be erected should it not be located with our other buildings of that same type, rather than to be placed on the flat ground near the railroad, which is, from all ordinary points of view,

148

the least desirable residence section on the estate. Also if it is to be such an expensive building it would be much more desirable, in my argument, to give the building the usual elevation from the ground and have hardwood floors instead of concrete. Concrete floors require plenty of rugs to be comfortable for residence purposes, and the elevation above the surrounding grounds should be sufficient to insure excellent drainage or flood water might run in on the floor. To give a concrete floor considerable elevation requires a great deal of grading and team work which is expensive.

I hope you won't mind my bringing up these few points in a preliminary way, as it maybe some time before a complete report could be made and we might as well talk over these various things as they come up.

Mr. Schuller agreed to come in yesterday to get the plans and specifications in order that he might study them over night, but he failed to show up; I presume he will be in today. Also he asked me to please ask you to return the clippings which I loaned you in connection with the plan he submitted.

We have had a good rain the past two days, the mountains are covered with snow and tis very cold.

Yours as ever,

G.H. Hall

Janurary 21 1929
Singapore

My dear Parthaji, [A.P.Warrington]

It was a real pleasure to receive your letter. I have been thinking of you quite a lot and really sorry that you were ill again. Maysie has been giving news of you and she says you are quite well again. I know that you would be happy when you heard the announcement by Dr. Besant. I hope you have not forgotten the nice times we had together. You write in your letter about renewing our acquaintance and I almost began to think you and I had to be introduced to each other when we met again! But Maysie told me that you always write like that — very formal. But you being an American will understand that I am joking. You know I am looking forward to seeing you again. We are now on our way to Java and I am really glad to go there. Then we go to Sydney and from there to America. But don't forget that my rooms must be ready for me. I hope you have not forgotten that you talked to me, that those rooms are ours when we come there!

I am afraid people might be disappointed with me for I have done so little even though Dr. Besant said great things of me. I take no meetings for women, I don't like public speaking, and the 2nd number of the *World-Mother* magazine is not coming as far as I know at present. The reason is that I feel I am not ready yet for the work and dislike to talk at Woman's meetings about Birth Control, Infant Welfare etc. which is what people expect of me. I feel it is not the real thing and I must discover the Real Message for myself. I am sure you are one of the few to understand what I am driving at.

I was sorry to leave Maysie behind at Adyar. Amma is always touring and does not give enough work to Maysie, I mean personal work and so Maysie is not as happy at Adyar as she might be. I told her to try and come for the Chicago Convention. But I feel this is doing her a lot of good though she may not realize it till she leaves India.

I was not very surprised at John's marriage. I suppose they are happy.
With much love always
Your grandmother!!
Rukmini

January 28, 1929
A.P. Warrington, still in Santa Barbara at the Paso Robles Hot Springs.

My very dear Rukmini,

It seems remarkable that your letter dated at Singapore should have come to me today, for it was only this morning that I was discussing with Sarah the possibility of a birthday telegram to you. I concluded there were two insuperable obstacles; one that you only have a birthday once in four years, and this is not one of the years, and the other, I did not know what your address would be. So here you come marching in within a few hours and tell me all about it. How nice of you. Great Yogin undoubtedly.

Yes, certainly your rooms will be ready for you; both of you. You are expected. Please let me know when to expect you so that I may have guests up to the last minute, if possible. Will you and his lordship be traveling throughout America again? I suppose you will go to the Congress? There is one chance in so many that I may go. The present year is a Sabbatical year for me in which I am moving heaven and earth to regenerate this body of mine, and believe me I am making progress too. The sooth sayers and wise guys generally tell me that my next birthday is the turning point and I really must be careful until then, and as the Congress is being held practically on my birthday, maybe it will be wiser to keep still and write an immortal letter to the gathering.

So you think I am very stiff when I write letters, do you? Well that is my reputation, and I have often wondered whether it was my stiffness that my readers felt, or the stiffness of my very rectangular secretaries who perform all the details for me. Anyhow I have limbered up very considerably in this letter, do you not think, and have even condescended to use a few words of illumination slang!

I am glad Maysie is coming back. She would repine if she stayed. I do not think India is made for any white person: only such gods as Amma and your lord and master seem to be able to stand it.

I appreciate your thinking that I would understand your policy with regard to the World-Mother matter, and I am convinced that you are right when I tell you that I have said to myself frequently, "If I were Rukmini, I would go slowly and let the message develop itself." I am sure in time you will know all about it. Meanwhile, no time is being lost.

California has been perfectly glorious this winter. Just now the almond orchard is in blossom and no poetical imagery of mind will describe the beauty of it; and the orange groves are laden with golden fruit. Surely the gods have blessed this beloved little valley. With much love to you and George, I am,
Ever cordially yours,
A.P. Warrington

Santa Barbara Branch Office
Carleton Monroe Winslow Architect
Feb 2 1929

Dear Sir: (Mr. L. G. Schuler)
I am mailing to you a set of plans and specifications for the construction of two units (A and B) of the Bachelor Quarters, Krotona Institute of Theosophy at Ojai. I wish you to figure on this work and submit a bid on same on or before the 10th of February.

You are to figure on using Angulo 22 inch hand made tile for the roof.

I think it advisable that you phone me and make an appointment so that I may go over the plans and specifications with you so as to give you a clear understanding of the work before you hand in your bid.

Although we are only building two units at present the septic tank, gas and electric services shall be figured as large as originally specified.[*]
Your truly,
R. H. Pitman

February 4, 1929
A.P.Warrington at Santa Barbara writes to Dr. Besant

My dear Amma,

Referring to recent correspondence in which you and I developed a plan for funding the indebtedness upon The Manor at Sydney. I had intended to put the plan into effect about this time; but many changes have taken place since our correspondence, the greatest of which is the suspension of the E.S. In view of this and the fact that Krotona needs money very badly to pay what is due at Bank and also to erect a few buildings for residence and work. I have drafted a plan which I hope you will not disapprove. I enclose a sketch of it. In it I have referred to the Sydney indebtedness as one for which you personally were obligated, because you stated in one of your letters that if we could to arrange the matter, you would have to go out and make the money to retire this debt. The other indebtedness is the $10,000. which remains unpaid of the $25,000. which Krotona borrowed from bank for you and is due next year. It seemed to me that it would be a kindness to you if we could relieve you of both of these items at the same time.

I felt it best to refer to the "80 Years Young Fund" to prevent confusion. You had written me you expected to use that for Happy Valley.

Miss Poutz will have the circular printed and sent to the 2500 E.S. people who I am sure will be very glad to have something to do at this juncture that will be of real help to you. Incidentally both Krotona and Sydney will be served.
Ever devotedly,
A.P. Warrington

---

[*] At the request of Mr. Pitman, Floyd S. Lee, designer & builder of sewerage-disposal plants makes a submitting bid of "Thirteen Hundred Eighty Five Dollars" for one of the three compartment septic tanks complete together with seepage beds to care for sixteen single apartments for the Krotona job.

February 6, 1929
A.P. Warrington at Krotona to Dr. Besant

My dear Amma,

Mrs. Sarojini Naidu came to Ojai as you wished. She saw Happy Valley, Krotona and the Star lands. She was entertained at Mrs. Gray's and spoke to a small group. She lunched with me at Santa Barbara where I was stopping at the time. In Los Angeles she saw Dr. Ingleman, All of this I was glad to arrange in accordance with your wish.

Mrs. Naidu said her visit to Ojai and Santa Barbara represented her happiest day in America; but she no doubt will write to you her own impressions. I am very happy to have had the privilege of meeting so charming a person.

I hope you are feeling very well, and that freedom for India is progressing satisfactorily.
Devotedly yours,
A.P. Warrington

Feb 9 1929
George Hall to Louis Zalk

Dear Louis:

The enclosed letter is the one that Mr. Warrington intends mailing to all former members of the E.S. in the Western Hemisphere Monday afternoon. The letter will also be sent to South Africa, Australia and New Zealand, Mr. Warrington particularly asked me to state that this is a personal enterprise on his part and not an official activity of the Krotona Corporation; that he is doing this because he promised both Dr. Besant and C.W. Leadbeater that he would do it. He states that he has a letter from Dr. Besant saying that she would have to go out and earn the money herself if he was unable to raise it for her. He also states that he has a letter from her in which she says that she intends using the money from the "80 Years Young Fund" for Happy Valley.

I make all of the above statements for Mr. Warrington at his request, quoting him as accurately as I can, without comments or explanations of my own in order that you may bet his thoughts uninfluenced by my opinion. I have several times in the past few weeks discussed this letter with Mr. Warrington and he states hat he has given careful consideration to all the points I brought up in connection with it, and that the letter has been revised several times to take advantage of those factors in my point of view which he considered useful. I believe that our conversations on the subject have covered every important point involved, and that Mr. Warrington, having given consideration to all possible objections, considers that this is the proper thing for him to do and that it will therefore be done.

Since I am the one who has been instrumental in bringing up all possible objections to this matter, and who assumed also the responsibility of bringing it to your attention as a Krotona Trustee and a member of the "80 Year Young Fund" Committee. I wish to say that I would not feel justified in making any further opposition to Mr. Warrington's action and am quite content to let the letter go out and meet its own fate. I feel that everything I have done about the matter was done as a duty of a friend and that that duty has been fully performed. It may quite well be that I am wholly mistaken in my views, and in any case the responsibility is now entirely his. If you and Dr. Ingleman feel differently than this, I suggest that you talk with Mr. Warrington directly over the phone, and I hope that such a discussion of it will deal exclusively with the letter itself and not at all with my opinions or any thing that I may have said about it, as I have had full opportunity of expressing myself to Mr. Warrington directly and have nothing more to say or do with the matter.

Sincerely yours,

G.H.H.

Feb 9 1929
George Hall to Louis Zalk

Dear Louis:

I had a long talk with A.P. about this last night and he states that he is quite honest and sincere in his belief that this letter is the proper thing for him to send out. I cannot bring myself to agree with him in this matter but I do not feel that I should oppose it any further. If Mr. Warrington is right and I am wrong I will be glad that my opposition went no further than frank and open suggestions discussed with him personally. If he is wrong the consequences will be his, and I shall be glad that I have not added to his troubles by going further than I have gone.

I feel that I have been right in telling you about this for my own personal reasons, but also aside from this on the grounds that as a Krotona trustee you were entitled to the information, and also because Mr. Warrington proposed in my conversation with him just before your arrival to take the matter up with all members of the "80 Years Young Fund" before sending out the letter, and I dissuaded him from so doing. As a result of my discussion on that point he modified the letter by including the phrase referring to the "80 Years Young Fund". I therefore place no restrictions upon your action in the matter because of the information furnished being confidential.

Yours as ever,

G. H.H.

P.S. Please note that A.P.'s letter is so worded that it is a direct appeal for money for Mrs. Besant and made in her name, and that if it fails to produce the money, as I think it will, it will be a sad blow to her prestige.

"Krotona" Ojai, Calif.
February 9, 1929
A.P. Warrington to E.S. members

Dear Friends of the American E.S.,

It has occurred to me that during the period of the suspension of the E.S. its devoted members might be gratified were I to give them an opportunity of serving Dr. Besant who, as O.H., has been of such very great service to us for so many, happy years.

It is a special case and is this: Dr. Besant, in the course of her duties which affect you and me, has had to obligate herself for certain debts. Just now there are two — one for $10,000. concerning America, and the other for $20,000, concerning Australia and the entire Southern Hemisphere, neither of which will come under the benefits of the "80 Year young Fund." The first has to do with the new race activities, and the other with the founding of a Center south of the Equator in furtherance of a plan originating in very high places. Hence both have a peculiar importance, so much so that recently in writing in to me on the subject of one of these debts Dr. Besant said that if it could not be otherwise managed, she would try to earn the money herself to pay it off. Think of that and decide if I am bringing to your attention a service of very real helpfulness.

The total involved is $30,000. It looks large, but after all it bears ratio of only $12 to each of the 2500 E.S. members of the American

Division to which this circular is being sent.

Do you not think it would be splendid to relieve Dr. Besant of this burden during the present year? Our great leader is bearing impersonal burdens all over the world, none of which is greater than that just now of helping to set India free. While she is thus engaged, can we not at least set her free from the above financial obligations? As everybody knows, when she incurs a debt it is never for herself but for the work somewhere. I hope that we of the E.S. may soon be able to extinguish these obligations as an offering in gratitude to our beloved leader. The outlay will mean so little to us — just $1 per month per member for a year — if all respond. But the relief to Dr. Besant from having a $30,000, obligation hanging over her will be great.

Therefore, I am sure you will appreciate my having called your attention to the matter.

Those who can contribute to the "Besant Indebtedness Fund" may remit to Miss Marie Poutz, "Krotona," Ojai, California. Remittances may be in installments, or otherwise.

Fraternally yours,

A.P. Warrington

Feb 9 1929
2123 Beachwood Drive, Hollywood, Calif.
Louis Zalk to A.P. Warrington

My dear Mr. Warrington:

I feel, even in advance of seeing the proposed circular which you wish to send out and the purpose of which is to raise money toward the payment of Dr. Besant's and Bishop Leadbeater's indebtedness, that I should acquaint you with a few factors which are at the base of the whole matter, and which should receive our combined consideration.

The "80 Year Young Fund" was instituted at the urgent request of Bishop Arundale. It is an international appeal. The total sum to be raised was $50,000 of which Australia's contribution was $15,000, England's $15,000 and America's $20,000. Bishop Arundale stated specifically to the whole world, as it were, that Dr. Besant and Bishop Leadbeater owed $50,000 which was a personal indebtedness that they had contracted for the Theosophical movement. So about a year and a half ago a committee was formed to receive the $20,000 which was America's quota. We circularized the members, representing the above objects, and so far we have collected approximately $11,000. About $5,000 is pledged but not paid. We have approximately a year and a half is which to raise the total quota.

The committee thought it wise not to prress for the balance of the money at this time, because it is everybody's judgment that our members are suffering from an overburden of appeals. We have the Happy Valley Association collecting money; there are the appeals for Wheaton Headquarters; there are the appeals to maintain the necessary work of the Order of the Star; there must shortly be issued the international appeal for the Star; and Mr. Rajagopal is even now touring the United States in an effort to raise money to help lift the burdensome debt on Starland. Beside, there is the reasonable wish of a great many of our members who are also members of the Order of the Star to attend the Star Camp, and the railroad fare and Camp fees are putting a drain upon their resources.

It is for the above weighty reasons that the "80 Years Young" Fund Committee thought it wise to refrain from the effort to raise the balance of the $20,000 which America is morally obligated to pay.

Now the above description discloses the premises which we all of us must consider. If a letter goes forth making an appeal for money with which to help pay Dr. Besant's and Bishop leadbeater's indebtedness, how can we harmonize such an appeal with the "80 Years Young Fund" appeal? And if the proposed appeal even indicates that it is not out of harmony with the "80 Years young Fund", then must we not consider the impression which will be created among those members who have been told by Bishop Arundale that there was only a $50,000 private indebtedness which had to be raised?

Now dear Mr. Warrington, I feel it my duty to offer my advice and honest judgment. I beg of you to believe that there is not the slightest controversial or argumentative feeling on my part. I am in the Theosophical movement honestly, to serve it. I seek for no prominence, glory or authority, as these mean absolutely nothing to me. I have cheerfully stepped out of a position of authority and prominence in the business world in my community at Duluth, and care nothing whatever for personal prominence n any of the movements. I hope you know that. But I do believe I can serve my friends best if I give them honestly my opinion.

If the proposed appeal you have in mind will take over the functions of the "80 Years Young Fund", believe me, I would be heartily glad of it, and our leaders can be so advised, and also that the moral obligation to pay the $9,000 still due would be fulfilled by the new appeal. In that case the committee in charge would, I am sure gladly notify those who have already helped in the "80 Years Young Fund".

I am sure that we can harmonize this, and I am sure that I wish success to the new appeal. It would in a sense relieve the members of the committee, or I would rather put it that it would add your valuable work to the work of the committee. I am duly mindful of your high purpose and the instructions that you have in this matter, and yet is it not our duty to offer our best judgment to our superior officers, even to the Commander-in-Chief himself, as long as there is truth and affection in our hearts and as long as we are ready cheerfully to abide by a decision even if it is against our viewpoint? Believe me, it is in that spirit that I approach this matter toward your good self and toward our great leaders, with truth and affection in my heart and a cheerful willingness to abide by their judgment even if against my own viewpoint.

Just one more point — as to my sharing this problem with Dr. Ingelman. I knew of the matter of course, and when it became apparent that the sending out of the appeal was practically inevitable, then of course the members of the committee who are vitally involved in the position they have taken I thought should be acquainted with the circumstance, and as the sending out of the appeal was inevitable and as they were affected by it, did they not have a right to offer to your good self their friendly pint of view?

I hope you will see my position and I can only state, in conclusion, that I do not propose under any circumstance in my conversations with you or our work together to get out for a moment from the atmosphere of truth, affection and the other bonds that exist between us; and I am quite sure that no provocation of any kind will dislodge me from that attitude in which I am firmly fixed.
Always most cordially,
Louis Zalk

February 12 1929
Louis Zalk to George Hall

Dear George:
Referring to the appeal which Mr. Warrington has sent out, after a thorough consideration of the matter, which in justice to

the other members of the "80 Years Young Fund" Committee necessitated sharing with them opinions and views, I decided, and I think each individual of that committee agrees that there is nothing to be done, and that Mr. Warrington has assumed the responsibility. If his action is not wise, that will be for time to disclose, and all the rest of it will develop. In the meantime the "80 Years Young Fund" Committee and the fund will have to make the best of it, and we will have to correct mistaken impressions if these arise. It is just one of those things which come up and which have to be met manfully and in accordance with our ideals. I am sure that I am succeeding in keeping a brotherly attitude toward Mr. Warrington, which is the main thing, as, after all, he is working for Krotona and we all have its interests at heart. I am glad you told me abut it. I hope I have not acted unwisely in writing to Mr. Warrington and speaking to him. He felt distressed about my talking about it, and for that reason it has been a very painful experience to me; but what of it? We have to have painful experiences too. So that's that.

One thing bothers me, however, and that is if you, my friend, have had any particular grief or trouble because your deep friendship for me has prompted you to tell me of these things. If you have suffered any, then indeed I will feel as though the matter won't heal up so rapidly. But if you are satisfied and carefree as regards this whole matter, I can assure you that I will not permit it to burden my thoughts or my work any further.
With much love to you, I am,
Louis Zalk

About this time in 1929, a peacock is added to the residents of Krotona. Although a very beautiful creature, his human neighbors assert that he has a very *unbeautiful* voice, which he raises in expostulation. We shall read later that Catherine Mayes in the 70's will also bring white peacocks to be added with the others on the Hill.

April 13, 1929

G.H. Hall, to Krotona:

Received through Miss Marie Poutz the sum of $1,400. as a partial payment on one certain note for $10,000. to the Krotona Institute of Theosophy, signed by Dr. Annie Besant, said payment being endorsed upon said note on the 13th day of April, 1929. Signed Krotona Institute of Theosophy,
G.H. Hall
Manager

―――――――――――――――――

Krotona News Notes

Now that the Esoteric School has been suspended by the Outer Head "for a time," members will no doubt wish to know how Krotona is affected.

Krotona was originally intended to be a communal centre providing industrial, cultural and spiritual opportunities for those earnest students who might wish or need to withdraw from the strain of city life and do their work in a Theosophical atmosphere, under ideal conditions. Before, however, it became possible to concentrate on this plan further than to conduct the Krotona Institute regularly from 1912 to 1922, the great privilege came to us of furnishing a headquarters for both the T.S. (eight years) and the E.S. (sixteen years). The work required by these two headquarters and the lack of adequate funds to carry out our plans further served to delay the one pointed development of the original idea until the present time.

Since neither of the headquarters' offices needs to claim our attention of the time being, Krotona has begun to concentrate its activities in the direction of the untouched features of the original plan. To this end, a book business (The Krotona Book Shop) has been opened. A garden nursery has been established (called the Krotona Hill Nursery). Arts and crafts are being considered as well as other activities for the future. In addition, it can now be learned that residence sites will be discussed with those who may wish to build and bring

160

their families here to live, and to add to the virility of the community life.

To meet the enlarged activities, the work is now divided between three departments — (1) the Cultural, (2) the Production, and (3) the Financial and Real Estate Departments.

Of the first department, Miss Marie Poutz is the head, having the direction of the Library and the Institute (which it is hoped may be re-opened for classes as conditions mature) in which she is to be assisted by her E.S. headquarters' helpers and others.

Of the second department, Mrs. Maude N. Couch is the head, having the supervision of the Book Ship, of which Miss Angele Davis is the Manger, and the Nursery, of which Mrs. Marie Louise Hancock and Mr. F.C. Pragnell, Landscape Architect, are the directing spirits, assisted by Miss Louise Hall, Mrs. Diana Gillespie, Mrs. Inez Barnett, and Mr. V.C. Hill.

Of the third department, Mr. Geo. H. Hall continues as the Manger with Mr. Eugene W. Munson as Assistant. Mr. Hall likewise continues as Treasurer and Manager of the finances.

Before everything we need now to increase our housing facilities. At present we have only a cluster of small houses accommodating no more than those who have been conducting the activities up to this time.

A further statement of Krotona's affairs will have been found in the two circulars issued a few months ago. Financial conditions have not greatly altered since then.

It may interest those who do not know, that the Krotona estate and the Star estate adjoin one another, making one continuous property, and this nearness makes for mutual helpfulness. The teaching side of the work of Krotona will naturally embrace the ideals taught by Krishnaji, while the other side will include activities along the parallel line of the Manu, in which we have long believed we were working. It is most fitting that the activities devoted to the two lines should be established happily side by side in useful cooperation, and those of us who are helping in the work feel that we are most privileged and would like greatly to share the privilege with many others.

A.P.W.*

The following ellipses (three dots or points) at the end of paragraphs mean something has been omitted, but we did not change the context. That which was omitted was a great deal of rambling.

Spiritual Centres and Their Work

On Easter Monday morning in the Adyar Hall, Bishop Leadbeater and Bishop Arundale delivered addresses on "Spiritual Centres and Their Work."

Bishop Leadbeater: I suppose we must define our terms to some extent. I suppose we may safely take a Spiritual Centre as a place from which helpful, uplifting influence is radiated. Spiritual in this sense probably means something like non-material. The idea certainly is that there should be an uplifting or helpful influence of some sort radiating out from it...

Now, the question is sometimes asked: "How do you go to work to found a spiritual Centre?" The only thing you can do is to gather together a few people who are really keenly interested in these ideas, and let them live there and do their work. It is also necessary for the successful prosecution of the spiritual work of such a Centre that those people should all be on good terms with each other. I have known cases of people who gathered together to work for some high object, and yet were perpetually squabbling among themselves as to how the work should be done or whether this piece of it or that piece was the most important. Such a centre might do a great deal of work on the physical plane, but it would not be effective on the thought-plane, because the constant small jarrings would prevent the steady pouring out of currents of thought. One of the most important factors for the successful working of a

---

* Warrington, A.P., "Krotona News Notes", *The Theosophical Messenger*, Vol.XVII, April 1929, no.4, p.91.

spiritual Centre is that there should be perfect harmony. The people who compose the Centre are all working for a certain object, and they are all thinking more or less along those lines, and so they send out a definite current of influence...

If you want to have good results with your spiritual Centre, it is not only necessary that all the people should be working of the same object and thinking to a large extent about the same things; it is also necessary that they should set up a very high standard of brotherly feeling among themselves; otherwise you will be liable to constant friction which will absolutely prevent the working of such an influence as that of which we are speaking. It is very delicate and a very difficult matter to bring any kind of a Centre into such working order that it can be used for this higher work as well as for the lower. I have had some experience along those lines. We are very well-meaning in the Theosophical Society. We do all mean well, otherwise we should not be here at all; but of course we do not all agree as to methods of work in all details. It would be very dull if we did! You see we must be a little individualistic, or we should not have joined this Society, because to do so we had to come out of the ordinary thought of the day, whether it be ordinary worldly thought, or ordinary orthodox religious thought. We had to break away from all that, therefore you have shown already that you had a certain amount of independence, of individuality...

It is just that kind of very intimate association that to some extent, when you live in one big house, is so trying unless there is a real affection among all the people concerned. At The Manor, for example, we have some fifty people living in one big house. They need to see more of one another than they wish; they have their separate rooms; but in order to make a useful Centre, they must come to know one another, and they must get over any little friction that may arise. It does not matter though it may be only over very trifling things, the friction must be entirely eliminated, so that there is an unruffled surface. It is only when the unity is perfect that you begin to reap real results.

You ask what kind of work can such a Centre do? The

fact is there are so many kinds of ways in which it can be employed that in the time at my disposal I cannot possibly tell you all about it. Again I must make a little draft on your credulity with regard to higher things. I think we all hold the existence of our Masters. We all believe on good evidence that there are such Great People as these, and we have all read books which tell us something about Them. We know that They are all the time working for the advancement of humanity, and that They are ready to make use of nay opening which is offered to Them. Suppose there should be such a gathering as I am suggesting — a number of people coming together and trying to make themselves a unity. There is an opportunity for Them to pour in Their influence and let it radiate out.

You have heard that Masters sometimes take pupils. I am not at all sure that that is the right word to use. It would be must better to say that They take apprentices. They use these apprentices not only by setting them to do things, but by radiating out forces through them. I am not going to lecture on that; but the broad principle of the thing is this: This pupil or apprentice is directed to meditate. He fixes his mind very strongly upon the Great One who is teaching and helping him, and therefore he becomes a kind of channel open to that particular influence, because he is in the habit of thinking so much about the Person, and trying to reach upwards towards Him. He thereby opens a channel of communication from that very much higher level to himself...

So you have a funnel open to the higher thought, you conduct it straight down to the physical plane, and on the physical plane you are in the habit of radiating out this higher thought all round you. If you have a number of such people together, and their thoughts are (not all the time, of course, but on the whole) directed upwards, directed towards helping the world, you have there a very fine machine of the distribution and direction of such thought. Such a Centre will be a kind of labour-saving machine, a channel through which higher people can pour out their thought and their force. They would do that anyhow; but without the Centre they would have to expend a great deal of the force in pouring it down through the different planes, and pressing down into coarse physical matter. If they can find someone who has already done that part of the labour, they have nothing to do but pour it in, and the same amount of force will do much more work.

A Centre can do just that. It is not only the effect of the people's own thoughts and their own general attitude, but it is also that there are higher powers which are all the time ready, willing and glad to use any channel which you make for Them. A spiritual Centre from this point of view does make such a channel, and it is very largely used, and it is a good thing for any country or any neighbourhood in which such a Centre is established.

That is the theory of the thing. As to the establishment of such a Centre, the arrangements have to be made on higher planes as well as on the physical, and therefore if you can begin such a piece of work with a body of people who are already closely linked you have a much better chance of success. I know the whole thing is difficult. It involves the whole neighbourhood. Such a Centre would be best established a little away from the heavy pressure of ordinary life. It is not good that it should be in the busiest street of a great city, because there the pressure round it would be so much in the wrong direction. If you could establish it somewhere else it would be better, for it would hardly be possible to manage the delicate business of the formation of such a Centre under such conditions.

Adyar is meant to be such a Centre, and to a certain extent it is. It is far enough away from the big city; it is about seven miles away from the city of Madras — far enough away to be free from those influences of that city which would make such work almost impossible, and yet near enough to be able to exercise a good deal of influence. Here we have been trying to make a Centre at Clifton Gardens. We have done well, but frankly I think we might have done even better if we had been a few miles further out. We have round us a good deal of Government Reserve, and that is of course helpful.

165

Then there is the whole question, into which I will not even begin to go, of what is called angelic influence. There is another great evolution besides the human which lives and works in our midst, close round us all the time, and is exceedingly valuable for all this work of radiation of force. If you can enlist the help of the beings which in ecclesiastical history you call the Angels — which in India they call the Devas, the Shining Ones — that is of incalculable advantage in the work of any such Centre. I can testify that there are such great Beings, and that they are willing to enter into cooperation with us and to forward our efforts. I do not want to turn aside to consider that vast subject, but I may just say that we have obtained a good deal of this kind of assistance in our work at Clifton Gardens; and wherever anyone wants to form such a Centre it would be worth his while to try to get into communication with the angelic host, for he will find his work much expedited in many ways...

That is a slight sketch of what a spiritual Centre should be, and of part of its work on higher planes. It should radiate out all kinds of good feeling. It can aim its good feeling at certain particular points if it wishes, or it can just go on spreading it all round, and let it be taken up and used by any others who are also working of the good of humanity in other ways. On the physical plane, too, the Centre ought to be doing some good work for others. In the Theosophical Society we do that, I hope, for Theosophists have an especially good opportunity of being able to establish such work. But, as I have said, a number of people who are thus able to break away from ordinary life have usually sufficient individuality to make perfect harmony difficult of achievement, so a good deal of tact is required So if any of you are thinking of setting on foot anything of that sort, first of all choose your people very carefully, and do not forget that one of the prime requisites is that they shall be tolerant and willing to fit in with the idiosyncrasies of other people, as other people no doubt will have to fit in with theirs...

That is a little glimpse of the inner working of these things. I am not asking you to believe it, but that is the things as I see it, and if you provisionally accept that, you will understand the exceeding great necessity of ridding yourselves of your prejudices and not obtruding tem in the work.

C.W.L.

C.W. Leadbeater

This following statement is by Bishop George Arundale, and again ellipsis at the end of paragraphs indicating that something has been omitted, but we did not change the context.

Bishop Arundale: I think you would believe in Spiritual Centres if you were to read a certain book written by a very eminent physicist, Professor Eddington, entitled Stars and Atoms. It is one of the most interesting books I know, and in it Professor Eddington practically speaking, though not in so many words, points out how each one of us is not merely a spiritual centre but a tremendous conglomeration of spiritual centres. He goes so far as to say that there are, one might say, ten to the twenty-seventh power of spiritual centres — atoms, universes — in each one of us. How he arrives at that conclusion you will have to read for yourselves. It is far too difficult a proposition to put before you this morning. But he tells us that we are not merely individuals but tremendous universes; that composing us are innumerable sub-universes for which we are responsible, which we have to control, of which we are the Logoi, as it were, so that talking of spiritual centres one realizes that one is a spiritual centre oneself, that one has one's own work to do as a spiritual centre, one is oneself a great universe with innumerable other universes in one's charge, however small they may be, so as to fit us for the time when in the far distant future we may have to become great Solar Logoi and have charge of great universes similar to that of which we are to-day insignificant parts...

Apart from that aspect, however, we have in the outer world these centres of which Bishop Leadbeater has spoken; we know some of them. We know specifically of Adyar, we know of Ommen, we know of Sydney here, we know of the Ojai Valley Centre, we know of Huizen and of many other centres, and we realize that they are, as it were, great machines developing, receiving and sending out in splendid pulsations, power, force, blessing, benediction, service, not merely to their respective surroundings, but to the whole world. I myself have visited practically most of the Centres, with the names of which we happen to be familiar, and I have abundantly realized that each Centre has its own specific peculiar work to d. Each is a machine *sui gneris*; it has is own exclusive work to do. If, for example, we take Adyar, it seems to me — I am speaking from my personal observation — that we have there a great machine of power, specifically for India and generally for the whole of the world.

Adyar is the great nucleus of the Theosophical Society, each section of which Society is a kind of planet revolving around Adyar. We have the Australian planet, the Indian planet, and so on. We have a whole Theosophical system revolving round and drawing its nutriment from the Adyar nucleus, from the Adyar centre. The dominant note of Adyar is power. I feel I am born into power anew when I enter the Adyar Centre. It is not in the least unnatural that the Adyar Centre should be associated with power, both because of the particular line of evolution on which is our beloved President, and because of is world relation. She is, of course, the greatest power we have, not only in the Theosophical Society, but I do not hesitate to say in the whole of the world. The whole of the

Theosophical Society, every member, wherever he or she may live, should, even if not physically, at least otherwise, strive to contact Adyar in the spirit of gaining power. Even far away from Adyar we can all enter into the spirit of Adyar and be renewed by Adyar. We can take full advantage of Adyar by intuiting Adyar, bathing in the power of Adyar. I do not say there are not other qualities which we may also derive from Adyar, but Adyar is to my mind the great Centre of power. And if I go to Adyar in a spirit of receptivity, trying to draw from the Centre all I can, then I shall benefit immensely, and my own power will to a certain extent be increased because I have been immersed in that specific channel of life.

Now, supposing I leave Adyar and I go to Ojai. Before I went to Ojai I had a conception of Ojai which I have ceased to have. At all events which I do not hold now. Ojai seems to me to be dominantly a kind of place where one lives in the future. Ojai represents the future; it is the future, as it were, casting its shadow, or one would rather say the coming brightness of the future into the present. It is the future, as it were, laying hands on the present. I regard Ojai as most remarkable from that standpoint. Adyar is in many ways a present-day working Centre, it has to do with today. Ojai has to do with tomorrow, and the peace, the wonderful peace, of Ojai is the peace of tomorrow, and at Ojai we may readjust ourselves to today in the soft light of tomorrow. But I had no conception that Ojai was so powerful a Centre, so much what we should call a First Ray Centre — at all events the special part where I lived — and how intimately it is concerned with definite work in special directions to bring about the future which awaits us. And it was very interesting to talk over this with the President, who of course is in charge of that particular Centre, and to see how she, very slowly, of course, is making her plans to draw the spirit of the future closer to the present. Of course the moment Ojai was announced as bring a Centre everyone wanted to flock there, I am afraid for the most part seeking what they might devour, for people often go to Centres more for what they can get than for what they can give. The vast majority have had, for the time being, to be refused by the President because she wants to go slowly, but she is planning a very wonderful practical Centre there along her own line which will foreshadow that which is to be in the future. One realizes how the very atmosphere of Ojai is not an atmosphere to which one is accustomed in other parts of the world. It is an atmosphere entirely different from the atmosphere of Adyar, from the atmosphere of Sydney, from any other atmosphere. It is, as I have said, *sui generic.* It is not a little mysterious; it is strange, but while it is both mysterious and strange it is also very, very wonderful, and gives me at all events a sense of what must be the nature of Eternity. Living in the present and so much restricted by time, it is very difficult to grasp what the Eternal may mean. Curiously at Ojai, when you are there, you have an uplifting sense of Eternity which for a while dominates your life in time. You do not ignore time, but you see how much you have been looking at life from the standpoint of time and how different life looks when you try to look at it from your own particular appreciation of that which is eternal. One seems to live in Ojai in the past, in the present and in the future. And that is one of the most interesting features Ojai, which to me gives it very great value.

Now, if you come to Sydney, I have to speak with considerable care, because the nucleus and heart of the Sydney Centre is seated here. He knows much more about it than I do, but it seems to me that when I come to Sydney, especially if I come from Ojai or from Adyar, I come to an entirely different type of atmosphere. All atmospheres are the same in the long run. Everything is directed to the same end, but you discover there are different means of approach. When one comes to Sydney one seems concerned both with time and eternity. In Sydney we have a Centre in which mechanism is strongly at work. It does not seem to matter what you do in Ojai, if you will not misunderstand me. It matters infinitely how you live in details of life in Sydney and I sometimes think it would be good for all our Sydney brethren to be transferred to Ojai, so that they might se that things that here matter infinitely do not matter at all, and perhaps that the Ojai people should

170

come over here so that the things they think do not matter at all they discover to mater infinitely, so that one comes to the conclusion by swinging between those two Centres that everything matters infinitely and that nothing matters at all. So, perhaps, does one reach the true philosophy of life swinging strongly between Ojai on the one hand and Sydney on the other. I am always glad to be in Sydney. I may have all sorts of aimless thoughts or feelings elsewhere; it is not safe to have them here because we are dealing with mechanism, with aspects of mechanism, which you may call forms and ceremonies of all kinds. This is most refreshing. I feel myself benefited immensely, and I feel sometimes the reason why we are dealing with mechanism in Sydney is because Australia has a baby body. It is a very good thing to have a baby body. There are a great many of us who would benefit by having a young body instead of the aged, ramshackle vehicles some of us are wearing. Australia has a baby body. That baby body must be very careful how it is fed. When we come to years of discretion we can afford to indulge in late suppers and to eat indigestible food. At least I ought not to say we can afford to do it, but at least it may not be disastrous if we do. Now the Australian baby must not eat indigestible food, must not stay out late at night, must not go to many shows, must not have too much riotous living. It is still a baby and needs careful nursing, and the Sydney Centre is trying to help in this direction. All the mechanism which is being used is — amongst other work — trying to nurse Australia's baby body into fine youth, in to fine manhood. My hope is that while this Centre will remain the heart, other subsidiary Centres may be formed in Australia so as to help to bring Australia to her own manhood, more quickly than might otherwise be possible.

Let us now look at Ommen. I am not able to say what Is its latest spirit, but one feels there in touch, more than perhaps in many ways in ay other Centre, with life universal, with the unity of life apart from all formal manifestation whatever. You are, as it were, immersed in the essence of things, yet not from the standpoint of eternity, but from

171

the standpoint of every-day life and can live or can train yourself to live more from the essence than from the form. Then there is another fascinating Centre in Huizen. There we have another mechanism Centre of very great interest, of very great value, of very useful purpose. Remember that each Centre has its own work to do. And no work is antagonistic to the work of other Centres, but is supplementary, gives another aspect of life. Just as the light of our Lord the Sun breaks up into rays, so does the work which is a reflection of our Lord the Sun break up into different centres of the fruition of the work he desires to do. I have sometimes urged my Indian brethren to make a great triangle of Centres in India, so that the power of the Sun may flow round that great country. Of course the apex of that triangle is Adyar. We have another very remarkable Centre in Benares. That is another very splendid Centre which should concern itself, though I do not think it yet does, with the intuition side of life, with the side of wisdom. Then there is the remaining angle. I suppose a triangle has three angles, although with Professor Einstein's new discoveries one cannot be quite sure. As at present advised we shall assume that a triangle has three angles. The third angle should be somewhere in the vicinity of Bombay. Bombay is, as it were, the key to India's commercial prosperity, and if we could have a Centre there to influence that particular and very important aspect of Indian life we might do a great deal of good.

Well, let us remember that in addition to all these Centres each one of us has to be a centre in himself, every member of the Theosophical Society should himself be a spiritual Centre, not only as regards himself but as regards his surroundings. Each should be able to gather round himself those who will form with him a larger universe so that the work of our Lord may be advanced. That is our duty. There are different kinds of universes according to differences of temperament, but each one should realize he is a spiritual centre already, that he can make a universe of himself, he being the nucleus, he being its sun, shining more and more upon his universe. And when one realizes that there is nothing else but sunlight, that we are all radiations of that sunlight, that we are all of us more or less splendid schemes of colour, at all events in the becoming, then when we look at our Lord the Sun, when we see how He shines, we cannot but realize that we have no other purpose in life than to strife to begin at our own humble level to shine in our surroundings, even as He shines so splendidly over the whole of His universe.

Let us take from this meeting the thought that we are little tiny suns, shining to our own measure and, as we grow in wisdom and in brotherhood, shining not only to our own small measure but to an ever-increasing measure of purpose until some day we shall shine even as our Lord the Sun. G.S.A.*

The following article is most interesting.

Startling Relationships
Between some Spiritual Centres of the World
Rt. Rev. Irving S. Cooper

Some months ago, while glancing at a map of the world drawn to Gall's stereographic projection, my interest was aroused by noticing that the three centres of spiritual power: Ommen, Adyar and Sydney, were on a straight line with one another. I began to wonder whether Ojai bore any relation geographically to the three. This attitude of wonder, as I shall relate, led to the discovery of a most startling set of relationships between all the spiritual centres known to Theosophists.

It will be helpful to state, for the sake of those not acquainted with theosophic thought, that a spiritual centre is not merely a place where there are spiritual activities. Of such places there are thousands in the world: Shrines, Temples, Churches and so on. A centre, like those mentioned in this article, is a place used for the distribution in a special way to spiritual force to vast areas of country. Such areas are in

* Arundale, George S., "Spiritual Centres and Their Work", *The Australian Theosophist*, April 15, 1929, pp.12-21.

no way limited by national boundaries, but include one or more continents, or even a hemisphere. They are linked in an intimate way with the activities of the Great Brotherhood, and are used to promote the evolutionary development of mankind irrespective of race or religion.

In the founding of the various spiritual centres no apparent plan can be seen. Adyar is an example. While H.P. Blavatsky and H.S. Olcott were touring southern India in the year 1882, they were urged by the son of Judge Muttuswamy to look at a property which was for sale in a suburb of Madras known as Adyar. As the Colonel had long been "observing places, people and climates, with a view of selecting the best place for permanent headquarters for the Society" he and H.P.B. consented to view the property and were driven out to the estate, Huddlestone's Gardens, on May 31st. They were so charmed with the palatial building, the bungalows and the tree-bordered avenue, and the price was so reasonable, that they bought the place. This estate, with the addition of many other acres which later were acquired, has become the Adyar of today.

Or take the centre at Sydney, Australia. It was about the year 1915 that C.W. leadbeater visited Sydney. He was first the guest of T.H. Martyn and then of Gustav Köllerström. While actively engaged in much good work, there was no thought then of a spiritual centre for the southern hemisphere. For some time the need for a community house had been discussed, but no action was taken until 1922 when The Manor was purchased. A huge rambling house of many rooms, its chief appeal was that it offered sufficient space for the needs of a number of young people and several families. The experiment was so successful that a little later The Manor became acceptable as a spiritual centre and it has been so used ever since.

The beginning of things in the Ojai Valley seemed equally casual. When Krishnaji and his brother arrived in California in July, 1922, they were invited, at the suggestion of A.P. Warrington, by Mrs. Mary Gray to be her guests. She rented for their needs a little wooden cottage near her hoe, now known as the Shrine, and there they lived for many months during a time of great importance in the inner life of Krishnaji. The brothers so loved the charm and peace of the Valley, that, with the generous aid of friends, they acquired four acres of land adjoining the cottage, on which stood a comfortable house. Still later, the Shrine itself and some additional land was bought, thus forming the Arya-Vihara of today. In the year 1924, about the month of January, Mr. Warrington, purchased one hundred acres of land at the other end of the Valley (the west end) and established there the new Krotona. Three yeas later, January, 1927, Mrs. Besant decided to take over the Happy Valley property in the Upper Ojai Valley, which had previously been acquired by Fritz Kunz for a school. One month later, the Starland, adjoining Krotona, was bought. In all of these transactions, the only person, so far as I can learn, who has any idea that the land was desired for the work by the Masters, was Dr. Besant when she purchased the Happy Valley property.

In much the same uneventful way Ommen became a spiritual centre. In 1923 Baron Ph. Van Pallandt van Eerde invited Krishnaji to visit the estate. It was then offered and accepted as the Headquarters for the Order of the Star.

In such simple ways were the various centres brought into existence physically. In their acquirement no ordered plan was followed. In most cases the agents concerned were not consciously aware that they were doing more than buying a piece of property, either which they desired or which was needed in the immediate work they had in hand. The fact that all of these centres, as well as several others, were linked together in an extraordinary manner geographically and inwardly was not taken into consideration, simply because the facts were unknown. But to resume the story of the discoveries made.

Some months after I began to speculate regarding the relation of Ojai to the three centres first mentioned in this article, I found in a house where I was staying a very fine terrestrial globe. One evening, I took a piece of string and passed it once round the globe so that it lay over all four centres. To my great delight I found that these four places lay apparently on one cleavage plane. That is to say, if I could have divided the globe into two unequal portions with one stroke of a sword held at exactly the correct angle, all four centres would have been on the line of division.

But this was not all of the relationships indicated. Upon joining Adyar and Ojai with one piece of string, and Ommen and Sydney with another, I found that the two pieces of string intersected one another approximately at right angles, thus forming the sign of the cross. And, most interesting of all, the point of intersection was the Desert of Gobi, where the fifth and greatest centre of all, the ruins of Shamballa, is found!

Naturally the discovery of all this was highly exciting as it seemed to hint at many things, and some time later, after my return to Ojai, I told a group of friends at Krotona of what had been found. One of those present, Hervey Gulick, who thrives on mathematics and adores intricate calculations, offered to check the accuracy of the observations. After hours of figuring extending over many days he finally emerged with data of rare interest.

It seems that instead of one circle which can be traced round the earth, there are two parallel circles lying about 11^0 sweeping round the world, which is at least 800 miles wide, but may of course be more. All of the spiritual centres of which we know anything lie directly on one or other of these circles. The common central point of the two circles is near the Kurile Islands, north-east from Japan, approximately at Latitude N 45^0 30´, Longitude E 150^0 30´. Let us call this point the Kurile Pole. From the Kurile Pole to the first circle, which we shall call the Adyar-Ojai Circle, the distance is 66^0 45´.

It will be interesting to trace the pathway of this circle after it leaves Adyar. Running northwest through India it passes to the east of Bombay and Karachi, but seems to pass immediately over Quetta beyond the Indus River. After crossing the middle of Afghanistan and the south-western part of Siberia, it passes over the Caspian Sea and north-west through Russia, the City of Moscow lying exactly in its course.

176

It passes over Helsingfors in Finland, and traverses Norway and Sweden about the middle of the peninsula. The circle reaches its most northern point when crossing Greenland. Running south-west now, it crosses Hudson Bay, traverses central Canada, passing a little west of the City of Winnipeg, crosses six of the western States, lying over Ogden and Salt Lake City in Utah and the Valley of Ojai in California. Still continuing south-west it traverses the Pacific Ocean cutting the equator at W 150^0, and passes over the Fiji and Loyalty Islands to enter Queensland, Australia, at a point near where the City of Rockhampton is situated. Leaving Western Australia at its northern part it passes north-west through the Indian Ocean to Madras once more.

The second circle, which we shall call the Sydney-Ommen Circle, lies 76^0 45´ From the Kurile Pole. If we trace its pathway from a point in this Indian Ocean 800 miles south of Madras, we see that it passes north-west through the Arabian Sea until it skirts the western shore of the Persian Gulf. It traverses Irak and Syria, passes the town of Angora in Asia Minor, crosses the lower end of the Black Sea, lies over Bucharest in Rumania, Budapest in Hungary, Prague in Czecho-Slovakia, Weimar and Munster in Germany, and over Ommen in Holland. From Holland the line crosses the North Sea to Newcastle, leaving the British Isles at Glasgow in Scotland. Entering Canada near the eastern point of Labrador, it traverses eastern Canada, passes over Wheaton in the State of Illinois, where the new Headquarters Building of the American Theosophical Society has been built, south-west over Kansas City in the State of Missouri, Oklahoma City in the State of Oklahoma, and then across Mexico to Lower California, which it traverses exactly at that point where the Sixth Root Race Colony is to be founded in the future. Continuing south-west it crosses the Pacific Ocean until it reaches Sydney, Australia. Passing over Australia, but not above any important city, it leaves West Australia in the neighbourhood of Steep Point and then passes on into the Indian Ocean.

The easiest way to determine these striking relationships

for oneself is to obtain the use of a small terrestrial globe and a large pair of compasses. Place one point of the compasses at the point mentioned near the Kurile Islands and the other point at Sydney, Australia. Holding the compass steady, revolve the globe so that the pathway of the larger circle may be seen. Similarly, extend the points of the compass between the Kurile Pole and either Adyar or Ojai, and then trace the pathway of the smaller circle.

By means of intricate calculations, Mr. Gulick also determined that the point of intersection of the two lines directly connecting Adyar and Ojai, Sydney and Ommen, was at Latitude N 38^0, Longitude E 92^0 . This point is in northern Tibet, between the Chamen and Atlin Ranges, about 150 miles from Lob Nor Lake. The lake lies at the east end of the Tarim Basin in Eastern Turkestan.

While I was discussing with Hervey Gulick the data which he gave me, I said: "The point of intersection of the two lines of influence is certainly in the Desert of Gobi, but this desert is a vast place. How do I know that the point you have given me is anywhere near Shamballa?" Mr. Gulick agreed with me that the uncertainty was there. Then an idea occurred to him.

"Have you a copy," he asked, "of the *Vade-Mecum* to *Man: Whence, How and Whither,* which was prepared by Mr. Schwarz of Adyar many years ago? If I remember rightly an interesting map went with that book." I thought a moment and went to my library shelves. In a few minutes we were pouring over that much desired map. We were greatly interested to find that Mr. Schwarz's map gave the approximate position of the City of the Bridge as N 37^0, E 90^0, While the position of Shamballa was given as N 40^0, E 94^0. We noticed, however, that the map was very roughly done and obviously not intended to be accurate. For example, the City of the Bridge and the White Island on which Shamballa is situated were much too far away from one another. However, the nearness of the calculation of the point of intersection of the two lines to the position of Shamballa as given on the map was more than striking; it was profoundly significant.

When these two intersecting lines were laid out flat and the angle between tem determined, it was found that they were not at right angles to one another, but that the angle was about 70⁰ 30´. If one were making the sign of the cross Christian fashion, the order of the centres would be as follows: from Adyar at the top of the cross to Ojai at the foot, and from Sydney at the end of the left arm to Ommen at the end of the right.

One additional point was noted. The distance from the North Pole to the Tropic of Cancer is $66^0 33´$, And from the Kurile Pole to the Adyar-Ojai Circle is $66^0 45´$. The distance therefore is practically the same. Has this anything to do with future shifting of the poles?

It is to be hoped that when these suggestive relationships are studied by members of the Society, other deeply interesting facts will be discovered. If so, the writer to this article would like to share in whatever is gained. This may be brought about by sending letters or other articles to *The Theosophist.*

April 19, 1929, announcements were sent out from the Krotona Institute inviting family and friends to attend a reception and tea to be given in honor of J. Krishnamurti at the Krotona Library.

April 26, 1929, Dr. Besant will leave India proceeding first to England where she will deliver four lectures on the general subject of "Life after Death."

June 1, 1929, at 3 o'clock, Beatrice Wood directed three one-act plays for the Star Camp: "The Dark Lady of the Sonnets" by George Bernard Shaw, "Michael" by Miles Masseson, adapted from Leo Tolstoy's "What Men Live By", and "Rosalind" by J. M. Barrie.

---

* Cooper, Rt. Rev. Iriving S., "Startling Relationships", *The Theosophist*, March 1929, pp.602-608.. A related article written later in 1968, and published in The Theosophist by Hugh Shearman: "Some Occult Centres," which deals with the same matter, but for those who are interested in studying his point of view, it may be worthwhile..

Another short article by Hugh Shearman, is worth the reading, published in *The Theosophical Journal T.S. In England* for November-December 1964, under the title: "Dead Letters" dealing with *The Mahatma Letters to A. P. Sinnett*, stating that one out of a hundred occult letters is ever written by the hand of the Master.

In spite of the recent fire that destroyed the beautiful Liberal Catholic Church, Huizen is not abandoned. The church is not rebuilt at this time. Bishop Wedgwood divides his time between Huizen and other cities on the continent, as Huizen is the principal center in Europe for the LCC and from an occult point of view is said to be the European center for the work of the Mahachohan.

L.G. Shuller has started constructions on apartments being built at Krotona. The first unit of four will be built around a patio on Krotona land fronting the old road across from the entrance to Villanova School. The plans call for a Spanish type of architecture and the units will contain unfurnished one-room apartments with Kitchenette, bath, dressing room, and garage. They will be ready for occupancy in June.

This year there have been no great construction problems for Starland.

Louis Zalk reports: The quiet groves of Ojai, with their pathways of "dancing shadows" await the tread of the many pilgrims who are coming, and "the mountains will for a brief pause awaken from their dream of eternity to witness an event, unique throughout the ages of their dream."

The completion of three bath houses and a cafeteria is ready for 1,200 people from around the world.

May 8 1929

> My dear Annie,
> Very many thanks for your letter of April 13th and for issues 1, 2 and 3 of the revived daily *New India*. Raja has already left us for America, but I will forward your message to him. I will myself write to Senator Reid and see Davidge and convey your wishes to them and I am sure that they will do their best to carry them out.
> I am afraid that our Krishnaji is a little complicating our work for the World-Mother by his statement to the American press that he knows nothing whatever about the matter. This statement may make some trouble among the more foolish of our members and no doubt the Darker powers will be quite ready to try to set his statement against yours, and perhaps even the Star Movement

against the Theosophical Society. I should be very glad to hear any pronouncement which you may find it desirable to make on the subject; meantime, my line will be to take it perfectly calmly and philosophically, and to say that while perhaps it may appear a little remarkable that in the physical body Krishnaji knows nothing about these developments, the whole situation is unparalleled; so have no criterion by which to judge how much of the higher plan should be known through the physical body and consequently it would be foolish to allow ourselves to be upset or greatly surprised by anything whatever that may happen. There are certain facts and there is not the slightest doubt as to their accuracy; it is not our business to dispute about them, but simply to note them and to go on with the work which is definitely given to us to do. That seems to me the best line to take, but I should be glad to know whether you approve of it, or whether you have any other suggestion to make.

With very much love,

I am ever,

Yours most affectionately,

A.P. Warrington

June 29, 1929

My dear Amma,

No doubt you would like to know the result of my circular of last February in which I asked for certain funds. So, I enclose Miss Poutz's report. This report, though not very thrilling at the present juncture, may bring forth further responses and perhaps may even awaken some brothers who have not responded at all.

Of the $6,512,60 cash received we have credited $6,000.00 thus:

> $4,000, upon the Sydney loan,
> 2,000, upon your note in the Ojai Bank.

Perhaps you would like to hear also from our venture in the garden nursery business. The nursery was started last September with a capital of approximately $500.00 contributed personally by a few workers at Krotona. With this small capital and the great devotion and enthusiasm given to the work by the handful of workers, the stock of the nursery has increased in volume to the approximate value of $5,000. Indeed, the business is growing faster than we can get volunteer workers to carry it on. I am very much encouraged over this experiment, especially as it points toward developing this community into a productive, self-sustaining centre. If we happily succeed in such ideal, with this and experiments along other lines contemplated, I think our effort will be a very valuable contribution to Theosophical social existence, one that could be followed elsewhere in the world, no doubt, by adapting the right principles found through experiment to varying local conditions. In any case, we here are in effect perhaps doing preliminary work for Happy Valley, for the experiences we gain here ought to be valuable there when you come to develop the industrial aspects of that centre.

We are just about to complete a row of bachelor apartments on the short block at the Krotona entrance with a view of later using them for shops and arts and crafts workrooms. Meanwhile they will help to satisfy the demand for residence quarters.

The suspension of the E.S., as the result of Krishnaji's attitudes, is having a rather disastrous effect, I am informed, upon Section Membership renewals. When a heart has been stilled can a body live.

We are naturally expecting to see you at the World Congress. Do you intend to come to Ojai afterwards? I hope so.

I hope your health is as wonderful as ever. My own is improving slowly. One or two soothsayers, whatever value their sayings may have, have volunteered the prophecy that after my nest birthday (27th of August) I shall be out of the woods as to health.
Ever with affectionate devotion,
A.P. Warrington

Krotona Hill Nursery had been doing so well, they purchased the nursery stock of Robert Perl who was in the plant growing and landscaping business in the valley for some time past, and removed the new addition to their business to the hill later in the month.

Meanwhile, A.P. Warrington, Mr. & Mrs. Williams Mayes, and Mrs. Catharine Gardener returned to Krotona after a few days in the desert.

By August 16, Southern Pacific Agent C.D. Chaffee completed arrangements for the special car, that took a group of Ojai valley residents to Chicago for the World Congress of the T.S. The party, included Miss Marie Poutz, Mr. A.P. Warrington, Mrs. M.L. Hancock, Mrs. Charlemaine Tower, Mrs. Sarah Mayes,

Mrs. Catharine Gardener, Mrs. Alma Kunz Gulick, Miss Eugenie Honold, John Roine, Mrs. Orline Moore.

It was around July 12 that the Chicago Tribune reported the death of Mrs. Katherine Tingley, who had been injured in an automobile accident some weeks before, and had succumbed to her injuries.

It was of interest to find in *The Theosophical Messenger,* Vol.XVII, No.8, August 1929, p.170 how historical facts can be twisted.

> Mrs. Katherine Tingley, although known as a Theosophist, was not head of the main organization, which had been founded by Mme. H.P. Blavatsky, who was succeeded on her death by the present head, Mrs. Annie Besant. Mrs. Tingley had her own cult at Point Loma, Cal., known as the Universal Brotherhood. She founded there a Raja Yoga school, of which she was the "purple mother" of the eighteen Theosophical Societies in Chicago, none are of her cults, but of Mrs. Besant's.

Some called Point Loma "Lomaland," and it, needed Katherine Tingley to thrive. Her death, coupled with the stock market crash, began its decline. By 1942, the land was sold to a developer.

In 1927 the name of the Order of the Star in the East was changed to Order of the Star, dropping "in the East" as its members realized that the days of expectation were over and Krishnamurti was for them the Teacher. As the head of that order, Krishnamurti at Ommen Camp on August 3, 1929 dissolved the Order of the Star. His reasons for this action are contained in a pamphlet: "January 11, 1911, Benares; Ommen, August 3, 1929." In the pamphlet we read: "The dissolution of the *Order of the Star* points to a new beginning. Founding of *The Order of the Rising Sun* was changed to the **Order of the Star in the East** in Benares, India, in the year 1911, to proclaim the coming of a World-Teacher and to prepare the world for that event." The goodwill and enthusiasm for Krishnamurti and his work did not cease with the dissolution of the Order, however, but found a more effective and concentrated expression during the following years.

The management of the Ojai camp made a very important announcement that the property was to be made available for the use of other organizations all over the nation who may desire such a location and such equipment for convention purposes, except for the time when Krishnamurti would occupy Oak Grove each May for his dialogues. (Around 1975, a primary day school, the Oak Grove School, was started adjacent to the Oak Grove.)

On the closing day, August 29, of The Theosophical Society's World Congress in Chicago, a group of artists and art-lovers met for an informal discussion on the ways and means by which the arts might be given greater prominence in theosophical activities. Mrs. Margaret Cousins, of Adyar, was appointed Liaison Officer for the promotion of all forms of art to be a more prominent feature in theosophical activities.

The Rt. Rev. and Mrs. George Arundale arrived on Wednesday, September 13, spending a short time visiting with Warrington at Krotona before going to Hollywood where they were the guests of Mr. and Mrs. Henry Hotchener.

Warrington gave a 5 minute talk to members of Krotona after their morning meditation, no date was given, but he does justify the purge of old style Theosophy, which may have led to the Back-to-Blavatsky movement.'

> I cannot help being impressed with the fact that we have come to a parting of the ways, and that we must make an examination of our Theosophical methods and lives. Many of our theosophist and theosophical bodies are still using outworn forms. The least informed are bringing to the outer world that has gone on just a little ahead of them in human progress, a Theosophy that is not quite in touch with it. They have not kept pace with the world's progress of thought, but still speak the language, so-to-say, of a bygone day. We really must not live in the past as we have been doing; we must not repeat the old forms that we used in the first stages of our Society when as scholars we were working more under the impulse of the Second and Third Objects, where Brotherhood in all its aspects must receive emphasis in daily life.

Theosophy needs to be laid before the world in more practical ways and less within sectarian limits. We must put it in terms of modern life which can best be understood, because it is of the utmost importance that the modern world should understand the principle underlying Universal Brotherhood and that it be assimilated into a fuller life.

If we do not pause long enough to get an understanding of the ways of the modern world, we shall be known as antiquated and shall miss our part in this great world today. Because fixed habits of thought exist in our minds in a highly specialized and academic way, it does not mean that the rest of the world is going to take Theosophy in the same way. Theosophists are rather unique and segregated in thought, and we must now learn the methods of thought of others, and find out how to deliver our philosophy with the utmost practical results. When we learn this, then shall be put into our hands a power to spread Theosophy which we have not today. In order to do this we must learn how other minds work.

Regarding the Theosophical Society, is it too orthodox in character; is it hard and fast and encrusted; or is it resilient and ready to receive the infusion of life that awaits it? Is it flexible enough to receive something a little different from that which we already have. Are we, as members, free and pliable.

Among the peoples of the earth there are vast differences of ideals, experience, and perception and multiple means will need to exist at all times for their helping. No one system, however wonderful could possibly prevail and be universally comprehended. Every phase of helpfulness that can be devised by man or inspired by divinity will undoubtedly be established.

For the theosophists, nothing ought ever to be settled in a Theosophical sense any more than things are every settled for the scientist in the scientific sense. One always waits eagerly for the next expansion of thought in order that the facts or traditions now possessed may be seen to evolve step by step and into constantly widening dimensions.

What we have of Theosophy today constitutes but the outer fringe of the full truth. We have it largely as something in the nature of a hint for our own original thinking and as a stimulant for the awakening of one greatest of instruments for seeing the truth — the intuition.

This following letter indicates the reopening of the Esoteric School.

Marie Poutz

September 14, 1929
E.S.T. "Krotona"
Ojai, Calif.
American Division

Friends,

With joy we accepted the suspension of the E.S., realizing the wisdom of that step. With greater joy do we welcome its reopening. Yet, let all pause before making a decision, ponder over the words of the O.H., and watch their reaction as they realize what strict discipline all will have to submit to from now on.

Is it a reaction of joy, even though the difficulties in the way may be fully understood? Is there present a determination to follow the special E.S. path gladly, as an expression of the free choice of the God within? Well and good, the E.S. is no doubt the life of work indicated.

186

Or will some, perhaps many, rather resent such discipline as something imposed from without, as an infringement on their individual liberty, and will they prefer to follow some other path more congenial to their natures? Again, well and good, for all paths lead to the Highest.

But a large number will probably be torn between conflicting thoughts and desires. Some, while wishing to remain in the School, may fear that the discipline required will be too strenuous for them or will antagonize those around them. Others may fear to show disloyalty to the O.H. if they leave the E.S., — as if we could be loyal to her by being disloyal to ourselves! Under the influence of that fear, they might try to force themselves to do the work required as a painful duty — not as the joyous effort which leads to success. Who can tell what obstacles may arise in the mind of those who do not yet see their way clearly!

So long as there is fear, doubt, shrinking from anticipated pain and difficulty, I would say, Wait — wait until you know unmistakably what you want to do.

All should realize that the E.S. exists for the very special purpose of acting as the heart of the T.S., and of forming a united and efficient channel for the use of those members of the Inner Government of the World Who wish to work through it.

Surely, not all the countless millions of human beings would want to take up such specialized work. Outside of it, men may equally well attain liberation and the fulfillment of Life. So, those who prefer not to re-enter the E.S. need not fear that they may be losing a spiritual opportunity or failing to do their duty. There is no failure except in being untrue to ourselves.

So, Friends, take your problem into the stillness of your heart, and let me have your answer.

Those who wish to remain in the E.S. will please notify me and let me know if they want their papers back, in case they have returned them to this office for safe keeping.

Those who prefer to follow some other path will also please notify me and return all their E.S. papers, including Pictures and membership cards, if they have not yet done so. No writing what ever should be sent by parcel post. If packages containing writing, such as old letters, etc., are examined by the postal authorities, they are reclassed as first class mail, and the higher rate of postage is collected from this office. So, instructions have always been to return papers by express, or by first class mail in the case of Candidates who have so few papers. Of course, the pledge as to secrecy is binding for the member's whole life.

Those who do not yet feel able to decide will please write and ask for more time.

I hope to hear from *all* in the near future one way or the other.

May the One Life we all seek to realize in our lives guide every one of you to the decision which shall lead to its fulfillment in you.

Every your friend,
Marie Poutz,
Corresponding Secretary

Sept 17 1929

My dear Rukmini,

Au revoir, my dear Rukmini. I feel that I have only had a glimpse of you, and that you are a soaring bird now, fleet of wing.

I hope that you and your splendid husband may have a very pleasant trip to Australia. You both certainly left behind you some highly treasured memories in the hearts of some of your friends.

By the way, a letter has just come from Neely. In it she says;

"I suppose you will be seeing Rukmini soon, won't you? Will you tell her that if I don't have time to write just now, I just want her to now how much it meant for me to see her again. She does something to me which seems to help a lot, without my knowing just what it is. I wish she needed a secretary! And would suddenly get the idea that I was the only one who would do!"

Again au revoir my beloved friends.
Affectionately,
A.P.W.

An announcement was sent out through *The Theosophical Messenger* by Annie Besant:

I have a special announcement to make about the international *Theosophist* issued at Hollywood, California, by the Co-Editor, Mrs. Hotchener, and published by Mr. Hotchener on our behalf.

From a literary and artistic standpoint the magazine has been a complete success, and is not only being internationally appreciated but is real credit to our Society. It has subscribers in nearly all parts of the world, and is upon the tables of a large number of public libraries.

But from the financial point of view there are some factors to be considered:

The preparing, printing, and publishing of such a magazine in America are exceedingly expensive, and at present the magazine is not only not meeting its costs, but it would have been impossible to continue its production during the first year had it not been that Mr. and Mrs. Hotchener gave not only their time but generously of their funds to augment what I contributed to start it.

I now again *appeal to members everywhere* to subscribe for it and thus to help me place before the international public an attractive, modern magazine worthy of our Society. Among the approximately 40,000 members in our Society less than 2,000 new subscribers responded to my former appeal, and this makes the possibility of the continuance of the International magazine a doubtful matter.

In Chicago, at the world Congress last year, when I decided to move the publication of *The Theosophist* from Adyar to Hollywood, I did not remember that Colonel Olcott some years before his death transferred the official magazine to the Society and requested its publication to continue at Adyar, and on my return to India this fact was brought to my attention. I was therefore compelled to continue the publication of the official organ there, and in order to do so I discontinued the *Adyar Bulletin* and called the old magazine *The Adyar Theosophist* (to distinguish if from the International), and have been issuing it ever since.

It has now been brought to my notice that unfortunately there has arisen a certain amount of competition between the two magazines. It is quite natural that members should want the "home" magazine form Adyar, but it seems to me that there ought to be a sufficient number of them who would also want the splendid International, and who would desire to help me in carrying out my original intention to make it a modern magazine, assisting in the worldwide dissemination of Theosophy.

American has every facility for publishing magazines on a large scale, and seems to be leading the world in doing so, and I felt, and still feel, that there is a decided place in our

189

Society for the present International and that its influence on the work is much needed.

There is another fact that has militated against its financial success this year. The many subscriptions of my Hindu brothers, which expire with the September number, were transferred by me from the old *Theosophist* to the International. This meant that they were receiving it at very much below its present cost. For nine months it has continue to reach them for the same price as the old magazine formerly published at Adyar — Rs. 9, or about $3 — the price of the International being $4. This has meant a heavy loss to my International.

Again, in starting it, there was the necessity for large outlays for machinery and equipment for mailing the magazine, and for the extensive supplies and clerical assistance that are especially needed at the inception of such an enterprise.

If the members had responded in the way I had hoped, there would have been no doubt of the continuance of the International. The fact must be faced that it cannot continue at its present loss after *January 1st of next year, unless many more subscriptions should come in before the first of January*, or some generous member or members should come forward and guarantee a sum sufficient to carry it on for another year or two, until it has time to establish itself on a paying basis.

In order to assist this plan, we propose now to reduce *The Adyar Theosophist* to about the same size as was the former *Adyar Bulle*tin (32 pages, and on special occasions, such as Conventions, a little larger) but it will continue to be a monthly, instead of a quarterly, *for official purposes* and my own comments and otherwise.

So I leave it with the members to try to carry out my original plan for the international *Theosophist*; and they will have from now until the first of January to see if they can send in two or three thousand more subscriptions, or generous private donations to secure its continuance. If they respond, well and good, and I shall greatly rejoice.

Annie Besant.*

* Besant, Annie, "An Announcement", *The Theosophical Messenger*, Vol. XVIII, no.9, September 1930, p.200.

In the September number of the *Messenger* an announcement was made of the shifting of the publication office of *The Theosophist* from India to this country. In relation to that matter the following was received from Dr. Besant:

> To All Whom it may concern:
> Be it known that I have this day appointed Mrs. Marie Hotchener my Assistant Editor of the monthly magazine entitled *The Theosophist*, to be issued in the United States of America on Jan. 1, 1930, and authorize her to perform all the duties belonging to that office, I myself remaining Editor-in-Chief.
> Be it known that I have appointed Mr. Henry Hotchener, of 6137 Temple Hill Drive, Hollywood, Cal., U.S.A., my Business Manager for the monthly magazine entitled *The theosophist*, to be published in the United States from Jan. 1, 1930, and that he is authorized from the date of this letter to enroll subscribers, to collect advertisements, and to perform all other duties of a Business Manager.
>
> Annie Besant

Sept. 20 1929
31 Ennismore Gardens
London S.W.7.

> My dear Charles,
> I decided, while in America, to move the publication of *The Theosophist* from India to the United States. The magazine reading public there is very large, and the publication facilities very great. I am making Marie Hotchener Asst. Editor with myself as Chief Editor. Henry Hotchener as Business Manager. I feel that the T.S. should be represented by an International Magazine better produced than is possible in India. Please send a very nice article, to arrive about December to Mrs. Henry Hotchener, 6137 Temple Hill Drive, Hollywood California, United States of America.
> I hope to be in Adyar again by the end of October or early November.
> Master (or rather Chohan) M. has directed me to make public the fact that the Hierarchy desires the uplift of India to her rightful place in the Empire. So that the white and colored peoples may be drawn together and racial war prevented.

You may remember that in 1917, as Congress President, I drew attention to the "Awakening of Asia." And the changes in China have possibly hastened the danger of conflict.

I have been resuming the E.S., but re-arranging it for "Those who mean business." Will send on details next week.

With love always

Herakles (Annie Besant)

78, Lancaster Gate,
London, W.2.
October 1 1929

To Members of the E.S.

Dear Brothers,

If you feel that you can try to live the Raja Yoga life; if you can accept Krishnaji as the vehicle of the World-Teacher; the Chohan Morya as the Inner Head of the E.S., and Brother Annie Besant as the Outer Head, appointed by Him, and if you are prepared to give ordinarily an hour a day to study and to mediation on the study, or on the Inner Head, with a desire to unite your consciousness with His, or with that of any Member of the Hierarchy, in order that you may offer more useful and loving service t all the lives that surround you; then I invite you to continue your membership in the E.S., reporting your acceptance of the offer to your present Corresponding Secretary.

There will be no fixed and formal meetings of the E.S., but informal gatherings will be held from time to time, that members may know each other personally, plan out useful work as needed, exchange ideas and enjoy the encouragement of mutual help and brotherly co-operation. These meetings will be called form time to time by a member of the E.S. Council; the names of the Councillor or Councillors in his country will be sent to every member who accepts this invitation.

To co-operate with the Great Plan as far as it is understood, should be the aim of our body, elders and youngers exchanging their ideas as to methods in each country.

In the Service of the Inner Head,

Annie Besant, O.H.

The Order of the Round Table was started in England on July 5, 1908. It rapidly spread to many other countries. The Dutch order of the Round Table in the Netherlands was founded by Corrie Dijkgraaf in 1911. The first report in 1913 show that there were Tables in Australia, New Zealand, France, Switzerland, England and America. There was to be a Round Table conference in London in the spring of 1929.

The records show that in 1918 Krishnamurti was appointed a Knight of Honour (Honorary title for life), and that he contributed to the Journal with wonderful articles of many talks he gave to the young people.

An article from the period that gives a history:

How the Order of the Round Table was Born
Ethel Whyte — Knight Libra

"How did our Round Table start?" Is a question sometimes asked of the older Knights. Well, as one of the first members, I can tell you something about its beginnings.

In 1895 a group for children was started at the headquarters of the Theosophical Society in London, and called "The Lotus Circle." The name came from America, where already several Lotus Circles existed. Dr. Annie Besant took advantage of the visit of an American F.T.S., Miss Stabler, to London, to ask her help in starting a Lotus Circle at the Society's headquarters in Avenue Road, St. Johns Wood.

The present writer recalls one evening at Avenue Road, when, before the Lecture, Dr. Besant announced that on the following Sunday, at three o'clock, the first meeting of the Lotus Circle would take place. Any children of Theosophists would be welcome, and parent might bring them, but apart from such parents "grownups" would not be welcomed. One member of the audience, already in her twenties, felt that this last remark closed the gate of Paradise, represented for her at that time by the house at 19 Avenue Road. Little did she guess how closely she would be associated in the future with the young people (and particularly with one of them*) who would form the nucleus of the Lotus Circle. For amongst them was a young man, still in his teens (known to the readers as Lancelot), and who very quickly became a most useful helper to the Theosophical ladies, placed by Dr. Besant in charge of the work.

The method of procedure, once the children had collected, in the conservatory of No.17, out of earshot of the residents of the community at No.19 was simple. Each child chose, and was regularly known thereafter as a flower name.

(Lancelot's name was Carnation), in the opening ceremony, as the name was called, the flower rose and recited a "Lotus Blossom," a short text or aphorism from some such book as *Light on the Path* or the *Bible* of one of the Faiths, which he had chosen and learnt by heart. A few songs had been collected by our American brothers. Three or four of these songs were sung at each meeting, the accompaniment being provided in the first instance by Miss Ester Bright, with her violin. Later, when she went abroad Miss Ethel Mallet (Libra) was invited to take her place!

After the Lotus Circle had become an established weekly activity, a great event in its history took place. For one Sunday a gentleman, who had recently come to live at Avenue Road, happened to enter the Library (where the meetings were then held) and enquired as to what was going to take place. "A children's meeting" he was told, and at once he asked "may I come?"

This was no less a person than the great Theosophist known to most of you as Bishop Charles Leadbeater (he was called Mr. Leadbeater). You will not need to be told that he was very quickly made welcome. From that day forward he became, and for many years

---

* The writer Ethel Mallet, married Herbert Whyte, the Founder of the Round Table on July 5 1908, and she became the first First Chief Secretary of this Order! (Editor)

continued to be the life and soul of the Louts Circle. Children and young people, and a few fortunate elders who were helping in the work, gathered round him Sunday after Sunday, listening to the delightful stories and the many interesting things he had to tell them. Nor were the meetings confined to Sundays. Every Summer in the long afternoon spent in the country in his company, and in winter visits paid, individually and collectively to this kind elder Brother (particularly after he had moved out to a London suburb) enabled the young people to get to know him as a friend, a privilege which Lancelot valued more and more as years went on.

In 1900 (if I remember rightly) Mr. Leadbeater left England for a lecturing tour in the USA, but before he departure, and with his approval, the name of this Youth group, for by this time many of the "Children" had become young men and women — was changed from "Lotus Circle" to Lotus Lodge," whose activities were organized by the older members, the chief worker being Herbert Whyte, whom Mr. Leadbeater had left in charge. The next occurrence was the starting of a journal — at first laboriously written and duplicated by the members of the Lotus Lodge, but later, with the assistance of a bank of theosophical guarantors (whose interest and help Lancelot had enlisted) published as a printed monthly Journal with illustrations.

Continuous help was given to this by Mr. Leadbeater, who each month wrote articles, and supplied illustrations of some of the wonderful sights he visited on his travels, but also furnished the editors with copy from the pens of J. Krishnamurti, J. Nityananda, Basil Hodgson Smith and others of the remarkable young men who came under his influence. So valuable indeed were some of the contributions generously placed at the disposal of the Editors — such as the original researches of C.W.L. into the after death conditions of children — and verbatim reports of several lectures given by the President of the T.S. (Dr. Annie Besant). These lectures had not at that time been officially taken down but she graciously allowed the little magazine to publish them, thereby of course, largely increasing its sales. Many adults became interested in the Journal. With such help it was possible to carry on the work for some 10 years, the reason for its cessation begin the start of *The Young Citizen* with which, of course, it did not wish to compete.

Twelve years had passed since the beginning of the Lotus Movement, to call it so, in England. Its members had grown up, married, and to some extent scattered (one had become the wife of the future General Secretary of the Italian Section) but some of the original group still carried on work for children, and most active of them was "Lancelot," who was always seeking ways and means of making more effective the work entrusted to his charge by his great Brother. The inspiration came to him to reorganize the Lotus work, and to make the ideal of King Arthur's Round Table its central feature.

Very vivid to the present writer is the remembrance of how, on a day of refreshment spent by the editors of the Journal, in the lovely country outside London, Lancelot outlined his scheme for transforming the Lotus Branch into Ceremonial Order, with grades to suit the various ages.

For weeks to come he spent all his spare time thinking out details of the plan. Service was, of course, to be the key-note of the Order. All such service being offered in the name of the highest IDEAL for each member — The King being the symbol of that Ideal. No limitations of creed or of race must mar the freedom of each soul who joined the Order to clothe his ideal in whatever form he most worshipped — but the desire to serve must animate each one, with reverence to those recognized as greater than himself, help to those weaker, in all kingdoms and courtesy to all.

Such were to be the informing ideals of the work; and such, through all the changes of the intervening years, have remained its basic conception.

The first thing was to ask the approval and help of one whom Lancelot and his colleagues regarded as their "Chief" — the President of the Theosophical Society, who had aroused in them the desire to qualify for service. Dr. Besant not only gave willing approval to the scheme, but allowed Lancelot (the name which he had chosen as leader in the new Order) to discuss with her many details of the work, and further wrote with her own hand a little Ceremony for the admission of "Companions" — the general title of all members at first, whatever their rank in the Order.

For herself she chose the title of "Protector" and to the work of the Order she gave her blessing and her help in every possible way. Nor was it from its Protector alone that help was forthcoming, Mr. Leadbeater, constant friend of all work for the young in body, wrote his approval to Lancelot and helped from that time until the end of his life. Some who have worked in it faithfully from the beginning are still working as "Chief" or "Leading" Knights. The form may change, but the spirit of chivalry and service can never lose their appeal, the coming years may see a new impetus, and a greater field of usefulness opening for the young workers in the service of THE KING.

When Lancelot returns shall he not again pour his love and added strength into the channel thus created?[*]

Later, these two letters from Dr. Besant and C.W. Leadbeater were written to Herbert Whyte.

7/5/1908

My dear Herbert,

I think our idea is an admirable one, your "Round Table" very

---

[*] Whyte, Ethel. "How the Order of the Round Table was Born", *The International Order of the Round Table Jubilee Book 1908-1983*, Beechwood Litho, Coventry, pp.13-15. Obor sit adipsus tinciliquis autat.

likely to be useful. If your knights have a vow like that noble one of Arthur's " I made them lay their hands in mine and swear" etc. "The King" being the Master or Perfect Man, any Master each turns to, you might inspire many young men and women to live nobly. I will gladly help you as far as I can.
Yours affectionately
Annie Besant

June 23 1908
My dear Herbert,
Many thanks for the papers referring to the Round Table; it is one of the noblest conceptions that I have seen, and I am very much pleased with it.
Yours affectionately
C.W. Leadbeater

Saturday, September 28, was the annual meeting of the Board of Trustees of Krotona. They authorized changes as an amendment of the Old Charter, rather than forming a new one, changing the place of business from Hollywood to Ojai for the duration of the corporation indefinitely, rather than for a limited period of years. They changed the number of trustees from fifteen to seven.

October 30, a 60-foot frontage on the east side of North Encinal Street. At this time, Meiners Oaks was a small suburb of Ojai. A comparative wilderness, offering peace and quiet, and a field in which there were no other churches. Meiner Oaks estimated population was about 200 families. Several large fine oak trees on the property made an attractive frame for the edifice. Members and friends literally built the redwood church in less than two months.

12 November 1929

My dear Brother, (A.P. Warrington)
I was delighted to receive your letter and especially delighted to know that you will be going to Adyar. Your conversations with our Presiding Bishop and with the other Bishops who will be there, are sure to be most fruitful of results. My only hope is that there will be no decision to abolish the Church, for I am afraid that I may be in the position of having to decide to continue it all by myself. Of

course, any direct communication from the Lord Himself would be most obediently and gratefully honoured, but so far as my own experience goes it is His wish that the Church be continued. Only the other day in Hollywood while I was standing at the Altar He was pleased to express His thanks to me for my "Discerning loyalty to the Church." We must go on. If we are misunderstood, well we must be misunderstood. I send you a little idea of my own which possibly may be right.

With regard to the gossip about your Centre and about the work of the Pupils generally, I have found it necessary to avoid crediting all I hear. There is no organisation, nor any gathering of people, immune from malicious gossip, not even a Star Camp! So one can only listen and pay no attention, or not listen at all. You maybe sure that not only do I stand by you shoulder to shoulder, but I never forget the very deep debt of gratitude I owe you for the privileges, the very great privileges I enjoy as a Priest and Bishop in one of the Churches of the Lord. Only last Wednesday I had a happy opportunity of bearing testimony to my gratitude to you for all you have done to help me, and wherever such opportunity offers you may be sure I hasten to take advantage of it.

I do not think that there can be any question of reconciliation between our line and Krishnaji's. I do wish he were a little more careful in his utterances. I do wish he did not attack as he does. But I suppose he knows his own business. At all events, as at present advised, I know mine and I know that both the Church and Masonry are radiant with life, and are full of promise for the future.

We must maintain them for the future which will need them, no less than for the present which has so largely benefited from them.

In many ways Rukmini and I wish we could have been with you at Adyar, but our work seems to lie here at present, and there is an enormous amount to do.

With all affection from us both.
George Arundale

November 17, 1929, only those who had been long in the Theosophical Society were called upon in Krotona for an old-timers' night to tell of what they knew of the founders of the Theosophical Society. Mr. Knudsen spoke of the first meeting with Colonel Olcott at Adyar in 1897 and the Colonel's two visits to America; especially the very interesting conventions in Chicago when Bishop

199

Leadbeater also was there. Marie Poutz had fifteen minutes and spoke of the value of the work and the existence of the Theosophical Society. There was no one present who had known H.P.B. personally.

John Forsell was original in his portrayal of incidents in Chicago, bringing in several of the characters now at Krotona.

Mr. Ross did a profile pencil sketch of Warrington that week, and spoke of Colonel Olcott's magnificent healing power and his contribution to the science of magnetic healing. Not the least of the values of the evening was an exquisite rendering of two violin pieces by Mrs. Monica Ros.

Eugene Munson was chairman of the evening and closed with an exhortation to hold fast and carry on the work into the future.

Adyar
10 December 1929

My dear George,

I wrote you at considerable length last week in answer to quite a group of letters, but since then yours of November 19 has arrived, for which many thanks. There shall certainly be a fine Christmas celebration at Adyar, both at midnight and at some convenient time in the morning. The idea that the Church is to be closed must be the personal invention of Mrs. Mackay; I have never heard the slightest suggestion of it, and should not countenance it under any circumstances whatever. If it were ever to be closed, it could be only by the direct order of Him at Whose instance it was founded. "Where two or three," you know; so you and I will carry on, and I do not think that we shall be left alone. The President speaks favourably of the Church and its work, though she does not think it wise to preach for it just now, when feeling seems to be running unnecessarily high. Also I think that she has heard some uncomfortable rumours about Huizen.

I quite agree with much that you say with regard to Krishnaji as sometimes inspired by the World-Teacher. Only last night at a meeting in the big Hall downstairs I had to reiterate, in answer to a detailed question, the statement that I published long ago in the *Australian E.S. Bulletin* as to the nature of the fusion of his consciousness with that of the World-Teacher; re-read that, and you will see exactly the facts of the case. The President is perfectly clear in her declaration that the manifestation is only partial; she is careful in her recent letter to the School to claim only that Krishnaji is the <u>vehicle</u> of the World-Teacher. She does <u>not</u> order that members should study <u>exclusively</u> Krishnaji's writings, but she does ask them to include his works in their curriculum. She no more approves his intolerant and exaggerated statements than you or I do; but she will put no obstacles in his way. She says: "He has his job to do, as I have mine; let each go on with his work without interfering with the other." Furthermore, she recognizes that, as the Lord Himself said, that he <u>must</u> be fanatical in order to make the necessary impression on the world.

You are doing splendid work down there in the Southern Hemisphere; keep it up in the face of all dangers and difficulties, so that we may "unite in forming a column of mutual defence and support." By the way, they are electing me R.W.M. of Lodge Rising Sun of India for next year, in spite of the fact that I shall be away for three months in the south. With very much love.

I am ever

Yours most affectionately

C.W. Leadbeater

A.P. Warrington acknowledges Dr. Besant's letter of October 22, 1930.

Dec 21 1929

My dear Amma,

When we were together in Wheaton recently I mentioned the fact that I keep in close touch with President Hoover in my thoughts and that I even have his photo to work with in my office.

Whereupon you said you'd like to have a photo also.

So I set to work to get one from no less a place than the White House itself.

Well, I have finally succeeded and I am sending it today — an excellent portrait with the President's personal signature affixed for your personal use. In this I am much indebted to the help of our friend Harry Carnes.

With love to you ever

Devotedly,

A.P. Warrington

21 Dec 1929
The Manor

> Dearest Parthaji, [A.P.Warrington]
> You may be surprised if you knew how much I am thinking of
> you. It makes me sad to hear that you are so ill. Perhaps by the time
> this letter reaches you, you are already much better. George and I
> often talk of you and we both send you our deepest love. Perhaps
> Sara will write to me on your behalf and tell me how you are getting
> on.
> Ever affectionately
> Rukmini

Although Warrington was still very weak, he wished George and Grace the best as they now prepared to move by January to Siete Robles in the East End of the Ojai Valley to live. Warrington expressed his deep appreciation for all they did for Krotona, and he wanted to renew his feelings of respect and affection so long enjoyed in their friendship. He wished them a loving Christmas and a Happy New Year.

To close this chapter, we turn to the pages of *The Theosophist*. We find played out in its pages the disruption that reaction to Krishnamurti's teachings has brought inTheosophy. Here it is in reaction to those who are attempting to frame theWorld-Teacher as limited by a "physical plane manifestation."

Supplement
Krishnamurti in relation to the World-Teacher

A good deal has been said, during the past two years, about the limitations which the Consciousness of so great a Being as the Lord Maitreya must necessarily take on, when expressing itself through a human vehicle, however delicately organised and however pure. The introductory footnote to Bishop Wedgwood's article, contributed by the P.T.S., refers to this point; and many will remember the paragraphs which were printed in the Watch-Tower Notes of *The Theosophist* about a year or eighteen months ago on this very subject.

As a statement of general truth, few who know anything of occultism will question this. The thing is obvious. No spiritual consciousness can ever function in its completeness on the physical plane; and this is true not merely of a wholly transcendent Consciousness like that of the World-Teacher, but (in, of course, a lesser degree) of the Ego-consciousness of each one of us. Every human being is, in reality, far more than he can ever express down here; and the fault is not with the human being, it is with the plane. This should always be remembered, since there is a tendency, we think, in some quarters, to regard this limitation of consciousness (now so much under discussion) as being something special to Krishnamurti and as, in some vague kind of way, his fault. So far is this from being (if we are to trust our occult authorities) a correct statement of the relation between Krishnaji and the Consciousness of the World-Teacher, that we have been told by our President herself that the World-Teacher reveals through him "as much of His Consciousness as can be manifested through a human body." The superficial hearer may regard his as not conceding very much. A little thought will, however, show that its concession is enormous. The world's history is full of human genius and capacity. It has its Golden Book of names which — quite apart from whatever loftier greatness such persons may have possessed on planes higher than the physical — have won the astonished reverence of mankind for what they have displayed down here. To say, therefore, that any man or woman reveals down here, in the highest degree possible under the conditions imposed by Nature, such a Life and Being as that of the World-Teacher, is to say something almost incalculable in its significance, since we all know how much (relatively to human standards) *can* be revealed on the physical plane — and we have our list of great men and women to prove this.

The standard which should be applied here is not that of some lofty region of Nature, about which most of us know nothing, but that of the world with which we are familiar. It may be true (any, it must be true) that Krishnaji cannot express, in its completeness, the Consciousness of the Lord Maitreya, as that Consciousness displays itself on higher planes. But if, as has been stated, he expresses *as much of it as is humanly possible on our own plane*, then this puts him, considered merely as a physical plane manifestation of consciousness, as much higher than the ordinary specimen of the world's great men as the Life and Being of the World-Teacher, in the inner worlds, is higher than the Ego-life of the great human beings in question.

This is not a matter which, we are sure, Krishnaji himself would care to have discussed; but, it is forced upon us by the fact that this limitation of consciousness, *vis a vis* that of the World-Teacher, seems by many to have been taken as in some way reducing Krishnaji, as a physical plane manifestation, to a level with themselves. This is not logical. To put it bluntly — any special manifestation of the Consciousness of the World-Teacher, however limited in relation to the full Consciousness of that great Being, must take precedence of any manifestation of life which has not this special task of representation. Too much emphasis, in our opinion, has been laid upon the limitations; too little upon that which is being limited. And this is the more to be stressed, since it s generally understood that the World-Teacher Himself was responsible for the choice of His instrument of self-expression and has planned to do a certain work through him. Either, therefore, the choice was a mistaken one, and the instrument not nearly so well adapted for what has to be done as would have been the vehicles of some of those who now criticise what he is doing — or the choice was a wise one and the plan is being carried out, however little the critics in question may understand it or appreciate it. To hold the former view is to cast a curiously bold reflection on the World-Teacher and his ability to choose His own instruments. It is also to negate, or at least to stultify, what has been told us on the highest occult authority for the past twenty years. To hold the view, on the other hand, that the choice has been a wise and a successful one, is to accept the occult authority in question; while the fact that many do not agree with it is also only a confirmation of what we have all along been told— namely, that there would unfortunately be many who, in spite of every advantage, would find fault whit the teachings of the Great One, when He came, and would fail to recognise His greatness.

It should be noted, in passing, that all this talk about the necessary limitations involved in the physical-plane manifestation of a World-Teacher, is of comparatively recent growth. In the days of expectation, it was the Greatness that we were enjoined to look forward to; little was said about the limitation of that Greatness. Every occult student must obviously have known, in advance, that the *whole* of the World-Teacher could not be manifested. But in the time of which we are speaking (how vague and far away it seems now!), we do not think that any one, however exalted, could have suggested what is now on so many lips, without evoking a gasp of astonished horror. We refer to the idea of the Great One would, when He came, have to be taken with a certain reservation; that in many cases, He would not mean precisely what He said; that His views on certain matters would be tainted by the personality of His instrument; that on certain other matters they would be definitely wrong. All this is being freely said to-day by people who would still claim to regard Krishnaji as some kind of manifestation of the World-Teacher. Perhaps only those who can remember the way in which the Coming used to be spoken about, can realise how far we have moved from the spirit of those days. And it has been one of the greatest shocks that they have experienced, that this critical and selective attitude — this attitude of appraisement, and of deciding what to accept and what to reject — should have succeeded the earlier attitude of wholehearted prospective acceptance; an acceptance (be it said) which was not by any means blind and grovelling, but of precisely the kind which any occult pupil would accord to the utterances of One, to Whom even is own Master looked up as a Being far greater than Himself. The World-Teacher being what He is, what other attitude — it would have been asked ten yeas ago — was either reasonable or thinkable?

It is unfortunate — but the conclusion is inevitably forced

upon the onlooker — that all this questioning has been caused by the fact that the teaching when it did come, was of an unexpected nature and of a character, to many, uncongenial. (And yet, how often were we told that this was just what it probably would be!) But for this, one doubts whether so much would have been heard about "limitations," "a fragment of consciousness," and so forth. All such, qualifications suggest that the reasons for their emergence has been simply the effort to bulwark up an older teaching in the face of a newer teaching which seemed to contradict it. The wiser method of examining the two teachings and assigning to each its proper place in the world of Truth has, up till now, hardly been attempted. Possibly the incursion of the new teaching was too sudden. Still, one feels that among the bitterest regrets, in time to come — when all that is happening now will be seen in its true perspective — will be the regret that, in the disorganisation of the moment, a line of self-defence should have been selected so derogatory to the greatness of the Lord and casting — many difficulties in the way of His manifestation.

It is not (let us repeat once more) the statement that all of the World-Teacher cannot be manifested on the physical plane that we dispute. That is an occult truism and does not need to be argued. It is rather the inference from this, which many have been encouraged (or shall we say, permitted) to draw; — the inference, namely, that the message, as given through the physical-plane instrument of the World-Teacher* is to be regarded as, in some degree, discounted by these limitations; that in points where it seems to contradict the older teachings, it is permissible to say definitely that he is mistaken. This, if we mistake not — and we do not think we have over-stated the situation as it is understood by large numbers of students to-day — is the thing for which, one day, the greatest sorrow will be felt. We have to remember that we are making history now — and history with a very large capital H — and there are those, whose names will appear on

---

* If we accept this as the true account of Krishnaji's position to-day. [footnote in original]

its records, who may well lament that the first few pages of the story were not other than they have actually turned out to be. Indeed, was it not thus last time also?

The serious thing about this depreciation of the credentials of the Teacher (as manifested in His physical representative) is its indirectness. It is like secretly discrediting a guest in advance, before he comes to stay at a house. Nothing that he does or says, when he does arrive, will after that ever seem quite right. Too much of this kind of thing (as we happen to know) is to-day being bandied about in reference to Krishnaji. We are thinking here more of the rank and file than of prominent personalities; but there have been public pronouncements by prominent personalities which, we cannot help feeling, must have given great encouragement to this kind of depreciatory gossip. Let us face the truth. If all that has been said on the subject of the Coming of the World-Teacher, during the past twenty years, was true; if it be true that the World-Teacher Himself selected His own instrument; and if, further, it be true that Krishnaji selected His own instrument; and if, further, it be true that Krishnaji was the instrument thus selected; — then no statement as to the relative smallness of Krishnaji, in relation to the greatness of the World-Teacher on His own plane, is relevant. If the World-Teacher is what He is, and if He selected His instrument with the definite purpose of giving, through it, the teaching which He deemed necessary for the world, then we cannot discredit the instrument without discrediting the Teacher. The Great Ones do not bungle. To hint at bungling, in the present instance, is to dismantle, by inference, the whole structure of occult statement on this particular matter, built up during the past twenty years. And if we do this, what is left of occult authority?

Of what avail to appeal to occult statements about ceremonial, etc., if, on this very much more urgent and important matter, occult statements have proved to be wrong — or, at best, right only in so very dubious and equivocal a fashion that they were hardly worth making?

It is high time, we think, that this truth should be frankly

207

faced. By all means let anybody, who will, reject the whole idea of Krishnaji's being the World-Teacher or in any way a representative of the World-Teacher. But do not let those, who make this rejection, appeal at the same time to the very authority which has, for so many years, been declaring that Krishnaji was the appointed vehicle of that Teacher, and which has since declared, in no uncertain terms, that its expectation has been fulfilled. To do so is a flagrant breach of logic, of which no self-respecting intelligence should be guilty.

Nor does the matter end here. To put some new interpretation upon Krishnaji's position — an interpretation hastily patched up, because his teachings do not happen to suit one's views — is equally illogical. If Krishnaji is only the World-Teacher in some sense which does not matter, and which every critic is at liberty to disregard — *then he is not the World-Teacher at all.* Surely words have their meaning! Have those, who take the attitude to which we are referring, thought what becomes of the significance of the words "World-Teacher," if they are right?

Nor again is it permissible to improvise some new general theory of the coming of a World-Teacher, simply because the theory formerly promulgated does not happen to have turned out according to one's taste. We were never told, for instance, that the Coming in the present instance, would merely vaguely centre round Krishnaji — with so little real centrality, that others might contradict his teachings and still be subordinate focuses of the general "movement." We were told that he would be the enbodiment of the Coming — that he would be the Teacher, so far as the world was concerned. If this was an incorrect statement, then the authority that made it is there impugned, and cannot be quoted as authoritative in any other connection. Surely this is only logical. To the plain man, we feel, it must be evident as such.

It is a pity that these things have to be argued. But they have to be argued, in order to clear the way for the correct attitude — namely, the attitude which is concerned with the truth or untruth of the message, and not with arcane statements about its bringer. Where the plain thinker must join issue with much that is being written and spoken to-day, is with the tacit assumption that the very authority, which is denied in one connection, can be appealed to for support in another connection. All this talk about the "limitation" of Krishnamurti, as the physical-plane expression of the World-Teacher's views on life and on what is important or unimportant in life, can only be valid in so far as it is accompanied by an honest readiness to discredit, if necessary, the authority which first told us about Krishnamurti and his coming destiny. If it will candidly do this, then no sensible man or woman can raise the slightest objection, since everybody is obviously at liberty to make up his own mind on such matters. But to discredit, or to whittle , the claims made on behalf of Krishnamurti during so many years of occult teaching, and then to appeal to another branch of the same teaching in support of one's rejection of these claims, is to do precisely what the common proverb means, when it says that you cannot have your cake and eat it. In so doing, it is assuming a licence, which no sensible person will be prepared to concede.

There is, of course, only one way of dealing sensibly with the matter; and that is to put aside all question of who, or what, the giver of the teaching may happen to be, and to consider the teaching itself on its own merits. The thing, for example, which, to our minds, taints much of the article by Bishop Wedgwood, appended as a supplement to the December *Theosophist*, is the implicit assumption that the value of Krishnamurti's teachings depends entirely upon the degree to which the World-Teacher is using Krishnamurti as a vehicle. This, one gathers from Bishop Wedgwood, is to be tested by "vibrations," or "influence." But surely it is to be tested by the truth or untruth, of the teachings themselves! And equally surely, it is this alone that matters, not the source! We make no reflection on Bishop Wedgwood's ability to trace an 'influence" to its right source, though one would like to suggest that other people might possibly detect such an influence, where he does not — and *vice versa*.

Our contention is that this is not the right way of tackling the matter. It seems to us, if we may say so, a little childish. We are doing small justice to a teaching — whether it be Theosophy or anything else — if we judge it merely how we feel in our *chakrams*, when somebody is speaking about it. It is even conceptually possible that a World-Teacher, in order to discountenance mere superstition or emotionalism, might deliberately tone down this vibrational side of His mission, thereby leaving the thinking part in His audience to judge of the teachings in the light of its best power of thought. In any case, the matter is not to be decided on these terms. It must be decided on its own merits.

Not only that — but in the interests of honestly, we should like to suggest that any pretence of accepting Krishnamurti as the World-Teacher should henceforward be discarded by those who cannot accept the teachings. We have the uncomfortable sensation that, where these two opposite attitudes are combined, they are combined rather in the interests of occultism than of Krishnamurti himself. We mean by this that the reason why the person in question does not openly proclaim himself a total disbeliever in Krishnamurti is the feat of thereby impairing the validity of the occult authority which he needs for the support of some other part of his position. This self-contradictory attitude should cease. Occultism, so far as its leading contemporary exponents are concerned, stands or falls by what has been so repeatedly and so emphatically (and we might add, so recently) said about Krishnamurti as the accredited representative of the World-Teacher; and no one has the right to deny all this, or to explain it away until it becomes meaningless, and then to quote the same occult authority for his views on some other subject.

Needless to say, most of the above has nothing to do with the situation as envisaged by Krishnamurti himself. He would regard (nay, we know, he does regard) all these discussions about himself as trivial. But trivial though they be, the circumstances that have given rise to them have, in our opinion, been occasioning him some little difficulty; and this (if he should *really*, after all, happen to be the World-Teacher, or the World-Teacher's selected vehicle) is a mater of obvious seriousness. The discussions have to be met, and can only be met on their own ground. It is for this reason that the above remarks have been made; and it is our joint feeling of the strong necessity of doing something to clear the air of its present unhealthy mists of equivocation, which has induced us to make this collective protest.

D.K. Telang
B.Sanjiva Rao
N.S. Rama Rao
B. Padmabai
Yadunandan Prasad

G.V. Subba Rao
Malatai Patawardhan
Jamnadas Dwarkadas
D. Jinarajadasa
C.S. Trilokekar *

* Supplement, "Krishnamurti in Relation to the World-Teacher", *The Adyar Theosophist*, February 1930, Vol.LI, n5, pp. xxxii-xlii.

Mr. George Hall, A.P. Warrington, Dr. Besant, Mr. C.F. Holland
80th birthday tea at Krotona

Chapter 4
1930

Sarah Mayes acted as secretary for Warrington while he was so ill again with arthritis in the Good Samaritan Hospital in Los Angeles under the care of specialists. Sarah reported that "the Boss" was improving nicely. The treatments were most beneficial and the doctor saw no reason why he should not be well and strong again.

The annual meeting of the Board of Trustees of the Krotona Institute was held Saturday, January 25, to vote on new Trustees appointed by Dr. Besant, and those in attendance were: Dr. Besant, A.P. Warrington, G.H. Hall, Grace Hall, E.W. Munson, C.F. Holland, Max Wardall, Bishop Cooper, Louis Zalk, Miss Sommer, Miss Miklau, Thos. H. Jalbot, Fred Smith, W.G. Field, and Marie Poutz.

An early visitor to Krotona in 1930 was Clara Codd of London, First National Lecturer English Section for the Theosophical Society. Clara took part in the Cristóbal Pankhurst raid on the House of Commons, and suffered imprisonment as pioneer in woman's suffrage movement in England. Upon being released, she began her work for Theosophy. Mrs. Elizabeth Price Coffey, Miss Rebecca Eichbaum, Emma Ewing and Clara Codd opened the Ewing School of Music at Krotona in 1930. Krotona often gave top entertainment for the Ojai Village with many operettas, under the direction of Mrs. Coffey in the Krotona Hall many times full to capacity.

Another character in Krotona's history was Tess McLean, F.T.S., living in a small house on South Signal Street given to her by the owner, Catharine G. Mayes. Tess, a white-haired lady who lived with her younger sister, and a member of the Ojai Scribblers Club, writing poetry by the hour. The house was torn down and replaced by the Ojai Festivals building.

Jan 17 1930

My dear George,
I had a letter from Bishop Arundale covering many matters. One of the items was that he wished to know wether he could borrow $15,000 at 5% on the Sydney Masonic Temple. He said he already had a loan for said amount on the Temple at 7%.

I have written him, through Sarah, (Mayes) that I was ill and could not attend to such enquiries and that I have referred it to you. I also incidentally remarked that if he had a good 7% loan on that property, he was lucky, as we could not get them over here for any less.

My reference to you is a mere matter of form for I know perfectly well that you will say the same thing; and if you are of that opinion, perhaps you would not mind writing to the good Bishop and confirming my judgement. I cannot conceive of our being able to arrange a 5% loan on a piece of Masonic property 7,000 miles away from here in a country governed by different laws. Can you?

I hope you and your wife are enjoying your new house. I am getting better and better every day.
Sincerely,
A.P. Warrington

George Hall answered Arundale's inquiry about a $15,000 loan at 5%. He said that he did not know of any loan agency in this country who would consider a loan in Australia on any terms. But he reminded Bishop Arundale that the interest due Krotona on December 31, 1929, was an even $600.

214

Jan 17 1930

My very dear Rukmini,

When I was at the hospital in Los Angeles yesterday, Mr. Warrington received your letter of December 21st, and he was so happy to be remembered by you. He regrets that he has been too ill to answer your most welcome letters, and has asked me to write and tell you about his condition.

I am so glad to tell you that he is getting much better. Perhaps you already know, but just after you and Bishop George left his home in September, he was stricken with this arthritis. The Convention was too strenuous for him, but he felt he just ought to go. The left foot and back began swelling and the pains crept on day by day. He tried many things, but nothing seemed to help. The gradual loss of vitality kept him from realizing his true condition until the pains became acute and he reached the point where he could help himself but little; then he knew something more would have to be done. On December 30th, he went to the hospital.

The examination was very thorough, and showed nothing malignant. There was a loop in the descending colon which probably has caused most of the trouble. His blood registered only 59, which did not give enough red blood to fight the disease. The doctor is a specialist in this disease (which he calls arthritis) and has told the Boss that he did not see why he should not be well and strong again.

The treatments are varied, but the principal one is the colonic irrigation which will relieve the congestion there. He is responding nicely to everything. I was surprised to see how much better he had gotten in a week's time. The swelling is going. The doctor thinks that in two more weeks he might begin to talk about coming home; but the patient will not be turned loose until he is sure everything is O.K.

While the Boss was so ill my husband (Billy) developed an ulcer in his stomach. (He is O.K. now.) This necessitated getting some extra help for the Boss. This came in the person of Ellen Meede who nursed Dr. Beckwith for a long time before he passed on. Ellen went to the hospital with the Boss and has helped greatly. I go down for two days a week and take care of his mail. The rest of the time I am doing things in his house that have been neglected, trying to make everything delightfully fresh nd clean for the homecoming. My! It will be wonderful to see him well. He has suffered so very much and so long he is so splendid and the American people do love him. It will be great to see him in the Work again.

He was very much touched to think that you were interested enough in his condition to write, and sends you his love. Bishop George also wrote him such a lovely letter, and this helps so very much. With my love and every good wish for the New Year, I am,
Devotedly,
Sarah Mayes

January 23 1930
Hollywood, California

Dear Friends:

Your splendid and loyal support of the Order of the Star laid the foundation for Krishnaji's work in America.

Now that the Order has been dissolved, two <u>business</u> organizations have been created to carry Krishnaji's message in a systematic and efficient way to everyone in our great country.

The Ojai Star Institute will organize Camps and gatherings at Ojai, California.

The Ojai Star Institute is now the legal owner of all Star property in Ojai, and assumes all its outstanding indebtedness. It also now own the various Starland lots and acreage donated to the order several years ago for Star Gardens.

The Agency Of The Star Publishing Trust, now established in New York, will be responsible for the distribution throughout the U.S.A. of Krishnaji's books and pamphlets and the *International Star Bulletin.*

The Star Headquarters, 2125 Beachwood Drive, Hollywood, will be sold when the real-estate market permits. The amount realized from this sale, after deduction of mortgage and one note, (together amounting to $8500) and the assets of the Order of the Star and the Star Book Shop, (consisting mostly of books) will form the nucleus of a small fund for the continuation of the work of The Star Publishing Trust in America, now located in New York City under the management of Mr. Ernest Osborne.

The remarkable spirit of self-sacrifice, enthusiasm and devotion from Star members, which it has been my privilege to witness during my three years as National Organizer in America, will always continue a most cherished memory. It offers also a fair guarantee for the future, that Krishnaji's great message will continue to be carried forward into the world. For Krishnaji expresses, in words of utmost simplicity and synthesis, the ideals of Strength, Beauty and Understanding which now and in the centuries to come will assist in molding a fine and glorious humanity.

May we all now do our part!

Ever sincerely yours,

John A Fugetman

P.S. The office of the Order of the Star is now closed, and henceforth no mail should be addressed to 2123 Beachwood Drive, Hollywood, California.

1. Please send all correspondence relative to The Ojai Star Institute to Mr. Louis Zalk, Ojai, California.

2. All matters pertaining to The Star Publishing Trust Agency in America, and orders for books, also subscriptions to *The International Star Bulletin*, should be addressed to Mr. Ernest Osborne, 100 East 42nd. St., New York City.

Rajagopal sends out an appeal to help with Krishnamurti's work.

January 25 1930

The Sinews of Life

D. Rajagopal

For those of us who believe that the World-Teacher is here that he comes for the world, the most vital and all compelling purpose of our lives should be to spread his message so wide that every man, woman and child may know of the Truth brings. Before that Truth was presented to us we may have had many occupations, many activities; we may have belonged to many organizations, religious and otherwise; we may have clung to half truths which were the best we knew. But that should have all changed for us with the coming of the Teacher who is the embodiment of Absolute Truth, who is himself Life, and who calls to that same Life in us to manifest. For us there should no longer be hesitation as to which organization we should support, which truth we should enunciate. The Teacher of all Truth is here and for us there nothing more vital than to endeavour to understand his teaching, nothing more urgent than to bring that teaching to the multitudes.

217

And here a word of warning is needed for there are many who say, "The multitude cannot understand the Teacher, his teaching is too difficult for them to grasp. The Goal he sets before us is not too abstract for their attainment."

Does not the Teacher of the world know his business better than we do? He says, "My teaching is for all, my way is for all, my attainment is for all. Throw away your crutches, leave your scared shrines, forget your half-truths, and climb in your own strength with me to the mountain top." If he tells us to do this it is that it can be done." How then can we carry out our duty as members of the Order of the Star and bring the world to the knowledge of the Teacher *By devoting our thought, our energy, our money to this endeavor.* To us, as members of the Order, the privilege has been given for building a bridge between the world and the Teacher. We may exercise our privilege by making that bridge ever wider and more beautiful.

How can the multitude be brought into touch with Krishnaji? First through the centres already established in Ommen and Ojai and later to be established in Benares. At these places yearly Camps are held. Until now these Camps have been confined exclusively to members. From 1929 onwards they will be open to non-members also. At these Camps some thousands of people are brought into direct touch with Krishnaji, and they in their turn make known his teaching to thousands more. But the erection of the necessary permanent building at these Camps is very costly and cannot be met by the registration fees, which only cover the opening expenses.

Our work carried on at Eerde is of particular importance, for it is the International Headquarters of the whole Order and from that centre the organization of the work all over the world is directed. The office expenses are necessarily very high. In addition to the permanent staff of workers at the Castle, there is a yearly gathering of members previous to the Camp, which enables many workers to come into touch with Krishnaji.

At Benares very important schemes will mature as soon

as the necessary funds are forthcoming. In this great centre in the north of India, a school is to be built where the young may be trained according to the principles being enunciated by the World-Teacher. It is impossible to exaggerate the importance of this, for it is those who today are children that must carry on his work when he has gone, and the value of that work for the world will depend upon the measure of their understanding of the Truth which Krishnaji now teaching. The land which has been acquired at Benares is on the site of the ancient Kashi, on the banks of the sacred Ganges, and within two miles of Saranath, where the Buddha preached His first sermon.

Yes, it takes very much money to build and equip and run a school, and its efficiency must depend, unfortunately, upon financial support.

We have the very important section of the work, the publication of Krishnaji's books, pamphlets, articles, and poems. Thousands may never be brought into touch with him personally, but may contact him by the written word. The Star Publishing Trust is founded in order that books and pamphlets might be published rapidly and cheaply as possible. But like every other business organization capital is a necessary preliminary for efficient and fruitful production.

It will at once be recognized that a very large sum of money is needed if the message of the World-Teacher is to be effectively carried throughout the world, and who shall supply the "sinews of peace" if it be not we, the members of this Order, so privileged in this that we may be companions in the giving of the Truth?

Individually we may be weak and poor, collectively we are strong and rich. *But in order to increase that strength, to add to that wealth we must conserve our energies and concentrate on one thing and one alone, the work of the World-Teacher.*

We must not let ourselves be side-tracked by other interests, however important they may have seemed in the past. The master has told us that it is more important to feed the soul than the body, and in Krishnaji's teaching, for those who understand its implications, we have the only food which

219

can satisfy the soul of the world.

Some of us in the past have helped to make concrete "the frozen thoughts of men" to use Krishnaji's expressive phrase, but the living Truth is far more important than the dead shells of Truth. For those who love animals — is it not going to be of infinite value to the animals themselves to make known the Truth of the compassionate One which will change the thought of the world so that kindness to all will naturally follow? It is an excellent thing to work for peace, but that peace which we desire to bring about will be only truly established when it is built upon the changed thought of individuals, for, as Krishnaji says, the world problem is the individual problem, and when all individuals have found peace within themselves, peace in the world must inevitably follow.

I hope that this appeal will not be misinterpreted and twisted to mean, that we should all cease from all activity. On the contrary, we should be more active than we have ever been before but we should direct our energies into the only channel which will eventually help most truly to solve all problems. *There is no work in the world, at the present moment, comparable in importance to this work of spreading the teaching of Krishnaji. That is, of course, for those who recognize in him the World-Teacher, and it is to those alone that I appeal.* I wish also to make it quite clear that I am not appealing for any individual organization. There may be many organizations of equal value with the Order of the Star, regarded merely as organizations. Neither am I thinking of Krishnaji merely as the head of an organization to be thought of in rivalry with other leaders of movements. I am appealing for the work of the World-Teacher to those who believe that he is the Teacher of the world and that the world needs the living Truth he brings.

For them, surely, there should seem nothing strange in my suggestion, but rather it would seem strange if it were not made.

In past years Krishnaji has himself made an appeal to members for funds to carry out his work. All will realize how unpleasant such a task must be for him and it is with the view of sparing him any such necessity in future, that I make this appeal myself. He is giving us of himself, is it necessary for him to invite our cooperation in trivial matters? I do not ask money for him, personally, I do not ask it to support merely an organization, but that the magnificent Truth he brings may be effectively broadcast throughout the world.

Those who desire to answer this appeal may write to D. Rajagopal, Eerde, Ommen, Holland. A yearly statement of accounts duly audited will be published in the *International Star Bulletin*.

At the same time Rajagopal sent out his appeal, Mr. Louis Zalk also issued an appeal to members for funds to carry out Krishnamurti's work under the Ojai Star Institute, which was a corporation now being organized to hold and manage the land at Ojai formerly owned by the Order of the Star, now legally dissolved.

Dr. James H. Cousins, noted Irish poet, educator and Orientalist, becomes the new leader of the Krotona Star Institute starting in February of 1930. Dr. Cousins' early educational activities were in connection with the Catholic University of Dublin, for which he prepared entrants from the high school in that city, himself being a student of the Department of Education at the University. He was also demonstrator in geographical teaching at the Royal College of Science, and reporter for the Royal Academy of Medicine in Ireland.

In India, Dr. Cousins became head of the Madanapalle College for Hindu Boys and a member of the Academical Council of the Universities of Madras. He was also a visiting lecturer at Universities throught out India: Madras, Bombay, Benares, Calcutta and Mysore; and in the schools of Mahatma Gandhi and Rabindranath Tagore. He spent a year at Keio University, Tokyo, as professor of English poetry (he himself being one of the poets of the Irish Renaissance) and won there the distinction of being the first non-Japanese to whom the Ministry of Education of the Empire of Japan conferred the degree of Doctor of Literature. His latest work at this time

221

in India was as Rector of a school of synthetical study where he brought into complete form his life's work towards a true scheme of education. Invited by American visitors to come to the U.S. and give the fruits of his 13 years of life in India, Dr. Cousins made a first lecture tour in the spring of 1929.

Dr. James H. and Margaret E. Cousins

On his way he lectured in the University of Geneva on Oriental Ideals in Education, and drew from the Rector, who presided, the compliment that the lecture was not only on education, but was itself an education. In America, Dr. Cousins lectured on his principles of synthetical study and also gave demonstration lectures in the occidental and oriental aspects of religion, arts, and literature, philosophy and science, particularly the science of education. A list of Universities where he spoke would include Columbia, Yale, Harvard, Boston, Iowa, Nebraska; colleges include Vassar, Wellesley, Doane, Mills.

A convocation address at Iowa State University on "The University of the Future" was published and distributed by the University. He delivered a special convocation address at the University of Nebraska entitled "Education for Liberation." On his way to Ojai he was to give the Fulton annual lectures, four in number, at the University of Nevada.

His keen interest in all aspects of human knowledge and culture, and his experience on three continents, gave him a special fitness to direct a course of synthetical studies such as outlined for the Krotona Institute. On his second lecture tour of the U.S., and while he supervised the Krotona Institute, he was in Los Angeles each Friday to lecture in the department of Oriental studies at the University of Southern California on the general subject of the "The Culture of India."

Dr. Besant, back in March, writes to Miss Julie Sommer in Egypt, that she thinks it would be quite useful to obtain information that might enable them to judge the time for starting the Theosophical University. Paraphrasing: The absolute building of the school must depend upon their success in collecting funds, for the school might be established before the colony itself is in working order. She writes that she is still considering speaking at the World Congress regarding the Theosophical University, due to the fact that the President of the Theosophical Society ought not to give opinions as to any details of the policy adopted in a Section, as each Section is autonomous.

L.W. Rogers writes in *The Theosophical Messenger* regarding Krotona becoming a Theosophical University:

What's In a Name?

One of the letters on another page suggests changing the name of the Summer School to College. I should never agree to that unless it really *becomes* a college. Things should be called what they really are. It is far better to have a school so useful that people are impelled to think of its in higher terms than to have a high-sounding name for something that does not fit its title. There has been too much of that in the Theosophical Society. Theosophists are great dreamers. Constantly new plans for some wonderful theosophical achievement arrive at Headquarters by mail. Occasionally one of them presents a sound business plan of doing something, but most of them are just rosy dreams. One of the easiest of all pleasant occupations is to make a fortune on paper, and every dreamer *knows* his plan will be a success.

Some years ago an enthusiastic young member actually

did start a Theosophical University at Krotona with a great hurrah, got the Board of Directors to let him use the building, organized a staff of teachers consisting of B.A.'s, M.A.'s, PH.D.'s, etc., got the University of California Extension experts on the job, formed the residents at Krotona into a student body, and created a wave of tremendous enthusiasm and excitement that was the wonder of the day. For a few weeks my life was made miserable because I was the only opponent of the great plan for "a practical, visible and immediate Theosophical University," and persisted in saying that from the business viewpoint it was absurd and impossible. Not being an officer at that time, my opinion was of no material importance to the promoters, but they wanted unanimous moral support, and other measures were resorted to to convert the mule. So flattery was tried. A University of California professor called upon me to say that they *must* have textbooks from the theosophical viewpoint and that I was the only one who could write them! Was I going to stand out against the great plan of giving the world a theosophical education? He must have been greatly shocked when I bluntly replied that I had no time to waste on an educational plan that was certain to die in infancy and that I declined to have any connection with it. The chief promoter became my mortal enemy and I was scorned as the one poor fool who could not grasp the fact that a new era in world-education was at hand.

For a short time the Theosophical University flourished and the tide of enthusiasm ran high. Then an awful calamity occurred. At the main entrance a brief notice was tacked up. It simply read, "The University is closed." It must have lived nearly two months! The only echo ever heard from it since was when the chief promoter sued a contributor for $15,000 which he had refused to pay in after he had at last grasped the fact that the great university was really on the toboggan slide, with the gulf of oblivion at the lower end!

Many of the theosophical schemes and dreams have names reminding one of Frank Stanton's poem which ends with the words, "and we find the smallest kind of possum up the biggest kind of tree!" Let us stick to the rule of modesty in naming our activities.*

On January 23, Mr. F.W. Houstone, Treasurer at The Manor in Australia sent a draft for 50 pounds to apply on interest due Krotona Institute. George Hall acknowledged the funds, but tried to explain that drafts in English pounds vary in American money according to the exchange rate. He kindly asked that the interest be paid in American dollars, as required by the terms of the loan. The exchange rate was $4.86 and not an even $5.

Mr. Hall reminded Mr. Houstone that the income of Krotona from rents is not sufficient to meet the expense of maintenance, and it was most important that the interest due from this loan should be received promptly when due. By September 1931, George Hall will receive the quarterly check from Herbert A. Staggs, Cleveland Heights, Ohio instead of from Australia. There is apparently some misunderstanding with The Manor, as they have been paying the interest with a check on a Boston bank by Catharine Gardner. So an adjustment on the next payment will be accounted for. No further payments were going to be made by Catharine Gardner, for Herbert Staggs has arranged to pay the interest on the Krotona mortgage for the time being. It seems that all the letters were passing in the mail. According the Herbert Staggs, he made an arrangement with Bishop Arundale personally and not with The Manor. He expected to pay the interest on the indebtedness from The Manor to Krotona as long as he remained in business or until the principal was paid.

The money loaned by Krotona to The Manor at Sydney was originally $20,000, but $6,000 was paid on the principal so that the remaining amount due was $14,000 even. The interest at 5% is $700 a year, or $175 quarterly, due on January 1, April 1, July 1 and October 1.

---

* Rogers, L.W., Personal Opinion, "What's In a Name?", *The Theosophical Messenger*, Vol.XVII, February 1930, n2, p.38

Krishnamurti and Mr. Rajagopal returned to Ojai in October, instead of going to India as was planned, because of Krishnamurti's health.

George Hall now had three new homes at Siete Robles with one or two others in project for the future, but even at that the development seemed to be much slower than he had expected.

Charles Leadbeater at Adyar, wrote to George Arundale in Australia, that he felt the Esoteric School should once more be the mighty power for good that it use to be; but the suspension was a very heavy blow, and it would take several years to recover from it.

Jan 30 1930
Adyar Madras India

My dear George,

Thank you for your letter of the 8th. It is rather a striking innovation to introduce a new Collect and an insertion in the Consecration Prayer, but I do not see that anyone is likely to object to it, and assuredly that for which you pray is very sadly needed. I suppose that before this you have received from Bishop Pigott the minutes of the proceedings of the Synod, and will have been able to put into force some of its recommendations. You will have noted that many of the points are left optional; we do not wish to disturb local customs in unimportant matters, but we should like a general uniformity. Your hymns are vigorous, though rhyme and scansion are sometimes unusual. They will be distinctly helpful in stirring up patriotism, which is so earnestly desired.

All your activities sound good, but take care not to over work yourself. I shall be glad to help in any way that I can when I arrive. I am not much in favour of set lectures, but rather of conversations and answers to questions — something along the line of our Monday night meetings. I greatly approve of bringing the Brotherhood together, and also the pupils but when they have gone "Star" they are for the time practically useless. We need to establish commonsense in our people most of all! We must try to make the Esoteric School once more the mighty power for good that it used to be; but the suspension was a very heavy blow, and it will take years to recover from it. You might think over something appropriate for a service for Good Friday, in place of the Eucharist of the Presanctified; we shall have quite a number of delegates present then.

226

Krishnaji has been very markedly less bigoted, aggressive and fanatical in his speeches here than he was (by all accounts) at Ommen; I do not know whether that was out of compliment to our President's attitude or whether more of the true Life is now beginning to come through; anyhow, be careful not to say anything about it, for we must not quench the smoking flax. The Synod wished, as you will have seen, to alter the phrase "ever-virgin Mother," which, however beautifully symbolical, seems out of place at that particular point in the Liturgy, but could not find exactly the right title to substitute for it; can you think of one? The general feeling was not in favour of "World-Mother," though I personally see no objection to it. "Mother of all the World" was one suggestion; "Mother of Mankind" another.

I wish you could have been with us, though I think you will approve most of our decisions. I shall be very glad to see you again.

With much love to you both.

I am ever

Yours most affectionately

C.W. Leadbeatear

C.F. Holland, attorney at Law in Los Angeles, on February 5, 1930 had the Articles of Incorporation of the Ojai Star Institute, ready to be signed by George Hall and his wife which was to be sent to Rajagopal to be signed by the other Trustees with instructions to return it back to Mr. Holland for his seal and then sent to the Secretary of State.

Feb 18 1930
Attorney and Counselor
2300 North Gower Street
Los Angeles, Cal.

Dear Mr. Warrington:

Greetings after these several years!

Enclosed is a paper which I believe should be brought to your attention. Last autumn while spending the week-end at the Rosicrucian Headquarters in Oceanside several of us drove down to Point Loma to attend one of Dr. De Purucker's meetings. Shortly after this I was shocked to receive a letter which informed me that their organization was to be operated as "The Theosophical Society" and that their magazine was to be renamed "Lucifer." Immediately I forwarded these letters to our beloved President. Today I have received the enclosed.

That you may understand that the Theosophical tail is attempting to wag the Theosophical dog will, I think, be clear to you after reading this illuminating letter. A former letter described the opening of a Chicago Lodge of their "Theosophical Society" in the Fine Arts Building in Chicago. It spoke of members of the "Besant Theosophical Society" attending the meetings of the Theosophical Society and congratulating them on their superiority.

As De Purucker ways, he is very anxious that all of the several varieties of the Theosophical Society should be brought under one Head with himself as the conquering hero Head. In a former letter he openly stated that the Master Morya had materialized in his office, I believe the number was three times, since the passing of K.T. He believes that the Master Morya is personally using and directing him to the exclusion of any person else as an active leader of the Theosophical Society. I place the matter before you for such action as you may care to take, if any, towards preventing a much involved mix up easily foreseen in this attempt to confuse the public re/the Theosophical Society.

I do not know whether their magazine has yet appeared under its new name "Lucifer." Should they volunteer a copy I shall send it to you if you would be interested.

Expressing my entire loyalty to our Beloved President and to her great co-workers, as always, I remain with fraternal greetings to you.
Most cordially,
Najan A. Courtright

The paper mentioned above was attached to the letter, dated February 17, 1930, and titled "My Comrades On The Path." Stating that it was "Written in the Masters' names, and under the authority that has devolved upon me, [G. de Purucker] this seventeenth day of February, 1930, according to the current calendar, at the International Theosophical Headquarters, Point Loma, California."

The following question issued on May 20 1930 contains Dr. de Purucker's appeal for Union among Theosophists the world over.

What is the difference between your Theosophical Society

and other Theosophical Societies, and what is your attitude towards members of these other societies?

This question is easily answered. I will not, however, point to the differences, but will merely remark that a tree is known by its fruits. Instead I want to emphasize the points of union, the points of contact. I love to notice friendliness and kindliness in human hearts, not diversity of opinion, not unkindliness, not criticism.

We DO NOT ASK MEMBERS OF OTHER THEOSOPHICAL SOCIETIES TO RESIGN THEIR FELLOWSHIP IN THESE SOCIETIES. We simply say; Our doors are open, We extend to you the glad hand of fraternal goodwill.

I want to emphasize the points of union, not the points of difference, those unfortunate and unhappy differences of opinion which in the past have caused the Theosophical movement to be separated into a number of different branches, societies. I want to gather under the wing of the one protecting spiritual light all true hearts. That is what I live for. I am true to my word and I am willing to take other men as true to their word also.

February 20 1930
Theosophical Society
Adyar, Madras

To the Corresponding Secretary, E.S.T.
Dear Friend,

I have to inform you that the O.H. has fixed April 1st next, or as near to that as convenient to your office, allowing for the delay in post of this letter, as the date on which the final reply must be received from those members, who have not yet decided whether to continue in the E.S. or not. From all members who do not desire to continue, please ask for the return of all E.S. documents. When we know by April next how many remain in the E.S., it will be possible to plan the details of the work to begin with October 1st next.

There are many details concerning which I hope soon to get instructions from the O.H. in the meantime, she asks me to say, regarding what interpretation is to be put on the phrase "to accept Krishnaji as the vehicle of the World-Teacher," that she does not mean any kind of a mere intellectual acceptance of him. The

C. Jinarajadasa

intellect should never be forced to go against its natural direction. The O.H. intends by the phrase, that all E.S. members must be sufficiently free in their mental attitude as to *keep themselves open to the life which Krishnaji is pouring out to the world as the vehicle of the World-Teacher*. The O.H. desires no examination whatsoever of a member as to how far he accepts Krishnaji.

She desires the attention of all E.S. members to be especially drawn to the following two paragraphs, which are a transcription of the direction given by our Lord the Maha Chohan in January of this year:

*We wish to warn Our older pupils against the tendency at present unfortunately prevailing in the world to lower all standards and to relax all requirements; and we ask them to impress anew upon candidates the absolute necessity of the "clean life" which was the first of the steps of the golden stairway explained to you by Upasika * half a century ago. They should understand that this applies to the physical plane as well as to higher levels, and demands at least the observance of the Five Precepts laid down by the Lord Buddha, including the avoidance of flesh, alcohol and tobacco.*

This which all pupils should undertake is no easy task; mere sentimentality will not carry them through this Kali-yuga of doubt, slackness and failure; they must develop robust common-sense, steadfastness and self-sacrifice also. Reverence to those worthy of reverence, gratitude to those who have helped them, unswerving loyalty to their highest ideals, utter avoidance of uncharitable thought and speech, unfaltering love to the brethren and to all — these are among the qualities which Our true pupils must possess if real progress is to be made.

---

* *Upasika* means a disciple using a feminine body—a title often applied by the Masters of H.P.B.

You will find these two paragraphs quoted by Bishop Leadbeater in his article "The Daily Life of a Master" in the February issue of *The Adyar Theosophist* (the article will appear in the *International Theosophist* as well).

After three active months in Adyar, which is now his permanent home, Bishop Leadbeater leaves today on a brief visit to Australia. It is not yet certain when the O.H. will leave for Europe, but when she does I shall accompany her.

Your sincerely,

C. Jinarajadasa

The following letter was sent from the Adyar Theosophical Center in St. Michael's Huizen, Holland.

Rt. Rev. J. I. Wedgwood
April 1 1930

My dear George, (Arundale)

I am sending you a couple of letters, received from Andor Steinacker. You will notice that they are both very courteously written, which is a welcome change from the tone adopted by many of our friends who get "Star-itis" and want to resign from everything. I released him from Egyptian Rite obligations and told him that in regard to obligations in the outer Co-Masonry he must write to his Lodge in Vienna. I haven't got a copy by me of the letter I wrote. I think it must have been sent from Adyar or on the return voyage. I certainly said something about Pupilship and as you are his link in that respect, I told him to write to you. Most of the people who get taken this way formally resign from Pupilship, though just a few of them want both to have their cake and eat it.

Bishop Leadbeater told me at Adyar that in regard to all this Krishna movement, the attitude of the Initiates as regards their faithfulness to the Hierarchy was being made something of a test case. I have had a good deal of experience myself in regard to Pupils who have chosen the "freedom" ideas of Krishnaji, and my net impression, especially since this year, is that unless Pupilship is still an intensely vivid, and living and real thing to the person in question, the arrangement made is put into abeyance. I have increasingly the conviction that there is to be no halfway-house tolerated in all this kind of thing.

I am sure that in a good many cases the people who go "Star" do experience some very real inner change. But because that is real, it does not also imply that they can continue with Pupilship which is no longer truly real to them. This man Steinacker seems about the most sincere of all who have had to do with me. I think, of course, that he is quite mistaken in saying that the link of Pupilship cannot be broken, and Krishnaji has most definitely said that Pupilship and reliance on the Masters are "bunkum" so far as he is concerned. He had a personal talk with Gardner last year and told him categorically that he did not believe in this Pupilship business. So far as I can see, he is a little inclined to fluctuate and change his mind from time to time about these things, but he has spoken quite definitely in this way at one time.

I dare say that Bishop Leadbeater will have told you something about the state of my health, but in case not, I may as well pass on one or two details to you, in case mutual friends ask. I have recollections of occasional absences from the body when I have suddenly realised that I didn't know what house or city I was in. I think these absences have been more frequent than I thought, because people have been telling me about their occurrence and I have had no knowledge of them at all. My memory has been exceedingly bad, both in regard to people's names and to the past and ordinary daily events. The doctor thinks all this can be put quite right. It is the consequence of persistent overwork, and I must be very careful for the coming months especially, and during the next two years. I have been suffering rather much from nervous colitis, which is very weakening, and from a long-standing nasal catarrh which involved five operations to the nose. These bodily things are not so serious as the overwork. I have been under a number of specialists, and the man generally in charge, who is very intuitive fellow is sensible enough to recognise that I am much better here among friends and doing a little congenial work, than kicking my heels in some strange and isolated spot. Fortunately things are improving.

I gather from current literature that you and Ruku are both as busy as ever, and am wondering when we are going to meet. I shall be travelling a great deal less than heretofore, because Miss Dodge is withdrawing supplies. We are getting a new Centre going near Camberley, in Surrey, which seems very promising, and where a number of our best English workers are going to have houses. This house at Huizen is going to be sold, but a large part of the estate below the lawn where the church stands is being kept on as a self-supporting Centre. It is proposed that I should come here from time to time. I think I shall have to give up a great deal of the European work, for want of money. I started the Church in a great many different countries, and took responsibility for people as Pupils, because the original promise of support from Miss Dodge for a certain moderate sum was a life one, and for another larger sum, made two years ago, was for another five years. This work has now been very badly let down owing to her breach of faith. But I suppose we have to go on just as best we can. The people here have been very faithful while I have been away, and things are in quite good working order. Excuse such a lot about oneself, but I know of course that you are interested in this place and look back to very happy times when you and Ruku were here.

Much love to you both,
Yours affectionately,
J. I. Wedgwood

Miss Mary Hoadley Dodge was a very wealthy American friend of Lady Emily Lutyens. She settled an annual income for life to Krishnamurti and Nitya, his brother.

April 30 1930
San Diego

Dear Miss Poutz:

Mrs. Mays, asking advice just telephoned giving me information contained in "Day Letter" just sent you.

There was no time to receive any response from Wheaton prior to this evening's Lodge meeting. In fact our Secretary had only just been appraised concerning intended visit of President and delegation from Point Loma at this eve's meeting to Besant Lodge.

Object of this visit is to ask cooperation in a joint observance of White Lotus Day.

Of course, I am but one member of a group. Lodge will have to make its own decision in this matter. The lessons of the past still linger on. Shall advise courtesy, friendliness, due consideration, also prudence.

Did not write to Mr. de Purucker after receipt of yours of the eighth inst. Intuitively feel that if they be really sincere in their desire then they must take the initiative and apply thru the proper channels.

And now the first offer of cooperation is made. Know not what this may lead to. No doubt Besant Lodge will communicate in this matter direct with headquarters.

Personally shall be very happy to see harmonious relations reestablished and thru proper channels. Shall keep you duly informed.

It has been raining all day; an aftermath of the Eclipse.

With greetings both to Miss Sommers as well as to yourself.

Fraternally and Sincerely,

Yours in Their Service,

Mina B. Brust F.T.S.

Miss Poutz replied that her answer must have been highly unsatisfactory; because she had no right whatever to approve or disapprove any T.S. move especially of such an unexpected nature. She trusted that Mr. Rogers would send his instructions.

May 1 1930
San Diego

Dear Miss Poutz;

It was an eventful meeting, last eve at A.B. Lodge. May nought but great Good for Humanity ensue!

In spite of the inclemency of the weather, the delegation from Point Loma, with officers of their local Lodge, seven in number called as announced. In their midst was Mr. Maurice Braun, the artist, also a member of the Inner Council.

They all addressed the meeting, bringing each one in turn a Message of Love; asking that the past be forgotten; saying that as this was the dawning of a new Era, that all members of the various sects of the T.S. henceforth endeavor n behalf of a needy, hungry, world, eager for the Truths, which alone Theosophia has to give, that all unite in the name of that BROTHERHOOD which we profess, and in behalf of Humanity go forth hand in hand to work in the great opportunity now offered.

Furthermore they asked us to participate with them in a joint program on White Louts Day, at their Lodge. Likewise an invitation to come to their Lodge meetings was cordially extended, promising that likewise would they attend our group meetings.

They also told us that Adyar Lodge in N.Y. and the Boston Lodge of our T.S. were cooperating in this joint memorial also; that thru out the world the invitation has become general, meeting with responses.

They went into many details about the work which they are doing, Youth Movement, Young Men and Young Women's Groups, Lotus Groups.

Am sending a copy of this same letter to Mr. Rogers, as I think that he should be informed.

Many thanks for response to my "Day Letter." Apropos, does our Society publish any literature, or magazine for the Lotus members? As a Grand 'mĕre, I am vitally interested.

No more for the nonce, duties call, and the mail man is on is rounds.

Am not a Biblical student but these words ring in my ears, "Be ye wise as Serpents, but Gentle as Doves."

Ever Fraternally and Faithful
In Their Service
Mina B. Brust

May 14 1930
San Diego

Dear Miss Poutz;

Since past few days have sought for this opportunity and will no longer delay answering you.

First to assure you in all sincerity that the Group mentioned in mine of recent date referred simply to our Theosophical Lodge, that is A.B. Lodge members. By what authority could I presume to abrogate unto myself that of any E.S. work? And of all things with any, tho very splendid and earnest students from over on the Point Loma?

Now as to the White Lotus observance, as promised herewith a few words. All passed off beautifully, just in the spirit warranted by the unusual event. Hall was well decorated; members from both factions working in the furnishing of flowers, pictures of our Beloved H.P.B. in decorating, and in the program as well.

Our Mr. Smith made an exceedingly eloquent address. That by Mrs. Clemensha from Pt. Loma likewise was good; Mr. Fussell read Dr. De Purucker's letter to Mr. Rogers in its entirety, and made a sincere appeal to all Brother Theosophists to allow the past to be forgotten and to work harmoniously henceforth in the name of

Humanity, realizing our responsibility in the meeting of present world conditions.

And then on Sunday we journeyed up to Laguna Beach and had the privilege of both hearing Krishnamurti speak and of actually speaking with him.

So much of the unusual; one has to be very quiet and keep a very level head also feet to earth. The pendulum is bound to react and one must be ready.

Distributed several hundred of the enclosed extracts on the White Louts evening observance. Mr. Fussell actually informing me that it was quite correct and that he was happy to be able to thus cooperate.

As much as should have cared to, the question of attending the meetings at Ojai next week is not to be even broached. I will be patient and soberly acquiesce.

Tonight A.B. Lodge will obverse White Lotus day. So I must away to duties. With greetings,
Sincerely and Fraternally
Yours Mina B. Brust

May 14, 1930

My dear Amma, (Annie Besant)
Interest in India and her troubles is spreading in America. The British are good propagandists and they will not be backward in presenting their side of the case to the American Editors, for England respects highly American opinion. There are a few earnest Hindus and white men here, however, who want to see India obtain justice and articles from their pens are appearing from time to time.

Would you think well of the idea that has come to me of placing copies of one of your books dealing with the oppression of the Indians by the British in the hands of the leading Editors of America? I think I could raise the funds to enable me to do this. But first, I should appreciate having your counsel as to which one of your works would be the best adapted for this purpose. If I should not hear from you, I will drop the matter But if you wish me to go ahead, it will be my happiness to do so with the book you may suggest.
Devotedly,
A.P. Warrington

It could be that the following letter is an answer to the one above since it was written without a date on it.

My dear Parthe, [A.P. Warrington]
Here I am, and very much alive. I have started a "House Rule League for India," for I think the plain "Home Rule" (the same as "Svarāj" Self Rule") is better than the new very variable "Dominion Status."

Thank you for the idea of placing one of my books in U.S. Libraries. That would be fine. "India a Nation" would be the best. It is small and readable. Three of our Universities have adopted it as Text Book of Indian History, and even are printing the fourth Edition, so it is well approved.

I am so glad you are better. We need your continued help both in East and West. I feel quite respectable, being adopted in Universities. See what comes of growing old.
With loving regards
Annie Besant

May 21, 1930

My dear Amma,
I had a visit of an hour or more from Krishnaji recently, and when he went I felt that I had been blessed. Indeed, to think of him is to receive a blessing.

But the more I learn from him, the more deeply I feel the very great need for Theosophy in the world, and that the Society should be in time strengthened in a splendid, purposeful program, rather than be treated to a diminished interest as some eager Star people would seem to wish.

Some day when I can persuade myself that it will not be an impertinence, I should like to lay before you a thought which, if accepted on the part of yourself and Krishnaji, would, I believe, ease many hearts and be of great benefit to the Great Work.

We are very sorry to learn that you may not be able to come to America this year.
With much Love
A.P. Warrington

May 21, 1930

My dear Amma,

I have been shown (1) a proposition signed by Mr. Frank Kilbourne to buy *The Ojai*; and (2) a petition signed by 55 valley citizens on Mr. Kilbourne's behalf, both which were about to be sent to you when I saw them.

Is it out of order for me to suggest (1) that if you have any idea at all of ever selling the paper, you could scarcely hope to find a more all-round satisfactory purchaser than Mr. Kilbourne.

May I suggest further that (2) if one reads between the lines, it is not difficult to find that the real motive force behind the petition is a revolt against the same source of trouble as Mr. Kilbourne speaks of in his letter. I am sorry, but that is the trend of the facts that have been laid before me.

Devotedly,

A.P. Warrington

The Ojai Star Institute held the third annual Camp Gathering in the Oak Grove on May 24th to June 2nd.

Trustees were: Mr. Louis Zalk, Mr. C.F. Holland, Mr. George Hall, Mrs. Ethel Casselberry, representing The Ojai Star Institute as District Agent for the States of Arizona, California, Idaho, Nevada, Oregon, Utah, and Washington, Mr. S.W. Williams, Mr. Y. Prasad, Mr. D. Rajagopal. The Management was: Mr. Louis Zalk, Mr. D. Rajagopal, Mr. Geroge Hall. Mr. Ernest B. Obsorne, directed the distribution of Krishnamurti's books and pamphlets. "The Little Book Shop" was located at 1705 North Vine Street, Hollywood, and was run by Mrs. Ethel L. Casselberry.

According to notes among A.P. Warrington's papers, during 9-9:45pm, on June 2nd, 1930, Warrington and Geoffrey Hodson were in the drawing room at Warrington's residence discussing Krishnamurti very earnestly when Master M. (Morya) suddenly appeared saying to them, "*inter alia*: Cease from discussion of the past and the present. Let your lips be sealed concerning that which you know."

Because of a painful, personal incident that had occurred in Chicago at the time of the World Congress in 1929, Warrington had suffered the impression that he had been abruptly and informally shelved, and this produced a shock which had not helped his recovery from arthritis from which he had long been suffering. The Master, seeing that he was harboring a secret thought of being no longer needed, says acoording to these notes:

> "Never for one moment have you (A.P.W.) been absent from my heart or away from my gaze. Rise up, my son; there is still work which I have for you to do. Your life work is not yet ended. A healing ray will descend upon you. This is a holy hill; you its spiritual guardian; wield your initiate powers to consecrate it and all who dwell hereon. Use your spiritual powers through your mind. (Consciously directing them). Live according to your spiritual stature."

Geoffrey questions Warrington on his secret thoughts of being on the shelf. Warrington admits it, at which point Warrington's notes have the Master saying:

> "The past for many lives has bound you too closely to that living heart which is our Brotherhood to permit a rupture in the present. Gratitude is among our sovereign virtues."

The notes show that Geoffrey Hodson sees Warrington as the Master sees him (to some extent as a spiritual nobleman) and that he perceives the Master's great affection for His son. The Master comes, according to these notes, to re-establish Warrington's spiritual self-confidence and maybe to heal deep seated and still bleeding wounds.

June 4 1930
San Diego, Caifornia

> Miss Poutz:
> Dear Co-Worker:
> This letter is the result of a conversation with Mrs. Brust. She

suggests that I notify you of the following.

One of our Co-M. members has a Masculine Maso. living in her home. The tie between him and her husband is stronger that that of many brothers born to the same mother. This man received his training in Europe where one needs "prove himself" before advancement. He has been of great help to our Lodge.

One day last summer I meet him on the street and he said, "The one you know as Master R. is visiting here." I was pleased and expressed the hope of meeting Him. This friend said, "You will know Him by His rings. He is to visit Pt. Loma."

Well I never met the Master at Lodge and never heard Him mentioned there, only as heresays. Of course I was disappointed. The next remark that linked up with the Master in my mind was said while I was helping decorate the hall for our joint Lotus Day meeting.

A lady said; "We were very much surprised at Dr. G. de Purucker being put in as Head and he is making so many radical changes." Another lady spoke up quickly saying; "O, Yes. But Mde. Tingley has had these ideas in mind for some time but things were not ready. She desires these changes and was working for them."

So I see that there were two factions working. Then articles in our different papers contradicted each other and I linked them in some way with the Master's visit in my mind. And in my inner most self I wondered wherein our Lodge had failed, so that the Master did not visit us. Well I thought I will call again on the link that I have and see what I can learn. So I phoned to my Masonic member and asked for their friend. I asked him when the Master was here. He said in the summer, two weeks before Mde. Tingles's death. She died July 11.

We had planned on a little Co-M. social that evening at my home and this friend said he would come. As it happened no none else came so we had a talk, of which this is the substance:

That the Light and Dark Forces are massing their members on this coast to have strongholds when the continent rises from the Pacific. That the Dark Ones are getting a foothold in many societies and creating terrible conditions and that sex worship and its kindred societies are springing up everywhere and that the Master R. was here trying to destroy as much of that as possible. The Rosicrucian Center at Oceanside, to which this man is connected, was also one that is being watched very closely. He was afraid that its spiritual source would be cut off by the Master. This friend said that Their help had been withdrawn from Pt. Loma. That They would not permit the one to take charge that Mde. Tingley had intended. And that this Leader was to turn back to the Light all those that he could. That he had been given a great task and great would be his reward if he succeeded. That he must be true to Them (the Masters but that he has to work alone). He said that the Master did not always bestow a blessing when They came. That under the circumstances I should be pleased that He did not visit my Lodge. (I am truly glad.)

Well that explained much to me. I plainly see the two divisions over there. I have been over to hear Dr. G. de Purucker twice, about six weeks apart. With this understanding I sense that he is seriously appealing for help. This last visit showed him more worn than the first. He says quite clearly that he knows what he is expected to do and asks our cooperation. I think he realizes that the continued existence of that Society depends upon its uniting with others which still have a link with the Brotherhood. He said at the last meeting a week ago Sunday that he was going to ask for a Congress of all Societies of Aug. 11, 1931, to try and formulate a plan by which all could work together. He is having all books reprinted, removing the introductions of his predecessor. He asked for co-workers not traitors and spies also at that Sunday meeting (to me that was a rap at his own members who resented him as a Head). His crown has many thorns. O! How I hope he wins in his fight, and I assure you he is a fighter.

None of their members visited our Lodge last week, whether they have quit coming I do not know. Some of them think we ought to be very thankful that we have been given a chance to join the Theosophical Society, and are slighting in actions that we do not jump at the chance. Well I smile to myself and watch the "play go on."

Dr. G. de Purucker has my best wishes, even if he fails he has tried but no effort for the Brotherhood is lost, so his struggle will not be in vain.

I do not know if all this will be of any help to you or not but Mrs. Brust thought I should tell you. Hope it is not too long drwan out.

Now there is a little mistake somewhere with regards to my connection with the E.S. You speak of me as being suspended. I had in mind being inactive for another year. Does inaction and suspension mean the same?

Your Friend,

Mrs. Mildred D. Mays

A note was attached to the above letter that Mina Brust had sent to Miss Poutz a copy of *The Theosophical Forum*, Volume I, No.12 for August 15, 1930. She mentioned that they were like "Soeur Anne in Perrault's Barbe Bleue" still looking on and awaiting coming events.

Krishnamurti's message was concerned with life, and how to set it free. Bear in mind that the *how* doesn't mean a method, but is an enquiry to understand what it means to be psychologically free.

The following was among A.P. Warrington's papers with no date on it. Although, he was to arrive Porto Rico (Puerto Rico) by the end of the year as the guest of Mr. Enrique Biascoechea, one of the devoted little band of workers who so effectively represented Theosophy in the island.

A Center
A.P. Warrington

I am speaking to you for the last time before leaving for Cuba; and in doing so I wish to clear up a point on which some seem confused. At least, I wish to give you my conviction derived in the same way and with the same certainty as on all other matters which have turned out to be accurate and sound.

The confusion is as to what constitutes a Centre spelled with a capital C. So, I would define such a Centre as a group in a community form, rendering service to our great cause, headed by an Initiate, who constitutes the link with the Great White Lodge, and Adyar to which all Centres are subsidiary. Krotona could not be such a Centre until the spring of 1921. Its head then became an Initiate, [Mr. Warrington] and in 1928 his special co-worker also reached that Status. [Miss Poutz] Since Krotona thus became established with two Initiates at the top, let's see what Bishop Leadbeater thought of it. I'll read from a letter addressed by him in 1927 to a member of this Community: "It is of the great Centres of our movement, and I am sure that under such conditions you will make the most rapid progress which Karma renders possible."

There are many different kinds of Centres as well as what we might call many degrees of Centres. There is Huizen with a very special duty in turbulent Europe, and there is The Manor at Sydney which has a most specific duty to extend for a very long period of time. And there is Adyar which is always to be the Chief Centre, as all others are to be subsidiary to it, occultly of course. Krotona is a quietist Centre, and E.S. Centre. Dr. Besant says in her memorandum on Krotona: "It is hoped by the O.H. that the work carried on at Krotona will create there a Centre of Peace and Strength, not only for the E.S. itself, but also for the whole T.S. in the U.S.A., and that those who live there will remember that their lives are dedicated to the service of the Hierarchy, and through Its help to the service of Humanity. Hence they must endeavor to be worthy of their high calling." Krotona makes no noise outside. It is headed for the wok of what let us call some special training. Future Manus begin the various aspects of the first steps of Their colonization a long time ahead, some times thousands of years. Is 600 years too soon for the 6th Root Race Manu to make some of His preliminary activities seen? And what of the activities of the 5th Race Manu Who incarnates in America before to start the 6th Sub-Race? That Manu has referred to Krotona as "My new Home," speaking through Dr. Arundale. That recognizes the capital C very substantially I should say. The future Manu, the Master M, is the real Founder of Krotona and He has for 26 years been represented by one who for seventeen years has been an initiate. For ten years there have been two and three Initiates active in the work here, forming the basis for a channel with the Great White Lodge.

In 1930 I received a message from Master M. through Mr. Hodson, who was then visiting here, saying in part — this is a Holy Hill, you its spiritual guardian; wield your initiate power to consecrate it and all who dwell hereon. Use your spiritual powers through your mind (consciously directing them)"

Of course these explanations and distinctions cannot be given outside; so, confusion may continue to abide there, but it shouldn't do so among ourselves. So far as we are concerned, let's drop the subject. We know what is here, — the peace, the power, which even casual visitors feel, the affectionate living together, and the extent to which the Krotonians have given themselves to the work. These are signs of the Great White Lodge, nothing less. So, we can be happy, happy all the time. And if C.W.L. can call this one of the great Centres of our movement, we can be happy about that too, knowing that our particular Centre will become whatever we make it. Let us not forget too what the Deva said. We here were not to be ordinary people, but to become keyed up to our spiritual status.

Geoffrey Hodson expressed his deep gratitude to the American Section of the Theosophical Society for the wonderfully kind and generous way in which he had been received . While he was visiting Krotona, he made contact with the Deva of Krotona. Warrington quotes the message the Deva of Ojai Valley addressed to George Hall, A.P. Warrington and Geoffrey Hodson who received the message on June 7:

> The Deva of the Valley says: This valley is a holy place, consecrated to a great purpose, destined to be fulfilled in the future. Great power has already been concentrated here with ourselves in charge (meaning the devas). Our group is chiefly situated below the slopes of the mountain (Topa-Topa) and the valley to its South Eastern side.
>
> There is focused in the invisible worlds a centre of power from the human Hierarchy of which we are the guardians. This hill is similarly consecrated as a subsidiary focus with its presiding angels. Between the two centres there is a continuous interplay of human and devic consciousness. These two centres are represented in the consciousness of the Great White Brotherhood of which they are an outpost; in which they are reproduced and from which their charge of energy is continually maintained at full strength.
>
> We wish to impress the human inhabitants of this consecrated place with the responsibility which they have for the physical maintenance and distribution of these forces. They do not sufficiently realize these responsibilities and this makes cooperation between them and ourselves not

only difficult but sometimes impossible. They are too much concentrated upon themselves and not sufficiently on the work of the Brotherhood. Not sufficiently dedicated to that work, so that its great purpose does not illumine their daily lives. Help them to recognize the forces, ourselves and the purpose for which the centre has been established. A unique opportunity is theirs; of becoming living embodiments of the force and the purpose and the cooperation between angels and men. That cooperation will later be established here, even on the physical plane. Experiments in this valley will be made with a view to carrying forward occult and scientific research side by side. A special centre is needed for much experiment and this is the place.

You (Geoffrey) will be given an opportunity of leading and helping this work if you care to accept it. You (A.P.W.) you are the Spiritual father of the valley and much of our work centres round your inner consciousness which we use continually. Live therefore more in that consciousness that it may manifest itself increasingly in your brain. Our healing power will be added to that of HIM whose "son" you are, that in your declining years your health and strength may be renewed. Think frequently of Him and of us, for gladly do we serve you both. When wielding the power of your station, permit us to be your messengers, more consciously than theretofore. Open yourself still more to the occult life which is all about you, as well as to that which for many ages has been deeply rooted within you (He bows to A.P.W. as one who would say, forgive the personal reference; he, a very high Deva, the Overlord of the Valley). He adds to A.P.W.: "Like yourself as servant of the KING:" and the Star shines forth over him." He continues: "My visit is necessitated by the fact that the human brethren here are not living according to the standard of their ideals, they are not alive to their privileges and responsibilities. They are allowing themselves to become ordinary men and women. If they fail another group will be chosen and their opportunity will pass.

No one comes to the valley by accident. Every one has a place here, a work to do, a part to fulfill, yet the brethren are far from being sufficiently occult minded for the deeply occult work which is expected of them. You sir (A.P.W.) must quickly get well and lead them. Do not fear, they will follow, for leadership is perhaps their greatest need. All those who are not able to attune themselves to this work and these ideals will automatically be ejected from the valley and that process has already begun. Their places will be taken by those more valuable, more deeply consecrated to the work of the Brotherhood.

We hail each newcomer to this enchanted vale, seeing all as children of the dawn. Arouse in them their first enthusiasm, stir up again the fire of devotion, the flames of which are dying down; reminding all who seek a greater freedom that in His Service may perfect freedom be attained.*

A.P. Warrington also received a message from Master Morya through Geoffrey Hodson, saying in part — "Krotona is a Holy Hill, you its spiritual guardian; wield your initiate powers to consecrate it and all who dwell hereon. Use your spiritual powers through your mind consciously directing them."

Krotona Institute of Theosophy is a subsidiary activity of the E.S., not of the T.S. Just as the various activities classed as subsidiary in the usual annual report of the President of the T.S. are such as to the Theosophical Society, so is this such as to the E.S. it was founded under direction of the head of the E.S., who has continually been its President, and has training of its objects, training which if properly carried out ought to contribute strength and steadiness to the work of Theosophy in America.

By June, the two existing Lodges in the Ojai Valley were united into "The Ojai Valley Oaks Lodge." The officers of the new Lodge were: President, Augustus F. Knudsen; Vice President, William

---

* A brief Theosophical synopsis as background: The Topa Topa Deva is called Helios—the being residing in the sun. (The Greeks captured the idea of the sun deity who drives his fiery chariot across the skies, giving man the light by which he lives, moves, and functions on this earth.) Since the earth is the only human-bearing planet in this solar system, the sun-being has a more specific interest in the planet earth. Therefore, Helios has a more direct relationship with man—the other aspects of nature being left to other deities. The physical light of day correlates with the illumination of mind. Therefore mental activity can be enhanced by the cooperation of Helios—angel of sunlight.

W. Kent; Recording Secretary, Harold M. Rider, and Librarian, Mrs. Thomas J. King.

John Ingleman, 3 years as National Organizer in American for the Star, announced that the office on Beachwood Drive, Hollywood, had been closed and the building will be sold.

It was the Ojai Star Camp. Krishnamurti was talking again to people from all the world who had gathered together of the third year in the Oak Grove on Starland. A visitor at the camp asked the meaning of the five-pointed star painted on the tents and official buildings, and the answer was typical of the unorthodoxy of Krishnamurti. He said, "Symbols had no significance whatever to him, that a star, or a flower, or a man, or a woman, were all merely symbols, whereas he was interested alone in life, which creates symbols. One day the camp management might change or remove the star."

From the *Adyar Theosophist*, March 1930, is an article "Dr. Besant Discusses Krishnaji."

> Dr. Besant reminds the members of the Theosophical Society, that Krishnaji does not share that omniscience of the Lord Maitreya, but a fragment of the World-Teacher's consciousness is in him, and his own is merged in it. And you must remember that that consciousness in him in the ordinary affairs of life behaves like that of an ordinary man. He puts down as it were a sort of finger of Himself into a human body specially prepared to stand the strain, a body absolutely pure, a life which for years has been a perfect human life. The consciousness of Krishnaji is merged with that Consciousness. It seems to be a merging of consciousness but we cannot expect to understand its details. Treat him with great respect. Do not force yourselves upon him with a kind of physical devotion. It is very tiresome for anyone to live in a physical body while every one is staring at him. He has taken this body to help the world by it.

In the *Australian Theosophist*, June 1920, pp.19-25, was an article by Rt. Rev. C.W. Leadbeater, "Art Thou He That Should Come?"

Leadbeater reminds the readers that they are caught in the attitude of John the Baptist, who sent his disciples to Jesus to ask: that question. This is He who should come, and there is no need to look elsewhere; and that, it is impossible with our limited intellectual power we can fully comprehend the mystery what has happened or is happening to Krishnaji. Whatever Krishnaji says, we must take it upon its inherent value, we must use reason and commonsense to be our guide, and not upon the authority of the speaker.

London, August 1930
The Esoteric School

Dear Brothers,

This School is one of the doors of admission, for members of the T.S., to the Probationary path. The normal conditions of admission to the E.S. are:

A period of membership in the T.S., the length dependent on the work done, as estimated by the Outer Head of the E.S., Brother Annie Besant. The Inner Head is the Chohan Maurya, whose decision on any matter is final

The applicant must be willing: (1) to try to live the Raja Yoga life; (2) to accept Krishnaji as the vehicle of the World-Teacher; (3) to accept the Chohan Maurya as the Inner Head of the E.S. and Brother Annie Besant as the Outer Head, appointed by Him; and (4) to be prepared to give ordinarily an hour a day to study and to meditation on the study, or on the Inner Head, with a desire to unite his consciousness with His, or with that of any Member of the Hierarchy, in order that he may offer more useful and loving service to all the lives that surround him; then I invite him to apply to the Corresponding Secretary for the Section, who will instruct him as to the next step to be taken.

To co-operate with the Great Plan, as far as it is understood, is the aim of our body, elders and youngers exchanging their ideas as to methods in each country.

In the Service of the Inner Head,
Annie Besant, O.H.

August 1 1930
Esoteric School

To Corresponding Secretaries
Dear Brothers,

I am asked by the O.H. to notify you of the following matters affecting the E.S.

The O.H. particularly desires that the organization of the E.S. shall be a as simple and flexible as possible. The Corresponding Secretaries have had in the past far too much office work to attend to.

The O.H. does not desire a large E.S., so much as one composed of earnest members, who have placed before themselves the goal of becoming some day Disciples of a Master. This was the basis of the E.S. when H.P.B. founded it, and is the sole reason for its existence now. The E.S. is Their School, and exists to serve Their work — this is the essence of the matter. A beginner may have no definite knowledge as to the existence of the Masters; but if he has a reasoned belief that They exist, and if he has an earnest desire to work for Them, the E.S. will lead him sooner or later to his Master.

Once again it must be emphasized that each E.S. member must pledge himself to some definite work, which he does with the object of serving the Masters, and must notify his Corresponding Secretary, sending two copies, one for the O.H.

The Teachings of Krishnaji. As already announced, every member must study the teachings of Krishnaji "as a part of his E.S. study." I do not suggest, of course, that everyone should immediately apply all Krishnaji's teachings to his own life; practice must follow only upon understanding. The O.H. herself has stated that there are parts of his teachings which she does not understand, and therefore cannot apply, but that she hopes to understand them some day. But since Krishnaji is the vehicle of the World-Teacher, and is giving an aspect of Truth necessary for the growth of mankind, and since the E.S. exists to serve the work of the Hierarchy, the O.H. points out that every member in the Master's Esoteric School should try to understand Krishnaji's teachings, and apply to himself any which he understands and agrees with. Under these conditions his understanding will evolve.
Yours sincerely,
C. Jinarajadasa

August 30 1930
100, St. Ermin's
Westminster, London, S.W.1.

Dear Friend,

I am directed to send out to all pupils the enclosed letter, to which I am sure you will give your most earnest attention, endeavouring perseveringly and strenuously to live your life according to its contents. The Great Ones can only help us when we remember that we must pass from our world into theirs; we must not presume to enter it unless we do our best, and after every stumble renew our efforts. The end is sure if we persevere, but the goal of perfection may be distant, as we reckon time. Keep that Goal ever before you, and never forget that "Love is the fulfilling of the Law."

With kindest wishes,

Annie Besant

London, August 1930
The Esoteric School

To The Members of the E.S.

In order to leave the field clear for the World-Teacher in His priceless work, I suspended the E.S. for a period. But the Theosophical Society suffered in its world-wide duty for lack of the organ which is its real heart on our earth. This was therefore revived on October 1st, 1929, but is confined to those who can accept the Raja Yoga Discipline as their rule of life, so as to form a more useful instrument in the Hands of the Members of the Hierarchy Who are willing to use it.

1. Members must obey, as far as it is physically possible, the Law of Ahimsa, Harmlessness. They must abstain, unless temporarily under medical orders, from eating the corpses procured by the slaying of sentient animals, involving, as it does, the terrible sufferings caused by the cattle trade. They must not use the skins or feathers of animals killed to supply them. Fabrics are now in the market as impervious to cold winds as are skins, so health will not suffer by the change. Hands which are outstretched to the Masters of Compassion must be free from the stain of the blood of our younger brothers. (Those who already have fur coats may wear them out, if for financial reasons they are really unable to replace them.)

250

2. In their service to God they must reverence and help to preserve natural Beauty, remembering that He is the Beautiful, as well as the Good and the True.

3. They must abstain from all stimulating and stupefying drugs such as alcohol or tobacco.

4. They must strive strenuously to preserve physical, emotional, and mental purity.

5. They must be engaged in some unselfish service of others as a regular part of their life, remembering that "the unselfish service of the world is the Heart of the honour of Our Brotherhood," and that "service in the little things of daily life counts as much with Us as the so-called greater services."

Every Member of the E.S. is, of course, expected to be a good citizen of his Motherland, and to manifest a constructive and co-operative spirit in both National and International affairs.

As the duties of the good citizen are not as well known as they should be, I add this from an oration delivered by Pythagoras (the Chohan Kuthumi) in the Greek Temple at Naxos (Taormina) in Sicily.

Hear His words:

"Listen, my children, to what the State should be to the good citizen. It is more than father or mother, it is more than husband or wife, it is more than child or friend. The State is the mother and father of all, is the wife of the husband, and the husband of the wife. The family is good, and good is the joy of the man in wife and son. But greater is the State, which is the Protector of all, without which the home would be ravaged and destroyed. Dear to the good man is the honour of the woman who bore him, dear the honour of the wife, whose children cling to his knees; but dearer should be the honour of the State that keeps safe the wife and the child. It is the State from which comes all that makes your life prosperous, and gives you beauty and safety. Within the State are built up the Arts, which make the difference between the barbarian and the man. If the brave man dies gladly for the hearthstone, far more gladly should he die for the State."

6. Every Member is expected to study the writings of Krishnaji as a part of his E.S. study.

7. Every Member must keep his body in health by perfect cleanliness, by clean diet, by exercise, and by the control necessary for its health and activity, remembering that these depend largely on control of the passions, emotions and thoughts, and that serenity and steady, quiet cheerfulness are necessary to health.

To physical cleanliness must be added complete abstinence from sexual relationship outside the married life.

8. He should abstain from frivolous and useless chatter, and cultivate the habit of silence; but so as not to attract attention, or to give the appearance of indifference to the interests of others.

If the daily obedience to these rules of life is too great a task, then he should not enter the life of the Raja Yoga.

Annie Besant,
Outer Head

The members of the E.S. school were passing through a strenuous period of readjustment since its reopening; they were all on test. As Miss Poutz reminded them, it did not decry practices and mental exercises. But it saw the study of E.S. material and the like, in much the same way as the use of mantrams, incense, etc., useful for a time, but requiring to be left behind as unessential when a certain point was reached, lest they become fetters rather than useful tools. She reminded them that the Masters need servers, and are watching Their School; how many of them will They find *meaning business?*

Since its reopening, the former conditions of membership were replaced with the following and which all E.S. members were required to accept, if they wished to remain in the School.

A.P. Warrington was still staying at the Paso Robles Hot Springs California, where the waters, baths and climate excel.

Harold Kirk and his little family were asked to move into the home of George and Grace Hall at Krotona since the house was likely to run on in a state of vacancy till winter.

Before A.P. Warrington returned home for his Birthday, Sarah C. Mayes is asked the Krotonians to give him something useful, and something he needed was a comfortable couch to lounge on in his study. She ordered an all metal, double coil spring legget couch bed with mattress. The cost was $21.25 from the Rogers Furniture store in Ventura.

August 21 1930

My dear George,

At your convenience, and as soon as you can make up a statement of what is due by the Nursery for water, you can come and have a conference with Mrs. Hancock, Mrs. Couch and myself on the subject of the Nursery; as I now have in my possession all their statements.

I have been thinking about the Lodges here in the Valley. I have never asked you what you are doing for them to make it easy for them to meet at Krotona, and at the same time make them feel Krotona's friendly interest in them and desire to cooperate with them, and even to contribute something to them in their struggle for existence. Offering them a meeting place is the least we could do. What would you think of the plan that Miss Poutz has always observed of having a contribution box for voluntary contributions for those who attend, as they go out? We cannot do too much to avoid prejudices and unfriendly feelings on the part of our own people, can we?
Sincerely,
A.P.W.

September 1930
E.S.T.

I regret to learn that a sentence of mine — a quotation from a conversation some of us had with the O.H. — has been entirely misunderstood. I refer to some words spoken by the O.H. last year.

She said: "Krishnaji should be their study." This I find has been understood as meaning that there should be no other study than Krishnaji's teaching! And some people have in consequence left the School! If the fault is mine I regret it, and would ask you all, if you know of any such person, to explain to him the misunderstanding and ask him to write to me, if he desires still to retain his membership in the E.S.

I shall also notify members whom I know were influenced by the remark. The School was closed in order "to leave the field clear for the World-Teacher in his priceless work" — the O.H.'s words. I never for one moment thought one should drop any studying order to study Krishnaji. He would be horrified I know to think that his ideas were being pressed upon any unwilling heart. As all of you should now know, he desires us all to judge for ourselves what we

253

do, what we feel, what we think — also he asks us not to judge another, for, by such judgment, we take way his freedom. I delight in Krishnaji's teaching. My heart has always been free, but I have more happiness in my freedom now and more understanding than ever before.

Another point: pray read carefully the O.H.'s words with regard to the Karma Discipline. This is not made for the *convenience* of members.

The O.H. herself will make exceptions to the R.Y. rule. It is distressing to find how many people who were Raja Yoga, and therefore vegetarian, before the School closed, took to meat again when the *outer discipline* was removed. Had they no ideal then of brotherhood to animals? Were they *only* bound by an outer "authority"? This proves how true are the words of Krishnaji when he urges us to live by *self-discipline*, not by an outer law imposed by another.

I beg of you to consider this matter earnestly. It touches so many points in our daily life. An outer discipline, a strict rule is meant for those not accustomed to rule themselves.

The one hour's study (Shravakas will only be asked to do half an hour) referred to by the O.H. may be arranged as convenient to students; for instance, a student may find it more convenient to do his study in two periods of half an hour each, or three of twenty minutes.

Students should understand that the O.H. desires to leave them all great freedom in their study and their work, trusting that that they will take a big view of their duties.

So, my brothers, we enter upon a new period of work in the E.S. — may we grow big and strong, tender and true.

Your friend,

Esther Bright

Mr. Jinarajadasa asked A.P. Warrington to quote the following extract from his letter of March 20th, 1930, to the Corresponding Secretaries:

"The O.H. asks me to say, regarding what interpretation is to be put on the phrase 'to accept Krishnaji as the vehicle of the World-Teacher,' that she does not mean any kind of mere intellectual acceptance of him. The intellect should never be forced to go against its natural direction. The O.H. intends by the phrase, that all E.S. members must be sufficiently free in their mental attitude as to *keep themselves open to the life which Krishnaji is pouring out to the world as the vehicle of the World-Teacher.* The O.H. desires no examination whatsoever of a member as to how far he accepts Krishnaji."

Around August 1, 1930, C. Jinarajadasa was requested by the O.H., Dr. Besant, to notify the Corresponding Secretaries regarding matters affecting the E.S. Dr. Besant wants the E.S. to be as simple, flexible and not a large body, but composed of earnest members, who have placed before themselves the goal of becoming some day Disciples of a Master.

As already announced, every member must study the teachings of Krishnamurti "as a apart of his E.S. study." It was not suggested that everyone should immediately apply all Krishnamurti's teachings to his own life, practice must follow only upon understanding. Since Dr. Besant states that Krishnamurti is the vehicle of the World-Teacher, and is giving an aspect of Truth necessary for the growth of mankind, and since the E.S. exists to serve the work of the Hierarchy, she points out that every member in the Master's Esoteric School should try to understand Krishnamurti's teachings, even though she does not understand all of it her self, and therefore cannot apply that part of it, but that she hopes to understand them some day.

Marie Hotchener reported that she was at Adyar when Krishnamurti was found, and when she attended one of his meetings, she reported: "I was at a recent meeting when he (Krishnaji) said that he wrote *At the Feet of the Master* as a child, and that later he found he must always return from the Master's feet unto himself. But that, to me, does not preclude Theosophical service in the long path between the feet of the Master and one's own."

Becoming some day Disciples of a Master was the basis of the E.S. when H.P.B. founded it; the sole reason for its existence was to learn to live the Raja Yoga life.

Marie continued to report, that it seems to her that Krishanmurti until quite recently, gave Theosophical teachings. She refers one to read in *The Star* magazine, published in America, for December, 1929, his article, "The Spark and the Flame," where he speaks of the personality, of the three bodies and the beings in them, the elementals, and how one should deal with them. She claims this is Theosophical teaching, most beautifully expressed, and in perfect harmony with their literature.

Unity; or Separation?
by A.P. Warrington
(Vice-President, Theosophical Society)

It does not require a very extended observation to enable one to perceive that the Theosophical Society at this time is beset with evidences of a near crisis quite as serious as any it has ever had. In former crises there had been somebody who was made the object of blame and unbrotherly treatment, but in the present the differences existing are created chiefly by a form of idealism, making it more deep-seated and vital. At present even old and devoted memberships are being cancelled and newly placed enthusiasms are being aroused. Those who are less wise have entered into their change of attitude with a fanatical zeal so one-pointed as to cause them to feel that every attitude, thought, or opinion that does not harmonize with their new one is wrong, unnatural and even an affront to the newly chosen leader. They are turning their backs upon things they once regarded as sacred, and in some cases even with feelings of antagonism and resentment against hands that gave them generous assistance in the past. This is what many of the less wise are doing even now.

Naturally this state of affairs has aroused in the more stable members of the Society feelings of amazement and even of alarm for the future welfare of the movement which has meant so much to them and still stands as the most important undertaking known to them in the world today.

It is not my purpose in this brief discussion to touch upon the general controversial topics which have arisen in this connection, but definitely to avoid them for reasons best known to myself. But what I do wish to remind my readers concerns rather the very great importance of the Theosophical Society to the generations of the future and how, in my belief, the new evangel which is being spread to a worldwide extent, in one of its aspects, should be allowed naturally to strengthen Theosophical idealism rather than otherwise.

During the past twenty yeas I have seen something of the very remarkable young Brahmin of whom we affectionately speak as Krishnaji, and who in the course of the work he happily feels called upon to do, has perhaps unwittingly been made the indirect cause of much of the disturbance in the Society, to which I have referred. Although during this period I only came into touch with him, for the most part, on certain widely separated occasions, yet there was a period — a period which no doubt may sometime be known as the most significant in his career — when my relationship to him was distinctly more than casual. The intimacy of that relationship enabled me to gain an advantage in a certain understanding of Krishnaji which few have had the privilege of enjoying. Thus I feel that perhaps I ought to be in a position to recognize whether or not there has ever been in him any modification of personality that would be significant, and why.

Now, with that as my background, I would respectfully venture to state that subsequently to the period referred to (the nature of which I at this time am not in a position to disclose) I *have* observed a difference in Krishnaji; there has been an atmosphere, a wealth of spiritual feeling about him which was not observable before, and which has had the effect upon me of arousing my deepest affections. I say deepest because there has seemed to be nothing peculiarly personal about the emotion, but rather something, shall I say, universal. Indeed, there has scarcely been a meeting between Krishnaji and myself that did not afford to me this same rare and valued experience. Thus from personal experience I have come to recognize a new and uplifting power about him that has had a greatly appreciated value in my life.

257

And I have likewise observed the play of this new power over audiences addressed by Krishnaji. I have seen the people sitting with rapt attention and listening in a kind of ecstasy to words which, had they been expressed by another of wholly different degree, might never have bound them to such stillness and absorption; and I have asked myself while analyzing the thoughts Krishnaji was then expressing; "What is it that holds them so vitally?" And answering the question out of my own experience, I could but say: "It is what he *is*; it is the Life that he brings and pours out in such abundance." While many have said they did not understand him, yet there have been others who said they did. No doubt there was *an* understanding. Many of us have felt that way, and when we got away, were hard pressed to explain even feebly what that understanding was. The upliftment felt showed that we were under the influence of a compelling, beneficent force. Would it be out of place to compare it with that which Christian devotees feel at the elevation of the Host in the Eucharist; or with other ritualistic activities wherein conditions are made favourable for the abundant outpouring of Life usually called blessings?

It is because of my experience and observations that I have felt that the constructive side of Krishnaji's work might lie chiefly in his ability to make Life more abundant for the world at large, and for those nearest him in particular, accomplishing this as a vehicle or channel for the Life; and that, no matter how wise his teaching might be (and I could not discount a teaching that has been so uplifting to me) it was not what he said so much as what he *was* that gripped his hearers, for after all his teaching is, for the most part, a much neglected and very important side of Theosophy itself, and, therefore, theoretically, at least, is not unfamiliar to theosophist, especially to those who have been students of Buddhism. Furthermore, one can see that certain statements of his have been construed even in a disruptive way, as witness the present controversy in Theosophical ranks over the inclusion of our Society with ritualistic and creedal orders upon which he has placed the mark of spiritual futility.

Although there is much that I could say in discussing this side of the question, I shall not do so, for I am not particularly interested in controversial details; I am willing to see those who *are* to carry on to the full limit of their sincerity, and I presume there will be many such. For my own part, I prefer to wait and discover what the teaching will be, say, ten or more years hence. Besides, my interest is really confined to that mystical manifestation of Life to which I have adverted, and for which Krishnaji is showing himself to be, in my humble judgment, a most wonderful channel. He brings to the world, if not a new concept, indeed a renewal of an ancient concept that beings highly developed in spirituality and constitution in their own person a veritable River of Life do sometimes exist on earth.

It is this that intrigues me. For it is this that unites, stimulates and vivifies one's finer qualities, whereas, socially considered at least, intellectual athletics, theological discussions, scriptural exegesis, and in general critical analysis, so universally practised in this old world of ours, have seldom escaped a harvest of division, separation and pain, since few have yet learned to stand up happily under vital differences of fundamental opinion. If they had, those who are leaving the Society because of a changed viewpoint, would not be separating themselves and criticizing their old friends for not following directly in their footsteps. Many are quoted as saying: "I really can't understand how you can do other than what I am doing." Truly it has been said that the mind is the slayer of the Real, for the Real in this case is our fundamental solidarity, symbolized and expressed by the unity of our hearts and the tolerance of our minds; through these there must constantly flow that River of Life when we can place ourselves in righteous relationship thereto.

One may ask why I lay so much stress upon the value of Krishnaji's presence and do not place equal emphasis upon what he says: how I can draw a distinction between the two, he being the origin and source of both? Perhaps I cannot answer better than to quote the reply I gave recently to a friend who was interested to know my opinion of the situation that is causing so much discussion. I then said: "I feel no doubt that Krishnaji's inner self during the present life has become merged with Spiritual Reality, and that thus his Spiritual Self and that Reality are eternally one, so that merely to be in his presence is to be blessed. But I doubt that Krishnaji's outer self, which belongs to the world of time, has succeeded as yet in continually manifesting that inner reality, however fully this may be achieved at time goes on. The art of expressing intellectually in a time fashioned structure that which is real and eternal is a stupendous feat on the part of the personality, and requires at least time for its perfection. Would not the critic do better, therefore, if he waited for the natural law of time to assert itself in the time-body before expecting it to manifest truly the divine miracle within?"

I ventured the above personal opinion with a great deal of diffidence, as I really never feel that I am competent to judge one who is manifestly so greatly my superior; and yet, Krishnaji himself has urged us to criticize him; "Tear me to pieces," he would often say in his eagerness to have us understand him from the standpoint of our own individual uniqueness. Well, I have merely taken advantage of that privilege and have expressed nothing more than an opinion, subject to fluctuation according as my understanding may grow deeper with time.

In view of all the above I have, for the time being at least, come to relate the mystery of the great and beautiful psychological outpouring that flows through Krishnaji with the heart side of nature, or the "direct path," understood by some as the Path of the Mystic; and to relate some of the teaching he gives (surely not all) with the head doctrine, or the "indirect path," sometimes called the Path of the Occultist. With this understanding I can appreciate better the world-wide blessing that proceeds from the mystery that has taken place in his Spiritual or timeless Self and is manifesting as direct heart force, a force so greatly needed in our present-day world. And I can also appreciate how phases of his counsel, pertaining as they do to the time body, or brain self, are necessarily limited by laws and inhibitions naturally imposed upon that time body by the time world in which it lives, and would require more or less time for perfection through understanding born of experience.

Krishnaji himself says that truth cannot be organized. Then it would be equally correct to say that truth cannot be organized into speech or teaching, would it not? Moreover, the moment someone attempts to teach what he believes to be truth, he becomes instantly an authority to someone else who determines to follow him as such, and thus a new cause of differences arises. We all know that Krishnaji does not wish to be considered an authority, any more than did the Lord Buddha. But he cannot escape it, any more than did the Buddha. For nether was the latter able to escape having followers, who created just one more island of teacher-following in the mass of humanity.

And so of the two aspects of Krishnaji's work I can see in the heart aspect, or that flow of divine Life through him, a feature tending toward social upliftment and solidarity, and this I do not yet see in the aspect of mind illustrated in some phases of his teaching.

Now, if theosophists could but take some view of the situation kindred to that outlined in the above discussion, would they genuinely feel that they were justified in leaving the Society and becoming followers of a teacher who does not want them as such? Would they not rather see that, after all, Krishnaji's message is a spiritual one and that no truly spiritual message can really depart from the mere enunciation of principles; and that he does not usually undertake to enjoin people along lines of physical details of action? Would they not find that it was possible to remain in the Society and at the same time to maintain a perfectly free attitude towards life in all its relations, meditative, devotional, or actional, and thus be able first to prove for themselves on a logical basis how much of the truth of is teaching they are capable of realizing before taking an action they might come later to regret? If this practical suggestion were not wise, then what of the poor creature who did not happen to be a member of any church or ethical society? Would he be barred from spiritual progress

261

merely because he had nothing from which to resign? Of course, looked at from this standpoint, the misunderstanding of Krishnaji's spiritual counsel leads to endless absurdities.

Why not let us stand by the ship that has brought us to such a beautiful harbor of Life? Why not realize that it was this ship that brought Krishnaji himself to the harbor, and has been of incalculable value to him and his work? And why not realize that if we continue to help his good ship to sail the seas of life, it will without doubt bring into the harbor other great spiritual teachers at time goes on, and thus continue to help the world in this magnificent way age after age?

Those who see in Theosophy an ever-expanding avenue to truth will remain firm and help to deepen the unity, the solidarity of our very great movement; and those who only see in it a concrete system upon which to lean will naturally not be held by it any longer than some other concrete concept that shall appear to be more attractive to them. Theosophy is the essence of the highest tradition regarding Life that has ever been offered outwardly on this planet, so far as we can know at this time. It penetrates deeper, rises higher and extends over a vaster area than any known concept. That we should realize this is a very great privilege, for it carries with it the inestimable opportunity of co-operating with a movement of such priceless value to our unawakened race and the races of the future.

Brethren, let us remain; let us go on with the work; let us embrace all that we can of that pure heart force and spiritual idealism that emanates from Krishnaji, and let us express it in the vitalization of our Theosophical ideals and life; and let us leave to the futile theologian the discussion of those things which so distinctly do not matter. It is in the realization of the soul power that lies in the unity of the mass in which every man has his right to partake, and in the social living of the life of truth and love, that service, kindness, friendship and happiness have their true expression; from this they proceed as the shadow from the substance.

---

* Warrington, A.P., "Unity; or Separation?," *The Adyar Theosophist*, Vol. LII, n1, October 1930, pp. 7-14.

NOTE: Is not the fact well expressed in the text: "He has come that ye may have Life, and that ye may have it more abundantly"? A.B.

A lecture given by Dr. Besant in Wheaton, Ill., during the Wheaton Summer School of 1929 was published in a special edition booklet. It contained all the lectures given on August 31, 1929 titled *The Mystic and Occult Paths;* pp. 17-27 are worth reading.

London

My dear George Sahib, (Arundale)
You were good enough to send me a nice letter sometime ago. I am ashamed not to have answered it before, but have been travelling about a great deal and in many countries with dear C.W.L. He has been perfectly wonderful in regard to the amount of work he could do. I think too he has saved the situation in regard to Ommen, there were many who could not accept all that Krishnaji said, but it has given a great many people more courage to follow their real instincts and judgement in the matter to know that the Great Man continued with his convictions. He has shown the most wonderful energy and fitness in his work, he managed to do more in a day than I could have done. Just at the moment he is far from well. A pain developed behind one eye while he was at Huizen. We took him to a good oculist, who could see nothing wrong with his eyes at all and said that in fact he had very young eyes without a sing of hardening. Things got worse, especially at Brussels, which he dislikes thoroughly, he has seen a great specialist here who says that it is due to overstrain in the brain and has ordered him a rest. The pain is less now, but he has been through difficult times and felt on the occasion of two or three nights that he might pass away. He is much better again at the time of writing. I always felt that he would pull through. It seems that he had something similar some time ago, and it got healed. There are already signs of the eye turning round a bit. Please keep this more or less private, as I don't think he would like the intimate details talked about. I thought, dear George, that you might hear some report of it, and would be glad to have authentic news.
He has been exceedingly kind to me. I find that all sorts of silly

stories were current as to my love affairs with various ladies in this part of the world. He went to different countries and had wonderful success. He shook hands with thirty people in succession in Berlin and showed the most wonderful kindness to the Germans. He says that some high egos are being born into their country. Then we went to Geneva to the International Congress, after a few days in Huizen, and back to Huizen. He has been very happy there, and eventually told me that news that Huizen is directly linked with Shamballa. I remember very well the Star shining there during a service some time ago, but I never ventured to think this great and wonderful thing. I am so happy that he is well satisfied with the work in Europe. He attended one of the Pupils' meetings at High Leigh in England, and was very happy about it. Then, after Ommen, we had a Priests' Week as usual at Huizen. There were close on 70 Priests and Deacons who attended, from 20 different countries including Iceland; and a large number of visitors from 15 different countries.

The Great Man has been wonderfully and unfailingly kind to me, and one has learned a lot from this contact with him. Following on the pamphlet which Raja, rather as I thought unhappily, issued without any consultation with me, he has spoken frankly about the position of many of the Pupils, which is belonging to one of us. He has spoken of the great strain that we people were under after the rapid march of events in 1925, and explained that we could well have made mistakes or not quite understood such things under such strain. Dear George, I have let him say all this, but the fact is that I got no instructions through into the waking consciousness at that time, and did what I did on the Chief's instructions and mostly at the beginning in collaboration with her. There are lots of people over here who distinctly remember her saying that in view of the pressure of work in connection with the New Race and the Coming, they were no longer taking pupils directly but entrusting that work to us. Raja's pamphlet was the first I heard of this other arrangement. I did discover myself that we had to find assent to them from our Lord the Mahachohan. He refused three or four that I proposed, smiled very graciously about some, but mostly gave some kind of formal assent. I get these things mostly not by clairvoyance but by direct illumination of the mind. However, there is not a great deal of trouble or disturbance abroad about the situation. I have always in recent years, dear George, laid tremendous stress on the necessity of pupils getting some personal experience for themselves, and have done my level best to help them to do so. Accordingly, the great majority have testified that, whilst they cannot recall seeing the Master face to face on very many occasions, there is complete change of consciousness and outlook on life since the event of Probation. One explains to them that the intimate knowledge of the Master and the remembrance of seeing Him comes at a later stage, and that the first change to expect is the strengthening by the Master's strength of the work that we do down here. Most can readily testify to that. The Prince told me some months ago that He preferred to use me as an unconscious instrument on most occasions than to give me direct instructions. He does, of course, sometime give these direct instructions. Dear George, I have written you all this quite frankly and also for Ruku's information, so that you may have all the facts before you. The Great Man is as charming as can be, and is not at all, I think, dissatisfied with the situation over here. We have got some more Initiates through -Mev. Schoonderbeek, Countess of Clonmell, Prof. Marcault, Bohle of Birmingham, Narve Ellingsen, Dr. or rather Bishop Nyssens, Peter Freeman, Peter Robinson and Katherine Patriccio. Charlotte Woods and I have lately been striking up a friendship and she has been put on probation.

The question of Huizen and of the Centre at Camberley has been settled. I was asked to keep on responsibility for Huizen for another two years, as the Hierarchy had poured so much force into it. I agreed to this, and expect to keep it on as a Centre which one constantly visits. But the withdrawal of money by Miss Dodge from the Centre and from myself cripples things very badly. The Chief at the beginning agreed with me that the English Centre might be more useful, and a number of our workers have built houses there. It is now understood that we can continue with this, and that I may go there from time to time on condition that I give due attention to Huizen for at least two years. I have the impression that we are to start centres with groups of Initiates in several European countries, there are already such groups in Poland, Austria, Hungary and Britain; and that one's work will have much to do with the starting and helping of these.

There, dear George, I have to go out now. I have been at work on this letter at various times of the day, as I wanted you to be au courant with the existing situation. You know how I have always felt in closest sympathy and understanding with you and Ruku, and I just want to say I have never swerved in that attitude. My very best love to dear Ruku and to you.

Agni (James I. Wedgwood)

Oct 5 1930
Auckland N.Z.

My dear Parthe, (Warrington)

Isn't it awful that I have not written to you all this time! But I have often thought of you and the coming of our American friends has brought you quite close. By this time, Mrs. Green, Max and Lillian Wardall must have reached San Francisco. It has been pleasant for everyone in The Manor to have had them all and Catherine. You probably know that Catherine is staying on with us till we go to Europe. All this has been a great experience for her and I am sure you will find her changed and grown. We all love her and I am glad to have this chance of getting to know her.

Here we are touring again and it reminds me of our tour in America. Do you remember it?

I hope you are well again — and I hope by now, you are 63 years of age so that you will never get ill again.

I have very little to write but this is to send you very much love in which George joins me.

Ever your most affectionate,
Rukmini

Oct 5 1930

Dear Mr. Warrington,

I am glad to have your little note and hear that you are better.

I have been helping the Harts with their business affairs for some weeks, and think they are now all set again for a while. Mrs. Hart has some idea of a possible move to Krotona, but I don't think the matter has been decided yet.

Hazel [Miss Hazel I. Crowe] is away on a month's vacation and I have been more or less ill with a peculiar cold, both of which circumstances have made it difficult for me to keep my correspondence up to date.

Louis arrived in Hollywood the first and I expect him up soon. Also Mr. Knudsen has returned from Europe where he consulted with Dr. Besant about a proposition of his to take over the Happy Valley project, and this is one of the first things to which Louis and I will have to give attention.

Mrs. Coffey has done much to improve the old farm house and surroundings, and I am helping where I can. I think her being at Krotona is a great asset, and undoubtedly the best opportunity you could ask to make a beginning in the establishment of your scheme for an Academy of Fine Arts.

Let me know when you get home and ready to see your friends.
Ever cordially yours,
G.H.H. (George Hall)

A great riff began back in August of 1929 when George Hall told Louis Zalk that Warrington was planning some kind of stunt to place Krotona more absolutely under his personal thumb, and this worried George more than necessary. A year later we find Mr. Zalk and George Hall calling on Miss Poutz, bringing up the matter of referring to her, as head of the E.S., all questions of residence at Krotona, to which she objected on the grounds that Warrington was the head of Krotona and not herself as head of the E.S., and that if such questions were referred to her she would pass them on to him. This conversation also brought out the statement from her that Zalk and George had not treated Warrington fairly at Chicago in August 1929, regarding the reorganization of the Krotona board. It would not be until December 18 that Zalk would go and see Warrington alone, in which Warrington expressed fully and at length his grievances in connection with Krotona and against Zalk and George. It would then be on December 29 that George had an interview with Warrington hoping to have a frank discussion of the matter which might clear up many obvious misunderstandings. George listened while Warrington stated at length his grievances against him and Zalk. Briefly his principal statements follow as:

(1) That by their action at Chicago "we boys" had destroyed the sacred relationship of pupil and guru which had heretofore existed between himself and Dr. Besant.

(2) That they had acted dishonorably in bringing before Dr. Besant their recommendations for the reorganization of Krotona without inviting Warrington and Miss Poutz to the conference. [George Hall admitted his mistake later on.]

(3) That Warrington had second-hand statements from three separate persons quoting George as having said that he went to Chicago "to get him," and that George had bragged

on his return that he "had got him," and that George referred to him in these statements with a foul epithet.

(4) That Warrington was constantly hearing reports of unfriendly and unkind statements supposed to have been made by George about Warrington, showing a distinctly unfriendly attitude on George's part. [According to George they were false.]

(5) That Krotona was Warrington's project, that he alone was responsible for its creation, its continuance and its success; That it has always been under Warrington's complete and personal control and should remain so; That because of the reorganization of the Board Warrington's hands were tied so that he could do nothing; And that if George's intention is to show a friendly attitude toward Warrington, the least that George could do to make amends for the wrong he had done Warrington was to change the By-Laws at once, deleting the clause providing for Business Manager and turn over to Warrington all the details of management connected with Krotona, subject to a budget established by the Board of Trustees.

George made an effort to correct his point of view wholly on the point of one of personal relationship rather than a difference of opinion over events and circumstances. George's listened carefully and understood Warrington's point of view, even though he built up his case against George, and only asked that he should be given the same consideration to his. Warrington agreed. George than began to answer the points of fact in Warrington's statements in an effort to clear up his misunderstandings and gain a fair hearing for the opposite point of view.

(1) George called Warrington's attention to the fact that from the beginning of their relationship in 1919, he had considered it exactly the same as his own relationship with Dr. Besant, and that George's esteem and affection for Warrington as his spiritual superior, particularly from 1925 onward, was the exact parallel except that George disillusionment with regard to it was caused by Warrington's own treatment of George since November, 1927, rather than

268

the action of a third party.

(2) Warrington was present and knew of the procedure that took place and had ample opportunity to speak for himself. However, this was not at all that happened. George sought an Interview with Dr. Besant, so far as business matters were concerned, regarding her other interests, *The Ojai*, and brought up the subject of Krotona wholly on the grounds of my personal relationship with Warrington. George told Dr. Besant of their fundamental differences of opinion and of his long service to Warrington personally and to Krotona, in which Warrington had the full cooperation of George even in those things with which George thoroughly disagreed. George told Dr. Besant that Warrington's attitude and actions towards him and his wife were so unfriendly, and painful, that he could not go on working with Warrington at Krotona in the close official relationship necessary. George therefore suggested that unless the financial integrity of the Krotona enterprise was important to Dr. Besant personally, he would be glad to sever his connection with the corporation. Dr. Besant stated that both these things were important, and that she wished George to continue, and that she would like such reorganization effected as would place the control of the Krotona corporation in the hands of few trustees to be selected by herself. She asked Zalk, Holland and George to help her in bringing this about as quickly as possible.

(3) It was a month or more previous to the interview under discussion, that Warrington said to George that someone had told him that in speaking of him George had used the phrase "to hell with Warrington," which statement George absolutely denied having ever made. George repeated it to his wife on his return home, and on the morning of December 29, before going to Warrington, he asked Mr. Kilbourne if he had carried that gossip to Warrington. Mr. Kilbourne said he had not, but that Warrington had told him the same thing, stating that Warrington had heard it from John Roine. Warrington disclaimed any knowledge of having repeated such a statement to George, but claimed that on the other hand what he had said was the same as he told Zalk, which was

an entirely different statement. George not only denied these statements absolutely but he tried to explain to Warrington how impossible it would be that he would have said any such thing, and how his knowledge of him should make it impossible for him to have believed such statements from any source. George made every possible effort in carrying out Dr. Besant's wishes regarding the reorganization of the Krotona Board, to save Warrington every possible embarrassment or hurt.

(4) George made it clear that based wholly on gossip and such statements as Warrington quoted to George were so distorted and twisted in the telling as to be unrecognizable.

(5) Warrington ignored the fact that George had also given ten of the best years of his life to the service of Krotona; and that George was the one who was responsible for having saved Krotona from bankruptcy and disintegration during 1920-21, and that its financial condition at the present time was largely due to George's supervision and management of its finances. However, by August, 1929, George was willing to sever his connection with the enterprise forever. Dr. Besant wanted the reorganization of Krotona in the hands of a Board of Trustees rather than a single person.

George felt the whole interview with Warrington was one of insincerity and unfriendliness on Warrington's part. Honesty, he felt, compelled George to state that future conversations with Warrington were useless.

It would be on December 30 that we read a note from Warrington to George that he forgot to tell him that he had no word from Dr. Besant at any time that any change had been made in the Krotona organization, either verbally or in writing, and when Warrington called to tell her good bye and asked her what plans she had for him, she replied very distinctly and positively that she wished him to return to Krotona and to carry on as he had always done. This represented to Warrington the sole instruction that he had received from her, adding that this may help George to understand Warrington's position.

The following memorandum regarding A.P.W. is written by George Hall on the following dates:

Oct. 17, 1930: Mr. Zalk and I called on Miss Poutz and brought up the matter of referring to her, as head of the E.S., all questions of residence at Krotona, to which she objected on the grounds that Mr. Warrington was the had of Krotona and not herself as head of the E.S., and that if such questions were referred to her she would pass them on to him. This conversation also brought out the statement from her that Mr. Zalk and I had not treated Mr. Warrington fairly at Chicago in August, 1929, regarding the reorganization of the Krotona Board. Following the conversation with Miss Poutz we had an interview with Mr. Warrington from which Mr. Zalk gathered the impression that he was unhappy or dissatisfied with his new relation to Krotona but which he did not seem to wish to discuss with both of us.

Dec. 18, 1930: Mr. Zalk went to se Mr. Warrington alone in which interview Mr. Warrington expressed fully and at length his grievances in connection with Krotona and against Mr. Zalk and myself. Later, in telling me about his interview, Mr. Zalk recommended that I should go to see Mr. Warrington and talk over the same subject matter in an effort to promote a better understanding between us.

Dec. 29, 1930: By appointment I met Mr. Warrington at 10:00a.m. for a two and one-half hour interview. I opened the conversation with the statement that much of what he had said to Mr. Zalk was news to me and not in accordance with the facts as I understood them, and that I had come to him in the hope that a frank discussion of the matter might clear up many obvious misunderstandings. I then listened while Mr. Warrington stated at length his grievances against me and Mr. Zalk. Briefly his principal statements were:

(1) That by our action at Chicago "we boys" had destroyed the sacred relationship of pupil and guru which had heretofore existed between himself and Dr. Besant.

(2) That we had acted dishonorably in bringing before Dr. Besant our recommendations for the reorganization

of Krotona without inviting him and Miss Poutz to the conference.

(3) That he had second-hand statements from three separate persons quoting me as having said that I went to Chicago "to get him," and that I bragged on my return that I "had got him," and that I referred to him in these statements with a foul epithet.

(4) that he is constantly hearing reports of unfriendly and unkind statements supposed to have been made by me about him, showing a distinctly unfriendly attitude on my part.

(5) (a) That Krotona is his project, that he alone is responsible for its creation, its continuance and its success; (b) That it has always been under his complete and personal control and should remain so; (c) That because of the reorganization of the Board his hands are tied so that he can do nothing; (d) And that if my intention is to show a friendly attitude toward him the least that I can do to make amends for the wrong I have done him is to change the By-Laws at once, deleting the clause providing for a Business Manager and turning over to him all the details of management connected with Krotona, subject to a budget established by the Board of Trustees.

To all of which I made reply in an effort to correct his point of view, which seems to me utterly one sided, distorted as to facts and in the nature of a legal argument such as one would use in a trial at court; whereas the point at issue, from my point of view, is wholly one of personal relationship rather than a difference of opinion over events and circumstances. I stated that I had listened carefully and understood his point of view, and only asked that he should give the same consideration to mine. I then proceeded to answer the points of fact in his statement as numbered above in an effort to clear up his misunderstandings and gain a fair hearing for the opposite point of view. I did listen without interruption while he built up his case against me. I then tried to answer as follows:

(1) I called his attention to the fact that from the beginning of my relationship wit him in 1919, I had considered it

exactly the same as his own relationship with Dr. Besant, and that my esteem and affection for him as my spiritual superior, particularly from 1925 onward, was the exact parallel except that my disillusionment with regard to it was caused by his own treatment of me since November, 1927, rather than the action of a third party.

(2) This statement could only be true on the grounds that Mr. Zalk and I sought an interview with Dr. Besant for this purpose and planed an official action as trustees. Even then "dishonorable" is a strong word, since Mr. Warrington was present and knew of the procedure that took place and had ample opportunity to speak for himself. However, this was not at all that happened. I sought an interview with Dr. Besant, so far as business matters are concerned, regarding her other interests in the Ojai, and brought up the subject of Krotona wholly on the grounds of my personal relationship with Mr. Warrington. I told her of our fundamental differences of opinion and of my long service to him personally and to Krotona, in which he had my full cooperation even in those things with which I thoroughly disagreed. I told her that his attitude toward me and my wife, and his actions understood by us as unfriendly, were so painful a thing, feeling toward him as I had, that I could not go on working with him at Krotona in the close official relationship necessary. I therefore suggested that unless my services in the financial management of Krotona affairs were absolutely necessary, that unless the financial integrity of the Krotona enterprise was important to her personally and to the work, I would be glad to server my connection with the corporation. Dr. Besant stated that both these things were important and that she wised me to continue, and that she would like such reorganization effected as would place the control of the Krotona corporation in the hands of a few trustees to be selected by herself. She asked Mr. Zalk, Mr. Holland and myself to help her in bringing this about as quickly as possible.

(3) A month or more previous to the interview under discussion, Mr. Warrington said to me that someone had told him that in speaking of him I had used he phrase "to

273

hell with Warrington," which statement I absolutely denied having ever made. I repeated it to Mrs. Hall on my return home, and on the morning of December 29, before going to Mr. Warrington, I asked Mr. Kilbourne if he had carried that gossip to Mr. Warrington. He said he had not but that Mr. Warrington had told him the same thing, stating that he had heard it from John Roine. In denying the gossip referred to above, I mentioned this other matter, and Mr. Warrington immediately disclaimed any knowledge of having repeated such a statement to me but claimed that on the other had what he had said was the same as he told Mr. Zalk, which was an entirely different statement. I not only denied these statements absolutely but I tried to explain to Mr. Warrington how impossible it would be that I should have said any such thing, and how his knowledge of me should make it impossible for him to have believed such statements from any source. He however reiterated his belief that the statements were true. In the first place the epithet quoted is not one that I would be apt to use about anyone, and secondly I have made every possible effort, in carrying out Dr. Besant's wishes regarding the reorganization of Krotona Board, to save Mr. Warrington every possible embarrassment or hurt. In this I have undoubtedly been unsuccessful in little petty matters of management at Krotona, but my lack of success was more largely contributed to by the gossip of some trusted friends and associates than by any intention on my part.

(4) This is based wholly on gossip and such statements as he quoted to me were so distorted and twisted in the telling as to be unrecognizable.

(5) This is entirely outside the point of issue, being an official matter connected with the organization and management of Krotona and only indirectly influencing the relationship between Mr. Warrington and myself because of the misunderstandings involved. (a) True as regards Krotona as a project with such exceptions as appear below. He ignores the fact that I also have given ten of the best years of my life to the service of Krotona; that I am the one who is responsible for having saved it from bankruptcy and disintegration during

1920-21, and that its financial condition at the present time is largely due to my supervision and management of its finances. However, I was quite willing in August, 1929, to sever my connection with the enterprise forever. (b) True as regards the past up to its point of reorganization, but not Dr. Besant's wish as regards the future. (c) Not the intention of the Board, and not true except as regards the expenditure of the corporation funds for promotion of various activities outside the routine management and maintenance. (d) This I would have right to do unless I wished to break faith with Dr. Besant, since the reorganization of Krotona was for the very purpose of putting this responsibility in the hands of a Board of Trustees rather than a single person. Neither have I the power personally to do such a thing, since the control of Krotona is in the hands of the Trustees and not in mine personally.

I was constantly interrupted in putting forward these statements, and everything I said was ignored that distracted attention from the central idea of Mr. Warrington's statement; namely, that all of the wrong was on my side, that he was the injured party and that a friendly relationship could only be established between us as he suggested. While he stated that his feeling for me was one of kindness and friendship, except for his disappointment in me because of my own actions, and while I did not deny the truth of any of his statements, my whole feeling and reaction from the interview was one of insincerity and unfriendliness on his part which honesty compels me to state. I did not attempt to discuss in detail his actions toward me, as any hint of criticism of him on my part rendered further conversation useless.

The following letter from C. Jinarajadasa indicates that Dr. Besant is showing mental impairement.

Oct 14 1930
P & O.S.N. Co.
S.S. Rajputana

My dear Warrington,

This letter is for yourself only, as you will see. You are the Vice-President and so should have information on come points in that capacity.

The President and I reach Bombay in 3 days. Her health is far from satisfactory. She showed a little improvement after getting to the cooler climate of Europe, but after a few weeks it was not maintained. She was beginning to feel the cold, and so I am glad she is returning. Her appetite is very poor, due to faulty digestion. But the changes in diet which we tried have not greatly helped. I think it is just due to old age.

But more serious than the physical is the mental. Her memory sometimes is very poor; more than that, there is a lack of grip. She varies; sometimes one can take up business matters with her, but often she fails to grasp the point. To those of us who stand close to her, and have a deep affection for her, matters are painful to watch, but we can do nothing. She is wilful, and dislikes assistance preferred.

Sometimes she looks very weak, and shows very little vitality; one half-feels she might then pass away in her sleep. At other times she is stronger. On her birthday night, she gave an admirable half-hour address in London — almost at the top of her prime; but at other talks, she is apt to digress, and be too long. I think she realises that matters are not right with her. Of course she is intensely worried over India; if that way were to cease I believe she could live on for some years.

You will have received the notification by her of myself as her "Deputy" on matters she delegates by writing. This was a surprise to me and happened while I was in Holland. Of course my deputy role cannot infringe your functions. Naturally at her Death, the Deputy vanishes, and you are in full charge by the Constitution. She told me the other day why she made me her Deputy. Last year when she toured Europe with Wedgwood's party, she saw an attempt being made to make Wedgwood a candidate for the Presidency. She does

276

not want him in that role, and so to forestall any such move, she has made me her Deputy, during her life-time. That will show the Society that she does not approve of any move pushing W. forward.

If anything happens to her, the Executive will carry on as usual at Adyar, regarding all matters at Headquarters. For the rest of the T.S., that is, the General Council, you will no doubt send instructions to Wood as Recording Secretary. I remind you and I don't know that anything is going to happen. But this letter will show that sometimes I am worried about the President, because the vitality seems to be so low.

C.W.L. had a breakdown at Brussels. He nearly went then, and also once in London. He is much better; at Port-Said, he came over from his ship to ours to see the President, and then after went off to the train. His mind is "all there." I rather think he had a slight stroke. One result is that his right eyelid muscle is paralyzed. In Dec. 1927, the same thing happened with the other eyelid; it got better after 3 months. If that was the first stroke, then this year's the second. So, there is danger ahead for him. Of course, I think it is quite out of the question for him to tour again, or go to USA next year.

At Port Said, we learned that Wedgwood had become somewhat mentally unbalanced. Mrs. Jackson, who was with C.W.L., told one that she lad seen signs of something wrong. I thought W. would have a bad physical breakdown — he looked as if he would have a stroke. But I did not expect his mind being affected. It seems he has gone to a psychoanalyst in Sweden. If he will knock off all occult matters, I believe he can be normal again. I don't know how serious it all is. He has been most rash about the matter of putting Pupils on Probation and so on. Even after the Mahachohan's letter, and C.W.L.'s gentle hints, he seems not to understand. Things have been so serious, in that regard, C.W.L. told me at Port Said, that the Masters have gravely discussed whether it might not be advisable to suspend all advancements for 5 years. Wedgwood made a bad blunder trying to transfer the centre from Huizen to Camberley; but C.W.L. came over to Europe and stopped that.

So, you see, we must be ready for emergencies.

I believe George leaves Australia with Rukmini after Easter. I suppose he will come to Adyar, enroute for Europe. If so, I presume the President will go with him. I can't, for one simple reason — no money. Very confidential. One thing more; the President made a new will in London — the old one was made I believe some thirty years ago. Graham Pole is executor. She has written instructions from her about her various obligations of a financial kind. I am glad she has delegated someone to see to all that, because, now, that business side will be properly attended to.

I don't think there is anything else to write about.

Schwarz leaves for India on Feb. 7 from Venice.

I hope your health is better. I fear you have had a bad time, but evidently that is the lot of all of us who mean business.

Ever yours,

C. Jinarajadasa

Mrs. William Kerfoot, who served so capably as hostess of the Ojai Country Club, is discontinued her work there due to medical treatment for an ailment affecting her back.

Mr. & Mrs. Irving S. Cooper and Miss Sarah Peacock Rogers purchased a tract of approximately five acres of Grand Avenue and named their place "Spreading Oaks Ranch".

The Ojai Valley Oaks Lodge resumed its 8 o'clock Sunday evening meetings at the Meiners Oaks Community Hall. A. F. Knudsen, just returned from Europe, was the guest speaker for the evening. Knudsen also lectured at the Shakespeare Club at the Woman's Club describing a mystery play.

During the early part of October, before a large group of picnickers from the Ojai and Ventura Theosophical Lodges who sat under a great oak tree approximately in the center of 300 acres under cultivation of beans, hay and walnuts, George Hall, manager of the Happy Valley property, gave a short history of the150 acres that remained in a wild state for the present.

Miss Clara Codd, by 1915, was a distinguished author, who, from early age wrote on Theosophy for very little children. By 1930, she was a Senior National Lecturer in England, and expected in November at the Community Hall at Meiners Oaks, California. She had begun public work over twenty years previously during the movement to enfranchise women in England, under the leadership of the famous Mrs. Pankhurst. Miss Codd was one of the most successful lecturers on the Theosophical platform.

Krotona Institute wrote to Mr. Will Clark that they would lease for pasture purposes all the flat land between the hill and the railroad track, as the same was now enclosed by fence, for the sum of $50 per year, payable in advance. If they installed a meter attached to the water line, Krotona Institute would let him connect a pipe to their water for the purpose of furnishing water to his stock, and they reserved the right to cancel this lease at any time on thirty days notice.

―――――――――――

Nov 14 1930

My dear Raja, (C. Jinarajadasa)

Your confidential, informative letter written from the S.S. Rajputana on the 14th ultimo is greatly appreciated.

I regret exceedingly to learn some of the things which you have mentioned; nevertheless, one can but see that the inevitable must happen sometime. I have been hoping , and especially since I was made the Vice-President, that the Master would keep our Great President's health in working efficiency, as He did in the case of H.P.B., as that would enable her to carry on for a great many years to come, for I am not in the least eager to increase my responsibilities in life, much less to take up duties which have been laid down by an illustrious personage. It is fortunate for me, however, that at this apparently critical moment I am now emerging from a long siege of suffering wherein I have apparently relieved myself, by a very painful process, of a great deal of cumbersome karma. At the moment I feel as one might who had been wandering around in a dark and dangerous jungle and was just beginning to emerge once more into the daylight where he could enjoy the sunlight and the blue sky again. Curiously enough, my restoration to health is taking place according to a plan which, when told me by astrologers and other soothsayers, inspired no faith in me whatsoever. They said, even as far back as fifteen years ago that my most important work would not come until after the age of 65, nor would my health completely return till then. I am now 64, and my bark is sailing toward the 65th harbor in comparative freedom from rocks and shallows. For this, the gods be praised.

I have put myself in the fore part of this letter in order that you may understand better what I should mean when saying to you, as

I now do, I am ready to be called, if anything should happen. In such unfortunate emergency, it would be my purpose to sail at once for Adyar. Meanwhile, I should hope that you would be willing to carry on under an extension of your present deputyship, the authority for which it would be my purpose to cable to you, so that the proper functioning of the executive and administrative offices might continue unhampered.

As to the other matters mentioned in your letter, I can but say I have had a dim feeling of the possibility of those things, but, of course, felt no keen assurance of the accuracy to my impressions. This refers to all you said about C.W.L. and J.I.W. I have wondered if it might not be the part of wisdom that C.W.L. remain at Adyar where the climate suits him so very much better than any other climate, and where his keen far-seeing, logical mind might collaborate with the dashing faculties of our over-burdened President? I should think he would be a god-send to her, and that it would be a blessing if the two could remain in close touch with one another at least during her life. We will never know what a priceless channel we are privileged to contact in the person of that great man, I fear, until after we have lost it. It would be the kindest thing to his marvelously constituted body, I would humbly suggest, if he could now remain at peace in the centre where he is happiest, and not be dragged around the world through conditions which, unfortunately, have been made so foreign to the delicate nature of his body. And so, I hear you say with some satisfaction that it is quite out of the question for him to tour again, or to come to the U.S.A. next year.

As to Point Loma: It has been made very clear by Dr. de Purucker that the Great Man, as Mr. Fullerton always called him, could never, under any circumstances, expect to visit the place as a welcome guest.

As to J.I.W.: Well, has not this present result been lying on the lap of the causes set in motion years ago? And in the world of occult law, is there ever such a thing as pardon or condonation? We have always been told there is not. So, while one's sympathies go out in an affectionate stream of understanding, yet the pupils who follow will understand better in the future the invariableness of occult law. The things I have heard directly from Europe about our unfortunate brother have been even less cheering than what you write.

In this connection, since the thought of pupils arises, I hope the situation in Europe may not cause Ammaji to clamp down the lid entirely. One by one some of us are likely to discover even better and more promising material than the majority of that which has hitherto been offered to and accepted her. Recently I wrote to her of one instance, that of Mrs. Betty Robertson, of Houston, whom you no doubt know, and who is now the Hostess and Assistant-Librarian at Krotona. The only reason that she was left out when Dr. Besant was in Houston was one which had to do not with herself, but the trouble which Mrs. Laura Wood was making in Houston at the time, and Ammaji thought it best to consider no applications there, as she desired not to augment the forces in Houston under the circumstances. Then sometime later when Bishop Arundale came around, there were some who were made pupils at Houston, and Mrs. Robertson was on the list but happened to be unavoidably away from the city at the time, and later was very ill when a further visit was made. So, not because of any disqualification on her part, but due to these untoward circumstances, she was left out of Dr. Besant's considerations.

Now, however, being one of our most valued workers, and very eager to reach the Master, and being, as I have suggested, so worthy of consideration, in my belief, I recently sent her name to Dr. Besant, and I hope that if she is not attending to her correspondence, and it falls to your lot to look it over, you will kindly bear in mind what I have said and try to see, if you kindly will, that the matter receives her attention at sometime when she is best able to do her work.

I am exceedingly happy to learn from you that Schwarz will soon leave for India, for we all know what his presence at Adyar has meant.

And now closing, with another word concerning our beloved Ammaji: I feel keenly the true meaning of your words when you say that those who have a deep affection for her at times find it painful to watch recent developments. This was also true in Chicago a year ago. There some of us had our very hearts torn watching procedures carried out, not at her initiative, but upon the easily imposed wills of others. A situation which I have recently learned, has since been many times duplicated in Europe. I had occasion to write to Ammaji with honest frankness three months ago telling her what it was she had done in respect of Krotona and myself, and which Miss Poutz and I look upon with increasing alarm as the time approaches for the pressure upon the T.S. and Krotona to increase in intensity, as it is sure to do, as certain eventualities grow nearer and nearer. If my letter falls into your hands, and its date was August 18th, I hope you will read it sympathetically and understandingly, for then you will appreciate, I hope, how clear it was at the time Amma's action was taken, that the great soul, having such impressive duties to look after from the higher worlds, was not down here at the time and, therefore, the body was an easy prey to the desires of others who used her authority to accomplish purposes more satisfying to their personal ambition than helpful to their spiritual life. And so your sad information but confirms that which I have painfully been made to realize, through the circumstances related above, and which could never have occurred, if Ammaji had been "All here."

Thanking you for your kind thoughtfulness in communicating with me, I am, with affection,
Sincerely yours,
A.P.W.

Oct 5 1930
Auckland, N.Z.

My dear Parthe, (A.P. Warrington)
Isn't it awful that I have not written to you all this time! But I have often thought of you and the coming of our American friends has brought you quite close. By this time, Mrs. Green, Max and Lillian Wardall must have reached San Francisco. It has been pleasant for everyone in The Manor to have had them all and Catherine. You probably know that Catherine is staying on with us till we go to Europe. All this has been a great experience for her and I am sure you will find her changed and grown. We all love her and I am glad to have this chance of getting to know her.

Here we are touring again and it reminds one of our tour in America. Do you remember it?

I hope you are well again, and I hope by now, you are 63 years of age so that you will never get ill again.

I have very little to write but this is to send you very much love in which George joins me.

Ever your most affectionate
Rukmini

The following letter refers to the constitution of A.P.W.: that Krotona is his to control, making trustees merely figureheads as before re-organizations in 1929 by order of Dr. Besant.

Oct 7 1930
Berkeley

Dear Friend, (George Hall)

You have no doubt heard by this time from Mr. Warrington about renting your Krotona house to the Hart's. I had to refer the matter to him, as he is the Head of Krotona, appointed by the Master as well as the Outer Head to establish our spiritual centre.

Of course, I need hardly say a thing which you know as well as I. I simply want to explain why I did not write to you direct before ascertaining his wishes.

I am glad we both agree to welcome our good friends the Harts at Krotona.

This is my last stopping place before getting back home at last. Just think,, I will have visited 48 places and traveled over 16,133 miles.

With much love to you and Grace,
Ever your old friend,
Marie Poutz.

According to the records, at the Chicago Convention in 1929, Dr. Besant told Henry Hotchener that she wanted Warrington to serve on the Krotona Board to help him as Manager, and that she had full confidence in Henry; also that Warrington was to have his cottage for life, free of rent. Henry Hotchener reported that Dr. Besant did not say to him that Warrington was to be divested of all control over Krotona.

The following letter refers to Warrington's letter on 12-21-29.

Oct 22 1930
Adyar Madras India

Dear Parthe,

Thank you so much for the portrait of your admirable President. [President Hoover] It is being nicely framed to hang on my left hand as I write. I am very pleased to have it for my "personal use."

With loving regards
Annie Besant

My dear George,

I did not think to mention to you yesterday something about the bachelor apartments. There are two things on my mind there, and have been on my mind for over a year about them.

First, when the rains set in I doubt if the people will be able to drive in and out of any of the garages.

Second, I think the place has remained unimproved so long now that we can see at this time that it would be good business to complete this investment. To be left incomplete, crude, in the raw, so to say, so far as the outside is concerned, discourages rather than attracts tenants. I am sure it would be wise, therefore, to complete the improvement by the proper roadway, which in the beginning we all went over and designed, and by doing a practical amount of planting. These, therefore, are the two points I am bringing to your attention: making the roads suitable for travel, both in the front and in the rear to the garages, and the doing of a necessary amount of planting to make the place look attractive.

I can tell you that there is a lot of stuff in the Nursery which soon may have to be thrown away. It is good material and would be very suitable for planting in just such a place as the bachelor apartments, and the material will cost Krotona nothing. Mrs. Hancock offers to co-operate in setting it out as fully as possible. I should think that if you would assign our bunch of men, Gene, V.C. and James, to the task, the whole thing could be accomplished in a very brief space of time. The time for doing this, I would suggest, would be after the first rain. There are enough men down there now to look after the stuff in moderate amount, especially during the winter season.

I think you will agree with me in all of the above, because outside Krotona the general practice of investors is to make their places attractive to their tenants, and I believe Krotona ought to realize now by this time that the same principle applies here.
Cordially yours,
A.P. Warrington

Oct 25 1930

Dear Mr. Warrington,

I am sorry to have you bother to write me as I am often at Krotona and would always be glad of an excuse for me to call and see you, if you will have your secretary phone either my office or my house.

You are quite right about the improvements needed at No. 10, and I supposed you knew as well as I that lack of money is the cause of the delay. We had $500 a short time ago available for such purposes, but I thought it more important to repair the main entrance road first. I am glad to hear of Mrs. Hancock's kind offer about the landscaping and shall take the matter up with her when the time comes.

Most cordially yours,

G.H. Hall

For more than two years, members of the E.S. were left to themselves to see what use they would make of their freedom. The results had not been encouraging: many had ceased to work and serve. Lodges had suffered; more than one earnest T.S. member shrugged his shoulders and felt they might never apply for membership in the E.S.

But it was hoped that members were now eager to grasp their opportunities of service, and it was now the duty of the Corresponding Secretary to ask everyone what work he or she had chosen as their special offering to the Master.

Marie wanted definite facts, not aspirations as regards the future or work done in the past, nor statements such as "I am doing all I can." She reminded them that the Master said, "Service in the little things of life counts as much with Us as the so-called greater services."

A.P. Warrington gave an informal talk to the Krotonians at the library on October 31, about the paper on the subject of Krotona's relationship to the Devas of the Valley, and to the plans of the Great White Lodge as they were known to the Devas and as they applied to the present and future uses of the Ojai Valley.

> You will remember in the paper I read that the Deva who spoke was disappointed in us. He thought that we were not sufficiently mindful of the plans of the Great White Lodge, and that, as a matter of fact, we were too self-centered, that we were thinking too much of ourselves and making ordinary human beings of ourselves instead of a big group of the Masters' servants — that because of the occupations of our

hearts and minds we, the agents in the world of that Great White Lodge are not doing our part. I am not unsympathetic with you all because of that state of affairs because I understand you — because I understand myself. I agree with one member of this group, who has expressed himself very strongly, and he contends that one trouble is we haven't been told anything about the existence of these invisible beings and therefore we do not know enough of Their plans and what They expect from us. Well, now that is true, and yet it is about that exactly as it is about all invisible revelations which have come to us through psychics, namely, if after we had gotten the fundamentals of Theosophy we had applied to these fundamentals the strictest rules of logic, we might even have reached the same conclusions as to the invisible worlds as the revelations show. I have studied it and I believe that, in a measure, I am right about it. So if we had applied the strict rules of logic to the fundamentals that we are confronted by, the fact that we have come to this Valley, the fact that Dr. Besant has placed her stamp upon our coming and our work here, the fact that she points to this as a sort of hatching house for the great colony of the future, added to which goes our own theosophic and Theosophical views, could not we, with the applications of a little bit of logic, have reached every conclusion which was revealed in that paper there? So, if we have not had enough revelation it has been good for us that we have not had it. It has given us the opportunity to do our own thinking and to reach our own conclusions, and how much greater good it has done to each one of us appears when we do reach those conclusions without the aid of revelation — well, as it was in the nursery "Mama" and "Papa" business. We have got to be adults and do our own thinking.

Now what I wish to do tonight, in this little talk, is to make some suggestions to you, if possible, which will help you to keep your minds on the Brotherhood, especially in respect of the work which the Brotherhood wishes to be done here in this Valley. I know (no one knows better than I do) how difficult it is to keep the mind on an ideal. When one has a thousand and one diverting agencies talking his mind away during the day! Of course you all remember that our great spiritual leader, Dr. Besant, has indicated, from time to time, my thoughts. She recognizes that our minds must be occupied by the daily duties, and all that she hopes for is that we develop the habit of turning our thoughts automatically to the Masters when we are through with those duties from time to time during the day. That all and everything is a counsel of perfection — it is just what we ought to be able to do; but I am going down into human nature just a little bit further and see if there is one other little thing that can be done that will set up the machinery of a constant reminder to us of that attitude of mind. Now when we have set up the mechanism of the reminder then we have got something. And it is that mechanism that I wish to explain to you tonight, for I believe that I have something of real value to you in a dozen different directions and which will be especially valuable to you in this particular direction which is the subject of our talk tonight. I want to go off for a moment and see if we can discern what quality we are perhaps lacking in that would be of special value to the Devas and to the Great White Lodge if we possessed it. There is no doubt in my mind as to what that quality is. I believe it is the quality upon which Krishnaji lays so much emphasis. You will remember that in his talks for the past two years now how he tells us that we could gain liberation by a number of methods — and one of them is by the possessing or by the experiencing rather of a great love, "A great affection," as he puts it. I know that Krishnaji had a great, burning affection — for his brother, who was taken away, and from that came the great sorrow that he talks about. I believe almost anything that would jar us from stem to stern might accomplish the same thing, shaking us out of our little selves into our big selves, but I am one of those who believe that a great affection, a great love, a great emotion that thrills from stem to stern, is the constructive force that will enable us to be of the greatest use to the invisible workers for the good of humanity. How there are not many of us who are young enough to be subject to those thrills — a thrilling affection between a man and woman in youth or in middle age, when

287

they have the capacity for such things in strong measure, if rightly used — mark you, if certain ideal restraints are put upon it and all those restraints are considered as sacrifices and dedicated to the Master as a gift — then you have got just what I am talking about, something very powerful and very wonderful in the use of the Great White Lodge. Why is it that the greatest of the Masters will write and say to his pupils, "Love is the fulfillment of the Law"? We have never yet as occult students had great affections. We flip along in human affection, experiencing these things just as the animals, when we have all the elements of heart and mind in us, and religion, especially where sacrifice comes in; and we have never yet applied those powers to any general development, experiencing a use of affection as we would use the power in a dynamo for a definite and specific purpose. The power in the two hearts that are thrilled with one another is a joint power constituting a dynamo of force, and it depends only on what we do with that force as to whether it is high or holy. We can waste it in mutual follies; we can specialize it in a force that will lead us to the very presence of the Master. *

Nov 5 1930
E.S.T.

Dear Friend, (George Hall)

I talked with Mr. Warrington this morning after you left, and we both agree with you that our dear Mrs. Goldy should be where she can be happy. So I just talked with her and put the whole matter up to her for her decision. I think she intends to speak to you about it.

Of course, as I told you, it means that the room in the Library Building will be vacant most of the time, as it should be occupied only by a High Degree Mason who is also a pupil and an E.S. member. But all will work out well, I am sure.

With best wishes to you and Grace,

Ever your friend,

Marie Poutz

---

* Warrington, A.P., Informal talk to the Krotonians at the Library, October 31, taken from rough draft notes in his handwriting.

My dear Ammaji,
    Thank you cordially for mailing to me from Port Said, the book entitled "Must England Lose India?"
    I will see what can be done with it in this country.
Heartily,
A.P. Warrington

The following instructions were received by Brothers Besant, Leadbeater, and certain other Initiates from the Inner Head of the School. All will remember that Brother Besant in 1928 transferred to the United States the International organ of the President of the Society, *The Theosophist*. She hoped that a better printing and binding than were possible in Adyar would create a larger circulation. On receiving the instructions given below, the magazine was at once transferred back to Adyar.

From the Chohans Morya and Kuthumi to Annie Besant, O.H. December 9, 1930

It seems necessary to make clear to your workers that, though Our Society is always and everywhere progressive, it has nevertheless to maintain its continuity. It widens out its usefulness, it enters upon new fields of activity; but it must never alter its original work, nor relax its effort along the lines for which it was founded.

It exists for the promotion of Brotherhood, and therefore for the promulgation of the great basic truths upon which the doctrine of Brotherhood is established. it has a very definite revelation to give to Western people, a definite gospel to preach; and along that line it has met with considerable success. That work is still needed, that gospel must still be preached with unabated vigour; much energy is and must be thrown into the branches, but the main trunk must not be allowed to show symptoms of decay.

Our present Commander-in-Chief (our Lord the Maha Chohan) whishes to utilize Our Society for a fresh facet of the Great Plan. It is by His direct command that efforts

289

are being made to establish centres for His use in different parts of the earth — centres through which His power can be radiated for many purposes which are at present beyond your knowledge. Hence the necessity for the founding of Sydney and Huizen, and Our insistence that these should be supported and strengthened.

We have other spots in mind. But Our Commander is most explicit and emphatic in asserting that all these are subsidiary to Adyar, the true centre chosen by Us fifty years ago, the only centre in which Our emissary Upāsikā* was directed to reside for this purpose.

This centre has been somewhat neglected and allowed to lapse; it was once a centre of fire and life even on the physical plane; build it up again and restore it to its pristine glory. Consult among yourselves how this can be done, for there is no time to lose. True, Our Society is world-wide, yet its root is in this sacred land. The centres of commerce and material civilization (so-called) may be elsewhere, but this is still the focus of spiritual power. Distracted though this Our beloved Motherland may be at the moment, she still remains the land most suited to reflect the glory of Shamballa, the spot on earth through which the light and life of higher planes may be most easily transmitted. An influence flows hence which no other country in the world can give; for fifty years you have sent out that influence of Ours to far-away lands through Our magazine *The Theosophist*, and We wish that sanctified channel restored to Our use.

We allowed (though with regret) the trial of your recent experiment†; it has not succeeded, for it could not succeed; the magazine has lost its unique character, but it must now be restored immediately to its former position. This is not the time when India can afford to be deprived of an important channel through which she spreads her special message and blessing through the world.

Offshoots, reflections, may of course exist; an *Australian* Theosophist, and *American* Theosophist — that is well, that

---

* H.P.B.
† See Note I at the end.

such nations as wish to do so may emphasize their own aspect of the truth, and give their local news. But Our magazine, published at Our Headquarters, and edited by Us through your hands as Our representative — that alone can claim the proud title of *The Theosophist* — a copy-right which We cannot consent to abrogate!

What we have already said about Our chosen home at Adyar will have indicated to you that if there is to be a special commemoration of the centenary of Upāsikā's previous birth, it is *there*, in *her* old home and in the heart of Our spiritual influence, that the principal celebration should be held under the highest auspices; though there is of course no objection to any Section, any branch, or any gathering of her admirers outside of the Society also solemnizing the occasion in any way that they may see fit.* But your dignity as her successor should be clearly maintained, though with perfect gentleness and courtesy.

Let no one in the least be troubled by the recent shaking out from Our Society of some of its loosely-attached members; brothers should remember that a similar event has several times happened before, and that on every such occasion Our organization has emerged stronger and more useful than ever. We blame no one; let every one obey his own conscience. It is merely necessary for Us to know upon whom We can absolutely depend. It is no mean epitaph: "Losing or winning, he played the game, and *stood firm* until the end." And the end is sure.

It should be clearly understood that while We always welcome progress, We do not look with favour upon the spirit of unrest, so prevalent at the present day, which desires perpetually to make changes merely for the sake of change. You have an example of that in the proposal to alter the form of the very object of Our Society.† After many minor fluctuations We gradually guided your officials towards a formulation of these objects in 1896 which was satisfactory to Us; why should they wish to modify it now? Unnecessary

---

* See Note II at the end.
† See Note III at the end.

changes in fundamentals give impression of instability which is manifestly undesirable. It is not a change in the objects pursuing them and applying them in daily life. I would say to you: Do not waste your time and strength in tinkering at your machinery, but go ahead and produce results. With Us it is work that tells, not barren argument; and in that work the Brotherhood stands behind you.

You must not impose even *belief in Our existence* upon your outer Society.* But in Our Inner School and most of all among Our Pupils it should be understood that there are two aspects of the work — that which Our members can do themselves, and that which We can do *through* them if they will make themselves fit channels for higher influences. I spoke to you before of the necessity of gathering round you a band of stalwarts upon whom you can *depend* — men not liable to be tossed to and fro, and carried about by every wind of doctrine, but men of selfless devotion to the great Cause of Humanity.

Such men you need in your centre, and also in the outer world as representatives and agents of your centre. Weld them into a unity, and doubt not that we shall use them; they will be a mighty weapon in the hand of the Lord as well as a channel for His power; and never forget that We stand behind you, and over you shines the Star of THE KING, the oriflamme of Victory.

Notes by C. Jinarajadasa

NOTE I
From the Presidential Address
December, 1929

For the sake of producing a Magazine in a form which would make a special appeal to the modern reader, I have transferred the publication of *The Theosophist* to America, where, in Los Angeles, Mrs. Marie Russak Hotchener wil act as Editor and Mr. Henry Hotchener as business Manager. In this I had the hearty support of the General Council, and the

---

* See Note IV at the end.

most generous help from my two American collaborateurs. At the same time I found it necessary — in fact, binding on me as President by Colonel Olcott's bequest— to have an Organ at the Presidential residence at Adyar; so I continue to publish from here what is now called The Adyar Theosophist. I hope the Magazine started by H.P.B and H.S.O. will in both parts of its new bifurcated form, continue to win the support of the members, and those sections of the public for which they are especially intended.

The last issue of the old form of *The Theosophist* was of 106 pages; the name *The Theosophist* was however withdrawn from the proposed American magazine and the title *World Theosophy* substituted. This title was an error, as the intention in the cable sent to Mr. and Mrs. Hotchener was that the title should be *World of Theosophy*. When the American *World Theosophy* began, *The Adyar Theosophist* shrunk to 62 pages. *The Theosophist* reverted to its old form in January 1931, with 125 pages. *World Theosophy* continued till December 1933.

The transference suggested, to which Dr. Besant and the General Council consented, was due to complaints in U.S.A. that the "get up" of *The Theosophist* did not have the distinction of American magazines, and that members who desired to pass it on to friends felt that it was not worthy of the message of Theosophy. Some enthusiasts held that if it were printed in America in a different format, the magazine would have a greater appeal to the public.

When this change was first suggested at the Chicago Convention of 1929, I would have pointed out, had I been consulted, one important factor against transferring *The Theosophist* to U.S.A. The magazine represents an attitude to world problems "as from the centre." This is possible from Adyar, but impossible to be the keynote of *The Theosophist* if it were to be edited by anyone living in U.S.A. The atmosphere of the country, so strong in every way, and needful to the country's growth, does nevertheless create a kind of fog through which international problems are surveyed. On the whole this fog is less at Adyar than anywhere else, for reasons which I need not enumerate. I was however lecturing in

Mexico at the time and could not break a long planned tour to go to Chicago for a few days' Convention meetings.

NOTE II

The reference by the Master is to an incident which took place in Geneva during the Tenth Congress of the T.S. in Europe, held from June 26th to July 1st. At one of the evening meetings of the Congress there was present sitting on the platform a Mr. Lars Eek, who had been brought there by Mrs. M.R. Hotchener who introduced him to Dr. Besant as a member from Point Loma. As various speakers announced were giving their addresses, Dr. Besant asked Mr. Eek to address the gathering. He then stated what nobody expected, that he came as the representative of "Universal Brotherhood and the Theosophical Society," The Theosophical Society at Point Loma whose leader was Dr. G. de Purucker. He brought an invitation from Dr. de Purucker to Dr. Besant and members of the T.S. to be present at Point Loma on August 11, 1931 to celebrate the Centenary of H.P.B.'s birth. Dr. Besant responded to the invitation and sent a cable to Dr. de Purucker ending, "I also accept personally, as does my brother, Bishop Leadbeater, the invitation to be present at Point Loma on August 11th next year to celebrate the centennial of the birth of our great teacher, Madame Blavatsky,"

Brother Leadbeater intimated to me privately that the President's acceptance so cordially to go to Point Loma for the celebration was utterly distasteful to him, though he would go with her, as she was his leader and he would follow where she led. Point Loma, however, did not follow up the invitation, possibly not caring that Brother Leadbeater should come along with Dr. Besant. The whole matter fell through and H.P.B.'s Centenary was celebrated by us at Adyar. To commemorate the occasion I, then Acting Editor of *The Theosophist*, issued a special H.P.B. Centenary number August 1931, composed (except for the Watch Tower) of various writings and drawings of H.P.B. and other interesting Material.

NOTE III

I recall that sometime previously to December 1930, there was talk among some members about changing the wording of the Objects of the Society. Dr. G. S. Arundale, when he became President, opened the matter again and many discussions took place in several National Societies, and much correspondence appeared in *The Theosophist* about proposed changes.

NOTE IV

In all my work in public lectures and even to members of the Society I have scarcely ever mentioned the subject of the Masters. I have long felt that the attitude of older members to the new member who has joined us is not quite just. We proclaim that the new member need only express assent to the First Object of the Society, yet when he enters the work of a Lodge he is so often met with positive assertions concerning the Masters, that They desire this and the other thing for the Society. In other words, he very quickly begins to feel somewhat in strange waters when he is expected to assent to certain ideas to which he has not in any way committed himself. It is as if he had joined a new sect, with a creed, where if you did not believe you were considered merely a "beginner" and in a sort of outer darkness.

There is a beautiful lecture of Dr. Besant. "The Masters as Facts and Ideals." It was a public lecture, but in no way imposing a belief in Their existence. If ever I have had to mention the Masters outside of the E.S., it was always with some qualifying phrase: "Some Theosophist believe," and so on. Naturally, within the E.S. I take for granted that all believe in Their existence, whether they have in any way realized that fact in their brain consciousness or have not yet done so.*

The following is a personal letter to readers of the *Theosophist*.

---

* Jinarajadasa, C., pamphlet, *Esoteric School of Theosophy*, "From the Chohans Morya and Kuthumi to Annie Besant, O.H." 1946, pp.1-12.

February 1931

Dear Mr. Cook:

In the absence of Mr. Rogers we are sending you this letter for the *Messenger* about the magazine *World Theosophy*, as there seems to be some confusion in the minds of members, judging from letters received, about the return of the title *The Theosophist* (international) to Adyar.

It is clear that Dr. Besant has decided the *The Theosophist* should be published at Adyar — not, as she says, because of any dissatisfaction with the magazine here, but because of necessity. What that necessity is we shall probably know in time, by mail, as cables are expensive and unsatisfactory.

But what we should like the members to know is that we are continuing a publication, *World Theosophy*, in Hollywood, the same character and price magazine as before, and that we are publishing it at the urgent request of Theosophists all over the world. Dr. Besant and others of our Leaders have given us the greatest encouragement in our last year's efforts, sufficient to convince us that such a magazine is really needed. Changing its name to *World Theosophy* will not alter its character, and Dr. Besant has given it her approval and blessing.

Apropos of this need we have received the following letter from our national President, Mr. Rogers:

"I am pleased to hear that you have decided to go on with the magazine, and shall help you all we can. We greatly need a Theosophical publication in the United States for general circulation, and I am glad that you are willing to make the sacrifice, for of course it will be that."

We firmly believe that if members will help us by sending additional subscriptions, articles we shall be able to publish a magazine that will increase in quality and value as time goes on, and will help to place, in popular, practical, and artistic form, the verities of Theosophy before its readers.

At the end of his last tour in America, Mr. C. Jinarajadasa said:

"There is a great need that in America there should be a magazine presenting our truths in simple and attractive form to the general public. I have myself no fear that such an American magazine would in any way interfere with the circulation of *The Theosophist* at Adyar.

...I can only point out that the magazines which I have seen in America of other organizations are attractively written for the general public, and are, I presume, financially successful. If we could

296

have a suitable magazine to back up our propaganda work, I feel there would be slowly a larger addition to our membership."

This is what we are endeavoring to do — make an artistic, presentable, and practical magazine that will have a general appeal for Theosophy's sake. It already is on many newsstands, in public libraries in many countries of the world, has many subscribers who are not members, as well as those who are, and not a day passes that we do not receive letters of appreciation for the work it is doing.

Even though publishing the magazine takes every hour of the day, and often a large part of the night, we so gladly give this service, not only our time, but our home, and what money we can spare, to carry on this avenue of service to the Masters.

So, dear friends, we make an urgent appeal for your help in Their work.

Sincerely yours,

Henry Hotchener, *Publisher*

Marie R. Hotchener, *Editor*[*]

The following appeared in *The Theosophical Messenger*, Vol. XIX, January 1931, n1, p306.

Dr. Besant has decided that Adyar being the International Centre should reserve the title *The Theosophist* for the magazine there. She approves continuing the magazine in Hollywood with the new title, *World Theosophy*. It will retain the same character and price as formerly. Will you please announce this in *Messenger* and say that Dr. Besant cables we may retain here the donations already sent for the magazine, and also all subscriptions, unless members instruct otherwise. We hope they will let us keep them, and urge others to subscribe, to help to continue this work, which is truly a great, but joyful responsibility. Happy New Year.

Marie and Henry Hotchener

---

[*] Hotchener, Henry, "World Theosophy", *The Theosophical Messenger*, Vol.XIX, February 1931, n2, p.320.

November 1930
Krotona E.S.T.

To All Members of the E.S.

Friends,

To the enclosed papers I will add only a few remarks, calling your special attention to the following points.

1. "The O.H. does not desire a large E.S., so much as one composed of earnest members, who have placed before themselves the goal of becoming some day Disciples of a Master. This was the basis of the E.S. when H.P.B. founded it, and is the sole reason for its existence now." (C.J.)

2. "The applicant must be willing to try to live the Raja Yoga life." (O.H.)

3. "Each E.S. member must pledge himself to some definite work which he does with the object of serving the Masters." (C.J.)

4. The applicant must "be prepared to give ordinarily an hour a day to study and to mediation on the study, or on the Inner Head, with a desire to unite his consciousness with His, or with that of any Member of the Hierarchy, in order that he may offer more useful and loving service to all the lives that surround him." (O.H.)

On those points, I wish to make the following remarks:

(1) The E.S. is the Way only for those whose ideal is the Ancient Path of Initiation, and whose heart turns to the Masters in *living* devotion and whole-hearted service.

(2) Many members, even among old workers, have almost ceased all service to the Theosophical Society, some out of weariness, others in order to "express freedom." It is when the Masters' Society is passing through a difficult time that all E.S. members should serve it all the more lovingly.

(3) Many alas! have not yet begun to realize what the Raja Yoga life of Harmlessness means... That will come gradually, I hope.... .

(4) I know of cases where the Daily Practice is omitted on the slightest pretext. Members should understand that to be released from monthly reports and placed on THEIR HONOR should make them all the more regular in their practices. Those practices are for the purpose of harmonizing the three bodies and making it possible for the SELF within to manifest. Negligence closes the door.

Brothers, we are passing through a strenuous period of readjustment; we are all on test, the Masters need servers and are watching Their School; how many of us will They find *meaning business?*

Every your friend and co-worker,
Marie Poutz
Corresponding Secretary
P.S. Your attention is also called to Circular No.1 which replaces the former Conditions of Membership and which all E.S. members are required to accept, if they wish to remain in the School.

Betty Robertson was a registered nurse as a young woman joining the Theosophical Society in October 1915.

The following announcement from *The Ojai*:

Mrs. Betty Robertson and A.P. Warrington were privately married at Mr. Warrington's residence at Krotona on Wednesday morning and left at once on a motor trip north. They expect to return to the Valley in three weeks.

The ceremony was performed by Bishop Irving S. Cooper on December 31. Their honeymoon trip will be to San Luis Obispo.

A.P. Warrington was a devoted worker from the very beginning of his connection with The Theosophical Society, and for many months he had suffering from a painful illness, but kept in close contact with all its affairs and constantly interested in its welfare. Glad tidings of his marriage come from all over the world.

A Personal Letter to Readers of the *Theosophist* December 1930.

Dear Friend:
We take pleasure in writing you about Dr. Besant's international *Theosophist* magazine published at Hollywood, California, for we feel that you would like to know of some plans which are being instituted for it.

You will perhaps remember with what high hopes Dr. Besant decided its publication a year ago, and how earnestly she appealed to the members to aid it. She said in the January *Theosophist*: "I send my affectionate blessing to all who will help me to plead the Cause of Theosophy among the huge reading public of the United States and elsewhere... Theosophists should try to spread the magazine everywhere. I appeal to them."

She also said that the Theosophical Society, being international, should have a magazine to appeal to Theosophists and others by affording them matter which, from the informative, stimulating and cultural standard, should be worthy of Theosophy and should quicken the evolution of its readers.

Almost a year has passed, and recently Dr. Besant has expressed her pleasure and satisfaction about the artistic and literary success of the magazine, but regretted that out of over 40,000 members less than 3,000 have subscribed. She has made another strong plea for subscriptions and donations, as she thinks it would be much to be regretted for such a fine channel of Theosophic work to lack support.

So anxious is she that it receive greater recognition and assistance that she is reducing the *Adyar Theosophist* to one-half its former size — to only thirty-two pages — and will use it for her official notices, reports, etc. Her international Theosophist will continue. They are convinced that the members will continue to respond to Dr. Besant's appeal. They will take the risk of continuing, and rely on the members to come forward and help.

We, the undersigned, are among those who want to aid in making this response of the members complete, and so we are asking your personal help. We know what a fine work the magazine is doing and feel sure that you will help if you can.

If you are already a subscriber you may perhaps be able to present another subscription to someone as a gift. Perhaps you can give a donation outright, no matter if only a small sum. Or you may be able to pledge a monthly donation.

Let us all do what we can, realizing how happy Dr. Besant will be that the members have recognized the importance of continuing her magazine to help the Cause of Theosophy.

Yours sincerely,
A.P. Warrington,
Marie Poutz,
Mary Gray,
May S. Rogers,
John A. Ingelman*

———————————⌘———————————

* Warrington, A.P., *The Theosophical Messenger*, "A Personal Letter to Readers of the *Theosophist*", Vol. XVIII, Dec 1930, n12, p.276.

The Siete Robles tract amid orange groves, originally known as the Mead Ranch, contained over 50 acres. Property owners, Walter J. Field and John D. Carey, two Hollywood gentlemen, left it in the hands of George Hall, who acted as manager and who later subdivided and purchased it. Hall was also at this time property manager of Krotona.

George Hall sold the largest lot in the subdivision, less than an acre, to Rev. and Mrs. Edward Martin in 1930. Edward and Rhoda Martin, born in England, became members of the Theosophical Society in Southampton in June 1910, and were acquainted with Dr. Annie Besant and C.W. Leadbeater and other leaders of the society.

Edward Martin joined the then Old Catholic Church (which later became the Liberal Catholic Church) in its early days in London where he was ordained to the priesthood by Bishop Pigott in 1925. Martin was a friend of James Wedgwood who was the first Presiding Bishop of the new Church. Martin was retired from the army, after having served the British Raj in India.

The Martins lived briefly at Krotona while Rhoda designed the mystery house of the valley with the assistance of John Roine, architect and builder, well known for his unusual work. They built together what is known as the "Taj Mahal." Rhoda had the tiles and some of the outside décor shipped from England, although not quite up to building code in that area, permission was granted by authorities on the basis that such a unique structure would surely attract visitors to the Valley.

Rhoda told the author that on one occasion on a full moon, J. Krishnamurti drove up and sat in his car watching the full moon rise over Topa Topa which shown like a great golden orb over the cupolas of the "Pleiades" and its glittering rays sparkling in the lily pool.

The house had a separate apartment in each wing of the U-shape for the Martins and for her parents when they came for visits. Rhoda's mother was one of many ladies-in-waiting for the Queen of England. Rev. Martin used the middle section under the largest dome, as a private chapel for Liberal Catholic worship. The chapel area itself contained a small stage and music auditorium as the room was designed around star points painted on the ceiling representing the Pleiades, an astronomical constellation.

After the construction was completed, Rhoda and Edward often sat on the roof outside of a little room within the center dome, which was the shrine and meditation room. There they watched the stars after the sun sank behind the Topa Topa Mountains, bathing the ridge in mauve and pick. One particular beautiful summer night, Rhoda saw the seven beautiful stars overhead, and asked Edward, an ardent astronomer, what they were. He said they were called "Pleiades" or the Seven Sisters, an thus was their home named.

The "Pleiades" has had several owners since Edward and Rhoda Martin moved to Berkeley, California, for a short time before settling in Walnut Creek in the late 1940s. Southern California's balmy climate has long inspired exotic architecture. This fantasy structure, replete with domes, mosaic tile and a small reflecting pool can be found on Avenida de la Verada looking incongruous among the ranch-style houses that surround it today.

Rev. Edward Martin passed from this earthly life May 13, 1965, at his home in Walnut Creek, California where he maintained an oratory, and Rhoda maintained a Theosophical and Metaphysical Library where the author first met Mrs. Martin, helping her with the work of the Theosophical lodge and served in her small Liberal Catholic chapel.

After the Hollywood Krotona Institute of Theosophy moved to Ojai in 1924, the influence of Krotona Hill did not stop with those who lived there. The devotion and effort of the members connected with Krotona throughout its years spurred them to engage in a number of activities for service to Brotherhood. The word had gone forth — be doers and exemplars.

By the late 1930's such avant-garde virtuosos as Ted Shawn and his wife, Ruth St. Denis, and Pavlova did much to revise the prevailing attitude of the dance in India (since it had deteriorated to a listless, minor function of the temples' votaries), and to rekindle the country's enthusiasm in its rich heritage. Uday Shankar, himself a

Brahmin and a man of tremendous personal magnetism, returned to Madras to play music composed by Shankar's younger brother, Ravi. Both musicians, two of India's greatest musicians, were recorded on RCA Victor records in the 1930s. These recordings are highly prized by collectors to this day.

At the end of 1930 Dr. Besant returned from Europe in broken health, and never recovered, but it could not stain her heart.

Farewell reception for Krishnamurti at Krotona

Dr. Besant on one of her last journeys.

Chapter 5
1931

In 1931, controversy still rages over Krishnamurti and his attitude towards the Adyar Theosophical Society.

Louis Zalk writes to Geroge Hall January 19, 1931: "We have such momentous problems connected with the Order of the Star Institute that the Krotona worry in proportion is as a small stick to a giant oak. We must turn our 'master minds' in the direction of solving the O.S.I. problems."

Mrs. Fred Hart moves in 1931 to Krotona into the Hall's house, and opens at her home a little tearoom for noontime dinners. Evening meals were only served on prior arrangement and catering for parties was undertaken in the same way. Mrs. Hart had a very pleasant living room in which she accommodated a dozen diners at a time. The cuisine was strictly vegetarian.

Before Marie Poutz left on a three month speaking tour, she reminded George Hall that though she knew he had the interest of Krotona at heart, he nonetheless had to promise during her absence he would not rent a room to *anybody* without first speaking to Mr. Warrington. She reminded Mr. Hall that there was an unseen spiritual side to Krotona, affected by everyone who came to live there, and that regarding this aspect, Mr. Warrington and herself were wholly responsible. George rented his house to the Harts, and Marie Poutz reminded him again that he had to refer the matter to Warrington, as he was the Head of Krotona, appointed by the Master as well as the Outer Head to establish a Spiritual Centre.

Krotona opened its door to the Junior class at the Nordhoff high school in the Spring of 1931 to entertain the seniors with an elaborate reception, dinner and dance with Miss Mary Nye as chairman. About 40 were seated at small tables in the music room for the feast which Mrs. Russell Andruss prepared, and after there were games and cards and dancing. This was an annual party that Krotona offered to the public.

In April, the Ojai Valley Tennis Club rented the Krotona hall for $10.00 to have their Friday night dance party from 8:00 to 11:00. The dance with Hank Wilson's orchestra of Ventura was a great success and all the young people enjoyed themselves thoroughly.

Bishop Wedgwood is under nursing care at Camberley, England; Dr. Besant describes it as "serious nervous collapse".

The following letter is from C.W. Leadbeater to Bishop Cooper, but the top half is missing.

February 17 1931

> I notice that you speak of "the Fiasco of the Coming"; I must say that I cannot quite agree with you there, for I do not regard it at all in that light. The line principally emphasized by our Krishnajee is necessarily so different in many ways from that which we had to take in preparing the way for it, that it has had a disintegrating effect on some of our institutions, such as the Liberal Catholic Church and Co-Masonry, but it has shaken out of those only the members whose faith in their efficacy was insecurely founded; and at any rate this Coming has been very much more successful than that in Palestine was during the same space of time. You will remember that in that case the full result of the teaching appeared only after some centuries; is it not likely that history will repeat itself in that

respect? Those for whom this Mystic Path is the natural and easiest way will follow it and succeed in it; those who truly belong to the Occult line of development are still following it with as much enthusiasm as ever. Others who drop away from it merely with the idea of following something new, which may perhaps seem easier to them, are in many cases already drifting back again, while others of them remain suspended, doing nothing in particular. Whether they will really be better or happier remains to be seen. Anyhow, differences of opinion on minor points must never be allowed to interfere with private friendships. With all heartiest good wishes
I am ever
Yours affectionately
C.W. Leadbeater

Why the following two letters were attached to the above letter, the author does not know.

The four gospels were written at Alexandria, and are all variants of or improvements upon the original story written at a monastery in the desert by the abbot Matthaeuw (in Hebrew). It was his idea to cast the life-story of every Initiate into allegorical form for popular consumption, weaving into it some recollections or rather traditions of the story of the Christ and some of the world-traditions common to the stories of older Saviours (which he knew from his connection with India and Persia), all intentionally confused with and centred round the life of a quite obscure prophet or reformer who preached about a century later than the real Christ. Matthaeus sent his sketch to the Alexandrian chief abbot, asking him to have it worked up and translated into Greek. The Alexandrian set a number of his young monks to work at it; each tried it in his own way, and four of these attempts have been preserved to our day, that is all.

I have considerable doubt as to whether <u>anybody</u> ever really was crucified except perhaps among some of the barbarous African tribes; the Romans, you know, were after all a highly-civilised people. The crucifixion story is borrowed straight from the Egyptian ritual; I have never traced the origin of the story of the two thieves, though I daresay I shall come across it some day. Many people seem specially interested in the life of the Master Jesus and of the Christ, and have asked that its story should be written. Perhaps some time I may do this, but I have several books in view which must be finished first, and a man of sixty cannot look forward to indefinite periods of labour in his present body. With all heartiest good wishes

I am ever

Yours affectionately

C.W. Leadbeater

I found in C.W.L.'s handwriting various odds and ends about the Church, (L.C.C.) and I think you will be glad to keep them.

I am just sending to the Press a good deal of material about the L.C.C., consisting of letters written by C.W.L. to Dr. Besant in connection with the interviews that he and Bishop Wedgwood had with the Lord, and instructions given about the re-arrangement of the Ceremony of the Mass, etc! I will send you a copy as soon as it is published. Of course, there were clear instructions from the Lord about the use of the First Ray Benediction.* The Synod of Bishops who met here agreed, however, to omit it. Later I asked C.W.L. why? As you know, though he was Presiding Bishop, of course he was a Bishop on the same level as the others. He told me it was Wedgwood who wanted the Benediction omitted, and I rather think also Cooper, if he was here then. C.W.L. was never a fighter, and furthermore, he told me that Wedgwood was already

---

* The First Ray Benediction mentioned above is as follows: "May the Holy Ones, Whose pupils we aspire to become, show us the Light we seek, give us the strong aid of Their compassion and Their wisdom. There is a peace that passeth understanding; it abides in the hearts of those who live in the Eternal; there is a power that maketh all things new; it lives and moves in those who know the Self as One. May that peace brood over us, that power uplift us, till we stand where the One Initiator is invoked, till we see His STAR shine forth."

a sick man, so he consented. But when he got to Australia, he gave strict injunction to Tweedie, the Regionary Bishop, never to omit it.

The Church made a supreme blunder, and since then has been definitely ansemic. I do not think there is any other religion through which the Lord has attempted one reform after another where He has failed. I won't write any more about this.

Ever Yours,

(The author believes it is from C. Jinarajadasa written about 1952 to Dr. Henry A. Smith)

From this material we can see that, for some reason, despite D. Besant's admoniton on the falseness of comparing the present to the past, we find theosophical leaders in this period comparing what is taking place with Krishnamurti to what happened 2000 years ago.

———————————————

C.W. Leadbeater was asked many questions regarding Krishnamurti and the World-Teacher. This article from May of 1931, "Questions and Answers," gives a sense of the questions and his replies:

Since you state that Mr. Krishnamurti is only a manifestation of the World-Teacher and not the World-Teacher himself, is it possible that that manifestation may not be expressing itself perfectly all the time, and therefore that Mr. Krishnamurti can make statements that seem condemnatory of certain movements that the World-Teacher has stated should be supported for the benefit of humanity?

Answer: There you are again, setting the two things against one another. I do not want to dogmatize, but you must try to realize the fact that the World-Teacher is a being of stupendous power on an elevation which we cannot imagine to ourselves even. He can never express one-hundredth part of himself in any physical manifestation. If you will kindly compare the present with the manifestation in Palestine two thousand years ago, you will see that exactly the same questions arose in people's minds then. You say here that I say that he is a manifestation. Don't you see that all you can ever have on the physical plane about the World-Teacher is a manifestation? How could particular people have the whole of that wonderful cosmic consciousness? You cannot have the whole of your own consciousness; happily, the ego is a much better fellow than the personality here. You can express just one phase or little part of it down here, but that is all. If you cannot manifest the whole of yourself down here how could so much greater a person manifest the whole of himself? You will see He did not manifest the whole of Himself last time, that is, if we are to believe the whole of the Gospel stories, which I do not believe are entirely reliable. If you read them, He is credited with saying things that the World-Teacher could not have said. What about the cursing of the barren fig tree for not bearing fruit when it could not possibly have fruit? You will remember the strong language used about Scribes and Pharisees. Look at the words the Christ is said to have addressed to his mother when she gently reminded him there was not any wine. He is said to have replied, "Woman, what have I to do with ye!" That, I am bound to say, is a mistranslation. What He really said was, "Gumi," meaning woman, but there is no other word in Greek that he could have used, excepting Mother or Queen. The word Gumi might be used to any land, and the real translation is "What to me and to thee,: or "What is it to thee and to me?" "What business is that of ours?": She knew very well what he meant, because she immediately proceeded to say to the servants, "Whatever he says to you, do it." She was not much shaken by the statement. A great many things are put down to Jesus which could not have been said by the World-Teacher, and quite possibly were not said by Jesus. You need not worry yourself about all this.

You say Krishnamurti makes statements that seem condemnatory. He goes further. He began by saying "Your ceremonies are all useless." I would not say "useless," but

310

unnecessary. What he said first was that ceremonies were all unnecessary. Throw them aside. The Lord Buddha said so two thousand five hundred years ago. You cannot take the Great Initiation without casting off a certain flicker, which means belief in any kind of ceremony. You must not hold that any ceremony is necessary because to hold it is a superstition. It may not be necessary, but it is very useful. Our President said, "A motor car is not necessary; I can always walk, but I can do more in the same time by taking a motor car," and Krishnamurti himself made a similar remark in quite a recent *International Star Bulletin*. He said, "Of course you can, if you like, go down on your hands and pickup every little bit off the floor, but you can do it in far less time with a vacuum cleaner." That is what we say about ceremonies. I could not myself produce the whole effect of a church ceremony, but I could produce a very great deal of it by a sustained thought of the will, but it would take two or three days. By using the machinery of a ceremony I can end the same thing in half-an-hour. Why not use the ceremony? That is my point of view.

Of course each of these two paths has its advantages, and I think each has its disadvantages. Undoubtedly the use of machinery and ceremonial has a danger that people may come to think in the ceremonial and nothing else. They will be pure ceremonialists. It has happened. I have seen church ceremonies performed — not in our own small church — where the whole thing has been hurried through, without any apparent attention to the meaning. Of course that is bad, and a thing of that sort might easily come to be taken a a useful thing, whereas it is useless. That certainly is a danger. One guards against that as one does against other dangers, by using one's own common-sense. It is better for you to leave these things alone. You may reasonably think — that it is true and incontestable — that no physical manifestation whatever can fully express the splendor of the whole. You may also remember that the position of the World-Teacher is one of enormous responsibility; that He has to carry on all religions and all educational work; He is under the great spiritual King

311

the minister for religion and education, and it is His business to endeavor to encourage all that is good in all the religions.

I know what is the matter. It is the old Christian illusion that used to be brought in my childhood. There was said to be only one religion, and that was Christianity. There were a few heathen religions, but all we had to do was to persuade people to come out of them and adopt Christianity. Little children were expected to have missionary boxes and go about collecting money to help the heathen. Many will remember that time. It was not logical, and now that we believe in Karma and reincarnation, we see that sort of thing was distinctly futile. Don't you see the world has a far more definite system of philosophy than is ordinarily given in orthodox Christianity? Orthodox Christianity really does not teach much in the way of philosophy. The more learned people in all the churches have their philosophical systems and try more or less successfully to fit orthodox teaching into these philosophies. They have to abandon quite a number of the old tenets in order to make them fit at all. They have not realized that many of these old tenets referred to symbols and not to facts.

All these so-called heathen religions have a great deal to say about philosophy; perhaps we might except Mohammedanism. There is a philosophy there, the Sufi, but it seems to be followed only by a minority. In Hinduism, Buddhism, and Parseism there is a fine system of philosophy; there are six in Hinduism, and you may take your choice. If you only knew a little more abut the old religions you would not be worrying about this. The one thing at present to remember is, Don't worry about it.

Many of you have heard Krishnamurti many times. If you are in the least sensitive you will agree with me that a most wonderful influence is poured out when he speaks. That, to my mind, is the greatest thing of the manifestation and the best evidence, if you want evidence that the World-Teacher does stand behind the manifestation. That influence flows out from him, and if you will only keep your lower mind quiet and let that influence sink in, you will take a very great deal.

312

I have seen them do it again and again in other countries; Krishnamurti will make some startling statement in order to arouse the people's attention, to catch them and wake them up. It is his main mission to pour life into the people. It is the lower mind that at once arises against that statement and says, "I cannot believe that," and you go on arguing about it in your own mind and miss the next ten sentences or so of what he says. You shut out the influence he tries to pour out. That is a very great mistake. I should say, listen to all that he says; if any of it fits your own case, apply it at once; see how far it applies. "Do I feel like that? Is it true that I am allowing myself to be subjected in one way or another?" Make a note of the thing. You will often hear things said that you won't understand. You cannot expect that your lower mind can understand everything all at once, but do not stop at the time to argue about it because you shut out that beautiful influence if you stop to argue in your own mind. It seems to me that what is said is really of such importance to us, that is my own feeling, but you must not take that as gospel. I do object very much to the people who will not think for themselves, but swallow everything they are told. It is not fair to a person trying to help. Lay yourself open to the influence and draw that in, and if what is said applies to you, then see whether you cannot modify your life accordingly, but if you are doing good work and can see that good is being done, then my own suggestion would be to continue the work you are doing. You cannot go wrong in helping your fellow men. The question at issue is, are you really helping them? Have you seen good results produced? I can bear testimony that I have seen a great deal of good done by the use of ceremonial. I have seen a person gradually educated through it until his own character was changed. I have seen a young man who was coarse and uneducated, trained through another type of ceremonial until he filled all the offices in succession, made a cultured gentleman merely by having to play his part in a certain form of ceremonial which I had better not discuss here, as it has nothing to do with the church.

I would not start criticizing or condemning. Listen to both

sides and use your own brains, and try to see which gives you the explanation most suited to you, bearing in mind that the other explanation is certain to suit some other people better.*

To all members of the E.S. throughout the world goes out an earnest call from Annie Besant for competent workers to come to Adyar and help build-up the "flaming Centre" asked for by the Masters.

C. Jinarajadasa also sent out a circular, and did not mention Krotona as an Esoteric Center. This caused a great deal of harm to the work at Krotona, since contributors asked why they should support Krotona in the Ojai Valley if it was not an Esoteric Center, blessed by the Masters. Warrington, Hall, Zalk, Hotchener, Wardall, and Holland request a pronouncement from C. Jinarajadasa as soon as possible.

Ms. Beatrice Wood announced that she had just completed a one-act play with four characters, suitable for Lodge production, dealing with life after death. The Ojai Valley Oaks Lodge, was interested in producing it after they moved into their new home on Founder's Day.

At that time the Ojai Valley Tennis Club Board Members were: Sidney W. Treat, President, Frank Cist, Vice-President, Sam Gorham, Secretary, W.W. Bristol, Treasurer.

April 10 1931
Ojai Valley Tennis Club

> Dear Mr. Hall:
> I want to thank you on behalf of the Ojai Valley Tennis Club for your kindness in consenting to let us use your hall for our dance Friday night, April 24th.
> I believe our understanding is that we are to have this hall from 8:30 to 11:00 on that evening with use of your punch bowl and glasses, that six members of the Club are to be on hand — three men and three women — to keep an eye on things, and that we are to pay for our privileges only the actual cost to you of our use of the

---

* Leadbeater, C.W., "Questions and Answers", *World Theosophy*, May 1931, Vo.1, p.344-346.

314

hall, which is a very generous offer on your part. I hope our use of it will be satisfactory in every way.

Unfortunately, I am compelled to leave for the East this following Tuesday and suggest that after that time, any question that might possibly arise in this connection be taken up with Mr. Sidney W. Treat, the President of the Club. A copy of this letter is going to Mr. Warrington.

Thanking you again for your cooperation, I am

Sincerely yours,

Frank Cist, Vice-President

P.S. I have spoken to Mrs. Gally of your cottages.

On February 18 1931, resolution presented by George H. Hall to Krotona Board of Trustees :

Whereas all money given to Krotona Institute was solicited and given either in the name of Dr. Besant or for the T.S. while Krotona was the T.S. Headquarters; and

Whereas all claims on such funds on the part of the T.S. have been paid, and the remaining monies in the possession of Krotona Institute are therefore wholly E.S. funds; and

Whereas none of the funds so solicited and given have ever been given to Dr. Besant; and

Whereas Dr. Besant borrowed from the Krotona Institute $25,000 in 1927;

Now therefore be it resolved that the unpaid balance of said note, both as regards principal and interest, be and is hereby canceled, and the Secretary is instructed to send said canceled note and a copy of this Resolution to Dr. Annie Besant at once.

This Resolution was opposed by Mr. Warrington, and as a result of his argument was not passed by the Board. It was subsequently collected without interest from her estate, A.P.W. was right about this.

G.H.

315

May 3 1931

Dear Mr. Hall,

I wish to thank you again with on my own account and that of the Tennis Club for your kindness in letting us have the use of your hall for our Friday night dance. With bad weather, I am afraid impressions of Ojai without this dance would have been rather bad. As it was and in your impression and lovely setting I am sure all our young people enjoyed themselves thoroughly. I hear that the dance was a great success and hope that you were equally well satisfied on your part.

Sincerely yours,

Frank Cist, Vice-President Ojai Valley Tennis Club

May 9 1931

Dear Mr. Cist:

Thanks very much for your good letter of May 3. We are very glad that the Tennis Club could have the benefit of our hall, and that the dance was such a success from every point of view. I regret that I could not attend myself, but I saw to it personally that my superintendent and building custodian made all necessary arrangements.

Should you or any organization with which you are connected ever wish the use of the hall in the future for any purpose whatever, I am sure we shall be happy to let you have it. And if you will kindly make the application to me personally, it will avoid any confusion or trouble with subordinates.

Very sincerely yours,

G.H. Hall, Manager

Krotona Institute

May 7 1931

My dear Mr. Hall

I have today O.K.'ed for payment your bill of $10.00 for the use of the hall. I wish to repeat Mr. Cist's thanks as expressed in his letter of April 10th for your very generous offer of allowing us the use of the building at only the actual cost to you. In the name of the Tennis Club I thank you and your organization.

I asked Mr. Warrington to be sure and let me know if any

damage was done to the building. May I repeat this request to you, for the Tennis Club wishes to take care of anything of that sort and leave only the pleasantest memories of their dance in the minds of the Krotona people.

Very sincerely,

Sidney W. Treat,

President, Ojai Valley Tennis Club

George Hall was not able to attend the dance, but he was glad to hear that it was a great success and everybody enjoyed it. As business manager of the Krotona Corporation, he wanted the people of Ojai to know that Krotona was always glad to have them use the hall, and the rental charge was only made to cover actual expense involved.

May 23 1931

My dear Warrington,

By President's order, George (Arundale) sorted out her letters. He has handed me some of your's when she cannot answer them. So I deal with them.

1. Re. Krotona Board, the only thing I can suggest is talk matters over with George; (Hall) draw up a full statement; authorize him to present it when, perhaps by then, if she is better, she may be able give some indication of what she wants.

2. You asked her to recommend your wife for probation. She cannot now take up these matters. What you can do is this. Every Brother's considered request will not be refused by the Mahachohan, but each Brother takes full responsibility for the developments of his request. If you care to write to C.W.L., he will pass on your request to Mahachohan and inform you of the results.

3. Similarly the case of A. A. Duany, about whom you write on Feb. 2.

C. Jinarajadasa

May 30 1931
Krotona Institute

My dear George, (Hall)

I do not know what you are doing to gain tenants for the Bachelor Apartments, but I hereby offer you two suggestions:

One, that notices be posted in the Lodges of Southern California to some such effect as I am suggesting in the enclosed memorandum.

The other, that non-Theosophists of respectable standing be admitted to the Apartments, and to that end they be offered for rent as other property in the village is offered for rent.

Miss Poutz and I have concluded to lift the E.S. and T.S. limitation on these Apartments since there is not sufficient demand from our own people to keep them occupied.

Cordially yours,

A.P. Warrington

George Hall agreed with the above regarding the apartments, and would send off to the lodges notices.

June 22 1931

My dear C.J., (Jinarajadasa)

I thank you for your kind letter of May 23rd advising me how to act with regard to those communications sometime ago addressed to our President, upon which she is now unable to take action.

I thank you also for the fortnightly report that comes regularly and keeps us posted with regard to Adyar. I look for these eagerly.

My own health is growing daily better. I am working in the garden every day and this is helping greatly.

I am planning to go to Convention where I have been requested to give the Blavatsky Lecture. I wish I were able to give as delightful a sketch of this great personage as that which appeared recently in the *Theosophist* from your pen. I am trying really to get the National President to modify his plan as to this lecture, so as to convert it into a symposium of H.P.B. to be participated in by leading lecturers in attendance.

I hope you won't allow yourself to work too hard. The neurasthenia that I thought was beginning to develop when you were here last, if really suffered by you, will be found a very difficult thing to overcome, except by the most relaxed methods. No one knows better than I, for I have suffered from it all my life in varying degrees.

Sincerely yours,

A.P.W.

C. Jinarajadasa speaking to members of the Esoteric School, at Adyar, who wanted to develop psychism, reminded them what Brother Besant said: "They like to be clairvoyant and such things; they like to hear about the Masters, *but they won't pay the price.*" The more the powers of mind are developed, the more extensive become the responsibilities of man, and the greater the crimes of which he is capable. Misuse of mental powers, and here misuse means *selfish* use, is incalculably more far reaching in its destructive effects than the abuse of physical powers.

Warrington was reported to have said:

> Those who wish for those powers evidently do not know what they really are nor how rapid and uncontrollable are their effects.
>
> If we are sure that no selfishness nor anger nor any other negative thing is within us, then we can take and use these forces, otherwise death and ruin will be in our path if we attempt to use them.
>
> Another reason is that much time is wasted in these practices inasmuch as all results flowing from them perish at death, leaving only a tendency to take up the practice upon the next rebirth.
>
> Lastly, complete renouncing of possessions, and complete psychological retirement from the world. Those who go in for it half way will surely be damaged.

The price of psychism still reigns throughout the Theosophical Society, especially within the Esoteric School.[*]

———————————— ❧ ————————————

Mr. Walter J. Field, passed away August 14, 1931, in Hollywood, a long time Trustee of the Krotona Institute.

By October, Mrs. Sarah Mayes went to Headquarters as a new worker. Along with her was Miss Mignon Reed to be an addition to the Staff.

---

[*] See Appendix, "On the Esoteric School and Psychism".

319

The Society was at a crucial point, changes were occurring, new ideas developing, and there was no better time to prepare to work cooperatively, and to face serenely the future and to work steadily on in its great purpose, that of being Their agent in giving the Ancient Wisdom to the world.

Warrington, International Vice-President, and Mrs. Warrington announced that they would attend the convention program under the Symposium on *H.P.B. and Her Work* to be held in the Sherman Hotel at Chicago on Sunday evening, August 16. It was reported that an audience of over 800 attended. Warrington gave the lecture "H.P.B., World Genius" at the Blavatsky Centenary Exercises on the ideals of the Society, and its purpose and place in the plan.

By the end of July, Krotona Institute had just closed its first session of instruction in general subjects presented from a Theosophical point of view. Warrington expressed his gratitude by the results obtained in this first tentative attempt to bring into renewed activity the instructions that were offered at the old Krotona, at the Hollywood location. He asked that each of the five teachers should hand in to the Chairman of the Faculty a thousand word summary of the work done by him or her during the Institute, laying stress on the spiritual idealism that always lies behind Theosophy, making the study of life more vital, and that the Chairman compile the same into the form of a transaction of the Institute for such circulation as might be hereafter deemed wise.

The following letter has a pencil written statement on it, that it was read to Dr. Arundale, but not given him to see.

September 2 1931

The Rt. Rev. George S. Arundale
Hollywood, Calif.

Dear Bishop George,
In response to your request for information with regard to the situation at Krotona under the 1929 re-organization, I beg to enclose copies of two letters written by myself to Dr. Besant; one

by Miss Poutz, and four other communications written to me by friends which explain themselves.

The reorganization, I was told, was ordered and communicated by Dr. Besant to Messrs. Zalk, Hall and Holland in a meeting of which I, the Vice-President, had no notice and from which I was thus excluded, although I was stopping at the same hotel where the meeting was held. When I learned what had taken place, it was impossible for me to retain my reverence for Dr. Besant. She was absent from the body and that decisions were directly or indirectly asked of her which normally she would have considered repugnant to her high ethical sense. It is because of this that I am of the firm opinion that Dr. Besant did what she was asked to do in a state of substantial absenteeism, or upon unverified representations; otherwise, she would have been more than equal to all of her responsibilities in the premises, as has been her life long practice.

That she was approached to carry out the present scheme is evidenced by the letter of Mr. Schuller [contractor who built large hall] forming a part of this correspondence. In this he states that Mr. Hall declared that he was going to see that I lost my right to give orders. In Chicago this was accomplished. Mr. Hall was told by me that I had intended to ask Dr. Besant to reduce our Board from 15 to 7 and to change the official headquarters from Los Angeles to Ventura County. This also was accomplished, but not by me. It is significant, also, that rumors reached me from others than Mr. Schuller that Mr. Hall had announced that he was going to Chicago to unseat me in my position here. When he returned to Ojai he crowed over his success, as stated in Mr. Schuller's letter.

The cause of Mr. Hall's turning away from me lay in the re-building of the old library. I found it urgently necessary to expand the building by adding a lecture hall. Incidentally, it became advisable to add three dwelling apartments, and to correct some of the errors of construction in the old building; also to replace its shabby furniture. This Mr. Hall opposed. But, as he had always opposed important progressive steps at Krotona, it was nothing new to me. So, I went ahead with the work without that assistance from him which we ought to have had, and succeeded in completing the undertaking by raising two-thirds of the cost in specially solicited donations, the remaining one-third (approximately $7,000.) coming out of the regular Krotona assets. Thus Krotona obtained a handsome new building, needed in every part, by the expenditure of only one-third its actual additional cost, on which we are now earning about 10%. This Mr. Hall condemned.

This spirit of opposition was shown recently in opposing the establishment of the Nursery here; and especially in his opposition to my arranging last spring for the re-opening of the three months' Institute Courses with Dr. Cousins as the leading teacher. He took me severely to task for the latter, fearing it might cost Krotona something. But I went ahead with it, made a great success of it, and closed the Courses with all bills paid and a surplus in hand for the next occasion.

Attention is called to Mr. Schuller's statement that Mr. Hall exacted of him the personal gift of $1100. or one-half of the commission to which he, Mr. Schuller, was entitled as builder. About $300. of this was evidently given back to Krotona, as Mr. Hall subscribed that amount to the building fund.

The reference in Mr. Schuller's letter to the gossip of Mrs. Hall, in which she imparted to him her opinions of my private affairs I should pass over without comment were it not for the assertion which he claims she made to the effect that I received donations which I did not record but kept for my private use. Perhaps I do not need to tell you that no greater falsehood could be told of me than this, and both she and her husband know it. I have taken every outer means to see that the current of incoming funds has always been directed to a fund treasurer other than myself, and by this and every other means I have been rigid in my avoidance of all contacts with money, knowing only too well how unkind associates are to make false accusations when they have something to be gained thereby. Mr. Hall himself has been one of those whom I have officially trusted with funds, even of large amounts, and it never occurred to me to have the slightest suspicion of his probity before this deeply false accusation was wickedly made by his wife. And even now I have no word to say, as my trust continues in spite of all that has recently emanated from the Hall family.

To show you that Mr. Hall's attitude to others has been widely different from the friendly one which he and his wife have shown to me, I have enclosed the letter from John Roine, a builder and architect, a brother Mason, Theosophist and E.S. member; and the one from Rev. Frank Kilbourne, likewise a brother Theosophist, E.S. member, also a Priest in the Liberal Catholic Church, and editor and manager of the weekly, "The Ojai." In both of these letters Mr. Hall calls me by a designation which one associates more naturally with habituees of bar-rooms and the like. Mrs. Couch's letter also shows the contemptuous attitude he holds toward all who reside at Krotona. And this is the man who has been made the Secretary, the

Treasurer, and the General Manager at Krotona.

To me he has never shown the front which is common to him when talking to others. Up to 1929 he was my trusted official employee and his direct attitude toward me was always one of deference and apparent kindness and friendliness, even though he always disagreed with every thought and proposal which I had for the welfare of Krotona, proposals which have always in the end proved their value. Thus he has continuously shown two faces; a deferential one to me, and a contemptuous one to those outside. His unpopularity in the Valley is, in my belief, greater than that of any other person living here. And old friend said to me recently that George Hall had ruined Theosophy in this Valley by his contemptible methods, and that the really fine Theosophists living here could not build up a favorable sentiment for Theosophy as fast as his conduct tore it down. And this is the man that Dr. Besant and Louis Zalk have jointly chosen to represent Theosophical interests in the Valley of the future. To do this they have measurably destroyed the good work and standing of the man who is responsible for establishing Krotona and bringing it up to its present status of success. I am sure that Dr. Besant's work in Ojai will never take on its proper dignity and hold the rightful respect of the people of this community, so long as the present situation continues. By one ill-considered stroke she played into the hands of the ambitious man who could least nobly give her the representation she deserved, and in doing so she, to all outer appearances, ruthlessly and without cause dismissed the man who had served her devotedly and successfully during the best years of his life.

Indeed, Mr. Hall has told me that her apparent intention to ignore me went so far as to exclude me utterly from the new Krotona Board, and that it was due to the persuasion of himself and Mr. Zalk that she finally consented to nominate me as a member. I was further informed that Mr. Zalk was to take my post of Vice-President, but that he generously refused it. He desired that I should continue to hold it. And so I do, but with every vestige of authority excluded from it. Mr. Hall also told me that Dr. Besant's instruction that I was to occupy my dwelling at Krotona for life without cost was suggested by them, and that she merely gave her assent to it. Likewise, as to the small stipend I receive out of the Krotona profits. Dr. Besant herself has written me nothing as to why I have incurred her displeasure, nor why I was given no opportunity to speak for myself.

There is one accusation which Mr. Hall admitted to me had

been made — that I was extravagant in spending money, and there was danger that I would mortgage the property: an accusation equally as false as the one made by Mrs. Hall. I challenge anybody to show, after the most expert examination of our books, that my administration has been anything but economical and careful; and I assert that which is of impossible for any person to mortgage the property of a corporation without due process of law, which includes a proper resolution of the Board and a transcript of the resolution showing the authority of the Board has been regularly obtained. Thus this accusation communicated to Dr. Besant, and evidently influencing her, was false throughout and was merely intended to accomplish the end that was gained.

Now, if the real Dr. Besant is satisfied with the present situation, I have no more to say.

But, if she wishes Krotona to be a living centre, as I am sure she does, and not merely a real estate proposition, there must be someone at its head who is capable of some degree of spiritual leadership, who lives on the place and whose hands are not completely tied as to its business affairs.

All this can be accomplished and the misfortune of 1929 be rectified by requesting the Board to elect either myself or some more capable Initiate as resident president, with Mr. Zalk, if need be, as Vice-President in charge of the property interests and sole non-Initiate, and the Board otherwise to be composed of Initiates who are really interested in the centre.

There would be the following experienced and trustworthy Initiates living in Ojai and within two hours' run of Ojai to choose from for the new Board.

Max Wardall, John Tettemer, Mrs. Gardiner, Henry Hotchener, Irving S. Cooper, Mrs. Rogers, Mrs. Hotchener, A.P. Warrington, Mrs. Gray, John Ingelman, Miss Poutz, Mrs. Elizabeth Sanford,

With Mr. Zalk sole non-Initiate.

Such a change might be useful for I have never had from Mr. Hall, nor any other member of the old board a single suggestion or thought looking to the interested, progressive developement of this place whereby it might increase its revenue and its usefulness to the Masters — only opposition at all times by its most active member when any progressive measure was proposed, his continuous attitude being exclusively static.

Mr. Hall can be employed to look after details which he will do very well under instructions, for Mr. Hall, the subordinate, is a very different person from Mr. Hall the boss. Mr. Holland would serve

324

as counselor as readily off the Board as on it, for he is impersonally interested in either case, though always very helpful and kind with his services.

I am not seeking in making this suggestion to acquire again any responsibilities for Krotona; I already have them, and merely ask that they be again officially recognized. Krotona was my dream; it has been my achievement; and it is my karma as an agent of the Masters. This karma I cannot avoid and others can only delay my fulfilment of it or helpfully make it easier for me.

And this does not mean that I am so attached personally to what I believe to be "my" work here that I am not willing to let go when a cause arises. On the contrary, I shall be glad to quit and do anything else when it is the will of the Master, or the will of whom I can only designate as the real Dr. Besant frankly conveyed to me directly, the Dr. Besant who still holds my affection, devotion and reverence.

Ever sincerely,

A.P. Warrington

It was around Spring in May, that Warrington and Miss Poutz concluded to lift the E.S. and T.S. limitation on the Bachelor Apartments since there was not sufficient demand from members to keep them occupied.

Another year, another elaborate reception, dinner and dance at Krotona Hall with Miss Mary Nye as chairman, seated about 40 around small tables in the music room for the feast which Mrs. Russell Andruss prepared. Later in the evening, there were games, cards and dancing in the beautiful hall. This annual party is one of the most anticipated affairs that the junior class at the Nordhoff High School anticipated.

In June, Mr. and Mrs. William Mayes, Mr. and Mrs. Ricardo Ros entertained a party honoring the birthday of Mrs. Betty Warrington at the Krotona library.

There are many reports throughout the world printed in the newspapers regarding Krishnamurti, and what he said. Here is only one report from the *New York-Herald Tribune*, for October 20, 1931. Krishnamurti having arrived in New York the day before on the Rotterdam is reported as saying he was misled by his early training.

Jiddu Krishnamurti, Hindu student, who was heralded upon his arrival here several years ago by Mrs. Annie Besant as the "Vehicle of Truth", "Second Messiah", and "Voice of the Great Teacher", reiterated yesterday that he had renounced Theosophy and the claims Mrs. Besant had made for him, upon his return here in the Holland-American liner Rotterdam.

Journeying up the Hudson yesterday he told how he had been chosen by Mrs. Besant to fulfill her claims that he was the "Voice of the Great Teacher". He was dwelling in the quiet of his father's house when Mrs. Besant learned of his eleven-year-old mystic leanings, he said. In justice to her and to his father, he said, they obviously believed in all sincerity that his grasp of Theosophy at that age and his remarks warranted their assumption that they had at last discovered the "Vehicle of Truth".

He recalled how he had been raised by Mrs. Besant in the belief that he was the "Voice of the Great Teacher", which he at first thought was his vocation. But later when his mental faculties matured he saw the error into which he had been led, possibly by emotional ardor. He said that gradually he drifted away from the beliefs held by Mrs. Besant, and, in fact, from all religious sects and beliefs.

"I learned that each of us must do his own thinking", he continued. "The Deity, the better life, lies within each and all of us. You cannot organize a system of truth; neither can you or I set a religious standard for another".

"His plans here were undetermined", he said.

Warrington, accompanied by Mrs. Warrington sailed on November 6 from San Francisco to attend the Convention at Adyar.

It was published in the Canadian *Theosophist* for November 1931, page 280, that:

"Dr. de Purucker made it known that his greatest desire was to bring about a unification of the various Theosophical groups throughout the world under his leadership. Failing unification, with a recognized centre at Point Loma, Dr de Purucker stated that he would be willing to have such sections as recognized his leadership exert their own autonomy, with a sort of super-society or structure, with himself to give the lead."

Dr. Besant, although told by her physician to stay in her upstairs room at Adyar, came down supported on both sides, her face wreathed in smiles. She apologized for her weakness, and asked for Mrs. Betty Warrington as she declared the 1931 Convention open, asking C.W. Leadbeater to speak for her. After A.P. Warrington read his address, he had to correct that reference to agree with the happy fact of her unexpected arrival. Although she was very weak, she was present much to the amusement of the audience. Dr. Besant gave one of the most significant talks of her remarkable career.

Dr. Besant's address to the 56th Annual Convention at Adyar on December 24, 1931 came across in a clear powerful voice, her first paragraph:

Friends, the point I want to impress upon all of you today is that only as you live Theosophy can you spread Theosophy. It is not our words, it is our life, that affects people. And I want each one of you and all whom you have influence with to remember that the man who lives a theosophical life is the best propagandist of theosophical ideas. It is not our words that influence people so much as our lives; our lives if they are unselfish, pure, loving and helpful are the best propaganda of theosophical ideal; for it is no good talk Theosophy unless we live what we talk.

---

* Besant, Annie. "Dr. Besant's Address to the 56th Annual Convention", *The Theosophical Messenger*, Vol. XX, Feb 1932, No.2, pp. 30, 43.

The whole address really was a summing up of her life's philosophy during a long career of selfless devotion to the welfare of humanity. She thought that most of us were afraid to trust ourselves, and urged that we go deep within ourselves and give our trust there. It matters nothing what you believe; it matters enormously what you are.

The following talk was delivered on December 25, 1931.

The Future That Awaits Us
By A.P. Warrington

I too was very greatly delighted to learn when I arrived at Adyar that Amaji was so much improved. I had within my heart of some time a picture of her great "comeback", as we say in America, after the Internment. It was told me that during the internment the body was as one deserted. Of course she was very busy on higher planes, but at the moment of release she came back with a bang, so to say. I have longed to see this repeated in the present instance. It is a thought I have held in my mind, and it has not left me; I still hold it.

Well; friends, I am going to ask the privilege of sitting down, and just talking as friend to friend. I will confide to you the fact that this is the first audience I have addressed for many years. I have been bearing very heavy karma on the physical plane, due to years and years of heavy over-work, a thing I would warn all enthusiastic Theosophists against. You may be able to do an intensive amount of good service for the time being, but inevitably, under the law, you will have to lie up and pay the karmic price of it. That is what I have been doing. So, I am not prepared to give a formal address to you, but shall just talk informally.

When Mr. Jinarajadasa asked me to give him a title for my talk, I could think of nothing but The Future That Awaits Us. That sounds pretentious — it means I am a prophet. Do not make any mistake, I cannot give a prophecy. But there is a way of looking into the future by judging of the past. Sometime if you have a broad scheme or plan laid before you, you can see

328

by looking over that scheme that it divides itself up normally into certain sections; and if you can see that certain sections of that plan have been fulfilled, you can fairly well make up your mind as to what is yet to come. Well, I shall approach my subject somewhat from that standpoint today.

In the beginning our Theosophical Society very obviously had a program laid down before it. Just for the moment, suppose we place ourselves in the position of wishing to organize a society, such as our own; to do a work such as we have been doing. The first thing that comes to our minds is, we must have a message; and then we must have a messenger. We start with a message and find a messenger; but that which is to be done we must have an organizer to do; and he must have an organization through which to do his work. In looking back over the history of our Society we see that this state of affairs obtained in the beginning. There was a great message — Theosophy, and a remarkable messenger — H.P.B., and Col. Olcott was the organizer. That was the nucleus of the great world work to be done in the name of the Masters.

The next thing was for our organizer to find his workers to get the organization well established throughout the world. It became necessary that he should gather together students who should thoroughly inform themselves as to the message. They should be able from the records of the past find evidence of the message through tradition in the ages of the past, so that its heredity should impress us all the more fully as to its reality. From the first we had the students. Gradually the philosophical aspect of our message drew to us those most capable of studying the subject and laying it before the world in their own words; in the forms which the world at that time could best understand and appreciate.

Thus we gathered round us some great figures, among them our great President and her faithful companion and collaborator who is now Bishop Leadbeater, our beloved Seer. (I never use that word that I do not remember what Col. Olcott said once when questions were coming in, and Bishop Leadbeater and he held the platform: "Don't ask me, ask Charles; he is the seer, I am only the overseer.")

These associated with these leaders have since built up a practical and understandable philosophy of life, the essence if you like of Theosophy; which is more comprehensible by the minds accustomed to think in Western and modern ways than the original message in its more recondite forms. The message as it came and was expressed through *Isis Unveiled* and the *Secret Doctrine* was not quite as easily understood as the interpretation which has come from the later writers and speakers; and so a very important work fell to their hand and has been very splendidly done. That represents the first phase of our work.

We see that our Third Object and our Second Object were predominant in the expression of Theosophy during the earlier days. Since then it appears that we have come to the point where we must throw the emphasis upon our First Object, where we must gather up the earlier work done and cast that into the form of life. We must give it expression in the daily life; we must show that the philosophy of life we have found in Theosophy is given to the people in the world in the forms which they can best understand. Some idealistic men of the world can understand it best in the form of Masonic principles. Others can understand best in the forms known as religious; still others will recognise the forms of art more easily. We must learn how to stimulate all these departments. Then even in the despised business, some of us will learn what the approaches are of rousing the business mind to a deeper appreciation of the Ancient Wisdom. Today we are using in business, in many departments, the methods of Theosophy; people are forming their business more and more in accordance with the ideals of the Ancient Wisdom — brotherhood is coming into the business world. Some of us would be surprised if we could go in to the finer aspects of the business and find out how much is based upon the principles of brotherhood. In America particularly there are business men who are beginning to speak almost in terms of Theosophy in expressing their ideals of what is best of their work This is very important because America is essentially a business country. Business meetings, associations, clubs, people are coming together constantly, forming organizations which have some of the principles of Theosophy at their foundations. I have myself attended some, and have been amazed at the degree to which this is true.

We are now, friends, where we must make an inventory of our Theosophical lives. I am impressed with the fact that we have come to a parting of the ways. Many of our Theosophists and Theosophical bodies are still using outworn forms in order to bring to the world our great ideals of the Ancient Wisdom. The least informed of our members are bringing to the outer world, that has gone on just a little ahead of them in human progress, a Theosophy that is not quite in touch. Some of our Theosophists are lagging behind in the progress of the world. They are still giving out their Theosophy in the old forms; they have not kept pace with the progress of the world; but still speak the language, so to say, of a by-gone day.

When I say that we have come to a parting of the ways I mean that we must awaken and come forward and ahead of other activities in the world which in the past we have stimulated with life. Again I say we must take an inventory of ourselves; we must not live in the past as we have been doing; we must not repeat the old forms that we repeated in the first stages of the history of our Society and when we were labouring more under the laws of the Second and Third Objects. We must awaken to the fact that we have come to a point where we must give vigorous expression to our First Object, where Brotherhood in all its aspects must receive emphasis.

We must first find out what the Brotherhood Movements of the world are doing, what their source of inspiration may be, to see what is lacking in their forms and supply that lack. So I say we must take inventory. We must awaken to the fact that the world is "cribbed, cabined, and confined"; we must help to release the spirit so that it may express itself in the new forms. This is one of the most important duties we have. There is a work which it would be well for some Theosophists to think over.

Another thing we need very much in our work a sort of encyclopedia of Theosophy; some fixed work, so to say, in which the opinions of all the writers on Theosophy are centred. That would be very valuable indeed. Now that we are coming to the time when everything is moving very rapidly, it would be well for the workers in the world, these working for the good of humanity, if they could have in encyclopedia form information on the philosophy of life. It has lain heavily on my heart for many years to find those who from a scholarly standpoint would have the ability to accomplish such a work. I mention it here because it is an opportunity I do not wish to let slip. It is part of the unfinished work of the Second and Third Objects and would further prepare the way for labour in the First Object in the future.

Just to give an illustration of what I mean, let me say that, when I was practicing law I used constantly an encyclopedia of law to give me the essence of the decisions in point; for it reported both for and against. Such an encyclopedia of Theosophy would be a very timely work of some scholarly theosophists to prepare because I feel we are coming now to a point where Theosophy must be laid before the world in more and more secular forms. That had not been possible in the past. There has been more or less of a religious fervour put into the expression of the Ancient Wisdom. It was necessary to stir up the enthusiasm of those who were to be its workers; but now we must gather round us men and women of the world who will not be appealed to by that.

There are many on the outer fringes of our work who do not believe, for example, in the Masters as we do, and yet who have the same spirit of response that we have when ever our Elders send out a call. We are highly technical and concentrated in our methods of thought. All this must now be diluted and carried out into the outer world in all forms of human brotherhood. That to my mind is the necessity of the hour. There are many movements in working order in the world which will carry the message of Theosophy to the world in their own forms; thus the people can draw from the central fountain source through forms a little more diluted than we are accustomed to use. It seems to me this is one of the opportunities that lies ahead of us.

As I have very briefly tried to show, our work was first to place emphasis on the Second and Third Object; and we centralised ourselves as strongly as possible. Now having come to activity under the First Object, there we come in contact with the outer world as never before, and now to give our message, we must give it in the other forms, not always ours. At first we used Sanskrit; to some it seemed easy, others difficult. Today we must take the forms of the outer life, understand them and infuse the life of Theosophy into these forms, — so impress them with Theosophy that they will put Theosophy into their outer forms and use if for the enrichment of life.

We cannot do without forms, and it is our work to use the forms which are most easily understood by our audiences and readers. These forms are changing constantly. Language is a form in which we express our thoughts and feelings. In America there are new legal forms. For the present they will be jarring to he conventional mind. I do not myself always understand them, but they are rich and vital. Of course we the elders call such corruptions slang; but the "language" of one generation becomes the language of the next. We must not be contemptuous of the method of the new generation. The future is in their hands; it is they who will be the future workers, whereas we shall die out.

We must help to give people the essence of theosophy and leave them to their own forms. Being now active in the realm of the first object, we must cultivate a certain expertness. We must be experts in the knowledge of the various living forms through which to express the Ancient Wisdom more practically. We must put it in terms of modern life which can best be understood, because it is of the utmost importance that the modern world should understand the Ancient Wisdom and assimilate it in its higher ideals and fuller life.

If we do not pause long enough to get understanding of the forms of the modern world, we shall be called "old fogies" and we shall miss our part in this great world today. Because older forms exist in our minds in a highly specialized even academic way, it does not mean that the rest of the world is going to take Theosophy in those forms. Theosophists are rather at the centre of things, and we must learn the language of the world, learn to deliver our philosophy in the forms that are being used daily in the world. When we learn this then all be put into our hand the power to spread Theosophy which we have not today. In order to do this, I feel we must go into the various activities of the world, and learn how other minds work. We must learn not only their language, but perfect ourselves in the knowledge of their other forms, and then infuse the life of Theosophy into those forms, using their materials because they understand them better. What they need more than anything is the life we have, the life of Theosophy.

If you could come to America and study some of the fraternal methods that are being used there today in public life and see the orders, societies, associations through which the people express their ideals in the vast life of the populace, you would be amazed to see how much Theosophy has crept into those forms. That is a very wonderful sign of the progress of the Ancient Wisdom in the world today.

You see, therefore, that the Ancient Wisdom has not rested upon us alone for its expression. We have given it in its concentrated essence, but in some mystical way the message of Theosophy which we have given out through our Theosophical Lodges and lectures seems to have been stepped down and to shave expressed itself in diluted forms in these orders and societies. One is truly glad to find how many of the forms contain bits of Theosophy. It would seem to me, therefore, that we have come to point where the need of the theosophical Movement is to study these diluted forms of Theosophy and to understand where to take advantage of the progress made by them toward universal brotherhood.

Do you know? It is not all of us who can do the thing needed today in the world. It would be very nice if we could take a leading part in these movements, but we have not the people who can do it. In the first place our members for the most part are a commonplace people; we are just a group of people who have been able to grasp the wonderful teachings of the Ancient Wisdom in their essence, in forms that the outer world will not take. The genius who is working in the outer world is working in their forms, and we have to learn to take our highly concentrated form of the Ancient Wisdom to those men and women of genius, to lay it before them in words they can understand, set them on fire with the beauty of our message, and then associate ourselves with them, and leave it to them to inspire the rank and file of human life with the message.

Now, friends, in a way, because I did not plan to give you a formal talk, I have gone a little beside my theme. And so in the few minutes left I want to come to a subject on which there is some difference of opinion. We all agree upon the very great importance of the Ancient Wisdom for the world today. We all agree that there is time in which to infuse public life with the message of Theosophy. I think we all agree that it now lies more or less in the hands of experts to successfully carry the true spirit of the Ancient Wisdom to the world, and give it to the world in forms which the world can best understand. It is not a matter of mere enthusiasm and fire; it is a matter requiring culture, training understanding of human nature, and comprehension of the nature of popular forms, if we would deliver our message. We do not want to burst these forms by infusing too great force into them. We have to learn to be careful, skilful, tactful, to have understanding in our work.

I know all this is the ideal that lies before us; but there is one thing that we must not forget in our enthusiasm of carrying Theosophy to the world. We have begun to receive an infusion of life, coming from none less than the World-Teacher Himself. Now, when the World-Teacher comes, when he vitalizes a vehicle through which to express His life to the world, I feel that no matter how splendid a vehicle which we have prepared for His use is fit. If we have got it too orthodox in character, if it is hard and fast and encrusted; whether it is resilient; whether we are really ready to receive the infusion of life that is to be poured out into the forms

335

prepared or His use.

It is time when those who have been sent before should stand to order and listen and observe, and be ready for the message which we have had the honour and very great privilege to help to prepare; to ask ourselves, "Are we ready, are our forms the forms that should have been prepared?" If so, excellent. We have done the work; has it been well done? Are our forms fitting, for are they over strictly orthodox and technical?

This is where we stand today. Again I say, we have come to a point where we must stand to order and listen and observe and see if our forms are suitable to the nature of the message that is coming. In doing so, that we must stand with our mouths and arms open and take things just as they fall in, without understanding. We have prepared ourselves to be the interpreters of life. We are now getting an infusion of life from none less than the World-Teacher Himself. Some bits of that Life have already come to us. We have not His message in full, we have only a bit of it. We who are the custodians of form made for the purpose of being held up to receive the life of the Holy Grail, to receive the blood of life that is to be poured down into it by the only One who has the true right to fill the Holy Grail with the essence of life; it seems that we should now be ready to receive that Life according to its intrinsic nature. We should bring to bear understanding and wisdom and practical thought, the ability to understand the essence of things, and put that essence into outer expression that the little children of life will understand and not mistake.

It seems to me, friends, that the physical vessel of the Life that is to be poured into the world by the World-Teacher, in some measure has already come. We must learn to receive that life. I know that we expect the forms of it to be certain things, and these things have not appeared. We have not the right to such expectations. Let us hold our minds free and open. If we already knew what the new forms were to be, what would be the good of His Coming? And there must be something new for us even though we possess some of the wisdom of the past. We have only a fragment of the Ancient

Wisdom; and we have come to a point where we shall get a greater expression of life than perhaps the world has ever had; and it falls to us to build a greater form through which to express the Ancient Wisdom than the world has ever known before. We who are at the very centre of things, entrusted with the secrets of life in the form of esoteric wisdom, we should know how to create the forms necessary now for the World-Teacher.

And so, friends, having brought you to this point and our hour having passed, I will leave you here for the moment to ask yourselves whether in all these years in which Theosophy has expressed itself to the world, you have built up these forms which are to express the life now waiting to be poured into the prepared vessels through which it may reach all departments of life. It would seem to me that this is the point where we are today. The spiritual life is there, standing ready to pour itself out into vessels fitting and adequate for the life.

It has been our inestimable privilege to be the ones sent to prepare the work. Our Society has been the John the Baptist to make ready smooth His way in the wilderness. Have we made the vessel adequate? Have we given it the strength? Is it resilient enough to receive something a little different from that which we have? Are we free and pliable, so that the message will be received even if it comes in a way we have not thought, if it is far simpler than we ever believed it would be — always the Messenger of the Ancient Wisdom comes in very simple form. The mind of the world is all crisscross, full of complications, stresses here and stresses there. And when we hear of the coming of the World-Teacher, we think of greater sources of complication.

But it is not so; He always comes with the simplest message, so simple even little children have understood it. But here we are surrounded by all kinds of complicated mechanisms; and yet the spirit of life is so simple. Friends, I think we are making life more difficult by the complicated forms in our midst, that we hold up before Him for expression and I feel that we must simplify our lives and philosophy, and get our vessels stronger and purer and more beautiful. If today we are

337

best fitted to pour down the Divine Life that is waiting for vessels simpler, down and down until the last human being has been able to receive the Divine Life that is now waiting.

Do we realize the central importance of our work? Have we any time to split hairs about doctrines? Have we any business with all these formal things? There is nothing to do but simplify our hearts to receive the message, and leave to the future the task of deciding whether we have received the true waters of life. We can most successfully pour these waters out into the other vessels, lesser vessels, so that they may spread and spread. For it is doctrine that always divides man, but it is life that redeems man. Friends, that is the work, the rare work that comes to us once only in centuries. Do we realize this? We are the Holy Grail lifted up to receive the life which shall be outpoured into other vessels in the outer world. Were we fit? Shall we be more fit day by day? That is the question that we should ask ourselves.

For we live, this time, gathered together as children of the Masters, the children who are called together to find ways and means of dispersing the Divine Life into the world's forms, and so we are children of the light.

And I leave you here today with the prayer that, first our hearts may be prepared unto childlike simplicity to receive the Life which is ever waiting for the forms we are building. Then the moment will come for us to use our energies to carry out into the world the Life which will have been thus richly poured into the Holy Grail of our hearts. We are now living of that outpouring, for that ray of the Divine Life which will continue to shine upon us in the future that lies ahead. Let us see that our forms do not fail that ever-waiting life. A.P.W.

Among Warrington's papers, is a very interesting short note regarding the prelude to the first Pythian Ode by Pindar.

The oldest Greek music extant is a fragment of the first Pythian Ode by Pindar. The Pythian games were one of the four great national festivals of the Greeks and were regarded with he highest reverence. They were held at Delphi in honour of Apollo. Pindar, the greatest lyric poet of ancient Greece, composed odes for the winners of the laurel wreath.

The celebration of the victor's success was of a religious character and consisted of a triumphal procession to the temple and sacrifices, followed by a banquet at which time the ode was recited.

Hiero, king of Syracuse, won the chariot race, and being a fine performer on the lyre, Pindar, as a graceful compliment, composed as a prelude to the ode sung at the palace banquet, this beautiful and poetical invocation to the golden lyre, expatiating on its powerful effects on gods and men.

This melody is restricted to the limits of the tetrachord except in one instance, its rhythmic and melodic character, its seriousness and majestic sentiment, place it in the Dorian mode, Pythagoras' favorite mode.

Pindar was himself an accomplished musician and a disciple of Pythagoras. This prelude to Ode 1 is regarded by acknowledge authorities as the only genuine specimen of his music in existence.[*]

———————❦———————

The following 1932 and 1933 letters are first-hand reports as an introduction to the next volume documenting the struggles and the unfolding drama of a dream recorded in these never released letters.

———————❦———————

A letter written by C. Jinarajadasa found among Warrington's papers which the author dates as from 1932:

I am glad to get all the letters you sent from Point Loma people, because I want to file them in the Records. So far as I can see, the value of your consorting with Purucker and

———————————————————
[*] The piece was played by Mrs. Hodson at Krotona, Christmas 1931.

Fussell is to have drawn out of them these documents for my Archives. I think your intuition was somewhat asleep when you jumped to the conclusion that the Point Loma people were definitely going to be brought by our two Masters into the plans. Their story is certainly a plausible one, but not to anyone who knows the whole history and the way that the Masters work. I have been in touch with the Judge affair since 1895, and have made a point of keeping in touch with all the different parties. I think you do not know how from 1894 and 1895 all the Judge people have persistently stated the only E.S. was that of Judge, and after, of Tingley, and that their E.S. was the sole channel of the Master's activities. They used to say very openly that our President was under the domination of the Black Powers, and they have not made a secret of dubbing all our esoteric doings as utterly spurious. That has gone on up to the present, and you know from Dr. Purucker's claims what his attitude is towards the esoteric side of the President and her relation to the Masters.

You might ask why, if that was the case, the President accepted in Geneva the Point Loma people's invitation to come together. She accepted it, not because she had the slightest faith in their occult pronouncements. On this matter I am fairly informed, because I was there at the time. She was, and is, quite willing to come together in a general sort of way with <u>any</u> Theosophical Group, for purposes of Brotherhood; but she knows all the same exactly that <u>the</u> channel of Their forces are the groups which she has striven so hard to build up. You must remember that she is something of a politician, and plays her own game; and as that game has been played you will notice that the false moves have not been by her but by the Point Loma people.

I will also file Smyth's letter to you. It is quite a specimen of his unscrupulous ways. Regarding his statement concerning me and the E.S., I have sent a reply.

Regarding the quality of Initiates and Pupils, the position is as described. But because a man has been given certain powers, it does not follow that he will use them rightly. That is the risk which was taken in advancing certain people.

340

Undoubtedly the high value to occult things n which I myself have been brought up has been lowered, seemingly by many things that have happened. But that is only seemingly, and all of us who fail to live up to the laws which go with each higher grade have to pay in karma for the failure to obey the laws. It is perhaps not such an evil thing that once again there should arise a certain amount of scepticism concerning occult things, because of late many have attempted occultism in a sentimental way, and not because it was the only thing to do in life. Occultism has been made too easy.

The following is the minutes of a Krotona board meeting of the matter of exchange of land for the $2000 note.

February 27 1932

> Dear George, (Hall)
> Henry Hotchener called me on the telephone and offered the suggestion that Mr. Warrington be advised of our Krotona Board Meeting and of that trade which was approved by the trustees whereby the Ojai Star Institute transferred that piece of land on the tope of the hill to Krotona, and Krotona cancelled the note of $2,000 which it holds, originally issued by the Order of the Star.
> I thought over Henry's suggestion and it is my opinion that while the trustees had full power to act, and that they acted most wisely and justly, it is a courtesy due to a fellow trustee that he be advised in the same way that we advised Max Wardall. I hope therefore, that you will write to Mr. Warrington telling him of the details. You can, if you think best, remind him of the origin of that note, and that the Order of the Star took over at par, bonds which were considerably under par; but that rests with you. I have it in mind because it is an integral part of the whole affair.
> With love,
> Louis Zalk

Perhaps a little explanation is in order regarding the resolution referring to the exchange of real estate for the note owed by the Order of the Star in the East. Krotona took an option on the Madge Mercer tract before Krishnamurti ever had any idea of coming to that

341

end of the valley with his camp. Krotona's intention was to purchase the land and then re-sell it as a subdivision in order that Krotona might have a chance to buy the rest of the hilltop directly south of Mr. Munson's house. However, before Mr. Zalk or George Hall had concluded the transaction, the option was turned over to the Order of the Star in the East, and the arrangements George Hall had made with Mrs. Mercer for absorbing two "Krotona" Sutter Basin bonds at par was continued by the Order of the Star, with Krotona taking a note for $2,000. As the Ojai Star Institute Trustees had arranged during the year of 1932 for the refunding of all the old loans, George Hall took advantage of the opportunity to secure this hilltop, which Mr. Mercer seemed quite willing to let go to Krotona in order to retire the $2,000 note. After many years Krotona's original purpose was accomplished.

Henry Bernhardt Donath, born in Milwaukee, Wisconsin, November 22, 1900, made his first contact with the Liberal Catholic Church at the Pro-Cathedral in Hollywood where Dr. Besant spoke. Bishop Frank W. Pigott from England was also influential and inspired Henry to enter the church. When Henry met Bishop Irving Cooper, an immediate friendship developed — a friendship which grew into deep love, and he was ordained by Bishop Cooper on Whitsunday of 1931. Henry was the oldest living Liberal Catholic priest in the United States, having served constantly over a span of fifty-two years. Henry Bernhardt Donath died on October 14, 1983.

Ubique, the official journal of the Liberal Catholic Church was founded in September 1931 by Father, now Bishop, Will Pitkin and his wife Ruby. *Ubique* was published on a nominal quarterly basis. The Church publishing, and everything that applies specifically to the work of the Liberal Catholic Church, is now under The St. Alban Press in Ojai, California, founded around 1968 officially.

In a single issue of the *Star Bulletin* we find this tension displayed between organization and Krishnamurti's rejection of organization as leading to truth. We find the statement that the *Star Bulletin* existed for one purpose:

"...to make available to the public an authentic record of Krishnamurti's talks and writings. To that end, Krishnamurti personally edits the reports of his talks before they are published.

"In view, however, of the misinterpretations of his viewpoint which frequently appear in the press and in certain periodicals, Krishnamurti was desirous that the *Star Bulletin* should always contain an accurate presentation of his ideas; and since his message is of permanent significance."

And we find Krishnamurti writing:

"To me, organizations which help to create physical conveniences are necessary, but institutions which are formed round Truth are absolutely unnecessary. You cannot give Truth to another. It is inherent in everything; therefore you cannot give it, you cannot organize it.

"To realize Truth, religious and spiritual organizations are unnecessary. For this reason I dissolved the Order of which I was the Head. You cannot organize a belief. It will at once become a dogma, a creed."*

———————————————

In a private interview with Warrington and Betty, Dr. Besant said: "Make young people welcome at Adyar. Let them come here and study Theosophy. It will not matter if they are members or not. After all, what is a Theosophist? Not just a member of the Society. A Theosophist is one who is searching for truth whatever his connection may be."

Warrington made some notes which he made in his diary March 13, 1932, soon after that interview:

"Saw Dr. Besant. She was 'all there.' Talked of taking non-sectarianism into the Society. Wanted to unite

* *Star Bulletin*, May 1931, n5, pp.10-11.

our lives and ideals with all spiritual people's ideals. She defined Theosophy as the living of the highest spiritual ideals with the greatest nobility. Evidently she feels we are in a dogmatic rut and wishes to see us really universalists."

Here it is worth noting that despite these intentions of Dr. Besant, in order to be able to stay on the Adyar grounds today one must be a member in good standing within the Theosophical Society, and more so within the Esoteric Section.

Roy T. Minor fortunately noticed a trim airfield where he could land when a broken valve crippled the engine in his airplane above Ojai. He mentioned to the reporter that he was surprised that more planes were not owned in the Valley, saying that "the view of the Ojai from the air is enchanting; that it is much more beautiful and appealing from above than when seen from below."

As the history of Krotona unfolds, we find two letters written by C. Jinarajadasa, 1933, to a lady called Zelma, and one to Esther Bright.

Miss Ester Bright, from 1890 was a co-worker with Dr. Besant through a voluminous correspondence with her in many humanitarian movements.

*Sishya** was launched as an idea for a publication back in 1928 when Dr. Arundale was instructed by the Outer Head, Dr. Besant, to gather together suitable material for publication as a Journal which she wished to issue specially to Pledged members living in India. It would contain unpublished addresses of the Outer Head, keeping the E.S. members in India in more definite touch with her. For various reasons since that date, Dr. Arundale did not publish any issues. The first issue he announced would be received from Port Said in time for publication in 1933, but he was waiting for a suitable name from

---

* Also found in documents of this period transliterated as *Shishya*.

the Outer Head. No communications was received from her, so Dr. Arundale temporarily chosen the name "*Sishya*" (a transliteration of the Sanskrit word meaning *chela*, or pupil) which seemed to him suitable both for the Indian audience and for an audience of readers who were aspirants on the Path of Discipleship. The name also gave India's place as the great background for the work of the World-Teacher: far different in 1928 than from what it is in 1933. These bulletins also contained notes of unrevised talks given many years ago by Bishop Leadbeater.

Adyar
March 6 1933

My dear Esther,

I have your letter, referring to the midnight communication of the O.H. *Shishya* is printed off, and will be distributed from Bhavanagar sometime this week. I suppose that what she said will make people think that there is something very seriously wrong with the T.S. I can only put down as a record what she said. I have no right to in any way modify her actual wording. Certainly, I could have condensed it into a few lines, but my aim has been to let the members have the facts and material, so that they could come to their own conclusion. I think many know that on most occasions there is very little of her down below, and therefore all the more on those few occasions when she speaks with precision and deliberation, my duty is to record as accurately as I can, and pass it on. No doubt many will think, as evidently you do, that what she has said is merely due to ill health and want of grip over things. I, who have so much to do with her, know the difference between the times of erratic thinking and those occasions when she is definitely down here. If she lays so much emphasis on four people as in some way vital for the Society's destiny, I can only say that that is what she said, and the members will have to make up their minds whether it was mere rambling thoughts, or whether there was behind her then a real great occult statement by the President of the Society and the O.H. of the E.S.

Right throughout, my aim has been to give a full record. Regarding the message from Shamballa which I found at last and have published in *Shishya*, you will note I allude to a statement of the O.H. when she used the word "disappointed" with regard to Krishnaji. Both Warrington and Dorothy have written to me, saying that this must be not from her real self but only due to ill health. I have no doubt many others will also protest. I can't help it, because my business is to put down as clearly as I can remember, sometimes of course, I have not pencil and paper on hand, what she did say. On that point, I do not want to publish it, if possible, during her lifetime, but to publish her actual words, but that word "disappointed" was used by her, and in a far more forceful way than I have put it in my statement.

We had rather a trying time last night. At 10:30 she moved from her sofa to her bed, and asked me to stay near. I was in her sitting room reading, till midnight. She was sleeping then, and I thought she would sleep through the night, but at two o'clock she was awake, and I heard her conversing with Miss W. and went to help matters. The President was up and restless, not disturbed about anything but chatting about all kinds of little things, and evidently not inclined to sleep. I waited till 3:15, when she went back to bed, at least sat on the side of the bed. I thought she would then lie down, and I felt a bit funny and thought I would leave. Rajagopal is better, but Dorothy is down with fever, so I did not know if I was getting into it. As a matter of fact, it is the other way about, and I found I had a temperature more than a degree below normal. A dose of fever would probably brighten me up generally. I thought she would go to sleep soon after I left, but Miss W. tells me that she got up again and walked in her rooms, and wanted coffee and nourishment, and that it was daylight, when Lukshman turned up, that she went back to bed. Though this is a little bit more than usual, it is something of what happens fairly frequently, which has no particular significance except of course that it calls upon the reserves of force of Miss W. and sometimes of myself. George walked up slowly yesterday, and was with her for two hours.

C. Jinarajadasa

Adyar
April 3 1933

My dear Zelma,

What you say is quite true, regarding that message published in *Shishya*. One or two have criticized that I added some remarks after it; but I am quite sure that were she publishing that message now, she would explain as I have tried to. I have only quoted her remarks, except that I did not give the actual words with regard to her "disappointment". They were uttered on May 12, 1932, and said to me after remarks about certain other persons. Looking at the picture of C.P., she told me certain things about him; and then looking at Wedgwood's picture, she spoke a few words about him. I mention this to show that she was "all there" at the time. Then her eye coming upon Krishnaji's big picture, as a boy, she said; "I suppose one ought not to be disappointed, but I had hoped he would do bigger things." I remembered the short sentence, which I wrote down about five minutes afterwards. The only point I am not sure about is whether she said, "bigger things" or "a bigger thing", which is a minor matter.

Again and again during the last three years, she has used the phrase, "I am sorry Krishnaji does not like Adyar" meaning, of course, what she and C.W.L. stand for with regard to the Society's work. Only as late as March 14th (last month), she touched on this same matter. She was going to C.W.L.'s room, and her hands were on George (Arundale) on her right and on me on her left, and just as she was coming out of her room to the verandah she said: "I am sorry Krishnaji does not like Adyar. I had hoped he would lead the Society as its head, but he does not seem to like societies". I have explained in *Shishya* her complete refusal to give up her loyalty and obedience to her Master, which is implied in one part of Krishnaji's teachings.

So many seem to think that any change in her attitude such as expressed above is due to the influence of C.W.L. and George. I think that is absolutely unfair. Nobody seems to realize that perhaps part of this confusion may be due to Krishnaji himself. I certainly do not think that the Masters ever meant him to put his teaching the form that he has, particularly with regard to the Society's work. Throughout my experience, both of him and of Nitya, there was very little cooperation on their part, particularly with regard to the instructions given us concerning their training. It was always an uphill task. One particular instruction was that both should know what Theosophy was, but my attempt to teach them Theosophy was a failure, as they were not interested. Of course, what he says about theosophists has a great foundation on fact, but the principal corrective to that would be to know what ideal we stand for. This he brushes aside. You will see in the *Theosophist* what he said at Adyar. There is a good deal of unfairness and harshness about it, but what I am most sorry for is that it is creating difficulties for his own work. His own people here in India never work together, and things are not satisfactory.

Of course, in 1927 I saw clearly the beginning of all this. Miss Dijkgraaf, who was at Erde, will remember the beginning of this movement, which then was phrased: "Amma is standing in Krishnaji's way". Mme. de Manziarly was one of the prominent people in this movement. I did my best to righten the boat that was being rocked. You will see what the President said and myself at the Amphitheatre meeting at Ommen that year. But matters went on from bad to worse. During this time Rajagopal was blind to what was happening, and did nothing; of course, he was wrapped up in the administration. When he came here in 1932, he saw how great is the gap, and then he tried to bridge it by wanting to dump his office here. Again and again he has not seen the danger. In 1928 when I was at St. Moritz and all kinds of people were interviewing Krishnaji, I interviewed him on behalf of Theosophy. My interview was given to Rajagopal, but it was not allowed to be published in the *Theosophist*. It would have eased the situation then; but Rajagopal says he gave it to Krishnaji, who wanted to make changes, and never finished it.

Similarly also there are those two disastrous interviews which Krishnaji gave in the United States when he landed there in October, 1931, when he definitely said that the President had put him on the wrong path when he was young, and he had to break away from it to find his own road. Rajagopal tells me that after the interview was published, they protested against it and wanted Krishnaji to send out a correction. He said he would, but has never done it. Rajagopal, instead of sticking to those important things, has allowed them to go by default, with the result of the present situation. It is one of the most pathetic things that this statement has gone on record as the judgment of Krishnaji about her. Never in one instance has he spoken of her work for the world; that she has always stood for truth, and has been full of the utmost sacrifice. Of course, I am not in the least disturbed, because I have my own visions; but I am profoundly impressed by the pathos of it.
Yours ever,
C. Jinarajadasa.

P.S. Of course, I don't forget the blunders made at Huizen, and that ghastly statement in 1926 about Krishnaji being influenced by the Dark Powers, at that time when the Lord took possession and the Star flashed out. I don't know what happened to her then, that she agreed with Wedgwood. This has, of course, been one element in the bitterness of some of Krishnaji's followers, and justly. It was

348

this incident that was alluded to in a question here, a question Rajagopal should never have passed. But he says Krishnaji insisted on taking it.

———————————— ❧ ————————————

After Dr. Besant's death on September 20, 1933, nomination for the new President caused many to be concerned as to what the candidates views were about Krishnamuti's outlook. There were considerable objections among themselves regarding who would stand. This is covered in the continuing history of Krotona, and the involvement of A. P. Warrington acting as Vice-President.

Warrington, in 1939, wrote an article "Recollections of Annie Besant." The following is an excerpt dealing with Dr. Besant's death:

"The last months of Dr. Besant's life were spent in quiet peacefulness. From her upstairs veranda she could look down the river to the sea, less than a mile away — the direction from which, it is said, the Masters approached in the early days — a view which to me for its sheer beauty is one of the most satisfying in all the world, and one I know she loved. None came to disturb her in these last days. Only those who were very near and dear to her came, those whose presence was always a happiness to her. The great Self was mostly absent, leaving only a fragment of itself in the failing body. Her great friend and brother, Bishop Leadbeater, is said to have remarked that he did not know why the spirit slipped away so slowly, except that the Masters needed to use the body as a focus for Their forces, which were so greatly needed in the world. She had made the vehicle for these forces such an effective one that it could be used even when the spirit had temporarily flown to other duties.

"When in the hushed hours of an early morning that great spirit finally kept its tryst with fate, the faithful and tired body lay still forever; and in a few hours that too was dissolved into the invisible. And thus closed a remarkable life."[*]

_____

* Warrington, A.P., "Recollections of Annie Besant", _The Theosophist_, April 1939, Vol.LX, n7, pp21-33.

Afterword
Are Krishnamurti's Teachings the Future Heart of Theosophy?

As a result of Krishnamurti's announcement that he would have no disciples and that he disapproved of the methods prevailing in the Adyar Theosophical Society, there was a stream of resignations from the T.S. during this period which lost the Society 28,000 out of 45,000 members. Today, however, Krishnamurti is the most talked about person in the Adyar Theosophical Society, and is the subject of many divergent opinions.

In the Convention of 1931, Dr. Besant appeared for a few minutes, and then for a brief moment she recovered her former fire, and said; "That each should seek the divine within himself and never in any external place or form." As the author understands it, this also was the core message of Krishnamurti: There is no secret passages to truth. No incantations, of word or of the subtler word that is thought, can light the central fire. The author's attention has been directed several times to certain passages by Krishnamurti that the Truth cannot be found through the Masters, nor through Krishnamurti's books, symbols, nor anything that thought has put together or created. Instead, enquiry itself into truth is a fire that burns up the false "I".

By hearing the teachings perhaps that light of inquiry is sparked, and a light discovered which can pierce through the soul—the ego, or content of mind. In Krishnamurti's teachings is reflected the whole story of man, there as a mirror for us to observe our self-created fetters of ignorance, and in so doing intelligently liberate ourselves.

Might this enquiry, this light, also be the future heart of Theosophy?

"The highest religion is truth."

351

Appendix
On The Esoteric School and Psychism

Is there a misunderstanding of the term *psychism?* The word *psyche* is of Greek origin, and originally meant just the vital breath and animal soul of our nature. In its next transformation, this term was given to the rational soul, or the human soul. Finally, it became applied to the highest, the spiritual synthesis, the crown of the human being. Thus, "psychism" today, should refer to the lower degrees of this energy, precisely those powers which are exhibited so strongly in mediums and psychics. This latter term is given in the West to those whose powers are somewhat higher than those of the usual medium. But, in both cases the spiritual energy is absent, as this spiritual quality can be manifested only when the chakras are open, and are purified by spiritual fire and transmuted. Many misunderstandings occur, and many peculiar interpretations and applications are made, because these psychic happenings are wrongly interpreted. We must understand that the psychic realm is vast, and it includes an endless diversity of manifestations. All of which has no connection with true spirituality.

One has often met psychics who were so pleased with their astral visions and visitants (considering these to be high achievements) that they lost all impulse toward self-awareness, the impulse to eliminate the personal self, thinking that they were especially privileged persons who had already reached the goal. This is so dangerous, leading to disorders of the nervous system, obsession, a neurotic existence, if not physical death.

Here, the author prints several short talks given by N. Sri Ram, Annie Besant (*Warrior*), and C. Jinarajadasa given to all Esoteric Pupils within the Esoteric School. The following talk was given by N. Sri Ram at Adyar.

To Members of the E.S.T.
Some Points from a Letter of the Outer Head
Adyar, June 17, 1960

Some members write that they have no particular experiences to relate, by which they mean psychic or dream experiences. But our aim in the Esoteric School is not the seeking of such experiences. Our dreams in many cases are a projection of our subconscious ideas and impulses. We should not attach too much importance to them except as an indication of our own mental condition. There is no great significance in the mere seeing of colors and forms or in the experience of some thrill or sensation in a particular part of the body. All that may have its proper explanation, but we must realize that psychic development and spirituality are two entirely different things. Humanity as a whole has outgrown that kind of psychism which was prominent in the earlier races. The "lower siddhis" (psychic powers), as pointed out in such books as *The Voice of the Silence*, are a hindrance to one who seeks to tread the spiritual Path for the reason that only too often they divert him from that Path. The "lower siddhis" are siddhis connected with the involuntary action of the vestures or bodies that function by that kind of instinct which we see in the sub-human kingdoms and not those which spring out of one's spiritual awareness and unfoldment.

Now and then I come across the statement "I cannot say how far I have progressed during the past twelve months." It is obvious that it is not so easy thus to measure one's progress, which is subject to fluctuations and has many aspects, but it would be greatly worth our while to consider what we understand as progress.

Progress, like Truth, is a difficult word to define. There are some books in our classic Theosophical literature, such as The Voice of the Silence, Light on the Path, and At the Feet of the Master, which are recommended in the Esoteric School and which indicate to us the general way of our progress. What has to take place most of all is an unfoldment from within, for which it is necessary to prepare the field, which is oneself, one's nature and consciousness. All that we attempt by the methods of the Esoteric School is to prepare this field, although there is simultaneously the beginning or at least the stirrings of the process of that unfoldment. To open one's consciousness to the beauty that is Truth (as well as Virtue or Goodness) is to let it unfold its nature in ourselves.

In meditation one has to be careful, particularly in the use of sentences that express our aim or aspiration. There should not be any emphasis on oneself, what one desires to achieve or become. In such a simple formula as: "I am the Spiritual Self," since the Spiritual Self is very vague to us, the emphasis may turn out to be on the "I," oneself as he is, with his ignorance, self-centeredness and illusions. But if our meditation is on Truth in any form, which is one with Goodness and Beauty, without reference to oneself or seeking anything for oneself, that makes a direct and intimate relationship between that truth and consciousness in its pure nature devoid of self.

Our meditation should not be an exercise in escapism or divorced from the reality of life. It would help us all, I think, to meditate on Life as it is in so many forms that we know of, proceeding from life to consciousness which is inseparable from life, and the way the consciousness opens out, responds and acts, seeking in every form such happiness and fulfilment as is within its reach. Thus when we come into contact with the reality of life and consciousness we would be spontaneously filled with sympathy and good-will towards all, which, as the Lord Buddha taught, is the very best condition to be in, a condition in which we can be centres of the utmost help to our fellow-beings as well as realize our own innate possibilities.

Our meditations, although they may represent some of our best moments, cannot but be limited by what we are normally. Therefore we need to be recollected in our daily lives so that we do not lapse from what we have realized in our best moments. Some of us have been for many years in the Esoteric School, and we ought to have developed awareness of how we are acting or behaving in different contexts in our lives, as well as of our inner reactions and ways of thought, so that when there is a lapse of some sort we should be able to pause and place ourselves firmly on the path we desire to tread.

In these days there are many who do not like the word "discipline," which is understandable, because anything that is imposed produces resistance. Nevertheless, we should realize that it is good to use a measure of control over ourselves and train ourselves in definite ways. Just as there is such a thing as a scientific discipline or a philosophical discipline, so there can be a self-discipline, moreover, which aims at removing the impediments to our free intelligence and will. The "Discipline" of the Esoteric School should not be an imposition. It represents partly a way of life based on certain fundamental realizations, that should have come to anyone who is ready to enter the Esoteric School, and partly methods of training oneself which have been found helpful and are therefore recommended. But these methods can be modified and varied to suit oneself and one's circumstances.

There are a number of old members who cannot be very active physically. They have their value for the movement. They are with us in spirit and they strengthen the work by their thoughts, influence and devotion. But there are others who are capable of being active workers in the Theosophical movement. They should realize the necessity of doing their best both to make the Society strong and active, and the work of the Esoteric School vital and inspiring. One of our members wrote to me recently that all the time his thought is turned to the work and its needs, using the word "work" in no narrow sense. There are others like him. All of us need such dedication, which is dedication not to some abstract cause but to "the good and happiness of the many," to use one of the Lord Buddha's phrases as given in the books. The whole Theosophical movement and our preparation in the Esoteric School is to that altruistic end.

There are very many members who can testify that their lives, their whole attitude towards persons and events, have been changed profoundly by their membership of the Theosophical Society and the Esoteric School, by which is meant, not the formal enrolment, but participation in the life that flows through these organizations. To what extent each of us so participates or is a channel of that life, it is for him to consider. Every Esoteric School Group and every Theosophical Lodge should be a channel, each in its own way, for the forces, the illumination and the blessing that ever flow from the Masters of the Wisdom. Each member of the School should be such a channel, a radiant centre of the Love and Wisdom which They embody.

It was said by the Inner Head some years after the passing of H.P.B. that while some members of the School had made progress as individuals, the School as a whole was not the instrument that it should be. That judgment holds good, I think, even after the lapse of all these years. The School should be a unity in the spiritual sense, not the mechanical unity that is produced by all members thinking alike. The unity should arise from mutual friendliness, a genuine interest in each other's progress, inner harmony, and the dedication of each one to all that the School represents and the work it should accomplish. Being an occult organization, to possess the necessary strength there should be the right relationship among the members, and also between the members and the person who happens to be the Outer Head. This latter relationship is translated by many as a loyalty on their part to him. There is something in that idea, but this loyalty is not to him personally but to the Work and to the Truth. I stated at the very beginning of my taking office, and might state here again, that though I have a certain responsibility for guiding the work of the School and maintaining its integrity, I consider myself a student along with my fellow-students, striving in that spirit to realize the unity of us all in the work of the Masters. *N. Sri Ram*

Isn't this one of the reasons this letter is important: if what Sri Ram says is true, then *why* maintain an Esoteric School when these truths could, and should be dispensed to members generally at all times?

History repeats itself, the happenings of the past are constantly susceptible to recurrence: the following reprint of an E.S. paper dated March 1959 would serve as a note of caution to be ever on one's guard.

The following is from C. Jinarajadasa, O.H.

A Warning

During the years since my two predecessors, Brothers Besant and Leadbeater, passed on to other planes, various persons, and some in the E.S., have "sat for communications" from them, as in Spiritualism. Here in London, three "Dr. Besant" have given communications through mediums, one to the late Mrs. Margaret Jackson, a prominent theosophist of England. A T. S. member lately offered to give me vital instruction from H.P.B. Soon after the passing of Brother Leadbeater, one E.S. member claimed to receive communications from him by automatic writing. I sent a message that if she did not stop, she would have to leave the E.S. One very faithful and devoted member, who held the position of a Corresponding Secretary, fell under the spell of these spiritualistic communications; an entity claiming to be Brother Besant gave orders *concerning the E.S.*, and the member acted upon those spurious orders without consulting me. He had, of course, to give up his post to another. The strangest of all is my supposed appearance to a spiritualistic circle in U.S.A. and there to have given teachings.

Everyone who had any intimate contact with Brothers Besant and Leadbeater knows that they were utterly opposed to spiritualistic communications. Why should they completely reverse their long sustained judgment on facts well known to them, merely because they have dropped their physical bodies? But members evade the issue by saying that the communications are not spiritualistic through mediums, but only received by clairvoyance. Even a little study of Astral Plane conditions will show that there is no *real proof* about the genuineness of any communications, since any astral entity can by a little training pick out of our aura every incident in our past, even if forgotten by us, even to revealing secrets known to us, and another now dead.

Even the most devoted of Theosophists can go astray on this matter. Mr. Sinnett ceased to receive letters from the Master K.H. towards the end of 1884, largely because he would not help the work in the manner the Master desired. From then on he had recourse first to various psychics, all women, whom he mesmerised into a trance, receiving through them what he claimed were teachings from the Master. Brother Leadbeater who knew him well could say nothing on the matter, as Mr. Sinnett had such blind relief in the communications, and was utterly certain that he was still in touch with the Master through them. Later, he employed a medium whose body was said to be taken by the Master. Mr. Sinnett assured me the year before he died that the Master M. had once taken possession of the medium, who was lying on a sofa, and got up and stretched his arms remarking how difficult it was for one of His height to fit into such a body. And Mr. Sinnett was convinced that that remark was a proof that it was the Master M.

I was once shown communications received from a so-called H.P.B., containing "strong language" characteristic of H.P.B. when the occasion demanded it. My informant held that because the spirit entity used similar strong language therefore it was a proof that the entity was H.P.B.

A group of Annamite mystics in Cochin China assured me that through their special method of spiritualistic communications they had received messages from the Lord Sanat Kumara and the three other Lords of the Flame.

There is in Cuba a person claiming to be a Tibetan prince born in Darjeeling, and to be the Master K.H., and chief agent of the Great Hierarchy. He signs his communications K.H. Some in Latin American countries have accepted his claims. Here in London is a person whose adherents claim that he is the Master K.H., or at least the Master's representative.

Without going further into this subject, I desire to make known:

No member of the E.S. may sit with another or with several, whether of the E.S. or not, "for communications". If the member insists on doing so he or she must leave the

School *at once.*

I have no right to prohibit a member sitting *alone* to receive messages or directions from any of the Masters or from my predecessors, H.P.B. and Brothers Besant and Leadbeater. I cannot *prohibit*, but I want to issue clear warning about the risk of doing so. The Masters do not send communications on the level of the Astral Plane. Even if They were to do so on the mental, the probabilities are that it is not a Master who communicates but some person adopting His thought-moulds and mannerisms. Brother Besanat told me that she had met an astral entity, one of the dark brothers who had for years assumed the form of the Master M., who tried to give her directions. The reproduction was so accurate as nearly to deceive her; she was however not deceived when she looked into the eyes, for she then knew he was not her Master. This impersonator did succeed in leading astray several good workers. The probabilities of deception by invisible entities, and the liabilities to self-deception, in one aiming to receive messages, are so great, that it is *not* advisable to ask for *messages* from a Master. Meditation on Them should be — if it is to be effective — an aspiration to be like Them, with intense offering of one's self to Their purposes, an asking for nothing, except for strength to "carry on." C. Jinarajadasa, O.H.

On November 23 1883, the Master M. wrote as follows to Mr. Sinnett: "It may so happen that for purposes of our own, mediums and their spooks will be left undisturbed and free not only to impersonate the 'Brothers' but even to forge our handwriting. Bear this in mind and be prepared for it in London."

Made in the USA
Charleston, SC
03 October 2012